British Generals in the War of 1812
High Command in the Canadas

The Canadian people have faced crises of leadership, but never more seriously than during the War of 1812. Despite the many studies of this turbulent time, there are still controversies over traditional issues, one being the quality of leadership on both sides.

In *British Generals in the War of 1812* Wesley Turner takes a fresh look at five British Generals – Sir George Prevost, Isaac Brock, Roger Sheaffe, Baron Francis de Rottenburg, and Gordon Drummond – who held the highest civil and military command in the Canadas. He considers their formative experiences in the British Army and on active service in European and West Indian theatres and evaluates their roles in the context of North American conditions, which were very different from those of Europe.

Turner answers questions about the quality of each general's leadership, particularly that of Brock, the best known of these five generals. He argues that Brock's charge up Queenston Heights – the basis for his heroic stature – was brave but hardly a demonstration of competent leadership. Turner also shows us that while the other generals displayed courage in combat, they had to face problems raised by American military successes and by the strains of warfare on the civilian population. *British Generals in the War of 1812* explores why these commanders succeeded or failed and why, except for Brock, they are all but forgotten.

WESLEY B. TURNER is a recently retired professor from the Department of History at Brock University.

British Generals in the War of 1812
High Command in the Canadas

Wesley B. Turner

McGill-Queen's University Press
Montreal & Kingston · London · Ithaca

© McGill-Queen's University Press 1999
ISBN 0-7735-1832-0

Legal deposit second quarter 1999
Bibliothèque nationale du Québec

Printed in Canada on acid-free paper

This book has been published with the help of a grant
from the Humanities and Social Sciences Federation of
Canada, using funds provided by the Social Sciences and
Humanities Research Council of Canada. Funding has
also been received from the Faculty of Humanities of
Brock University.

McGill-Queen's University Press acknowledges the
financial support of the Government of Canada through
the Book Publishing Industry Development Program
for its activities. We also acknowledge the support of
the Canada Council for the Arts for our
publishing program.

Canadian Cataloguing in Publication Data

Turner, Wesley B., 1933–
British generals in the War of 1812:
high command in Canadas

Includes bibliographical references and index.
ISBN 0-7735-1832-0

1. Generals – Great Britain – Biography. 2. Generals –
Canada – Biography. 3. Canada – History – War of 1812 –
Biography. 4. Command of troops – History – 19th century.
5. Great Britain. Army – Officers – Biography. I. Title.

FC443.A1T87 1999   355.3'31'092241   C98-901405-3
E353.T87 1999

Typeset in New Baskerville 10/12
by Caractéra inc., Quebec City

Dedicated to all those who have fought in defence of Canada's freedom

Contents

Maps

Preface

"The Legislature of Upper Canada has dedicated this monument to the very eminent civil and military services of the late Sir Isaac Brock ... whose remains are deposited in the vault beneath ... He fell in action the 13th day of October, 1812, in the 43rd year of his age. Honoured and beloved by the people whom he governed, and deplored by his Sovereign to whose service his life had been devoted." This is a part of the inscription on Brock's Monument, which rises 190 feet on Queenston Heights, overlooking to the north the village of Queenston, where he died, and to the east the Niagara River and the United States. At the base of the stone column are two tablets, one commemorating Major-General Brock and the other his provincial aide-de-camp, Lieutenant-Colonel John Macdonell, both of whom lie buried in the monument. Brock's Monument is a familiar sight to historians of the War of 1812, as well as to the many thousands of history buffs and tourists who visit the area.[1]

To Brock's military and civil superior, the governor-in-chief and commander of the forces throughout the war, there is no grand memorial. The remains of Sir George Prevost lie in the family vault in a quiet churchyard in East Barnet, Hertfordshire, England; there is also a plaque in the cathedral church of Winchester, Hampshire, installed by his widow. The inscription on the plaque reads in part: "Sacred to the Memory of Lieutenant-General Sir George Prevost ... He was interred near the remains of his Father, Major-General Augustin Prevost ... Catharine Ann Prevost, His afflicted Widow, Caused this Monument to be erected, Anno Domini, 1818."[2] Prevost's last resting place is neither a sight nor a site familiar to historians, much less to tourists.

Why this vast difference in the commemoration of these two men who served the same cause? Indeed, this question may be asked when one compares Brock's Monument with the memorials to the other

British commanders during the War of 1812, and it is among those that inspired this study.

During that war five men held the principal responsibility for the military defence and civil administration of the provinces of Lower Canada (Quebec) and Upper Canada (Ontario). Prevost was governor-in-chief of British North America as well as captain-general, vice-admiral, and "Commander of all His Majesty's Forces" with specific responsibility for Lower Canada. In the upper province Brock served as "Senior Member of the [Executive] Council" (president of the council or civil administrator), as well as "Senior Officer Commander of the Troops," as did each of his successors, Major-General Sir Roger Sheaffe, Major-General Baron Francis de Rottenburg, and Lieutenant-General Gordon Drummond.[3] Of the five, only Brock has entered the popular imagination in Canada as an unqualified hero, if not its outstanding military genius from the War of 1812, while the others have been blotted out from the collective memory of the people whose forerunners they defended. Nor have they received the respectful treatment accorded Brock by historians. This tendency to amnesia extends as well to Lieutenant-General Sir John C. Sherbrooke, who served as lieutenant-governor of Nova Scotia from October 1811 to June 1816, as well as commander of the forces in the Atlantic provinces and governor-in-chief of the Canadas from 1816 to 1818.[4] During the War of 1812 he and Rear-Admiral Edward Griffith commanded the invasion of Maine in September 1814.

Why, in Canada at least, has Brock been more commemorated than any other military or civilian leader from that conflict? This simple question was the starting point for my research. The idea for a book comparing the five generals arose when I asked fellow historians, Who won the battle of Queenston Heights? Most replied without hesitation, Brock, of course! But consider the fact that he was killed very early in the battle and that command of the forces there devolved upon Sheaffe, who went on to win a decisive victory. Why has Sheaffe not received the major credit – or indeed, any credit – for that success? Raising these questions inevitably leads to others.

Why is Sheaffe virtually forgotten? Why is Drummond scarcely remembered, even though he has to his credit the capture of Fort Niagara and, in the view of some historians, success at Lundy's Lane? If Sheaffe deserves historical obscurity because he failed to defend York in April 1813, it would seem only fair to apply the same judgment to Brock for failing to defend Queenston on 13 October 1812 and to Drummond for his unsuccessful siege of Fort Erie. Prevost held the important post of commander of the forces, but he is scarcely remembered, and not at all for his military prowess. There is a quiet, but continuing scholarly controversy about the abilities, merits, and contributions of commanders of the forces in the War of 1812, particularly about Prevost, Drummond, and Sheaffe. Perhaps the most enlightening approach is to concentrate on comparing the five, an attempt that has not yet been made in print.

All the above questions also raise the issue of how critical leadership was to the course and outcome of the war. Leadership certainly deserves to be examined if only because it has been included as a subject in so many scholarly studies, some of which are mentioned below. My research indicates that in the period under review, in both civil and military roles, a large degree of the direction, morale, achievements, and shortcomings of forces and governments were ascribed to the leaders. This attribution still occurs, and whether warranted or not then or now, it is a historical fact that deserves study.

In his general history of the war, G.F.G. Stanley comments briefly on the British generals, and Donald Graves in his study of the battle of Lundy's Lane critically examines generalship on both sides in the Niagara campaign of 1814.[5] These and other scholarly works on the war make valuable contributions to understanding how armies were commanded and how battles were won or lost. What they do not undertake – quite understandably – is a comprehensive or comparative examination of the generalship of the five British commanders; nor do they assess the significance of combining civil and military leadership on the British side. This particular arrangement, in contrast to the American system of separate civil leadership and military command, may be seen as assisting or impeding the defence of the Canadas.

These questions and considerations led me to undertake a comparison of the five commanders in a study of leadership during the War of 1812. By leadership I mean both the military role of these generals (their generalship) and the civil role of administrator, in the cases of Brock, Sheaffe, Rottenburg, and Drummond, or governor-in-chief for Prevost. As part of this examination, I thought that it would also be useful to include the aides-de-camp of these generals to see how these officers were employed and to estimate what their appointments reveal about the generals.

Let me make clear now that I have limited what I have attempted to cover in this book in order not to detract from the main focus. This work does not offer a collective biography of the five leaders or the story of their entire careers. It is not a study of the British officer corps in the Canadas during the war; important subordinate commanders such as Major-General Henry Procter, Major-General John Vincent, Major-General Phineas Riall, and Lieutenant-Colonel John Harvey are therefore touched on only in passing because they were not officers

commanding all the forces in Upper Canada.[6] Despite their importance, key military administrators such as Colonel Edward Baynes, adjutant general, and Sir Thomas Sydney Beckwith, quartermaster general,
will also receive only cursory treatment.[7] Furthermore, since my starting point is the image and reputation of Brock, in order for compari-
sons to be valid, they must deal with officers who held similar rank and
responsibilities. A succinct summary of the events of the War of 1812
and a chronology (appendix A) are included in order to save the
reader from having to refer frequently to a separate history. Native
perspectives and leaders are certainly important in our understanding
of the war, but again I have been forced to limit the material to what
appears relevant to the leadership of the five generals.[8] Lastly, the British army will be examined only insofar as is needed to understand the
backgrounds and roles of the five officers. Since the generals began
their service during the last quarter of the eighteenth century, the most
relevant points are the characteristics of officers then and the reforms
later undertaken to improve their performance.

It is also necessary to establish the role of these men in the military
and civil structures governing the Canadas during the war, for it is a
basic argument of this book that their leadership was crucial to the
successful defence of the colonies. Criteria for comparing the leadership of these five individuals must, of course, be identified. The sources
from which I have attempted to draw them are military history, biographies, and documentary sources rather than sociological or psychological studies, whose models or theories tend to be based upon twentieth-
century examples. But because the possibilities in this area should not
be completely ignored, I make passing reference to one such approach
in the concluding chapter.

Historians of military studies have remarked on the gaps in writing
about British army officers, and one has even suggested that "a 'DNB'
for all of the noteworthy officers of the eighteenth century would form
an admirable project."[9] Perhaps this study may make a useful contribution to the wider sphere of military history by its look at the attitudes
and conduct of five commanders during a time of great challenge to
leadership.

Acknowledgments

For a project that has taken so many years to research and write, my debts to individuals and institutions are almost incalculable. I sincerely thank all those who have contributed in any way to the completion of this work. They are not forgotten, although I may not mention them by name because of space limitations.

I was encouraged in the early stages by Richard A. Preston, Syd Wise, and Donald Goodspeed. Two others who deserve special mention for their continuing assistance are Donald E. Graves of Carleton Place and Stuart Sutherland of Toronto. They provided information, guidance, and invaluable criticisms that forced me to sharpen my thinking and hone my writing. Others who contributed in various ways were Bruce Wilson, David Owen, Carl Benn, Luc Lépine, Dennis Gannon, and my colleagues Carl Wolff and John Sainsbury. The Hon. Mrs Drummond, subsequently Baroness Strange of Megginch, Scotland, and James Jervois of London, England, made available the private papers of their ancestors. I appreciated also my conversations with these two individuals, which furthered my understanding of those long-ago times.

The institutions and their staff who deserve my thanks include the National Archives of Canada (in particular, Tim Dubé and Pat Kennedy), the Archives of Ontario, the William L. Clements Library of the University of Michigan, the Buffalo and Erie County Historical Society research library, the Special Collections department in the Perkins Library of Duke University, and the Baldwin Room at the Toronto Reference Library. The help that I have received from various people at Brock University has been unstinting and invaluable. In particular, I wish to thank the reference librarians, who readily answered my endless questions and who arranged interlibrary loans, and John Burtniak in Special Collections. That is the first place that a researcher should visit when undertaking a project on the War of 1812. Mary Pisiak and others in User Services (Computing) and Heidi Klose of the History Department unravelled the mysteries of computer disks and programs. The financial assistance provided by two SSHRC General Research Grants and grants from Brock University is very much appreciated.

At McGill-Queen's University Press, John Zucchi, editor, provided strong support for this publication, while Joan McGilvray, coordinating editor, assisted me in a great many ways to prepare and improve the manuscript. I am also grateful for the exemplary copy-editing of Elizabeth Hulse.

Every effort has been made to trace the ownership of copyright material reproduced in this book. The author and the publisher regret any errors and will be pleased to make necessary corrections in any subsequent edition.

The writing of this book stretched over almost ten years, long enough to try the patience of anyone. My wife's acceptance of my absence on research trips and my silence when I worked at home constantly amazed me, and I appreciate that quality more than I can say. The opinions, as well as the errors, in this book are my responsibility.

Brock's Monuments at Queenston
Heights: the first erected in 1824
and badly damaged in an explosion
in 1840 (NA, C-002316); the second
begun in 1853 and completed in
1856 (etching by Nicholas
Hornyansky, courtesy of the Weir
Foundation, Queenston)

Sir George Prevost's tomb at St Mary the Virgin Church, East Barnet parish, Hertfordshire, England (photograph by Carl M. Wolff)

Peace of Ghent 1814 and Triumph of America; engraving, probably by Alexis Chataignier, after a painting by Julia Plantou (courtesy of the Library of Congress, Washington, DC)

Lochée's Academy c. 1827–30. The academy was established about 1770 by Louis Lochée and continued after his death by his son, also Louis Lochée (courtesy of the Royal Borough of Kensington and Chelsea Libraries and Art Services, London, England)

Sir George Prevost, painting by Baptiste Roy-Audy (courtesy of the Musée du Château Ramezay, Montreal)

Captain Thomas Macdonough's Victory on Lake Champlain and Defeat of the British Army at Plattsburg by Genl Macomb, Sept. 11, 1814; engraving after a painting by H. Reinagle
(NA, C-010928)

Sir Isaac Brock; painting by B. Drines,
commissioned by Brock University
(by permission of the university)

General William Hull's surrender to Brock at Detroit; artist: Henry L. Stephens (NA, C-16404)

Sir Roger Hale Sheaffe; artist unknown (NA, C-111307)

View of the Taking of Little York by Commodore Chauncey & Genl Z. Pike
(Amasa Trowbridge Papers, Library of Congress, Washington, DC)

Lake Ontario entrance to the Niagara River, showing Fort Niagara on the left,
Fort George in the middle background, and Niagara on the right
(reprinted from Lossing, *The Pictorial Field-Book of the War of 1812*)

FROM THE CABOT CALENDAR.

SIR GORDON DRUMMOND.

Sir Gordon Drummond;
after a painting by Alfred Sandham
(NA, C-007880)

The battle of Lundy's Lane, 25 June 1814; engraving by Alonzo Chappel (NA, C-012093)

Sir James Lucas Yeo; etching and engraving, 1810
(NA, C-022895)

Lieut.-General Francis, Baron de Rottenburg, K.C.H.
Journal of the Society for Army Historical Research
10, no.40 (1931):237.

British Generals in the War of 1812
High Command in the Canadas

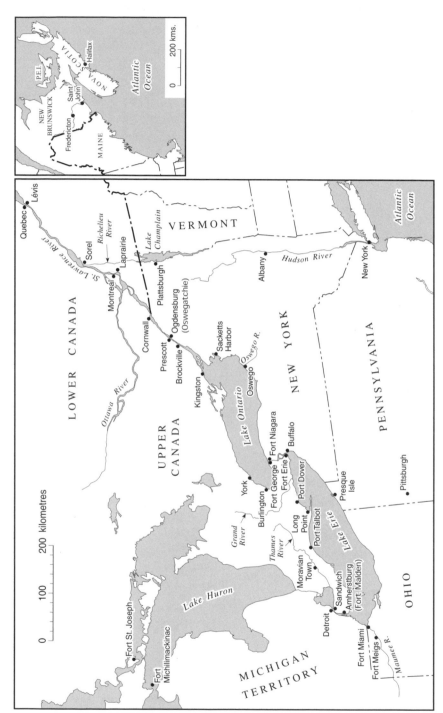

Map 1 The Canadas, the Maritime colonies, and the northeastern United States (courtesy of Loris Gasparotto)

Mr Madison's War

The principal reason for America's failure was poor
leadership.

Hickey, *War of 1812*, 90

"Scholars can learn from the War of 1812 how a war ought not to be
conducted," writes John K. Mahon in the preface to his lengthy scholarly study of the war.[1] The comment could apply to both sides. This
introduction is intended to help the reader to understand the following
chapters by offering a succinct account of the principal events of the
war with emphasis on the American side. In the appendices a chronology of events and a comparison of the years of service of the commanders on the two sides summarize a good deal of information that the
reader may find useful.

American anger at British actions and attitudes had been swelling for
years before 1812, particularly over Royal Navy interference with American merchant ships both on the high seas and in European waters.
James Madison, elected president in 1808, was coming under increasing pressure to resort to war, for neither American protests nor legislation restricting British trade softened that government's policies
because its overwhelming concern was to defeat Napoleon. Another
growing American grievance was what the United States believed to be
British encouragement and weapons behind Native opposition to the
advance of the frontier of settlement in the western regions from
Michigan to Kentucky. The only way to remove that malevolent British
influence was to conquer the Canadas. These and other reasons for war
were advocated by the "war hawks," who gained power in Congress in
the 1810 elections. Finally, in June 1812, they got their wish when
Madison sent a war message to Congress. In the House of Representatives the vote in favour of war was 79 to 49 and in the Senate 19 to 13.

Opponents to war came mainly from New England, New York, and New Jersey, with a few from the south and the west. President Madison was leading a divided nation into war, and regional opposition to the conflict would continue to grow.

Henry Adams at the end of the nineteenth century claimed, "The War of 1812 was chiefly remarkable for the vehemence with which, from beginning to end, it was resisted and thwarted by a very large number of citizens." More recently an American historian has written, "The War of 1812 was America's most unpopular war. It generated more intense opposition than any other war in the nation's history, including the war in Vietnam."[2]

The president was also leading a nation with weak military forces. Despite an authorized strength of 35,603, the U.S. army in July 1812 consisted of only 6,686 men, at a time when British regular forces in British North America numbered over 8,000.[3] The Navy had 4,010 enlisted sailors and the Marine Corps 1,523. British land forces in Europe amounted to about 220,000 regulars. The American army grew to just over 19,000 men in 1813 and to 38,000 the following year, still substantially below its authorized strength, which had been increased to 62,000. An attempt to raise an army of 100,000 men by conscription was refused by Congress in October 1814.

President Madison headed a cabinet rent by political disagreements and personal animosities. Dr William Eustis and Paul Hamilton, respectively secretaries of war and of the Navy at the outset of the war, proved unequal to their responsibilities and were dropped. Madison offered the War Department to several other men before turning to John Armstrong, who accepted it, and in January 1813 William Jones replaced Hamilton. Both James Monroe, secretary of state, and Jones had a very low opinion of Armstrong, who would resign in September the following year because of intense public criticism and presidential pressure. He was replaced by Monroe, who continued also as secretary of state. When the secretary of the Treasury, Albert Gallatin, left the cabinet in May 1813, Jones took over that department, and it took Madison a year to find a permanent replacement at the Treasury. Jones resigned as secretary of the Navy in December 1814 and was not replaced.

When the war began in June 1812, Napoleon had invaded Russia, but by the end of the year his army, suffering devastating losses, had retreated to German territory. He would raise new armies in 1813 and fight against the other great powers of Europe, but by the end of that year the allies were attacking him across the Rhine and the Duke of Wellington was invading France in the south. American success in its war against Britain would depend heavily on the latter's inability to spare army and naval resources from the European conflict.

American victories at sea began quite early in the war, but these were limited to the capture of single Royal Navy ships. The British could spare only limited naval forces to act against American warships and merchant vessels. In 1813, as naval forces were freed from European duties, Admiral Sir John B. Warren was ordered to extend a blockade along the Atlantic seaboard from New York City south and into the Gulf of Mexico. With the port of Halifax a centre of naval and military power, Nova Scotia and New Brunswick were safe from invasion throughout the war. On the Great Lakes and the St Lawrence River, the British army's Provincial Marine proved well able to move supplies and forces to reinforce Upper Canada and to enable Brock to act both offensively and defensively. This situation changed by November, when a small squadron of warships under the command of Captain Isaac Chauncey of the U.S. Navy gained control of Lake Ontario just before navigation ceased for the winter.

The war on land took quite a different course. The British capture of Michilimackinac in July and of Detroit in August exposed the western frontier to Native and British raids. These successes also freed Brock to concentrate on warfare farther east. American invasion efforts in October and November were repelled, but both sides recognized that Brock's death at Queenston Heights was a serious loss to the defence.

Prevost asked the British government to involve the Royal Navy on the inland waters, and this change was made in May 1813, when Sir James Yeo arrived with hundreds of seamen and officers. On Lake Ontario the British were constructing warships at Kingston and York (Toronto), and the Americans were doing the same at Sackets Harbor. On Lake Erie American shipbuilders were busy at Presque Isle (Erie) and the British at Amherstburg. Both sides had small shipyards at other locations on or adjacent to these lakes as well as on Lake Champlain. The "shipbuilder's war" would continue on Lake Ontario until the end of the conflict and on the other two lakes until American victories in 1813 (Lake Erie) and 1814 (Plattsburgh).

The year 1813 opened auspiciously for the Americans as their Lake Ontario fleet assisted the army in the capture of York in April and Newark and Fort George in May. At York the British lost two ships and large quantities of naval supplies badly needed for the Lake Erie squadron. After the fall of Fort George, General Vincent retreated to Stoney Creek, but took the risk of a night attack on his opponent's camp on 6 June. After this confused clash, in which they lost both their commanding officers, the Americans retreated to the Niagara River, where they remained virtually confined to Fort George and Queenston until the end of the year.

From 1 June until 21 July Chauncey stayed in Sackets Harbor, while Yeo dominated the lake; over the rest of the summer the two squadrons sailed in sight of each other, but fought only when they could not avoid it, as was the case in September. About mid-October Yeo brought his ships into Kingston and reluctantly ordered part of his squadron to move down the St Lawrence to support the defence against the American invasion under Major-General James Wilkinson. The latter led one prong of the strike against Montreal while Major-General Wade Hampton led the other. Armstrong had appointed these two generals to command on the northern front, and he expected them to cooperate closely in spite of their well-known personal animosity towards each other. The campaign ended ingloriously with Hampton's defeat at Châteauguay in October and Wilkinson's at Crysler's Farm in November.

In western Upper Canada there had been indecisive fighting south of Lake Erie, but the whole situation was transformed by Captain Oliver Perry's defeat of Captain Robert Barclay at Put-in-Bay on 10 September. General Henry Procter felt compelled to retreat from Amherstburg despite the vehement opposition of Tecumseh. Both were forced to stand and fight the pursuing Americans under Major-General William Harrison on the Thames River near Moraviantown. Procter's defeat and Tecumseh's death in this battle allowed the Americans to dominate the area north of Lake Erie until the end of the war.

On the oceans the weakening U.S. Navy gained few victories, and the tighter British blockade of the east and gulf coasts seriously impeded trade. Royal Navy captains raided eastern ports and ships almost at will, and Vice-Admiral Alexander Cochrane created an even greater threat by seizing an island in Chesapeake Bay to serve as a base for raids, including attacks against Washington and Baltimore. The British government hoped to divert American troops from the Great Lakes front as well as to pressure the United States into making peace.

The American people remained deeply divided over the war, one indication being the election of 1812, in which Madison was returned by a majority of only 39 votes in the Electoral College, compared to 75 votes four years earlier. Furthermore, strong opposition continued in New England to supplying the federal government with either militia or funds. Congress passed laws to end trade to Britain, particularly in foodstuffs, which were helping to feed Wellington's army in the Iberian Peninsula. This trade embargo was aimed particularly at New England and seemed to have been no more effective than earlier measures had been.

Despite their 1813 victories, the Americans had not conquered Upper Canada or successfully invaded the lower province. The end of the year brought them more bad news, as Fort Niagara was taken in a daring night attack and British and Canadian forces went on to lay waste the New York side of the Niagara River. The British retained Fort Niagara until the end of the war, thereby controlling the mouth of the river. After Major-General Jacob Brown crossed the Niagara (3 July 1814) and advanced northward, the British presence in Forts George and Niagara prevented Chauncey from using his fleet to assist Brown's army. The Niagara Peninsula was the principal scene of land warfare in 1814, with major battles at Chippawa and Lundy's Lane, followed by the British investment of the American-held Fort Erie. Brown's forces displayed discipline and courage throughout his campaign, thus brightening somewhat the army's badly tarnished image. His campaign, moreover, had prevented a British offensive along the Niagara frontier.

In response to a British suggestion made in November 1813, President Madison, early in the new year, sent delegates to Europe to negotiate an end to the war. The talks at Ghent dragged on for most of 1814, each side keeping an eye on events in North America and neither willing to admit defeat. But allied victories in battle forced Napoleon to abdicate in April, and that event freed the British to send reinforcements across the Atlantic during the navigation season. They knew that they would have to keep some forces in Europe because of disputes among the victorious allies, particularly over territorial changes, which might even lead to armed clashes. By the end of the year, European needs and war-weariness made the British anxious to sign a peace treaty.

American planning of campaigns in 1814, however, showed no improvement over the previous year. In February Armstrong proposed an attack on Kingston along with a pretended invasion of the Niagara Peninsula. But Chauncey and Brown, the latter the commander of the troops at Sackets Harbor, thought that their forces were too weak to attack the Canadian port. The main focus was therefore changed to the Niagara River. The intention was for Brown to capture Fort Erie and then advance against Burlington and York, but troops were sent from Detroit against Michilimackinac instead of being shifted to Brown's army. As well, an attempt was made against Lower Canada when Wilkinson invaded on 30 March. After a short skirmish just north of the border, he withdrew and found himself facing court-martial charges brought by Armstrong. Major-General George Izard took over Wilkinson's command. Yeo launched two new frigates at Kingston in April; they enabled him to dominate Lake Ontario until mid-June, when Chauncey, with two new vessels, outgunned and outnumbered his opponent. The Americans' control of Lake Erie allowed them to launch raids into western Upper Canada that devastated farms, mills, and towns such as Port Talbot and Port Dover, but had no wider strategic significance.

Yeo would regain superiority on Lake Ontario in October just before
winter weather shut down navigation.

Invasions of American territory at Chesapeake Bay, in eastern Maine
and northern New York, and in December at the mouth of the Missis-
sippi seemed proof that the Americans could not avoid defeat in the
war. But Captain Thomas Macdonough's victory on Lake Champlain
and the British lack of success in Louisiana greatly strengthened the
hands of the American diplomats at Ghent. In any case, the U.S. government flatly refused to surrender any territory, with the result that
the British proposal for a sovereign Native state south and west of Lake
Erie was unattainable. Nor would the Americans agree to changes to
the boundary with British North America, the end of American rights
to fish off its east coast and dry fish on its shores, or the removal of
naval forces and fortifications from the Great Lakes. As mentioned
above, the British were anxious to make peace, and when the Duke of
Wellington in November advised the government to conclude the war,
it dropped its main demands in order to achieve a settlement. The two
sides soon agreed and signed the Treaty of Ghent on 24 December.
The treaty required each party to return what it had conquered, but
did not address the American grievances that had been the basis for
the declaration of war. Nevertheless, when the news of peace reached
the United States in February 1815, people rejoiced, and in the Senate
not a single vote was cast against the treaty.

An engraving of *The Peace of Ghent, 1814, and the Triumph of America*
was published in Philadelphia shortly after the war. This remarkable
painting by the French artist Julia Plantou, with its abundant allegorical
imagery, suggests that Americans held romantic notions of heroism in
battle and the glory of war as strongly as did Europeans. It was first
displayed in 1817 in Washington and subsequently engraved, probably
by the French engraver Alexis Chataignier.[4] The caption explains that
Minerva is dictating peace terms, which Mercury then presents to Bri-
tannia; she is forced to accept them under the looming presence of
Hercules.

The people of British North America were less happy with the Treaty
of Ghent because they gained no territory or improved boundaries nor
exclusion of the Americans from the east-coast fisheries. Boundary
questions were settled later by commissions, and through negotiations,
agreements were reached about disarmament on the lakes and about
the fisheries.

CHAPTER ONE

Generals and Generalship

British officers require an authority of no mean description,
exercised with considerable strictness, to keep them in order
and within due bounds.

The Duke of Wellington, 3 May 1812

In order to establish the criteria for judging the leadership of Prevost, Brock, Sheaffe, Rottenburg, and Drummond, it seems reasonable to begin the search in the age in which they served. A broad picture of how British general officers performed needs to be sketched and a brief survey of the British army in the late eighteenth and early nineteenth centuries presented which touches on its main weaknesses and the reforms attempted and achieved. This glimpse will be based on contemporary observations and those of subsequent military historians.

Between the outbreak of war with France in 1793 and its final resolution in 1815, British troops fought in numerous battles and campaigns in a great variety of theatres. Although they suffered many defeats, these were outnumbered by victories, particularly in the years 1809 to 1812. Their successes were sometimes achieved under very capable commanders, such as Sir John Moore, the Duke of Wellington, Sir William Beresford, Robert Craufurd, Sir Thomas Graham, and Sir Rowland Hill,[1] and sometimes under those less able. Even when British soldiers were well led, however, their victories were not solely the consequence of higher leadership. For example, Wellington's success against French armies in the Iberian Peninsula owed much not only to his own abilities but also to the guerrilla warfare of Spanish peasants, virtually complete British control of the seas, and Napoleon's distractions elsewhere.[2]

Since only a brief survey of the faults of British generalship is possible, it ought to begin with the most crucial element, the professional inadequacies of commanding officers. Michael Glover claims, "During the Peninsular War and, to a lesser extent, in the Waterloo campaigns, Wellington suffered from many shortages … but nothing circumscribed his operations so much as the dearth of competent general officers … with more than 600 officers of the rank of major-general or above on the Army List, it might have been supposed that enough able men could be found to supply an army of nine divisions. Such, however, was not the case and the Horse Guards were constantly at their wits' end to meet Wellington's not very exacting needs."[3]

Wellington's exasperation with many of his generals is made clear in his letters. In 1811, for example, he complained, "I am obliged to be everywhere and if absent from any operation, something goes wrong. It is to be hoped that the general and other officers of the army will at last acquire that experience which will teach them that success can only be attained by attention to the most minute details; and by tracing every point of every operation from its origin to its conclusion, and ascertaining that the whole is understood by those who are to execute it."[4]

He continued to lament in 1812,

We have more General officers to command divisions than we have divisions … What we want in them is health, good will, and abilities to perform the duties of their situation. I am sorry to say that the perpetual changes which we are making, owing to the infirmities, or … wounds, or … disinclination of the General officers to serve in this country, are by no means favourable to the discipline and success of the army …

I have frequently mentioned to you the great inconvenience which I felt from the constant change of officers in charge of every important department, or filling every situation of rank or responsibility with this army … No sooner is an arrangement made, the order given, and the whole in a train of execution, than a gentleman comes out who has probably but little knowledge of the practical part of his duty … and none whatever in this most difficult of all scenes of military operation. Nobody in the army ever reads a regulation or an order as if it were to be a guide for his conduct, or in any other manner than as an amusing novel; and the consequence is, that when complicated arrangements are to be carried into execution …, every gentleman proceeds according to his fancy; and then, when it is found that the arrangement fails … they come upon me to set matters to rights, and thus my labour is increased ten fold.[5]

Wellington may have exaggerated the problems he encountered with army officers in order to impress the authorities at home, but he did not imagine or invent the faults he condemned. Their existence is proved by other contemporary writings and by his problems with subordinate officers.[6]

The quality of the British officer corps in the late eighteenth century was deplorable, as Richard Glover has shown, and even with the improvements brought about by the efforts of the Duke of York, the commander-in-chief of the army, and others, the professional standard of officers in the early nineteenth century remained low. Referring to much of that century, Anthony Bruce asserts, "If the officers were generally deficient even by the limited criteria laid down by the military authorities, they tended to be more so in comparison with their European counterparts."[7]

The deficiencies of British officers at the end of the eighteenth century may be briefly summarized.[8] They did not gather intelligence and consequently knew little if anything of the terrain or enemy commanders and their troops, intentions, and means. They lacked knowledge of the history and theory of war and showed no interest in studying to remedy this fault. Not surprisingly, their planning was often inadequate or incompetent – that is, if they planned at all, for they neglected their duties, were often absent without leave, and disagreed with their superiors publicly and frequently.

Several of these faults are illustrated in the following account of disobedience to Wellington's orders. "The most flagrant example occurred during the retreat from Burgos," writes Michael Glover. "In the rain-sodden final stages Wellington ordered the First, Sixth and Seventh Divisions to move by a certain road. The three commanders, William Stewart, Henry Clinton and Lord Dalhousie, decided that the road was too long and too wet and chose another. This brought them to a bridge which was blocked so that they could not cross. Here, eventually, Wellington found them waiting ... 'What a situation is mine!' he complained to London later. 'It is impossible to prevent incapable men from being sent to the army.'"[9]

Officers without a sense of responsibility or an interest in being competent professional soldiers usually knew little about the men under them. They failed to care for their men's needs, creating not only disciplinary and other problems but also exacerbating the conditions that already caused such problems in the British army. Desertion and drunkenness are frequently stated to have been the army's major problems, but neglect of duty and insubordination cannot have been far behind.[10] The problem of incompetent and unprofessional commanding officers was not simply the product of the personal characteristics of the men concerned. Who these officers were and how they functioned depended upon other conditions, in particular their social background and that of the common soldier, as well as the structures of higher control and direction of the army.

The social chasm in English society between lower and upper classes also underlay the army's structure, thereby perpetuating a basic difference in outlook between the officers and the rank and file. The British army, writes G.E. Rothenberg, "was composed of long-service volunteers, mostly uneducated, and contained a good proportion of social misfits."[11] These men, who had known little but deprivation and hardship, were given weapons and then expected to meet standards of conduct far removed from what they had been used to. The soldiers received low pay, were prevented from enjoying a stable family life, and too often were not adequately supplied with such basic needs as food, clothing, shelter, and even ammunition. Conscientious officers faced no easy task in trying to achieve high standards of discipline and morale with such raw material as they were normally given and with the often faulty organization of the army itself.[12]

The lives of the common soldiers were hardly brightened by the presence of spouses and children, since the number of wives allowed per company of about one hundred men ranged from six to twelve, depending on where the regiment was stationed.[13] The wives did the soldiers' washing and often nursed the wounded and sick. No allowance was paid to those left in Britain when a regiment sailed for duty overseas. A private earned seven shillings a week, from which several stoppages were made to cover the cost of his rations, personal equipment, washing, and cleaning materials. He would be lucky to see one shilling and sixpence actually paid over.

Discipline was harsh, if no worse than in the civil penal code and less brutal than in the navy. Nevertheless, the discretion of the individual regimental commander determined the savagery of punishments. The army's methods of attempting to deter, as well as to punish, breaches of discipline were execution, transportation, confinement, fining, branding, and flogging. The most common of these punishments was flogging, and sentences of up to three hundred lashes by a regimental court martial and up to one thousand lashes by a general court martial could be imposed.[14] Even though these brutal methods seem not to have been effective in deterring crimes, many officers continued to rely heavily on them. They were unaware of or simply ignored the effects that could be achieved by the methods used by other commanders, who sought to redress the grievances of the men and lessen dependence on harsh penalties. There is, moreover, evidence to suggest that this more enlightened conduct did in fact improve discipline and morale.[15]

The difficulties of creating an effective officer corps were increased by the fact that large numbers of officers held their rank not because of qualifications or interest but through purchase. The exceptions were the Royal Artillery and Royal Engineers, where commissions were obtained by merit or seniority. In the infantry and cavalry, commissions from ensign to lieutenant-colonel could be purchased, and at least

before 1800 the majority were obtained in that way.[16] The system therefore placed those without wealth, whatever their social status, at a clear
disadvantage, a problem that was increased because the official price
of a commission was not its actual cost (the extra payment being called
"over-regulation"); in addition, some non-purchase commissions were
sold illegally by colonels of regiments. Above the rank of lieutenant-
colonel, promotion was gained only by seniority. During wartime the
number of promotions naturally increased, and the evidence suggests
that seniority became overwhelmingly the predominant means of
upward mobility.[17]

Upper-class background and the purchase of a commission did
not necessarily produce incompetent commanding officers, although
Rothenberg is critical, claiming, "Officers were neither skilled profes-
sionals nor, with rare exceptions, dedicated idealists; they were representatives of the English upper classes"; "essentially the British officer
remained an amateur ... There was little sense of subordination or
attention to administrative detail."[18] Many officers who purchased commissions were not interested in a military career, but joined the army
for non-military or personal reasons, one being a desire to enjoy its
social activities. Even after they gained command of a regiment, officers
who lacked professional knowledge and skills could not be compelled
to acquire them. At the same time, an officer who was diligent in learning and practising his profession had slender prospects of promotion
in peacetime unless he belonged to the proper social group and had
money.

The consequences of this system were described by Lord Clyde later
in the nineteenth century: "I have known many very estimable men
having higher qualities as officers than usual, men of real promise and
merit, and well educated, but who could not purchase. When such men
were purchased over, their ardour cooled, and they frequently left the
service, and when they continued, it was from necessity, and not from
any love of the profession."[19] There could hardly be an incentive for
young men or their parents to invest in years of education for army
service. Officers therefore learned their trade by experiencing combat,
for which there were opportunities aplenty during the French Revolutionary and Napoleonic Wars. How they applied their experiences
depended almost entirely upon their own character and good sense.

THE STRUCTURE OF THE BRITISH ARMY

Problems for the army began at the top, where "the utter fragmenta-
tion of command and administration ... made it all but impossible to
carry out a military operation against a national enemy."[20] Although an

exaggeration, Michael Glover's statement is not far off the truth since many departments and officials exercised responsibilities for administering the army.[21] Only a sketch of its structure will, however, be provided here.

Infantry and cavalry came under the authority of the Horse Guards, an organization named after the Horse Guards building in London.[22] Here were the offices of the commander-in-chief, whose concerns were recruitment, training, discipline, and promotion. Also located at the Horse Guards were the adjutant general and quartermaster general. The former was responsible for the promulgation and application of regulations and for uniforms and equipment; the latter looked after movements of troops, encampments, accommodation, arms, and accoutrements. In British North America they were represented by adjutant generals and quartermaster generals to the forces there. The commanders overseas corresponded principally with the Horse Guards and with the secretary of state for war and the colonies, a civilian cabinet minister responsible for the size of the forces and in large measure for the "conduct of war and military strategy."[23] Robert Jenkins, second Earl of Liverpool, was secretary of state until June 1812, when he became prime minister. The new secretary was Henry Bathurst, third Earl Bathurst. These two politicians maintained a large, regular correspondence with Sir George Prevost.

Generals had also to be aware of the Board of Ordnance, which controlled the Royal Artillery and Royal Engineers, and its head, the master-general of the Ordnance, a military man with a seat in the cabinet.[24] Royal Artillery and Royal Engineer officers corresponded directly with the master-general; they were thus able to complain directly to that official if they disagreed with orders given by army officers commanding. In North America relations between Royal Engineers and army generals were sometimes difficult, whereas their relations with Royal Artillery officers seem to have been much more cooperative. The Ordnance was also responsible for providing war materials to the army in the field, guns and military stores for the artillery and engineers, and barracks and fortifications.

The role of the Treasury should likewise be noted, for besides its general control over revenue and expenditure, it had authority over the comptrollers of army accounts and the Commissariat Department. That department's representatives, known as commissaries, in overseas theatres obtained provisions for the army either by importing them from Great Britain or purchasing them from local suppliers, but in British North America they were also to provide specie and, at times, transport services. Under the joint control of the War Office and the Horse Guards was the Medical Board, which appointed doctors and surgeons and supervised the supply of hospital stores and medicines; the latter were, however, actually provided by other officials, while the Ordnance had its own medical arrangements.

REFORMS IN THE BRITISH ARMY

Reforms of the British army were attempted in the eighteenth century and continued in the nineteenth. This study is not concerned with technological improvements or structural changes, but with those that affected the professional skills and knowledge of the army's officers.[25] In these areas there was improvement, although certainly not enough to eliminate all the deficiencies mentioned above. In short, there was so much to be corrected that only a drastic and unceasing program of reform over a long period could have eliminated all the problems. Still, the efforts to raise the competence of the officer corps indicate that there was both a desire to improve the army and a knowledge of how to set about it.

Richard Glover and other military historians have argued persuasively that much of the impetus for reform came from the Duke of York during his first term as commander-in-chief, from 1795 to 1809.[26] Through his efforts and the choice of capable subordinates to perform specific duties, the changes required increased professional competence from officers and laid the groundwork for higher standards in the future. The duke aimed directly at the defects of the officer corps. In a series of regulations he sought to ensure that incompetent officers would not receive commissions or be promoted. The regulations also tried to prevent very young men from purchasing a captaincy or majority. To deal systematically with applications for promotion, the duke created the post of military secretary and appointed to it "able young officers with good active service records."[27] They were, in succession, Robert Brownrigg, Henry Clinton, James W. Gordon, and, from 1811, Henry Torrens. The duke was not, however, attempting a fundamental reform of the purchase system, but rather an alleviation of some of its worst abuses.

After his appointment he went on regular tours of inspection. As a result of these, he issued orders for the routine drilling of troops according to the prescribed manual. Officers who did not enforce these instructions were sharply reminded of their duties.[28] Here was an area of professional knowledge and application in which many British officers had been remiss. The effects were extremely significant, for in Richard Glover's opinion, "It is likely that no one reform of our whole period did more to make the British Army an effective force than this steadily applied system of training."[29]

The training referred to was for regular infantry, called infantry of the line. Light infantry required a different kind of training, and as early as 1791 the duke tried to institute this in an organized manner. He made little progress until 1803, when he was able to set up a training camp, assigning the task to Sir John Moore, who has been judged one of the most effective trainers in the British army. This appointment, together with others mentioned below, suggests that the duke possessed a sound ability to choose the right men.[30]

He also set out regulations that strengthened army discipline over officers and by this means reduced such notorious misconduct as drunkenness and absence without leave.[31] The duke also required officers to know their duties in commanding and exercising their troops, under threat of non-promotion or even dismissal. To improve officers' knowledge, he supported the establishment of the Royal Military College in 1801. This institution came too late to affect the education of the five officers in this study, but its stamp on the officer corps was becoming evident before 1812.[32]

The duke's efforts to improve conditions for the common soldier suggest that, in his view, officers should be concerned with the welfare of their men. Through his efforts, military hospitals were built, "with special wards for soldiers' wives,"[33] more chaplains were provided, cheap postal rates for soldiers on active service were introduced, and a school was founded to provide education for a thousand children of soldiers. These numerous, though minor improvements gave the impression that the duke saw the ordinary private as a human being, and he became known as "the Soldier's Friend."[34] Officers who treated their men in the same manner gained their affection without lessening their obedience. The Duke of Wellington's troops knew of his concern for their welfare, and it was clearly one reason for his successful leadership. Michael Glover cites one of the witnesses to this quality in Wellington, the veteran Sergeant William Wheeler, who wrote in 1816, "If England should require her army again, and I should be with it, let me have 'Old Nosey' to command. Our interests would be sure to be looked into ... There are two things we should be certain of. First, we should always be as well supplied with rations as the nature of the service would admit. The second is we should be sure to give the enemy a d——d good thrashing. What can a soldier desire more?"[35] Notice which quality the sergeant put first.

Improvement of the army was aided by the Duke of York's employment of able officers in important posts. Further examples of his good choices are Sir William Fawcett, who served as adjutant general from 1795 to 1799, his successor Sir Henry Calvert, and Robert Brownrigg, who was appointed quartermaster general. The duke employed Major John Gaspard Le Marchant to train cavalrymen in sword exercises and ordered cavalry officers to purchase Le Marchant's manual. He also helped to forward the major's scheme for an army training school, one source for the creation of the Royal Military College.[36] Earlier, in 1798, the duke had accepted the proposal of General Francis Jarry, an officer with much experience in staff work and education in the Prussian and French armies, to instruct British officers in the art of war.[37]

Whether they went to military school or not, British officers could learn something about the art of war from reading the books of great eighteenth-century military leaders and thinkers. Although many had not been translated, the highly respected studies by Marshal Maurice de Saxe of the French army, Frederick the Great of Prussia, and the French officer Jacques-Antoine-Hippolyte de Guibert were available in English.[38] There was no requirement, of course, that officers read these books or be acquainted with their ideas, but it was different with the drill manuals, including those for light infantry by Lieutenant-Colonel Baron Francis de Rottenburg and Francis Jarry.[39] In addition, every officer was expected to have a copy of the *General Regulations and Orders*, published by command of the commander-in-chief.[40]

Others besides the Duke of York attempted to improve the quality of the army. Colonel David Dundas contributed by compiling his *Principles of Military Movements* (1788), an abridgement of which became the standard infantry drill manual.[41] As master-general of the Ordnance until 1795, the Duke of Richmond instituted significant reforms.[42] But Wellington's testimony to an 1809 inquiry gives a very large degree of credit to the Duke of York. Wellington stated,

I know that since His Royal Highness has had command of the army, the regulations framed by him for managing the promotion of the army have been strictly adhered to, and that the mode in which the promotion is conducted has given general satisfaction ... the officers are improved in knowledge; that the staff of the army is much better than it was ... that the system of subordi- nation among the officers of the army is better than it was ... and everything that relates to the military discipline of the soldiers and the military efficiency of the army has been greatly improved since His Royal Highness was appointed Commander-in-Chief.[43]

Wellington later added, "The improvements to which I have adverted, have been owing to the regulations of His Royal Highness and to his personal superintendence and his personal exertions over the general officers and others who were to see these regulations carried into execution."[44] In summary, all these reforms reinforced the seasoning effect of serving under Wellington in the Peninsula and of combat experience in other theatres in improving the competence of officers.

TRAITS OF GENERALSHIP

The characteristics of what constituted good generalship during the period of this study may be organized in three categories. The first covers the martial qualities and professional skills of a commanding officer while the second relates to his knowledge of the "art of war"; lastly, because the five generals held both civil and military command, the commanding officer's ability to exercise civil leadership is important. Great commanders of the past have possessed certain innate traits along with professional skills learned from experience, training, and study. The quality usually given first place in the literature may be called courage, heroism, valour, or boldness. Whatever the term used, this trait may be taken as the basic requirement for outstanding generalship. Support for this view can be found in the literature from the eighteenth century to the present.[45]

We can begin with examples of two commanders in the eighteenth century Marshal Maurice de Saxe wrote: "The first of all the qualities of a general is valour, without which I would place little value on the others, because they would be useless. The second quality is inspiration; he should be bold and ingenious in his plans and actions. The third quality is good health."[46] Field-Marshal Earl Wavell in his lectures on generalship quotes Voltaire as praising the Duke of Marlborough for "that calm courage in the midst of tumult, that serenity of soul in danger, which is the greatest gift of nature for command."[47] On the "moral" or "natural" qualities of a great leader, Wavell writes,

He must have "character," which simply means that he knows what he wants and has the courage and determination to get it ... most vital of all, he must have what we call the fighting spirit, the will to win ... There is one other moral quality I would stress as the mark of a really great commander as distinguished from the ordinary general. He must have a spirit of adventure, a touch of the gambler in him ... Napoleon always asked if a general was "lucky." What he really meant was, "Was he bold?" A bold general may be lucky, but no general can be lucky unless he is bold. The general who allows himself to be bound and hampered by regulations is unlikely to win a battle.[48]

There can be no doubt of the personal courage of great commanders during the Napoleonic Wars from Napoleon to Wellington and down the ranks.[49] Yet these men were neither reckless nor foolhardy. They shared with their soldiers the risks of being at the battle both because it was still possible for a commander of an army to see the whole of a battlefield and because they led by example. They knew their conduct could inspire their troops to fight with determination. As one soldier was overheard to say, "I'll stand as long as the officer stands."[50] Being on the battlefield with all the responsibilities of command, Napoleon, Wellington, and others displayed "the first essential of a general, the quality of robustness, the ability to stand the shocks of war."[51] This is the quality of moral courage, the ability to continue to lead effectively while under great stress, beset with doubts, and enveloped in the fog of war. It is the sense to know when to continue to push for the objective, to drive troops ahead even if losses will be heavy in order to attain that objective.

The description of courage, therefore, needs to be qualified. This leadership quality did not feature what Rothenberg claims as the "hallmark of Napoleonic combat leadership at all levels," namely, "Supreme disregard of dangers"[52] Such an attitude, this author points out, led to heavy casualties among the officers.[53] But if losses were too great, there could not be a body of experienced officers capable of inspiring their troops. The brave ones would all be dead, and the only men left to command would be those who were cautious or extraordinarily lucky. Furthermore, the loss of commanding officers during an engagement, instead of inspiring the troops to fight more effectively, might throw them into confusion or uncertainty.

Courage must be governed by judgment, a term that covers most of the qualifications already suggested, and twentieth-century writers such as Fuller, Michael Glover, Liddell Hart, Wavell, Falls, and Sixsmith support this interpretation.[54] Judgment is not a term that can be easily or precisely defined. It is a quality that combines mental flexibility, the *coup d'œil*, "an expressive term for the combination of acute observation with swift-sure intuition. All the Great Captains possessed in high degree this faculty of grasping instantly the picture of the ground and the situation: of relating one to the other, and the parts to the whole."[55] There must a creative element (as well as the perceptive) in this judgment, which can produce original thought or surprise for the enemy.

The combination of courage with flexible common sense seems to derive basically from what is called in the literature the "character" of the individual. Can character be created by study, training, and association with others or from experience? Historical examples do not provide a clear-cut answer. The literature suggests that these circumstances do not determine character, although they can influence it. Rather, it appears that the character an individual possesses creates a propensity for study and training and for the effective application of lessons learned from any sort of experience.[56]

What other qualities ought a commanding officer to possess? The literature alludes to several, but the one that appears to accompany the three principal traits already mentioned is the ability to lead and inspire men. This quality may be called the professional skill of leadership, and the argument is succinctly put by Richard Glover: "The qualities of 'the man at the top' are all important; if he has moral courage, firmness, tact and a quick appreciation of good work, he will produce well-disciplined subordinates; if he lacks those qualities, he cannot."[57] Not surprisingly, Napoleon stressed the role of the leader, claiming, "In war men are nothing, it is the one man who is all," and on generalship, "The essential quality of a general is resolution."[58]

The Duke of York's reforms emphasized the need for officers to improve their conduct, a significant emphasis. In spite of this, many defects remained, which aroused the ire of Wellington. He provided a model of conduct for a commanding officer, with his self-control and his acceptance of the individuality of his subordinate commanders, combined with his clear vision of their responsibilities. What he expected of his officers may be seen from his general order issued at Badajoz on 16 September 1809:

The Commander of the Forces cannot avoid taking this opportunity of calling upon the field officers of the regiments in particular, and all the officers in general, to support and assist their Commanding officer in the maintenance of discipline, and in the preservation of order and regularity ... The officers ... are much mistaken if they suppose that their duty is done when they have attended to the drill of their men, and to the parade duties of the regiment: the order and regularity of the troops in camp and quarters, the subsistence and comfort of the soldiers, the general subordination and obedience of the corps, afford constant subjects for the attention of the field officers in particular, in which, by their conduct in the assistance they will give their Commanding officer, they can manifest their zeal for the service, their ability and their fitness for promotion to the higher ranks, at least as much as by an attention to the drill and parade discipline of the corps.[59]

What Wellington required would have been approved of by other great commanders before and after his time. Marlborough's concern for his soldiers, who nicknamed him "the old corporal," indicates his own sense of responsibility. Frederick the Great advised his generals in 1747: "The commander should practice kindness and severity, should appear friendly to the soldier, should speak to them on the march, visit them while they are cooking, and alleviate their needs if they have any ... they should not be treated in an overbearing manner."[60] Marshal de Saxe wrote, "A general should be calm and never ill-tempered. He should not know what it is to hate. He should punish without favour, above all those who are his favourites, but he should never get angry. He should regard himself as bound to comply strictly with the military regulations ... and must rid himself of any thought that he himself punishes, but understand, and make others understand, that he only administers the military law. With these qualities he will be loved, he will be feared, and, without doubt, he will be obeyed."[61]

In the nineteenth century the need was just as great as in previous centuries for a commander "to command himself" and to be capable of learning and practising effective discipline over subordinates in peacetime as well as in war.[62]

GENERALSHIP IN THE WAR OF 1812

The prominence of the commanding officer in battle and the immediate impact of his effective or ineffective leadership are not surprising, for most engagements involved small numbers of combatants over limited areas of ground. The men would be aware of the nearby presence of the commander even if they could not see him clearly through the smoke of battle. He, for his part, could either see all parts of the battlefield or move a short distance to view its other areas. He could issue orders or send them quickly to subordinates and expect immediate results. The commanding general came under severe pressure, as Graves makes clear: "Because of his direct involvement in the battle, the small size of his staff, and his high degree of visibility, a general's mental and physical state during a battle was a matter of greater importance than it is today ... not only did a general have to be cool and collected, he had to *appear* cool and collected."[63]

Land warfare in this period often came down to personal combat at short range. Graves provides a partial description of how a battle was fought. "The clash of infantry," he writes,

was the most important aspect of the Napoleonic battle. A typical action involved the manœuvre of opposing formations in line or column, covered by skirmishing light infantry and supported by artillery. When the formations closed with each other, typically, one side ... gave way, sometimes assisted on its way by the bayonets of the other ... Recent technological advantages had rendered artillery the most powerful arm in battle ... Guns were designated by the weight of the round shot they fired; a 12- [pounder] gun, thus, fired a shot weighing twelve pounds.

Artillerymen most often fired round shot, and it "had a fearsome effect," for "under optimum conditions a 12-pdr. shot could, at a range of 600 to 700 yards, penetrate thirty-six human beings or eight feet of compacted earth, while a 6-pdr. shot could cut through nineteen men or seven feet of earth." Coming down to the individual's level, this author writes,

The infantryman's experience of battle ... was truly terrifying. Given the primitive state of military logistics, the soldier often entered combat hungry, and usually tired after a long march. Blinded by powder smoke, packed in tightly crowded ranks, watching round shot bouncing towards him but unable to move, suffering raging thirst brought on by tension and the necessity of biting into cartridges containing bitter black powder, seeing men killed and maimed around him, the infantryman stood, fought, and died.

The importance of good health or physical fitness to a commanding officer is obvious. An individual is able to contribute to his own good physical condition by avoiding harmful actions and situations, such as over-indulgence in alcohol and food or excessive fatigue. But a person may not have much control over his mental and emotional health, and in the eighteenth and early nineteenth centuries, doctors could contribute little that was positive to physical or mental health. The primitiveness of public-health conditions and the inadequacies of the practice of medicine in this period are too well known to need elaboration.

Luck (chance or fate), therefore, must be regarded as the major contributor to a commander's good health. Brock was blessed with robust health, as was Drummond up until the battle of Lundy's Lane, but Sheaffe suffered bouts of sickness while he was in command of Upper Canada. How much each man's leadership was affected by his physical and mental health can only be guessed at. Certainly, Brock could not have acted as energetically as he did unless he had been in excellent physical condition. Yet he cannot be given all the credit for his good health, nor should Sheaffe be blamed for his sickness.

A general's age could also affect his leadership, but historical examples do not prove that the young ones were always bold and old ones timid. In the subjects of this study, the small difference in age between Sheaffe (born in 1763) and Brock (born six years later) does not explain the differences in their characters. Prevost (born in 1767) was a dashing commander when serving in the West Indies in his twenties and thirties, but not when leading the forces in the Canadas in his forties. Yet even for that period he should not be considered an old man; after all, both Napoleon and Wellington were aged forty-six at the time of Waterloo.[64]

BROCK'S GENERALSHIP

We now come to the central question of this study. Its core is, Why has Brock become the standard against which other British commanding officers of the War of 1812 are compared? Despite occasional criticisms of him, Brock continues to outshine all the other British army commanders in North America. More significant, a historian has to argue the case to pull him down from his pedestal to the level of the other generals. In other words, whether or not he was as extraordinary as earlier authors claimed, he still provides the benchmark for assessing other leaders.

The disparity between Brock and the others is starkly evident in the field of biography because there have been many full-length studies of his life but none of Sheaffe and Prevost. The absence of a biography of Sheaffe is perhaps understandable, but it is surprising for Prevost in view of his distinguished career, at least before the War of 1812, and the high-level posts that he held. Aside from the biography in the *Dictionary of Canadian Biography*, the student of Prevost's career will find the most informative source to be the obscure *Some Account of the Public Life of the Late Lieutenant-General Sir George Prevost, Bart ...* (1823). Written on behalf of the family by Sir George's former civil secretary, Lieutenant-Colonel E.B. Brenton, it is of limited value.[65] In addition to that source, there are two useful, but not readily available MA theses by A.M.J. Hyatt and M. Sutherland.[66]

The five commanders in this study were professional soldiers who were capable of exercising military command, that is, organizing, training, and leading troops. As well, they were competent to deal with the problems of civil administration and able to provide leadership in that sphere. In other words, the men with whom Brock will be compared were not stupid, foolish, uninformed, or unprepared. In order to judge the competence of the five generals, the characteristics of good generalship and the criteria with which to assess both the civil and military qualities of their leadership in the War of 1812 have been established. Chapter 2 looks at Sir George Prevost; subsequent chapters examine each of the other officers commanding the troops in Upper Canada.

CHAPTER TWO

Disappointment:
The Leadership of Lieutenant-General
Sir George Prevost

In the present state of politics in the United States, I consider
it prudent to avoid every measure which can have the least
tendency to unite the people of America.

Prevost to Liverpool, 15 July 1812

Sir George Prevost bore the highest responsibility for the defence and
government of British North America throughout the war. His position
and responsibilities make him unique among the five officers; he provides the link among the other four, for he appointed them to their
positions, replaced two of them, advised them on civil government, and
dictated the strategy they were to apply. His leadership abilities and
deficiencies, his strengths and weaknesses, therefore need to be examined first because they provide points of reference for all the other
commanders.

Prevost has been the most criticized of the five generals, and the
attacks made by many contemporaries, both military and civilian,
have dominated the historiography on him up to the present.[1] His
critics complained that he was an excessively cautious and weak-willed
military commander, indecisive in the field, and as civil governor, far
too conciliatory to francophone politicians. Recent historians have
tended to praise his political approach as shrewd and his conduct as
pragmatic, sensible, and effective, but few defend his military conduct
at Sackets Harbor and particularly at Plattsburgh. Their assessments
range from the severe (timid, indecisive) to the moderate (defensive-
minded).[2] Hyatt, the most vigorous supporter of Sir George, praises
his defensive strategy, claims that he was a brave man who would
choose to fight when the time was right, and sees his failure at Plattsburgh as arising from tactical errors rather than strategic misjudgment
or cowardice.[3] Rather than defending or criticizing Prevost, this

chapter attempts to assess him in terms of the three categories outlined in chapter 1.

Born in New Jersey in 1767, Prevost was the eldest son of a Swiss officer in the British army, Major-General Augustine Prevost, who served in several theatres with considerable distinction.[4] "Designed by his father for the military profession," George was sent to "Lochée's academy at Chelsea" and later to Colmar, France.[5] Augustine Prevost was appointed in 1775 to command in East Florida; his term there was followed by active service in the West Indies. By the time of his father's death in 1786, George was an ensign in the army, having joined his father's regiment, the 60th Foot, in 1779. He transferred to the 47th Foot in 1782 as a lieutenant, to the 25th Foot in 1784 as a captain, and then back to the 60th Foot in 1790 with the rank of major. These rapid promotions suggest that he purchased commissions, for both his father and his maternal grandfather were wealthy men.[6] The direction of George's life, and probably that of his brothers William (in the army) and James (in the Royal Navy), was determined by his father, while the other strong influences until his marriage in 1789 seem to have been his schooling and army service. Here we have the initial sources for Prevost's development of soldierly qualities, professional skills, and understanding of the art of war. His knowledge of civil leadership came later, out of his own experience in St Lucia, Dominica, England, and Nova Scotia.

Only in the West Indies had Prevost experienced combat before he came to Canada in 1811. Britain's efforts against France in those islands were neither diversionary nor backwater campaigns.[7] The area was a principal theatre of war because of the financial, commercial, and strategic importance of the islands to both European powers. Campaigning there was far from easy or comfortable, for climate and diseases made the West Indies extremely unhealthy for European troops. British military and naval leaders had to be able to mount that very difficult form of warfare: amphibious operations. In this adverse setting Prevost showed himself a courageous and determined commanding officer and a capable civil administrator.

His service in the islands began when he took command of the third battalion of the 60th Foot on Antigua. In 1794 he was promoted lieutenant-colonel. During the next two years he commanded the defence of St Vincent against French attacks (and briefly the forces on Dominica), but he was so severely wounded that he had to return to England. In 1798 he was promoted colonel and then brigadier-general, and appointed commander and lieutenant-governor of St Lucia. The island was restored to France in 1802, and Prevost, in ill health, returned to England. The commander of the forces in the West Indies at that time,

Lieutenant-General Sir Thomas Trigge, wrote to Colonel Brownrigg, secretary to the Duke of York, that Prevost's "zeal and unremitting exertion ... and the exact attention which he has paid to the several duties of his situation, point him out as a distinguished and excellent officer."[8]

Perhaps because of such a favourable report, Prevost in 1802 was appointed to Dominica as captain-general and governor. The next year he was second-in-command of the successful expedition to retake St Lucia and Tobago. He won lavish praise from the commanding general, Lieutenant-General William Grinfield, who wrote of Prevost's "cool and determined conduct" in leading one of two attacking columns and acknowledged that "to his counsel and arrangements the Commander of the forces attributes the glory of the day."[9] In 1805 Dominica was attacked by a French squadron, which landed a force of about 4,000 men. They burned a village and seized some loot, but suffered heavy losses as Prevost fought a series of tough defensive actions during his retreat across the mountainous island to Fort Cabril. Rather than undertake a siege of that strong fort, the French warships sailed away to Guadeloupe. Again Prevost received praise from his superior, and the Duke of York wrote that he would be "happy in availing myself of any opportunity to recommend him for a mark of His Majesty's favour."[10]

Promoted major-general on 1 January 1805, Prevost returned that year to England, where he was created a baronet. He served in command of the Portsmouth district until 1808, when he was appointed lieutenant-governor and commander of the forces in Nova Scotia.[11] The next year he served as second-in-command of an expedition that captured Martinique. The commander of the forces, Sir George Beckwith, described Prevost's generalship as bold, swift, and decisive.[12]

Prevost then returned to Nova Scotia, where he governed until 1811. In his colonial appointments he proved popular, mainly because of his personal charm and political skill; his reputation as a resolute military leader probably also enhanced his appeal.[13] Moreover, the apprehension in Nova Scotia of conflict with the United States required his improvement of the province's defences, by which he furnished another example of his competence in simultaneously handling civilian and military roles in time of danger. It is therefore easy to understand why the British government would see him as well suited to exercise supreme command in British North America in 1811, when war with the United States threatened.[14]

There was the additional benefit that the bilingual Prevost had successfully governed a French-speaking population in St Lucia. To understand the problems facing him in Lower Canada, we need to glance at the constitutional structure created by the Canada (Constitutional) Act of 1791. It provided for a government by appointed executive and legislative councils and an elected assembly in each division of Canada, Lower and Upper. In the former the governor headed the government, while in the upper province a lieutenant-governor presided except when the governor was present in person. Although the people would have a voice through the lower houses, the real authority rested with the governors and their councils.

In Lower Canada a francophone majority dominated the elected House of Assembly, and from the early years of the century there had been disagreement between it and the appointed councils dominated by English-speaking members. The issues had involved taxes and the role of government placemen in the assembly, but underlying these disputes was a conflict between the defenders of the traditional French-Canadian way of life and the advocates of change, principally in directions more suited to the English-speaking commercial minority. Governor Sir James Craig began his term in October 1807, and by summer the next year he had taken up the cause of the "British" party, which included supporting the anglicization policies promoted by the Anglican bishop, Jacob Mountain.[15] Craig's partiality brought him into direct conflict with the *parti canadien*, led by Pierre-Stanislas Bédard, who was also one of the founders of its outspoken newspaper, *Le Canadien*.[16] By the time Prevost arrived at Quebec, the province appeared deeply divided between two hostile language, social, and economic groups. With an American war imminent, internal political and religious discontent could only imperil the security of the Canadas.

During his term as governor, which began on 21 October 1811, Prevost placated the politicians who had opposed Craig by giving many of them government appointments, and he won the confidence of Bishop Joseph-Octave Plessis, who headed the Catholic hierarchy of Lower Canada.[17] Prevost was seeking to broaden the base of political support for defensive military preparations. When war came, there was widespread willingness by French Canadians to serve in the militia and by their elected representatives to pay for the war effort. Prevost deserves some credit for this outcome, although the exact amount may be debatable.[18]

But if he enjoyed good relations with the French and Catholic community, his policies alienated the English-speaking minority, in particular Mountain and Herman W. Ryland, clerk of the Executive Council of Lower Canada. Although this group had no choice about their loyalties in a war between Britain and the United States, their animosity towards the governor remained, and in 1814 they would seize on his military failures to broaden their attacks on him. This assault would blight Prevost's career and reputation, but would not affect the course of the war.

At the same time as he assumed the helm of government, Prevost had to prepare the Canadas for a possible war. Before the end of September 1811, he had appointed Major-General Isaac Brock to take charge of Upper Canada and had inspected the forts of the Montreal District.[19] In the following months he ordered officers to examine the overland route from New Brunswick to the lower St Lawrence River. Usable only in winter, this route had been travelled by couriers, but Prevost may have been thinking that it could be a means of moving troops from Halifax to Quebec when navigation was closed on the St Lawrence. He requested weapons, equipment, and clothing from England for the militia, and proposed cavalry forces and sent arms and ammunition to Upper Canada. The building of another warship on Lake Erie was approved, and Prevost asked the naval commander on the Halifax station, Vice-Admiral Herbert Sawyer, to send a warship to the St Lawrence.

In December the governor authorized the raising of a new corps, the Glengarry Light Infantry Fencibles. It was recruited among the Scots of the Maritime colonies as well as in Upper Canada. By May 1812 some companies had begun training, and by July the corps had reached its goal of 600 men.[20] Meanwhile, in Lower Canada, recruitment for a provincial corps of light infantry, or Voltigeurs Canadiens, had begun in April. This new militia corps had been earlier suggested by Brevet Major Charles-Michel de Salaberry, an experienced regular officer in the 60th Foot who also represented a distinguished French-Canadian family. Under his leadership the corps would give a good account of itself during the war.[21]

Prevost authorized Salaberry to recruit the unit, promising him the rank of lieutentant-colonel when the corps reached a certain strength. Differences soon arose between the two men which affected their relationship during the war. In October 1812 Salaberry complained that he had been promised the higher rank when the Voltigeurs reached a strength of 300 men but that now the governor was requiring 380. Salaberry thought that this figure would be very difficult to achieve and that his chances of ever receiving the promotion would thus be jeopardized.[22] Furthermore, he would not be satisfied with the "the Militia rank of Lt. Coll:" but wanted an army rank. Prevost seems to have been anxious to please Salaberry, for he made him a militia lieutenant-colonel, with his commission backdated to 1 April 1812 to give him precedence over other lieutenant-colonels, and promised him that rank in the army when he had recruited the required number of Voltigeurs.[23]

These difficulties were still in the future when the Lower Canadian legislature met between February and May 1812. It approved over £60,000 for training and arming the militia and a new militia law that strengthened Prevost's hand because it authorized him to embody militiamen when invasion was imminent, rather than only after it had occurred.[24] In case of war, the governor could call out the entire militia of Lower Canada. In May Prevost ordered four battalions to be embodied, and they were quickly filled. But the following month, when the militia was called out in response to the American declaration of war, there was a disturbance at Lachine, where some men refused to be balloted.[25] It was easily suppressed by regular troops and other militia, and there were no more such incidents in Lower Canada.

After the outbreak of war, Prevost's success with the legislature and his support from the people continued. In July the assembly approved his request to guarantee army bills, a paper currency. In order to overcome popular distrust of paper money, the governor sought and gained the backing of francophone politicians and clergy.[26] But although army bills met the government's need for a stable currency, they did not solve all its financial problems, particularly in Upper Canada. Nonetheless, varying numbers of army bills were issued every year until 1815, by which time the total had reached £3,441,993. Over the next two years the bills still in circulation were redeemed. The Canadas did not therefore suffer the severe deflation that undermined the American war effort, and Prevost deserves credit for his initiative and foresight in avoiding this major problem.

As a military commander, he also had to formulate strategy. In fulfilling this role, he revealed his professionalism, which included knowledge of the art of war. With the reassuring precedents of the sieges of Quebec in 1759–60 and 1775–76 behind them, the traditional strategy of commanding British generals in the Canadas had been to concentrate the bulk of their forces at Quebec, on the assumption that as long as the fortress held out, the rest of the territory could be reconquered after reinforcements had arrived from the home country.[27] Prevost's instructions from England required him to adopt a strictly defensive policy, and this suited his professional outlook.[28] He argued from two premises. First, he believed that the forces in the Canadas were too few and, aside from Quebec, the fixed defences too weak to allow attacks on the United States or to defend effectively the territory above Quebec. On 18 May 1812 he wrote to the secretary for war and the colonies:

Quebec is the only permanent Fortress in the Canadas:– It is the Key to the whole and must be maintained:– To the final defence of this position, every

other Military operation ought to become subservient, and the retreat of the
Troops upon Quebec must be the primary consideration:– ...

If the Americans are determined to attack Canada, it would be in vain the
General should flatter himself with hopes of making an effectual defence of
the open Country, unless powerfully assisted from Home:– All predatory or ill
concerted attacks undertaken presumptuously and without sufficient means,
can be resisted and repulsed:– Still this must be done with caution, that the
resources, for a future exertion, the defence of Quebec, may be unexhausted.[29]

Secondly, Prevost believed that the Canadas could derive no benefit
from attacks on the United States. As he explained to Liverpool, the
prime minister, on 15 July 1812, "In the present state of politics in the
United States, I consider it prudent to avoid every measure which can
have the least tendency to unite the people of America. Whilst disunion
prevails among them, their attempts on the British American Provinces
will be feeble. It is therefore my wish to avoid committing any act which
may even by a strained construction tend to unite the Eastern and
Southern States, unless from its perpetration we are to derive an immediate, considerable, and important advantage."[30]

Prevost held to his belief in a passive defence throughout the war,
although his actions were not always consistent with his strategic
thought. His attitude towards combat, however, remained consistently
conventional and cautious. Military doctrine in the eighteenth century
emphasized campaigns of manœuvre to occupy territory or to come
between an opponent and his base rather than engage him in battle.
A commander was under pressure to preserve his army because of the
time involved in training soldiers and the costs of raising and maintain-
ing them. Battles should be avoided, or fought only if the commander
felt very confident of success. In a publication of 1770 Major Thomas
Bell expressed a widespread view: "Battles have ever been the last
resource of good Generals ... The fighting of a battle only because the
enemy is near, or from having no other plan of offence, is a direful way
of making war."[31] This approach to warfare was being changed in
Europe by Napoleon and Wellington. However, Prevost's education and
formative military experience belonged to the eighteenth century, and
his active service had involved capturing or defending very small areas
of territory. It is not surprising that he would regard the vast expanse
of Upper Canada, with its scattered population of mostly recent American immigrants, to be undefendable.

Besides a conventional and careful outlook, Prevost's generalship was
also characterized from the outset by pessimism about the possibility of
holding Upper Canada and by a tendency to appeasement in the hope
of promoting the cause of peace or of producing advantages for the

defenders. One explanation for this trait of Prevost's generalship was his heavy responsibilities as both governor-in-chief and commander of the forces. The transformation of a bold officer into a cautious one by promotion to a post of supreme command has precedents in North America, such as the careers of Sir William Howe, Sir Henry Clinton, and Sir Guy Carleton.[32] A brief summary of the principal reasons for each general's transformation may help to throw some light on the change in Prevost over thirty years later. Howe, it seems, was a prisoner of his eighteenth-century military upbringing, which stressed the importance of preserving the army. Hence, he would rather let his opponent escape than risk suffering heavy casualties in a decisive battle.[33] Clinton also worried about risking his army in battle, but he was disadvantaged by the reduction of his forces, by his lack of self-confidence, and by weak political support from the home government. Carleton tended to underestimate his enemy and seemed unable to appreciate the wider consequences of his actions in Quebec (the Canadas). He was also on bad terms with his superior, the secretary of state for the colonies. Howe and Carleton displayed their caution most obviously in the very slow movements of their armies, whether pursuing a beaten foe or invading enemy territory.

Like those predecessors, Prevost from 1812 to 1814 faced problems that were less serious or insignificant for generals commanding in Europe. There were the obvious difficulties of distance, climate, and land communications over large territories. Any commander-in-chief would have to be concerned to preserve his army and supplies because neither could be quickly replaced from their principal source, Britain. Both circumstances and his own character caused Prevost to seek to avoid defeat, which meant following a defensive, rather than offensive, policy, and as often as possible to prevent any fighting by negotiating a truce. Yet as war approached, Sir George's conventional, cautious, and pessimistic outlook did not deter him from acting vigorously to prepare the defences of the Canadas.

To ease the serious shortage of trained regular officers in Upper Canada, Prevost sent Captain Andrew Gray, acting deputy quartermaster general, and Captain M.C. Dixon, RE. In May 1812 he dispatched units of the 41st Foot and the Royal Newfoundland Regiment to the upper province. After the outbreak of war he continued to send supplies and men, including part of the 10th Royal Veteran Battalion and the 49th Foot. Lieutenant-Colonel John Vincent, a veteran of thirty-one years' service, was put in command of Kingston, the principal British naval base for the Great Lakes, and the experienced Lieutenant-Colonel Christopher Myers and Major-General Roger Sheaffe went to assist Brock.[34] Prevost was able to spare these troops and officers because, on his own initiative, he had kept the 100th Foot instead of transferring it to Nova Scotia and also because reinforcements (103rd and 1st Foot) had begun arriving from overseas.

But an examination of official troop strengths demonstrates that he did not provide Brock with increased forces on the Niagara since between January and September 1812 only one-fifth to one-seventh of the troops in the Canadas were stationed in that area.[35] The reinforcements of regulars that Brock sent to Colonel Henry Procter at Amherstburg, a village on the Detroit River near its entrance to Lake Erie, he took from the troops needed along the Niagara frontier and at York. Prevost may have provided increased means, including officers, to Brock, but it was the latter who would shoulder the risk of taking the war to the enemy at Detroit.

In spite of increasing troop strength, when war broke out, Prevost did not prosecute it vigorously himself; nor until the summer of 1813 did he encourage his subordinate commanders to do so. His letters to Brock after news of the declaration urged caution and abstention from offensive moves.[36] He sent orders to Captain Charles Roberts, in command of Fort St Joseph, "to observe the greatest vigilance and caution" and "to afford every assistance and Protection Possible to Promote the Interest and Security of the North West Company, Consistent with a due regard to the Security of the Post and in Case of Necessity the ultimate retreat of your Party."[37] This pessimistically cautious message contrasts strikingly with Brock's letters to Roberts, which included orders to attack Michilimackinac. Closer to home, Prevost placed a cordon of troops and militia under the command of Major-General Rottenburg around Montreal, sent supplies to the militia along the St Lawrence between Montreal and Kingston, and instituted a convoy system for boats going upriver.[38]

When he learned in August about the repeal of the orders-in-council, conditional upon the United States ending hostilities, Prevost wasted no time in sending his adjutant general, Lieutenant-Colonel Edward Baynes, to negotiate a truce with Major-General Henry Dearborn, the American commander of the frontier opposite Lower Canada.[39] The agreement, which confined each side to defensive measures, suited both men, for Prevost had no desire to launch attacks and Dearborn was unable to because of the inadequacies of his forces. The truce did not apply to Brigadier-General William Hull's command at Detroit; in any case, it could not have saved him because it became known in Upper Canada only after Hull's surrender. There is disagreement about the value of this ceasefire, which ended on 4 September, to the defence of the Canadas.[40] While it enabled Prevost to send supplies upriver unmolested (but without increasing troop strength), it also prevented

Brock from attacking Sackets Harbor, the principal American naval base on Lake Ontario, or the American side of the Niagara River, and it stopped the Provincial Marine's warships from interfering with the movement of American supplies and reinforcements. A significant result, notes Hitsman, was that "the American schooners which had earlier been chased back to Ogdensburg had been able to make their way to Sackets Harbor."[41] At this shipbuilding centre they were soon converted into warships and would help Captain Isaac Chauncey, the new American naval commander on the lakes, to gain control of Lake Ontario at the end of 1812.[42]

The governor's policy of passive defence may be accepted as a reasonable response to all the circumstances that he was aware of and the difficulties that he faced. Yet his later shortcomings as a military leader were foreshadowed as early as August and September 1812 in his reactions to the capture of Michilimackinac, as well as in his advice to Brock regarding the Detroit front. In his correspondence Prevost revealed a lack of boldness, an absence of offensive spirit, and a startling misunderstanding of American intentions. On 12 August he wrote to Brock commending Captain Roberts's "zeal and promptitude" in capturing the American post, but he fretted, "at the same time, I must confess, my mind has been very much relieved by finding that the capture took place at a period subsequent to Brigadier-General Hull's invasion of the Province, as had it been prior to it, it would not only have been a violation of Captain Roberts's orders, but have afforded a just ground for the subsequent conduct of the enemy, which I now plainly perceive no forbearance on your part could have prevented."[43]

Early in September 1812 Brock wrote to Prevost about the growing strength of American forces along the Niagara River and his expectation of an attack by them "almost immediately." He asked for "officers, men, and heavy ordnance," but indicated that he would put up a strong resistance to invasion.[44] Prevost's reply a week later showed excessive caution, for he suggested that Brock evacuate Detroit and the Michigan Territory. This move would enable him to reinforce his front with the forces from Amherstburg rather than taking them from the troops at Kingston. On the 28th Brock rejected this course of action. Prevost's advice conformed to the traditional strategy of concentrating on the lower St Lawrence rather than trying to hold on to the interior,[45] and it was not necessarily the wrong advice, given his view from Quebec. What it does show is his readiness to counsel retreat rather than resistance, much less attack; it emphasizes his caution and pessimism.

Prevost's misreading of American intentions might be contrasted with Admiral Sir John B. Warren's quite accurate prediction in October 1812 that the United States was not disposed to make peace with Britain but would likely continue to pursue the war, and that eventually the northern and eastern states would also take "a more active part," in spite of the many opponents of the policy among their citizens.[46] Warren's more realistic appraisal may have been the product of his long experience in Britain's navy, which had begun in 1771 and included service during the American Revolutionary War as well as against France in the 1790s. From November 1807 until July 1810 he had been commander-in-chief of the Halifax station; he was therefore necessarily well informed about American attitudes towards Britain. In August 1812 he took command of the North American station, and the next month he tried unsuccessfully to negotiate a peace settlement with the United States. He had no illusions that, while the British were fighting Napoleon, the Americans would be willing to end the war.

The commander of the forces revealed yet another quality of his generalship in these early months, a decisiveness towards subordinates who failed. On 4 October an attack by fencibles and militia from Prescott against Ogdensburg was driven back before the men even got across the St Lawrence. Colonel Robert Lethbridge, the elderly commander at Prescott and leader of the raid, was quickly recalled to Montreal and his command given to the younger Lieutenant-Colonel Thomas Pearson. Sir George never tolerated failure in others.[47] Just as Wellington held officers responsible for the conduct of their men, so also did Prevost in Canada. After a court of enquiry reported to him about the "outrages committed by a Detachment of the 103rd Regiment under the command of Captain [James Bowie] on its march from Quebec," he blamed the faults on failures by the "Officers of the Detachment and most particularly by the Officer in the immediate Command of the first Division."[48]

During 1813, in the realm of civil government, the governor's success continued, although he did encounter minor frustrations. In the course of its session from 29 December 1812 to 15 February 1813, the legislature in Lower Canada voted large sums of money to provide equipment and hospitals for the militia and for general war purposes and again backed army bills. It did not give him a revision of the Militia Act or approval for any future use of martial law, thus leaving Prevost in the position that any application of martial law would rest solely on his own authority.[49] (As it happened, Prevost never declared martial law in the province.) His inability to achieve everything he sought cannot be attributed to a failure of his leadership; rather, it was the result of continuing disputes between the assembly and the Legislative Council.

The citizen-soldiers continued to give good service in 1813 and achieved particular distinction for their defeat of an American invasion force on 26 October in the battle of Châteauguay. On that occasion

Salaberry commanded the defensive forces composed of Voltigeurs, militia units, and Native warriors, but he afterwards believed that he had been unjustly deprived of his rightful credit by Prevost.[50] This feeling of resentment only worsened their relationship. Meanwhile the numbers of the Select Embodied Militia (a long-term force) were increased, and several other units recruited in the province.[51] These included infantry, cavalry, artillery drivers, and a provincial corps of Commissariat Voyageurs to help with the transport of supplies upriver, thereby relieving the Lower Canadians of an onerous duty.

In the second year of the war would come Prevost's first opportunities to take offensive action. His advice to subordinates and his behaviour would demonstrate clearly the traits of his generalship mentioned earlier. He passed through Prescott on 21–22 February 1813, on his first visit to Upper Canada. There he transferred Pearson to command at Kingston and replaced him with Lieutenant-Colonel George Macdonell of the Glengarry Light Infantry.[52] Pearson and Macdonell advocated retaliation against Ogdensburg for earlier raids on the Canadian shore, and Prevost agreed that Macdonell might make a demonstration on the ice. He later wrote to him ordering him not to attack without previously informing Rottenburg at Montreal, and only then if the situation offered an easy opportunity to inflict damage upon the enemy. Macdonell received this message during the course of his raid on Ogdensburg, an enterprise undertaken on his own initiative that was highly successful in eliminating that town as a base for American offensive operations.[53]

In his report on the action, however, Sir George claimed for himself a more positive role than he actually played. For example, he told Lord Bathurst, "I deemed it absolutely necessary … to dislodge the enemy from his position at Ogdensburg, to secure from interruption my line of communication with Lower Canada."[54] It is Hitsman's view that Prevost forgot Macdonell's disregard of his order because of the success of the raid. Furthermore, Prevost "doctored" Macdonell's report "lest anyone should suspect that he [Prevost] was too defensive-minded to take advantage of any ready-made opportunity for an easy victory."[55]

In the attack on Sackets Harbor on 29 May, Prevost had his first experience of combat in the war. The commander of the forces was at Kingston when he learned that Chauncey had sailed his fleet to the western end of Lake Ontario. He and the new Royal Navy "commanding officer on the lakes," Commodore Sir James Yeo, recognized the opportunity both to take the pressure off Vincent and to destroy the American naval base.[56] Yeo, who had arrived at Quebec on 5 May and hurried to Kingston, was a veteran of small-ship actions and coastal raids.

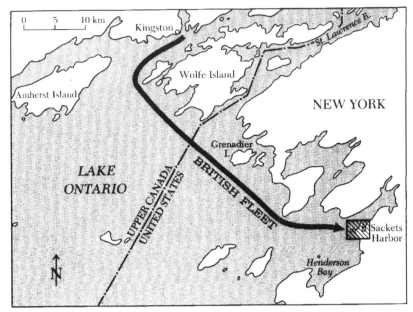

27 May

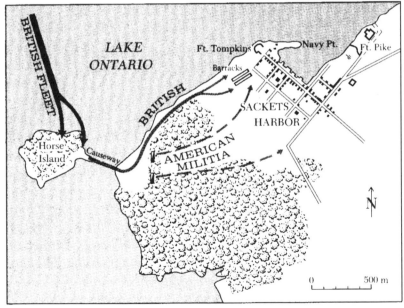

28–29 May

Map 2 The attack on Sackets Harbor, May 1813
(reprinted, by permission, from Stanley, *The War of 1812*, 236)

Details of this action are readily available in various sources, in particular an excellent recent study by Patrick Wilder.[57] Rather than a description of the battle, what is important here is Prevost's role in the expedition. He and Yeo prepared their forces on 27 May, hoping to storm ashore early on the 28th and catch the Americans by surprise.[58] While Yeo commanded the naval arm, Prevost put Lieutenant-Colonel Edward Baynes in command of the troops. A thirty-year veteran who had seen action in South Africa, Baynes may have been qualified to command an assault.[59] Yet without giving reasons, Prevost accompanied the expedition, and that meant he would have to be included in the decision-making.

The Americans had prepared warning and defence systems which worked effectively because unfavourable winds delayed the British landing.[60] The evidence of participants indicates that Baynes made the decision to delay the assault and, when conditions appeared more favourable, authorized it after obtaining Prevost's consent.[61] At other times, Sir George issued commands, in particular the final withdrawal of the troops from the battle.[62] He ordered the retreat, he later explained, because Yeo's warships could not approach close enough to shore to provide covering artillery fire. Other accounts suggest that different factors influenced the commander's decision, most especially the high rate of casualties, particularly among the officers, and a belief that the dust raised by retreating Americans indicated the arrival of reinforcements.[63]

Some accounts mention that the order for withdrawal was conveyed by a bugle call, which some of the soldiers did not understand.[64] It is no surprise to find differing and even conflicting reports about events during a tumultuous battle, but the vagueness surrounding this final stage suggests uncertain leadership. There was not the clear-cut decision to withdraw displayed by Sheaffe at York in April, by Vincent outside Fort George in May, and indeed by Prevost himself at Plattsburgh in September 1814. The British re-embarked without difficulty and returned to Kingston, while Chauncey arrived at his base on 1 June.[65]

The attack achieved only limited success.[66] The British failed to capture the base or even to inflict serious damage. During the action the Americans set fire to the barracks, a sloop under construction, and naval stores, but the flames were put out before much harm had been done.[67] Nevertheless, the raid did provide a lesson for the future about how to weaken enemy naval forces: namely, that destruction could be inflicted on an enemy naval base and ships simply by the fact of an attack, even if the base was not captured. During a raid the defenders might decide to destroy ships and stores to prevent them falling into the hands of the attackers. (Such had been the case in April during the American attack on York.)

Prevost's role during this expedition was ambiguous. After the landing Lieutenant-Colonel E.B. Brenton, an eyewitness, wrote, "Sir
George, who could not rest satisfied on board [ship] and yet who could
not consistently command the expedition, embarked in a canoe ... at
2.30 A.M." He not only went ashore, but advanced with the troops and
exposed himself to fire. After the retreat was sounded, Brenton
reported, "We retired with the hindmost, nor was it, I assure you, with
a quickstep, though showers of grape were falling about us. Fortunately
the enemy did not attempt a pursuit."[68] Brenton does not specify who
ordered the retreat, but Prevost in his report to Earl Bathurst stated
that he had. In effect, Prevost took command away from Baynes, and
even if he did so with Baynes's consent, it was clearly not a step taken
after the alternatives had been discussed.[69]

It is true that the attack was made under extremely difficult conditions. The British had lost the advantage of surprise, and on shore they
lacked the firepower from their navy's guns. They faced capable American commanders leading a determined body of defenders who were
able to fall back on a series of defensive lines and positions with artillery support.[70] What the commander of the assault did not need was
his superior's presence there, suggesting that Provost had doubts about
Baynes's leadership abilities. There was no reason for the commander-
in-chief to be present at what was simply a quick raid, rather than a
carefully planned and powerful invasion of enemy territory. In spite of
his demonstration of personal bravery in the midst of shot and shell,
Prevost's place during these events was in Kingston, not at Sackets Harbor, where he risked death or capture.

In July Prevost displayed an aggressive attitude when he sent an expedition of soldiers and seamen against American bases on Lake Cham-
plain, although the credit for this plan probably belongs to Rottenburg.
This operation, commanded by Lieutenant-Colonel John Murray, with
the naval element under Commander Thomas Everard of the Royal
Navy, completed its assignment without difficulty. The invaders burned
blockhouses, barracks, and storehouses at Plattsburgh, Swanton, and
Saranac, and Everard captured four vessels at Burlington, Vermont.[71]
This expedition confirmed British control of the lake until at least
September.

Prevost returned to Montreal from Upper Canada in the first week
of March 1813; he made his second visit to the upper province in May,
staying until the third week of September. Both times he went no farther than Fort Erie.[72] The purpose of his trips was to inspect troops and
fortifications and to assess the situation for himself. Once again Prevost
showed that he was a conscientious commander and not afraid to be
near a scene of fighting. But his leadership at Sackets Harbor in May

and near Fort George in August raised doubts in the minds of Upper Canadians about his interest in fighting battles as well as about his ability to command.[73]

On the Niagara frontier the Americans had retreated to Fort George and entrenched themselves in the fort and the adjoining town of Newark (Niagara-on-the-Lake). When Prevost arrived, he found Rottenburg and Vincent with their 2,000 troops "cooping up in Fort George an American force exceeding 4,000 men." He wished to ascertain "the extent of the enemy's Works" and their ability to defend them, and thus he "ordered [for 24 August] a general demonstration to be made on Fort George."[74] The British drove in the American pickets and temporarily advanced into Newark, but they could not capture the fort or force the Americans to fight outside their entrenchments. According to his report of 25 August, Prevost got "close to the Fort" during the skirmish and concluded that the position, which was strongly supported by the guns of Fort Niagara, could not be taken except by a combined assault on the two forts.

This affair raises questions about Prevost's tactical discernment. He hardly needed to employ such a large force simply to prove the obvious: that the American position was strong and that Fort Niagara dominated it. He could surely have gained this information from the veteran commanders Rottenburg and Vincent. If, however, he wanted direct knowledge, a reconnaissance or small-scale probes would have been sufficient.[75] Moreover, Prevost made no attempt to coordinate the movement with Yeo. The latter had reported from Kingston on 22 August that Chauncey had taken shelter in Sackets Harbor and "in my opinion will not come out until his new Brig is ready."[76] Yeo's fleet appeared off the Niagara River between 27 and 30 August.[77] It is hard to understand why Prevost did not wait to take that opportunity to plan with Yeo an operation combining a naval demonstration with his land assault. In September he would urge the commodore to undertake a combined operation against the same objective with Rottenburg, but by then Chauncey's squadron was on the lake.[78] Why it was urgent to launch the general demonstration on 24 August is not clear.

Whether or not a more ambitious enterprise was possible, Upper Canadians were disappointed that the commander of the forces, the officer commanding in Upper Canada (Rottenburg), and the highly regarded Vincent had together attempted no more than a reconnaissance raid.[79] Prevost's impact on the army's morale was not impressive, to judge by the comments of a couple of its members. Colonel Charles Plenderleath, 49th Foot, wondered, "What his visit has done, or is to do, no man can see ... I am afraid he has not thrown life enough into our *worthy* Generals" (he presumably meant Vincent and Rottenburg).

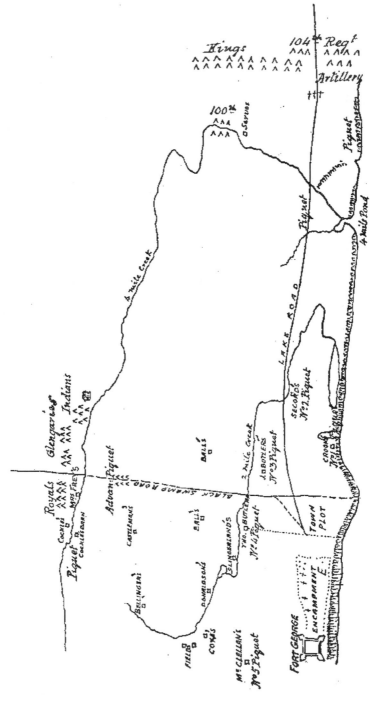

Map 3   American piquets around Fort George, summer 1813 (by permission of the Lundy's Lane Historical Society)

The subaltern John Le Couteur was ordered by Prevost to gallop off with orders to Major Robert Moodie and then twice recalled to repeat the orders. He concluded, "This hesitation and uncertainty reminded me of Sackets Harbor."[80] What was becoming clear in 1813 was Prevost's inability to inspire either his fighting men or the Upper Canadian civilian population.

He continued to make vigorous appeals to the British government for troops, seamen, and supplies, which he intended for the reinforcement of the Canadas rather than Nova Scotia and New Brunswick.[81] From his own garrisons he drew reinforcements for Upper Canada, and as troops and seamen began arriving from overseas, many of these were sent upriver.[82] In fact, from June until November the regulars in the upper province outnumbered those in Lower Canada.[83] Although Prevost was providing the means for offensive warfare in Upper Canada, this was not his declared intention. What he expected the commanders there to do was to keep their forces concentrated in order to repel invasion and always "to act with such caution as would enable you to husband your resources for future exertion."[84] That was his advice to Sheaffe in March, but only four months later he told Rottenburg that, if he was forced to withdraw to the Head of the Lake (Burlington Bay), he was to do it "with the fierceness and deliberation of the Lion and without leaving to the Enemy any Trophy of any kind."[85] In one direction only did Prevost press for offensive action, that is, on Lakes Erie and Ontario.[86] He wanted the Americans defeated on these waters in order to provide security to the flanks of the land forces and their supply lines.

The increasing commitment of troops, matériel, and money to Upper Canada was apparently for defensive purposes. Yet these commitments meant that a withdrawal from the province, in the event that the Americans severed the St Lawrence lifeline, would be virtually impossible physically and unacceptable politically. Naval control of Lake Ontario would assist such a withdrawal, but it could be effective for only a short distance east of Kingston.

What Prevost did during 1813 was to moderate slightly the traditional strategy for defending the Canadas by lessening Quebec's garrison, in order to shift more forces upriver to the area of Montreal and in Upper Canada as far as the Niagara Peninsula.[87] The key to control of the Canadas remained Quebec. But the Americans could not threaten it by water; nor was it feasible to launch an invasion through Maine, as Benedict Arnold had done in 1775. In effect, they had no choice but to attack Montreal or farther up the St Lawrence before they could advance on Quebec. Prevost was defending his capital by shifting his forces upriver. At the same time, these troop movements certainly gave the impression that he was determined to hold on to the interior.[88] Perhaps an indication of a genuine commitment to preserve Upper Canada was his concern that the commanders there act vigorously, even if they were forced to withdraw. Sheaffe, who had not retreated fiercely from York, was replaced in June by the veteran Rottenburg, and in December this uninspiring commander with the younger Drummond.[89]

While Prevost might look for improvement in the military situation in 1814, the political scene in Lower Canada promised him more frustration than success. During its session from 13 January to 31 March the Lower Canadian legislature extended the issue of army bills, but otherwise did not provide the governor with the measures that he sought, including a revenue bill. As in the preceding session, the principal causes of his setbacks were the disputes between the assembly and the Legislative Council.[90] Prevost was unable to prevent the assembly from instituting impeachment proceedings against the two chief justices, James Monk and Jonathan Sewell, and from trying to appoint an agent to prosecute the charges in England.[91] Another factor was the apparent security of the province, which allowed time for the luxury of political squabbles. Prevost reacted calmly, believing that the politicians were not motivated by hostility to his government or disloyalty. His cool-headed policy was sound, for he had the support of the Catholic Church, and the war still demanded his major attention.[92]

In the early months of 1814 Prevost faced a promising, but ambiguous military situation. In Europe the defeat of Napoleon appeared imminent, and partly for this reason the American government agreed to the British proposal to open peace negotiations. There was also the probability that large British naval and land forces would soon be released from Europe for use against the United States. In April Napoleon abdicated, and by August substantial reinforcements began to reach Quebec. But as he was unaware of these developments, Prevost's main concern naturally remained defence, particularly the line between Montreal and Kingston. Yet at the same time he proposed and approved attacks designed to secure domination on the lakes. In other words, he wanted Drummond and Yeo to act aggressively but with considerable caution and without expectation of help from Lower Canada.

On 17 January he wrote to Drummond suggesting an attack on the American ships held by ice in Lake Erie. Drummond consulted with Yeo, and the two agreed that the attempt would be worthwhile.[93] When he received this answer, Prevost urged haste while ice conditions were favourable. (He even laid down a timetable.) His letter contained a curious mixture of boldness and pessimistic caution: "It is allowed that in all great enterprises some risk must be run and something left to fortune." But he warned Drummond, "Whilst the enemy continues to concentrate a large disposable force near the frontier of Lower Canada ... thereby indicating his intention that the pressure of the approaching campaign should fall upon that Province, you must be sensible of my total inability of augmenting your present force. I give you this information that you may regulate your measures accordingly."[94]

Ten days later Prevost wrote to Drummond pressing him to act against American forces, including their vessels, at the Detroit River. "I am desirous of strongly impressing upon you the necessity of making every effort during the remainder of the winter for the destruction of the enemy's naval force on Lake Erie ... Nothing but the impracticability of the measure from the causes alluded to in my late letter to you on this subject will justify its not being attempted." He hoped that Drummond could follow his success by establishing a naval base on Lake Erie. To indicate his support for the enterprise, he sent Lieutenant-Colonel John Harvey to Upper Canada to assist him.[95] Drummond was prepared to make the attempt even without additional help from Lower Canada, but as he told Prevost on 3 February, because of the "uncommon mildness of the season," the ice was not sufficiently strong to bear the weight of the troops.[96] Prevost expressed "deep regret" that the plan had been abandoned.

Reinforcements trickled into Upper Canada. In February Prevost sent a detachment of the Royal Marine Artillery with Congreve rockets to Kingston, and in March the 103rd Foot began to arrive there.[97] By April Drummond was pleading for reinforcements.[98] Within the next two months Prevost had sent an additional 700 men, to make a total of 6,600 in the upper province out of 14,489 altogether in the Canadas.[99]

After Yeo had launched two new frigates on Lake Ontario in April, Prevost urged Drummond to consider an attack on Sackets Harbor to prevent the Americans from matching Yeo's fleet. If such an attack were successful, Prevost proposed that it be followed by aggressive moves against the enemy along the Niagara frontier and in western Upper Canada. Already planning such a raid, Drummond quickly agreed, but he laid down as one condition that he would need at least 800 troops from Lower Canada.[100] In his reply of 30 April, Prevost vetoed the plan because he could not spare the troops from the lower province. He calculated that he would have to send at least 1,000 regulars to make up the necessary force. But was he suggesting that Drummond act cautiously or boldly when he wrote: "The views of His Majesty's Government respecting the mode of conducting the war with America, do not justify my exposing too much at one stake. It is by wary measures and occasional daring enterprises, with apparently disproportionate means, that the character of the war has been sustained, and from that policy I am not disposed to depart"?[101] Prevost did not explain why this proposed attack on Sackets Harbor did not qualify as one of those "occasional daring enterprises." Such an assault would probably have diverted American attention away from the St Lawrence front. Based on his experience of American efforts against Lower Canada, Sir George need not have been so fearful of the effects of weakening his forces by 800 or 1,000 men.

Excessive prudence, however, was his frame of mind, and he maintained it when, in May, Drummond again advocated an attack on Sackets Harbor, with a request for 800 troops from Lower Canada. In the same letter he explained a plan that he and Yeo had developed for a raid on Oswego, a small port on the south shore of Lake Ontario southwest of Sackets. Prevost approved of this latter project, but refused to send any soldiers because he believed that he needed all his available force for the defence of the lower province.[102] He encouraged offensive operations in Upper Canada as long as they required no assistance from Lower Canada and endorsed them as long as they succeeded.[103]

At the same time as he was suggesting and approving offensive plans, Prevost was also agreeing to a ceasefire proposal made by the American secretary of state, James Monroe. Sir George learned of the request in March and asked Drummond and Yeo for their opinions. They both advised against it, making clear that they preferred to prosecute the war.[104] Nevertheless, even though he was not authorized to undertake peace negotiations, Prevost on 29 April selected Baynes as his negotiator in the belief that President Madison was acting with "a sincere desire of conciliation ... and not merely for the purpose of obtaining a temporary cessation of hostilities."[105]

If Prevost actually believed that the American government was motivated by a sincere desire for peace, why was he so fearful of reducing his garrison to meet Drummond's request for troops? The day after appointing Baynes, he wrote to Drummond refusing to send the 1,000 regulars and, because of the prospective negotiations, advising against action: "This circumstance renders it inexpedient that an extensive offensive movement against any of the enemy's positions should be undertaken until you shall again hear from me on the subject." On the other hand, he directed Drummond, "You will please to communicate to Commodore Sir James Yeo the subject of this letter, but I do not wish it to restrain him from any operation he may have in view until the armistice is officially announced."[106] Sir George's meaning and intentions cannot be described as clear when it is seen that only a week later, on 7 May, he wrote to Drummond approving his proposed raid on Oswego. No truce was made, and Earl Bathurst, when he learned of the American proposal, quickly forbad any consideration of it.[107]

It is clear that Sir George was concerned about British naval security on the lakes, particularly Ontario. He recognized the threat of Sackets Harbor, but as we have seen, he was reluctant to commit his own forces to any attack on it. In short, during 1814 he was unwilling to take any risks for that prize. In October an attack on Sackets Harbor before the end of the year received some consideration. On the 11th Prevost wrote to Bathurst from Kingston that such an action was not feasible because Yeo would not gain control of the lake until his new ship, the *St Lawrence*, was launched. Even then, it would be too late in the season to consider an attack because "the enemy have made Sackett's Harbour a place of considerable resistance against any force capable of being brought against it." Prevost went on to explain that he was arranging with Drummond and Yeo to launch an assault early in 1815.[108]

The most controversial facet of Prevost's career was the failed offensive against Plattsburgh in September 1814. After nearly 15,000 of Wellington's veteran troops together with some of his best brigade commanders had reached Canada, Sir George had a golden opportunity to lead a major invasion of American territory.[109] In July he received Bathurst's letter of 3 June informing him that the troops were to be used "first, to give immediate protection; secondly to obtain if possible ultimate security to His Majesty's Possessions in America … The entire destruction of Sackets Harbour and the Naval Establishments on Lake Erie and Lake Champlain come under the first description … The maintenance of Fort Niagara and so much of the adjacent Territory as may be deemed necessary; and the occupation of Detroit and the Michigan Country come under the second."[110]

According to these instructions, the prime targets were naval bases: Sackets Harbor, Plattsburgh (and possibly Vergennes on Otter Creek, which flows into Lake Champlain), or both.[111] The reasons why Prevost chose not to attack Sackets Harbor have been noted. He made a sound decision not to attempt it without superiority on Lake Ontario, but instead to advance against the more accessible objective of Plattsburgh.

So far in Canada when leading in combat, Prevost had demonstrated his overwhelming concerns to avoid defeat and preserve the army rather than to battle on under difficult conditions, seeking victory even at heavy cost. His habitual caution would hardly be lessened by Bathurst's injunctions:

it is by no means the intention of His Majesty's Govt to encourage such forward movements into the interior of the American Territory as might commit the safety of the Force placed under your command.

Should there be any advanced position on that part of our frontier which extends towards Lake Champlain, the occupation of which would materially tend to the security of the Province, you will if you deem it expedient expel the Enemy from it, and occupy it by detachments of the Troops under your command, always however taking care not to expose His Majesty's Forces to being cut off by too extended a line of advance.[112]

Even though Prevost's circumstances were very different from those faced by General John Burgoyne in October 1777, no British general could be unaware of the consequences of that campaign.

The next aspect to consider is the naval. Prevost knew that the British naval force at Île aux Noix, down the Richelieu River from Lake Champlain, would not be strong enough to challenge the American squadron of four warships and ten gunboats under Lieutenant Thomas Macdonough until the new ship *Confiance* could be put into service. It was launched on 25 August and was expected to need three weeks to be made ready for action.[113] At the end of the month Yeo transferred command of the squadron to Captain George Downie, who arrived at Île aux Noix on 1 September.[114] This change in command could not be expected to hasten the naval preparations. Nevertheless, gun boats were available to assist Prevost's advance, and by the 7th Downie had his squadron moving towards Chazy, about twelve miles north of Plattsburgh; the *Confiance* was towed there to join the other ships on 9 September.[115] These movements suggest that Downie was trying hard to meet Prevost's schedule.

Meanwhile, on the last day of August, Prevost had moved his headquarters to Odelltown, just north of the American border, where he learned that the American commander at Plattsburgh, Major-General George Izard, had marched westward with part of the troops from there, leaving Brigadier-General Alexander Macomb in command. In fact, Izard had taken 4,000 men, leaving behind 3,000, not all of whom were effectives.[116] Prevost could readily obtain intelligence of American movements and must have realized that the Plattsburgh garrison had been significantly weakened. The circumstances appeared propitious for his invasion, but the naval force would not be completely ready for a week or more. If naval support was crucial, Prevost would simply have to wait; but if the army could gain Plattsburgh, then the time had come to invade. The latter would seem to have been Sir George's conclusion, for his men crossed the frontier on 1 September. The army was formed in three brigades, one each under Major-Generals Thomas Brisbane, Manley Power, and Frederick Robinson, officers recently arrived from serving in the Peninsula under Wellington. A fourth brigade, under Major-General James Kempt, remained at Montreal as a reserve.

Prevost's army, some 10,351 strong, advanced "cautiously and by short marches," according to Macomb.[117] It took five days, including one day's halt, to march about fifty-seven miles. The roads were in bad condition, but probably Prevost's habitual caution had more to do with the army's very slow movement. On the 6th it arrived at the north bank of the Saranac River, which divides Plattsburgh in two.[118] No serious opposition met Prevost's forces, and as Macomb wrote, "So undaunted ... was the enemy, that he never deployed in his whole march, always pressing on in column."[119] It was prudent for Prevost to take care when invading enemy territory, but in view of the size and quality of his army, the nearness of his base and reinforcements, and the accompaniment of gunboats as far as Chazy, his caution seems excessive. His army appeared able to operate quite effectively without Downie's ships for transport or protection. In fact, when some of Macdonough's gunboats fired on British troops near Plattsburgh, the latter used artillery to drive them away.

In retreating across the Saranac, the Americans had removed the planking from the river's two bridges and withdrawn into the fortifications of three open redoubts and two blockhouses.[120] Prevost thought of attacking on the 6th, but decided against it when Robinson informed him that his men were exhausted from their ten-hour march. Night would be on them by the time the men were rested, and Prevost would not undertake an attack in the dark.[121] By the next day he had decided against an immediate assault. From the 7th onward, his intention was to attack only in cooperation with the British squadron, and he informed Downie of this decision on that date as well as on the 8th, 9th, and 10th (see appendix C for the text of this correspondence and the sources).[122] The initiative that Prevost had possessed so far was thus relinquished, never to be regained.

His men erected heavy batteries to deal with both the American fortifications and any ships within range.[123] Prevost learned the whereabouts of the ford three miles up the Saranac but not the exact route to it. He also discovered how far the American defences were from the river bank. Intelligence had been gathered, but not all that was needed, even though the *General Regulations and Orders*, in effect at that time, "particularly expected from General Officers, and others in considerable command ... An intimate knowledge of the scene of action, and its neighbourhood."[124] The knowledge was to be sufficient to enable troops to operate in combat without requiring guides. This requirement had not been met when the assault came.

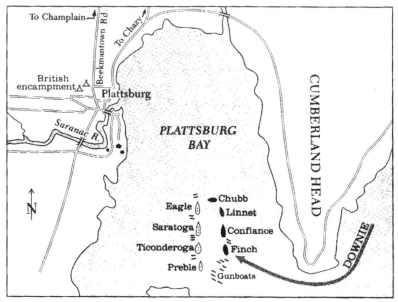

Naval battle

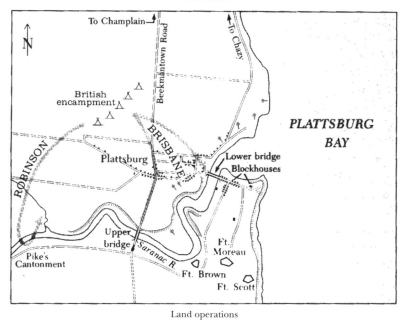

Land operations

Map 4   The attack on Plattsburgh, September 1814
(reprinted, by permission, from Stanley, *The War of 1812*, 347)

Prevost seems to have devised a plan that required Brisbane's brigade to make a demonstration against the two bridges, while Robinson was to lead a stronger force (his own brigade and Power's) across the ford to outflank the American works. There is no indication that Sir George discussed with his brigade commanders such other considerations as the role of Downie's force or the priority of avoiding heavy casualties. Aside from these measures, Sir George simply waited for Downie's squadron to appear and wrote letters to him urging speed. The need for haste depended upon what he expected of Downie. His first statement was given briefly in his letter of the 8th: "I only wait for your arrival to pro-ceed against General McCombe's position on the South bank of the Saranac. Your share in the operation in the first instance will be to destroy or to Capture the Enemy's Squadron, if it should wait for a Con-test, and afterwards Co-operate with this division of the Army." The idea of cooperation was repeated in subsequent letters. What they left unsaid was how Downie's action could assist the land attack and the exact timing of each operation. In the letter of the 8th, what was the meaning of "afterwards" and in that of the 10th of "at nearly the same moment"?

On the 11th the wind at last enabled Downie to sail from Chazy to Plattsburgh Bay. Before he came around Cumberland Head, which blocked the bay from his view, he fired his guns without using shot, "the signal by which the Land forces should be informed of the approach of the Naval Squadron, in order that they might know when their co-operation was wanted."[125] This signal was given about 5 a.m., thus allowing Prevost at least three hours to act before the naval engage-ment began at between 8 and 9 a.m.[126] The troops were ready before dawn, but Prevost gave Robinson a start time of 10, which seems rather late considering what he had told Downie. Robinson's men were delayed by at least an hour in locating the ford, and as they fought their way across it, the naval encounter ended with the complete defeat of the British squadron. Prevost immediately ordered Brisbane and Robinson to break off the action and return to camp. "Never was any-thing like the disappointment expressed in every countenance," wrote Robinson, expressing the dismay of both brigade commanders, who felt confident that in an hour or less they could have taken the American positions.[127] But Sir George's order had to be obeyed.

The events of the day suggest that he intended the land assault to follow the commencement of the naval attack. But this was not Downie's understanding; he expected assistance from the land forces and thought that the attacks were to take place simultaneously.[128] Since Downie was killed in the naval battle, his views were reported by naval officers at the naval court martial in August 1815. R.A. Brydon, the master of the *Confiance* during the battle, testified that, as the squadron rounded Cumberland Head, Downie told the crew, "There are the Enemy's Ships, our Army are to storm the Enemy's works at the moment we engage, and mind don't let us be behind." Brydon's opinion – and he believed that it was Downie's also – was that only with assistance from the land forces would it be safe for the squadron to attack the Americans. Captain Daniel Pring, commander of HMS *Linnet*, reported conversations that he had had with Downie, "some immediately after he had had interviews with the Commander of the Land Forces in which he informed me that the said Commander wished, as his Army had been so much annoyed by the American gun Boats in crossing dead Creek on their way to Plattsburgh that Captain Downie would come up with his Fleet, and draw off the attention of the Americans while the army was crossing the Saranac; and would attack their fleet at the same time the army attacked the works on land."

Before the start of the battle, Pring told his crew "that the Land forces were to attack the works on shore, at the same moment that we were to go into action with the Fleet, by which it was supposed the Americans would feel it necessary to quit their anchorage, and thereby give us an opportunity of deriving advantage from their confusion – With this Assurance and prospect our Officers and men went into Action with the greatest confidence."[129] Lieutenant Robertson, who took command of the *Confiance* after Downie's death early in the fight, supported the views of these two officers.[130]

Prevost's reports on the battle reflect the vagueness of his correspondence regarding tactics and do not explain the delay in the land attack (see appendix D).[131] His first report on 11 September gives a hint of why he hesitated to attack the Americans immediately, for when his forces reached the Saranac on the 6th, "I found the Enemy in the occupation of an Elevated Ridge of Land on the South Branch of the Saranac crowned with three Strong Redoubts and other Field Works, and Block Houses armed with heavy Ordnance."[132] Only at that time, he claimed, did he call upon Downie to cooperate with the army, while on the 11th he ordered the troops to attack as soon as he saw the squadron steering around Cumberland Head for Plattsburgh Bay. In his second report, on 22 September, he stressed the necessity of naval support for his invasion and asserted that before he advanced, the flotilla was equal in strength to the enemy's and ready for action; but he remained uninformative about tactical details and times. Even more than the previous letter, this report shows much concern to justify his conduct of the campaign.

After Downie's defeat, Prevost faced the choices of attacking Plattsburgh, remaining where he was, or retreating. In terms of the aim of the campaign, nothing would be gained by advancing south of Plattsburgh, and indeed, such a move would have placed the army in a perilous situation.[133] While the capture of Plattsburgh would have involved increased casualties, it would also have been a tactical victory sure to produce military and diplomatic benefits. (As it was, Macdonough decided to remove his ships to the south end of Lake Champlain to enter winter quarters.) The army would have withdrawn after a success rather than appearing to flee from a total defeat, an impression strengthened by the haste of the retreat, which left behind supplies and even wounded men.[134] A successful assault on Plattsburgh would have been helpful, whereas the army's failure was damaging to the British position in the negotiations then underway at Ghent. A positive outcome would also have gone a long way towards retrieving Prevost's military reputation. But throughout his career in the Canadas, Prevost had never shown himself to be a tough-minded battlefield commander. It is tempting to commend him for being concerned about the lives of his troops, but it was not a concern he expressed before the battle, nor was it known to be prominent in his defensive planning. While the concern could have been genuine, it was also useful as an excuse to avoid making a difficult decision to continue the push into Plattsburgh. The key to understanding Prevost's generalship appears to have been an intense anxiety not to fail.

At Plattsburgh he commanded an army easily capable of overwhelming the American defences, which Fortescue thinks "would hardly have stopped veterans, who had carried the entrenchments of the Nivelle."[135] With even less cause, Prevost showed the same lack of offensive spirit so evident at Sackets Harbor in May 1813 and at Fort George in August 1813 and no boldness whatsoever, even though the risks of being defeated in an attack across the Saranac before 11 September were low. Referring to the situation on Lake Ontario in the summer of 1813, Fortescue claims that "there are very few men who are qualified to direct the joint operations of a squadron and an army, and unfortunately Prevost was not one of them. Supremacy on Lake Ontario was the Navy's business; let the Navy look to it first, and the military operations would follow afterwards; if the Navy were slow, let it be hurried. Such were the principles which he cherished only too faithfully to the end of the war."[136] Whether or not this was the case on Lake Ontario, it certainly applied to the Plattsburgh campaign.

Prevost's reports were in part a response to the rising chorus of criticism directed at him and a contribution to the developing controversy over who was responsible for the fiasco.[137] He accepted no blame for himself or the army but put it squarely on the navy, in particular on Downie and those on his ships who had not done their duty. Even if those men were largely responsible for the failure, Prevost must share some blame, for he appeared to be pressing Downie to sail into action before he was ready.

Prevost's letters and messengers from 7 to 10 September were intended to compel Downie to act in accordance with the general's timetable. Prevost had had experience of amphibious operations in the West Indies, and in the Canadas he was aware of manpower shortages for naval vessels on the lakes, yet he seemed unable to comprehend Downie's difficulties in building and manning his little flotilla. In 1813 the commander of the forces had made the long journey to Upper Canada to gain first-hand knowledge of conditions there, but on this occasion he did not travel twelve miles north from Plattsburgh to see Downie's situation at Chazy. Moreover, the tactlessness of some of his communications was neither necessary nor helpful. It is not surprising that surviving naval officers regarded these actions as goading the captain to sail into action prematurely, and Prevost's enemies would pick up that cry.

To the political criticism of Prevost could now be added strictures on his military competence. In spite of Wellington's opinion "that the war has been a most successful one, and highly honourable to the British arms" (9 November), he had already advised Bathurst, "It is obvious to me that you must remove Sir George Prevost" (30 October).[138] While British ministers might disregard the political brickbats thrown at the governor because they were motivated by quarrels among Canadians, they could not ignore the impact on British public opinion of Sir George's failure to achieve a decisive military outcome even with his greatly enlarged force, augmented as it was by Peninsular veterans. They would look foolish trying to justify the retention of a commander-in-chief who with such advantages could not obtain a single victory.

Prevost's recall to England in March 1815 is not surprising. He departed from Quebec on 3 April, and after arriving home, he explained his conduct of the Plattsburgh campaign to the satisfaction of the government. But in August a naval court martial of the officers who had survived the defeat in Plattsburgh Bay agreed with Yeo's opinion that Prevost had hurried Downie into action prematurely and had failed to support him.[139] In order to clear his name, Sir George asked for a military court martial. It was scheduled for 12 January 1816 but was postponed to 5 February because of his ill health. He died on 5 January aged only forty-eight; the court martial was never held. Both supporters and critics thought that his anxiety over the forthcoming proceedings worsened his already poor health, thereby contributing to his early death.[140]

Prevost's recall, apparently under a cloud, followed soon afterwards by his death, which prevented him from presenting his side of the story, left a shadow over his reputation that has never dissipated. His critics proved to be more influential in their writings than did his supporters.[141] One reason may be Sir George's difficulties in other relationships.

His troubles with Charles de Salaberry sprang from a variety of issues and had wider implications than simply personal grievances. The usual view is that Prevost had the support of French Canadians, while his opponents were found in the ranks of the English-speaking minority, but it should not be assumed that this support was monolithic. Salaberry was an early critic, and his attitude towards Sir George became increasingly negative, particularly after Prevost's general order for the battle of Châteauguay. By December 1813 Salaberry claimed that Prevost was losing popularity among both French and English Canadians, as well as the confidence of the army. (Salaberry also described an angry encounter between Rottenburg's wife and Prevost which may have been simply gossip or may have indicated something more serious between the two generals.)[142] Whatever Salaberry's motives and however inaccurate or distorted his views, he was supported by other prominent French Canadians, one indication being the vote of thanks he received from the Lower Canadian assembly for his victory at Châteauguay.[143] Some of Salaberry's other complaints, such as that Canadians were less likely to receive official notice than other nationalities,[144] may have found sympathetic listeners among other officers and civilians.

Salaberry was no armchair critic, but a brave and capable officer who led his corps in some very arduous duties along the Lower Canadian frontier. In addition to the Voltigeurs Canadiens and the Frontier Light Infantry, in 1814 Prevost put a new militia unit, the Chasseurs Canadiens, under Salaberry's command and appointed him inspecting field officer of militia light infantry.[145] He and his sympathizers could not be ignored, but there seemed no way that Prevost could overcome that officer's hostility.[146] The fact that there were numerous military and civilian critics constantly at his heels waiting for any opportunity to discredit him might have increased Prevost's concern to avoid risks.

In relation to Royal Navy officers, Prevost had the authority to command cooperation based on the Admiralty's instructions to Yeo upon his appointment as commander on the Great Lakes.[147] These required the commodore to obtain Prevost's "concurrence and approbation" for his operations and to conform to the "Requisitions" given by the commander of the forces. Although Yeo was also instructed to follow the orders of Admiral Warren, that arrangement would have no practical effect on the inland lakes.[148] Yeo and Prevost cooperated readily in the raid on Sackets Harbor, but by late summer the latter had determined to make it clear that decisions affecting naval personnel would be subject to his approval, and in the following weeks the Prevost-Yeo relationship became less harmonious. In August Captain Robert Barclay, naval commander on Lake Erie, following Yeo's directions, dismissed George Hall from the Provincial Marine. Hall complained to Prevost, who promptly appointed him "a superintendent of the dock yard and naval stores at Amherstburg." Prevost went on to make it clear that Barclay had no authority over appointments made by the commander of the forces and was not to make dispositions of naval forces without "the concurrence and approbation of the Gen'l officer com[mandin]g the Right Division" (i.e., Major-General Henry Procter).[149]

Prevost's conception of the naval role was to serve the army's needs for transport and battle support. In specific situations (Barclay on Lake Erie and Downie on Lake Champlain), he even expected naval commanders to take serious risks. In August and September 1813, in letters to Procter and Yeo, Sir George made it clear that, for the sake of Procter's forces, Barclay should act aggressively against American naval forces on Lake Erie. The way he put his admonition suggests that he had little understanding of the enormous difficulties which Barclay faced in competing with growing American naval strength: "The experience obtained by Sir Jas. Yeo's conduct towards a fleet infinitely superior to the one under his command will satisfy Captain Barclay that he has only to dare and the enemy is discomfited."[150] Yet Prevost was not prepared to take similar risks with land forces.

Yeo recognized Prevost's authority and indicated his readiness to cooperate, but as early as September 1813 the general was expressing disappointment with the commodore for not achieving decisive command of both Lakes Erie and Ontario.[151] Such a criticism suggests that Prevost had no more understanding of Yeo's difficulties than he had of Barclay's, even though Sir George was at Kingston, the naval headquarters. The defeat of Barclay's squadron on 10 September raised the question of whether the naval captain or Procter had been responsible for the decision to take on Commodore Oliver Perry's fleet. Prevost claimed that Procter had "no alternative but to consent to Captain Barclay seeking a general action with the enemy's squadron,"[152] a statement which implies that Barclay took the initiative. Yeo, while somewhat critical of Barclay, put the principal onus on Procter. "I am therefore," he wrote to Admiral Warren, "of the opinion that there was not that necessity for General Procter to urge Captain Barclay to so hazardous and unequal a contest."[153]

Relations between Yeo and Prevost did not subsequently improve. They had a difference of opinion in October over whether it was the army's or the navy's fault that two companies of De Watteville's Regiment had been captured by American warships while travelling by water from York to Kingston.[154] Although Prevost repeatedly urged Warren to send more seamen and stressed the great needs of both Barclay and Yeo,[155] only a few months later Yeo felt that Prevost did not believe him.[156] Perhaps these differences of opinion lay behind Bathurst's recommendation in early 1814 that Yeo be more independent of Prevost's control.[157]

The aides-de-camp of the commander-in-chief and governor deserve a brief discussion for what they reveal about Prevost. He seems to have chosen capable ADCs but not men who brought with them much weight in either the military or civilian communities. His official "family" included Captain William Cochrane, 103rd Foot, who aside from becoming a brevet major in 1814, left no other mark during the war. Captain Foster L. Coore, 3rd West India Regiment, had served as Prevost's ADC in Nova Scotia in 1809 and 1810. Three years later he was promoted major and appointed acting deputy quartermaster general for Lower and Upper Canada. He volunteered for action in the assault on Fort Erie, for which he was mentioned in dispatches. Ensign Noah Freer, of the Nova Scotia Fencibles, had been Prevost's military secretary in Nova Scotia, and he held the same position at Quebec. He was probably never intended to be a combat officer, although he was promoted lieutenant in the New Brunswick Fencibles in 1813 and after the war a captain. Brevet Major James F. Fulton, 98th Foot, also came from Nova Scotia. He had been stationed with his regiment from 1805 there, in a colony where he was unable to gain combat experience.

Captain Robert McDouall, 8th Foot, had served in Egypt, Martinique, and Copenhagen before coming to Canada in 1810. He represented an experienced infantry officer, and he may have had a record for bravery, for that is what he displayed during the war, particularly in his successful defence of Mackinac in August 1814. Captain H.B.O. Milnes, 1st Foot Guards, was the son of Sir Robert Shore Milnes, an earlier lieutenant-governor and administrator of Lower Canada.[158] In 1813 the younger Milnes was appointed an acting deputy quartermaster general, but he died in July from wounds received in a skirmish at Goose Creek when the British tried to recover vessels seized by the Americans. Captain John S. Sinclair had begun his military career in the Royal Artillery in 1794, but there is no record of combat experience. Finally, there was Captain John Bagwell, 60th Foot, who received his appointment in September 1814.[159]

These men did not all serve as ADCs at the same time, and the reasons for their appointments are open to speculation. Coore and Freer may have been chosen because of their administrative experience and abilities, McDouall because of his combat record, and Milnes because of his father, but why the others were appointed is uncertain. There is the strong possibility that Prevost used these officers to keep an eye on the commanders in Upper Canada and to provide him with first-hand information about them.[160] That kind of role may explain why Fulton was in Upper Canada in September 1812 and again in June and July 1813, why Coore was with Drummond at the siege of Fort Erie, and why Milnes and McDouall were both at Stoney Creek.

Prevost's three provincial ADCs served throughout the war, but they were men of little importance in Lower Canada. Lieutenant-Colonel Pierre-Amable Boucher de Boucherville and Lieutenant-Colonel Michael H. Perceval were militia officers. When Boucherville was appointed in September 1811, he held no offices, a fact which suggests that his principal distinction was his descent from an aristocratic French-Canadian family.[161] Perceval was collector of customs at Quebec and a member of the Executive Council; in 1813 he was named a justice of the peace. He may have been sympathetic to the *parti canadien*, making him a useful contact for Prevost. The third provincial ADC was Edward B. Brenton, from Nova Scotia, who was deputy judge advocate general for British North America.[162] Prevost appointed him civil secretary as well as ADC. What seems characteristic of all these appointments was that they were safe men who would serve Prevost faithfully.

In generalship, Prevost's scope was that of a conventional eighteenth-century general. He appeared fearful of departing from established military doctrine regardless of circumstances. His anxieties about himself and his responsibilities as commander-in-chief meant that he could not respond spontaneously and positively to unexpected opportunities.[163] These anxieties may explain his misunderstanding of Downie's situation and, indeed, of Yeo's in 1813 and 1814.

A summary of Prevost's failures would include his lack of generalship in combat, his inability to inspire either military men or civilians, and his inflexibility in adhering to defensive strategy despite situations or changing conditions where offensive action was necessary. Among his successes were his policies as governor and his administrative achievements as commander-in-chief.[164] He had a basically sound perception of the political realities in Lower Canada, and as a result, he contributed positively to popular support of the war effort. It is not likely that a different governor could have secured more support for the war from the assembly or have prevented the political wranglings of 1813 and 1814. In any case, there is no evidence that those quarrels affected the war effort. Prevost's strategy of concentrating on the security of Quebec, Montreal, and the line up to Kingston was valid. Yet with all his concern for defence of the St Lawrence, he did provide considerable numbers of troops and quantities of supplies of all kinds to the commanders in Upper Canada. It is improbable that a different commander-in-chief could have obtained more aid from Britain, although he might have provided more engineer and artillery officers to the upper province. Sir George's generalship at Sackets Harbor, Fort George, and Plattsburgh was watched with intense interest and high expectations by Canadians and British alike. Perhaps for this reason, their disappointment at his weak performances was all the greater. With such a high level of disillusionment, it is not surprising that many contemporaries gave Prevost little credit for his quiet persistence, strategic ability, and administrative achievements.[165]

CHAPTER THREE

Audacity:
The Leadership of Major-General
Sir Isaac Brock

Thou, sixteenth of August, shall raise admiration
And oft be productive of proud emu'ation,
The Troops and Militia stood firm as a rock
Who fears thrice the number when marshall'd by BROCK.
To capture an army that counts three to one
A fortress and state, hardly losing a man,
Will long be remember'd a capital stroke
And quoted uniquely, "The glory of BROCK".

Quebec Mercury, 10 November 1812

In June 1812 Major-General Isaac Brock faced an intimidating responsibility: the defence of an extensive and sparsely populated territory with but seven fortified positions and defended by just over 1,000 regular troops, some Native warriors, and perhaps 11,000 militiamen of uncertain reliability, against an enemy much stronger in numbers and prepared to invade at times and places of his own choosing.[1] As a result, Brock's status and responsibilities, although on a lesser scale, were similar to those of Sir George Prevost. Like the governor-in-chief, he took over civil and military command of Upper Canada in peacetime, but was required to think of preparing for war. He was also forced to argue for a serious British commitment to defend Upper Canada, which he did by proposing a strategy at odds with that of the governor. Brock's successors did not face this need, for when they took command, the commitment to the upper province had been made, even though there might be a question of the level of resources it received. Indeed, Britain's stake in Upper Canada can be said to have increased with Brock's death at Queenston Heights. The glorification of Isaac Brock and the development of an image of heroic Canadian militiamen fighting in defence of their homes were well under way before the end of 1812.[2] These perceptions would affect conduct during the war, as well as subsequent interpretations of it. No other British general of this war had the same effect.

Isaac Brock was born on 6 October 1769 on the Channel island of Guernsey into a long-distinguished family connected through marriage with other leading families in island society.[3] His father, John, had married Elizabeth de Lisle, daughter of the bailiff of Guernsey.[4] John died at an early age but left the family independently wealthy. Isaac was the eighth son among fourteen children. Three of his brothers served in the army, while his other brothers followed civilian careers.[5] His sister Elizabeth married John E. Tupper, whose son, Ferdinand Brock, compiled *The Life and Correspondence of Major-General Sir Isaac Brock. K.B.* This work, which went through two editions, is a basic source of information about Brock and his family.[6]

Unlike Prevost's family background, Brock's was civilian. He did, however, have family connections that could help his career and sufficient wealth to buy his commissions. On the basis of family relationships, Isaac was exposed to aspects of military life (including naval) as well as to civilian careers. Although he was being prepared for a leadership role, it would not necessarily be in a military career. He was educated locally and then briefly in Southampton and Rotterdam. Even after leaving school to enter the army, he is reported to have devoted time to study.[7] Certainly, later in life Brock collected and read books both for instruction and for enjoyment.

He entered the army in 1785 at the age of fifteen by purchasing an ensigncy in the 8th Regiment of Foot. Thereafter he advanced fairly rapidly in rank by the same method, becoming a lieutenant-colonel in 1797. Speedy promotion was a characteristic of the British army in those years, but Brock's rise was helped by his family's wealth, and was possibly spurred on by his ambition to achieve as much personal success as he could in the army. This was a prominent theme in much of his correspondence.[8] Aside from occasional family concerns, he had no personal distractions; in other words, he remained a bachelor all his life, and there is no evidence that he formed an attachment with any female.

Brock's military career hardly prepared him to command the forces of a province. In 1790 he became a lieutenant and served in the Channel Islands. The same year he raised enough men to establish an independent infantry company and thereby gained the rank of captain on 16 December 1790; soon after, he exchanged into the 49th Foot.[9] Captain Brock served with that regiment in Barbados and Jamaica until 1793, when his normally vigorous health broke down, forcing him to return to England on sick leave. In his absence the 49th took part in the campaign in San Domingo, and although Brock therefore missed seeing combat, he also avoided exposure to the diseases that killed so many of the troops in that campaign.[10] When the regiment returned to England in the summer of 1796, Brock, now a major, rejoined it. By the end of the following year he had become senior lieutenant-colonel of the 49th but had had no experience of action.

That experience he first obtained in 1799, and on that occasion he displayed a trait which may have gained him recognition but which also proved fatal when employed thirteen years later. Boldness – indeed, recklessness – in the face of the enemy would not be surprising in a young officer not yet thirty and untested in battle. That Brock would continue to act this way even with the rank and responsibilities of 1812 suggests his belief in the value of this behaviour to a military leader. His willingness to act boldly probably arose from his powerful desire for fame, an ambition that remained with him to the end and was expressed in his actions in 1799 and at Queenston Heights.

In August 1799 Brock's regiment was part of a British force that landed on the Dutch coast in a campaign against French and Dutch defenders, and at the beginning of October the 49th Foot formed part of a column sent to attack Egmont op Zee. According to Brock's later account, when the enemy threatened to turn his regiment's flank, he led a charge of six companies (his second-in-command, Lieutenant-Colonel Sheaffe, led the other four) across the dunes. His bold action threw his antagonists into disorder, causing them to retire. Brock made light of the slight wound he had received, exulting to his brother John, "No commanding officer could have been more handsomely supported than I was on that day ... I got knocked down soon after the enemy began to retreat, but never quitted the field, and returned to my duty in less than half an hour."[11] In a later expression of this love of action combined with ambition, he would write from Quebec to his brothers on 19 November 1808: "My object is to get home as soon as I can obtain permission ... I must see service, or I may as well, and indeed much better, quit the army at once, for no one advantage can I reasonably look to hereafter if I remain buried in this inactive, remote corner, without the least mention being made of me."[12]

In his early career, a greater risk to Brock than combat was discontent within his regiment. For example, during the summer of 1797, while the regiment was stationed on the banks of the Thames River, it was swept with sympathy for the naval mutinies of that year. Brock took precautions for his own safety and acted to allay discontent and restore discipline, and his success won him praise from the commander-in-chief, the Duke of York. In 1800, during his own absence, Brock left Sheaffe in command. Upon his return, the men cheered him, for they had been unhappy under Sheaffe's command. Brock rebuked them and confined them to barracks for a week.[13] In other words, he was more concerned to maintain discipline than to enjoy a brief moment of popularity.

In 1802 the 49th Foot was ordered to Canada, and it arrived during the summer under Brock, Sheaffe, and Captain Charles Plenderleath. The regiment was ordered to Upper Canada early in February 1803, and this move marked the beginning of Brock's experience with the upper province. Prevost, Rottenburg, and Drummond would none of them have as long an acquaintance with Upper Canadians.

Again the 49th was threatened with mutiny. Discontent as serious as in 1797 broke out in August 1803 among the troops stationed at Fort George, where Sheaffe was in command. Men deserted and some plotted to mutiny, a scheme that spread to Chippawa and Fort Erie. Sheaffe and Brock took severe and probably just action of the type normal for the period. A pursuit was mounted, the deserters were caught in American territory, and the plotters at Fort George were arrested. Brock urged their court martial and stern treatment, and seven were shot.[14] Upon news of the executions, he addressed the garrison at Fort George, telling the troops of his "grief." It seems unlikely that such concern for his men would be soon forgotten or would have no bearing on the soldiers' willingness to follow his lead in combat. By 1807 his inspection report praised the state of the regiment, now in Lower Canada and under Sheaffe's command.[15]

When Brock was in command, discipline was well maintained and desertion low. The crises that arose in his regiment did so when Sheaffe was in charge, suggesting he had less understanding than Brock of the art of commanding men or of winning their confidence. Sheaffe's shortcomings would become even more serious when he was in command of Upper Canada.

The second period of Brock's career in the Canadas lasted from 1806 to 1810. He returned there in June 1806 after a visit to Britain at a time when relations between that country and the United States were extremely strained. In subsequent years relations between the two nations would worsen, and on each occasion the authorities in the Canadas would have to assess the seriousness of the threat of attack from their neighbour.

In September 1806 Brock became the senior officer in the Canadas and therefore commander of the forces there.[16] This responsibility ceased when, in October 1807, Sir James Henry Craig arrived to become governor and commander of the forces. The following March Craig appointed Brock a brigadier-general and put him in command of the Montreal District. Brock thus gained experience of wide, as well as limited, military responsibilities. He was also obtaining as broad a range of peacetime military administrative experience as was possible in the Canadas. Although it took place in peacetime, this exposure was hardly untroubled, for the Canadas seemed dangerously threatened.[17]

In C.P. Stacey's view, "During this period ... Brock worked with characteristic energy to improve the defences of the country."[18] That is no exaggeration. His activity was not limited to strengthening the fortifications of Quebec, important as that task was; he also put a good deal of effort into trying to improve conditions for the troops. Furthermore, he made administrative changes to the marine department, which Stacey credits with providing an effective naval force on the lakes, the Provincial Marine, when war came. Never one to tolerate mismanagement, Brock detected it in the financial affairs of Deputy Commissary General John Craigie and demanded answers.[19] These examples show that Brock had an eye for genuine problems and a keen understanding of administration. Nor could he ignore Upper Canada, where Lieutenant-Governor Francis Gore, alarmed by reports of warlike preparations at Detroit, asked for weapons for the militia. Having already sent 4,000 muskets and other military stores to the upper province, Brock decided that he could not afford to reduce his stock of muskets further. As well as refusing more aid, he suggested that the defence of the province might have to be concentrated from Kingston eastward.[20]

In September 1810, when Brock was sent to command the forces in Upper Canada, there were in Lower Canada two major-generals senior to him and with more combat experience, Gordon Drummond and Baron de Rottenburg. There may have been various reasons for Brock's appointment, one perhaps being the friendship between him and Governor Craig. However, it is clear that his superiors had confidence in his abilities. Adjutant General Baynes, an officer close to the governor, wrote to Brock that Craig thought it necessary to have "a person like yourself ... in the Upper Province, that a scrutinizing eye may correct the errors and neglect that have crept in, and put all in order again."[21] The emphasis was on administrative achievement and potential.

June to September 1811 saw Brock back in Lower Canada commanding the Montreal District, an appointment made by Drummond, who had assumed "temporary Command of the Forces in the Canadas" following the departure of Craig for England on sick leave.[22] After 12 September, when Sir George Prevost arrived, Brock returned to Upper Canada as "Senior Officer Commander of the Troops" and "Senior Member of the [Executive] Council."[23] He met the council on the 30th. Gore departed for England on 8 October, and Brock's term as president of the council began the following day.

He found in Upper Canada a very different society from that of Lower Canada. The upper province's first lieutenant-governor, John Graves

Simcoe, had hoped to use the Constitutional Act to mould a society and a government with an unmistakably British character, run by men of education and good breeding. These intentions had not been fulfilled. A majority of the population consisted of American-born immigrants who had brought with them attitudes favourable to social equality and a role by the people in their government. The elite, however, consisted of wealthy merchants and government officials who were descendants of the Loyalists or recent British immigrants. Ability, education, or hard work were not in themselves sufficient to achieve advancement without the support of those who decided on appointments or could exercise influence on such decisions.[24] Brock was well acquainted with this system of patronage and tried to use it to his advantage.

Yet his brush with civil authority in Lower Canada suggests that he was not tolerant of challenges to his authority when he believed that his duty imposed a certain course of action.[25] In short, it seemed that he might bring to his role as political leader, not the arts of negotiation and compromise, but rather the authoritarianism of the military hierarchy. He faced in Upper Canada's elected legislature a body of men uninterested in military affairs and unwilling to accept the administrator's decisions without question. There were critics of the executive but not an organized or systematic opposition.[26] These men appear to have been motivated more by personal grievances or ambition than by ideological drives, and Brock recognized this cause, particularly in the case of the government's leading opponent, Joseph Willcocks.[27]

Before the end of 1811 he began preparations for his first meeting with the assembly. One of his central concerns was the role that Upper Canadians would play in the event of war with the United States. The populace would have to be convinced that the government would indeed resist an American invasion, for he wrote that "unless the inhabitants give an active and efficient aid, it will be utterly impossible for the very limited number of the military who are likely to be employed to preserve the Province."[28] Besides a widespread sense of uncertainty, he believed he also faced an anti-war spirit promoted by a "number of improper characters." He intended to respond calmly, believing "that the best policy to be pursued ... will be to act with the utmost liberality and as if no mistrust existed." This comment suggests a political shrewdness not always evident in military men's dealing with civilians. For the most part, Brock would follow his own advice.

The militia system of Upper Canada, introduced originally by Simcoe, required all males sixteen to sixty years of age to provide military service when called upon by the government. Brock was well aware that the men's attendance at the annual militia muster was usually low and their standard of training very poor. He proposed to amend the Militia Act of 1808 in such a way as to encourage better attendance at musters and to provide greater security for and proper maintenance of the arms issued to the militia.[29] These seem reasonable aims when public property was involved and in keeping with Brock's well-established interest in the efficient use of government resources.[30]

At the time he took command of Upper Canada, Brock's knowledge of the art of war had been obtained almost completely from reading and observation. Now he commanded naval and land forces and was expected to win the cooperation of Native warriors. Perhaps, therefore, his reading materials and methods deserve more than a passing glance. One notable characteristic of his reading was that it was deliberate and organized. An officer who continued to study was unusual in itself. He told his brother Irving, about his habits while at Fort George in 1810–11: "I hardly ever stir out, and unless I have company at home, my evenings are passed solus. I read much ... I like to read a book quickly, and afterwards revert to such passages as have made the deepest impression and which appear to me the most important to remember."[31] Whether from his reading or his experience, Brock believed in audacity, a characteristic highly regarded by British soldiers. He had displayed this trait in his charge during the attack on Egmont op Zee, and it may have been reinforced by the success of Admiral Nelson's boldness during the attack on Copenhagen on 2 April 1801, which Brock witnessed while on board the flagship.

Knowledge of the art of war is also indicated by what officers thought about strategy and the measures they took before hostilities broke out. Here Brock's responsibility was more akin to Prevost's than to that of the officers subsequently commanding in Upper Canada, for both wrote about strategy before hostilities broke out. Traditional thinking was to concentrate forces at Quebec on the premise that as long as it was held, the rest of Canada could be reconquered from an enemy. The two commanding generals accepted this view, but Prevost's thinking never shifted far from this basic concept, whereas Brock showed greater insight into the changed conditions, namely, that the territory upriver from Quebec contained substantial settled populations and deserved protection just as much as did those in the region of Quebec. In other words, the consequences of abandonment in 1812–14 would be much more serious both to the inhabitants and to metropolitan security than they would have been in 1759 or 1775.

Brock never denied the importance of Quebec to his defensive plan, but he showed greater understanding of what might be accomplished and how British success might affect American behaviour. Two of his points may be emphasized. First, he believed that the British had the advantage of better-quality troops and leaders than the Americans and also the valuable assets of naval forces and potentially large numbers of

Native allies. Second, he argued that attacks would prolong the defence of Upper Canada, giving the British time to marshal their strength, and would probably distract the Americans from assaulting Lower Canada. Taking the war to the Americans might boost Canadian morale. He did not believe that the Americans would quickly put aside their disagreements and unite even when their country was invaded.

In December 1811, when Brock had developed these views, he sensed a change in the mood of many residents, at least in the Niagara area, towards the possibility of resisting an American assault.[32] They seemed to have assumed that the inadequacies of military forces meant that no resistance was intended, but Prevost's measures to strengthen Upper Canada's defences and the appointment of Brock had brought about "a determination on the part of the principal inhabitants [of Niagara] to exert every means in their power in defence of their property and support of the Govt." What was needed, Brock believed, was some expression of confidence in the loyalty of the people in addition to further military aid. Such a commitment would imply that Upper Canada could not be easily abandoned.

"My first care on my arrival in this province," Brock wrote, "was to direct the officers of the Indian Department at Amherstburg to exert their whole influence with the Indians to prevent the attack which I understood a few tribes meditated against the American frontier." Prevost considered Brock's statement so significant that he sent an extract from this letter to the British minister in Washington to be employed in rebutting American charges that Britain was inciting Natives against the United States.[33] If war were to come, Brock wanted "an active cooperation" of the western Natives because they would tie down large American forces protecting their western frontier, and he proposed to secure this alliance by seizing Detroit and Michilimackinac. (This was not an original idea of his, for Gore had suggested virtually the same thing in 1808.)[34]

Brock went on to survey the province, beginning with Amherstburg (which contained Fort Malden). This area could be crucial, he argued, for if it were provided with the means for active operations, the result would be to deter any attack against the province from Niagara westward. He proposed to reinforce Malden with 200 regulars (from Fort George and York) to impress on the militia and the Natives there that the government would actively resist an American invasion.[35] As a further boost to that sector's defence, as well as a means of threatening Michilimackinac, he urged an increase in the naval force on Lakes Erie and Huron.

For the Niagara frontier, Brock estimated that nearly 3,000 militia and 500 Native warriors could be collected and that, combined with a

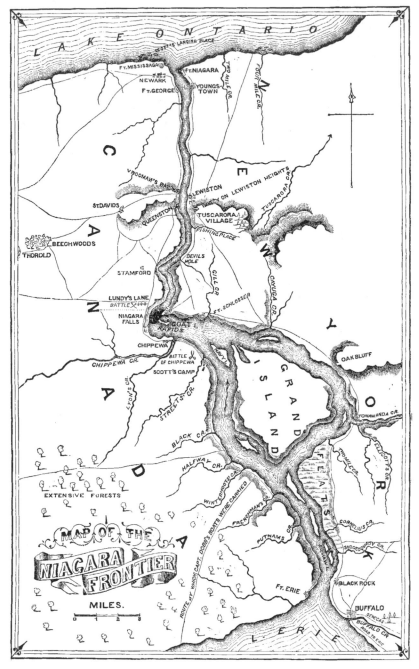

Map 5   The Niagara frontier
(reprinted from Lossing, *The Pictorial Field-Book of the War of 1812*, 382)

strong regular force, they could repulse anything short of a major invasion. He did request additional help, namely, gunners, drivers, and horses to complete a volunteer corps of farmers who employed their horses in drawing field guns for the army, and weapons to arm a volunteer cavalry.[36] He stressed the importance of a protracted resistance to American attack, believing that they would not come prepared for it and consequently would soon lose enthusiasm for war as the difficulties and expenses mounted.

Brock seemed most confident about the security of the Kingston District, where he believed the militiamen were the most dependable in the province. The initial role he saw for them was to watch the movement of American forces; if an invasion force moved down the Richelieu River valley to threaten Montreal, the militia and regulars could be concentrated quickly where needed.

This general assessment of what would be effective defence would prove closer to actual events than would Prevost's. Besides making strategic assessments and watching events in the United States, both commanders believed that they ought to take measures to prepare for war. We have seen that Prevost was vigorous in his preparations, and these also affected Upper Canada.

Brock was, in addition, much concerned with naval strength and security on the lakes, and he offered recommendations that included building sailing vessels and gunboats, fortifying harbours, and replacing older commanders with younger men.[37] Whether or not he needed Brock's urgings, Prevost took naval defence seriously, for he ordered the construction of another schooner on Lake Erie and in January 1812 sent Captain Andrew Gray to Upper Canada to consult with Brock. They met at York and discussed shipbuilding there and other ways to improve the naval forces. Prevost agreed to the changes in personnel that Brock asked for.[38] He also concurred with Brock's request to be allowed to make appointments to the new corps of Glengarry Fencibles and to permit recruitment west of Kingston.[39] These decisions indicate his confidence in Brock's judgment.

Prevost supported energetic measures while simultaneously urging caution on him, particularly in dealings with Native warriors.[40] In a sense, the governor was taking a large risk in Upper Canada, because his commander there had very little combat experience and none above the regimental level. Although he had had a brief time in higher command, that was during peacetime and it provided no certainty about how capable he would be under the stress of war.

Brock took other measures, such as seeking information about the fighting strength of Natives in American territory. In February he sent a confidential message to Robert Dickson, a British fur trader in what would become Wisconsin, asking what cooperation might be expected from "you and your friends."[41] He wanted to know their numbers, whether or not they would march under Dickson's orders, and what supplies they would need. In May Brock also visited the Mohawk village on the Grand River, where he spoke about the danger of war and urged preparedness.[42] When asked about British assistance to Natives in the United States to resist American encroachment, he said that he could not interfere in peacetime. Brock was aware of dissension among the Six Nations over land matters, but he refused to make promises that he doubted he could fulfil. The Mohawk war leader, John Norton, was impressed by Brock's honesty and spoke in favour of the British side.

Brock's public political role began early in February 1812 with the start of the fourth session of the fifth provincial parliament. In his opening address to the members of the Legislative Council and House of Assembly, he deplored American warlike preparations at time when the empire was fighting against Napoleon.[43] He spoke of his confidence in the militia, but reminded the members that to be effective it would need both money and improved instruction. He believed that Britain would never abandon the colony, but if it ever did lose imperial protection, Upper Canada would sink into poverty and insignificance. Brock's address was a call for action by the legislators on behalf of their community's self-interest if for no other reason.

Two measures that Brock proposed, an oath abjuring all foreign powers and a suspension of habeas corpus, were rejected in the assembly by small majorities.[44] He had expected opposition to his measures from opponents of the absent Gore, but he believed that those men would be motivated by personal grievances, not by disloyalty. However, after the votes had been taken, he complained about the influence of recent settlers from the United States.[45] Brock was further disappointed when the assembly limited the operation of the amended militia law to the end of the ensuing session. And this sentiment the administrator made quite clear in his address of 6 March closing the session: "The exigencies of the time alone authorize me to give my assent to the amended Militia Bill, for under circumstances of less urgency its very limited duration would oblige me to reject it."[46]

What the legislators did approve were measures to strengthen the colony's security without threatening civil rights. Such a response from civilians in peacetime is not surprising, and it is even less so when the American origin of the majority of the populace is taken into account. Brock's reaction as commander of the troops is likewise understandable. The assembly also passed a fairly stiff law for the apprehension of deserters from the army[47] and approved the act to reorganize the militia. The new bill provided for greatly improved training, particularly for the newly created flank companies, and £5,000 was voted for this purpose.[48] Brock's instructions for their training reveal a good deal of understanding about the limitations of militia as fighting men.[49]

Meanwhile, he faced other political strains as members of the assembly began an attack on a pillar of the merchant elite and a prominent supporter of the government, Robert Nichol.[50] Despite his strong annoyance at the assembly's conduct, Brock made no attempt to interfere, and his cool restraint proved politically more astute than decisive action would have been.[51] His support for Nichol's political career and his appointment of him as lieutenant-colonel in command of the 2nd Norfolk militia demonstrate his high opinion of Nichol. After the outbreak of war, Brock persuaded him to become quartermaster general of the militia, and in that role Nichol served effectively.

The administrator even made an effort to win the trust of former government critics. The most notable of these was Joseph Willcocks, who at one point openly boasted "at being ranked among the enemies of the King's servants in this colony."[52] Yet at Brock's request Willcocks agreed to try to convince the Six Nations to help to defend the province against an American invasion and served at the battle of Queenston Heights as a gentleman volunteer.[53] During the following year he defected to the United States and raised a force of Canadians who were willing to fight for the Americans. Willcocks was killed in September 1814, dressed in the uniform of an American colonel. Whatever the explanation of his conduct in 1812, perhaps some account of Brock's influence should be included. Although the general was no admirer of popular government or political opposition, he was clearly not engaged in politics for personal gain and did try to stay apart from political divisions. He was a man, too, of warm personality with a long-range point of view. It is highly unlikely that Gore would have sought Willcocks's support, and Sheaffe, even if he had been willing to try such a course, lacked his predecessor's winning nature.[54]

A contrast between Brock's activity and Prevost's passivity at the outset of the war is standard in most treatments of this subject. Again, Brock acted consistently and with a clear perception of the results desired. The American declaration of war on 18 June was known at Niagara at least by the 27th.[55] As soon as he was aware of the outbreak of hostilities, Brock sent dispatches to his subordinate commanders. As a result, Colonel Thomas Bligh St George at Fort Malden and Captain Charles Roberts at Fort St Joseph received the news on 30 June and 8 July respectively, giving them an advantage over their opponents. The American commander at Fort Michilimackinac, Lieutenant Porter Hanks, learned of the declaration when Roberts on 17 July summoned him to surrender.[56] In the matter of notifying outposts, Brock realized the value of promptness and acted accordingly.

Nevertheless, he should not be seen as a commander with a focus only on attack, for his vacillating orders to Roberts show understandable uncertainty, but also that he was trying to balance different needs. Roberts commanded a small fort situated at the northern end of Lake Huron with a garrison consisting of a small detachment of Royal Artillery and one company of the 10th Royal Veteran Battalion.[57] Some fifty miles to the southwest a small stockaded fort on the American island of Michilimackinac dominated the strait between Lakes Huron and Michigan. Located on a major fur-trade route, it was strategically and commercially important. Brock's aim was to catch the Americans off guard by seizing the island, but he had to take account of other considerations. One of these was Prevost's repeated commands to restrain the Natives and to take no action that would give the Americans a pretext for hostilities. Another was Upper Canada's military weaknesses. As Brock told his superior, "the reflection that at Detroit and Michilimackinac the weak state of the garrisons would prevent the commanders from accomplishing any essential service, connected … with their future security, and that my means of annoyance on this communication were limited to the reduction of Fort Niagara, which could be easily battered at any future period, I relinquished my original intention, and attended only to defensive measures."[58] His definition of defensive measures was not the same as Sir George's.

On 26 and 27 June Brock ordered Roberts to attack Michilimackinac if practicable. Both letters arrived on 8 July, but four days later there came two more, dated 28 and 29 June, ordering a suspension of hostilities.[59] On the same day Roberts received orders from Prevost to act cautiously, afford assistance to the North-West Company, and prepare to retreat "in case of necessity."[60] Brock's orders vacillated, but he never advised retreat. On 15 July Roberts received a dispatch from Brock dated the 4th, "with orders to adopt the most prudent methods of offense or defense which circumstances might point out."[61] In effect, the decision was left to Roberts's discretion, and he decided to act in what he could guess was the spirit, rather than the letter, of Brock's communications. His capture of Michilimackinac on 17 July had immediate consequences for Brock's advance against Detroit and also long-term effects.[62]

In the meantime, Brigadier-General William Hull had been moving slowly towards Detroit with an army of regulars and militiamen. Near the end of June, apparently still unaware that war had been declared, he decided to speed up his march by sending baggage, sick men, and officers' wives on the schooner *Cuyahoga* to Detroit. St George's force captured the vessel and found that it also carried Hull's official papers.[63] Hull nevertheless advanced and on 12 July crossed the Detroit River to accomplish the first American invasion of Canadian territory in the war. His troops outnumbered the defenders of Malden, and its capture would have deprived Brock of his only base for counter-attack. Hull delayed an attack and on 8 August withdraw to Detroit after hearing of the British capture of Michilimackinac, of growing Native support under the Shawnee chief Tecumseh for the British, and of Brock's departure for Amherstburg. Native warriors led by Tecumseh ambushed a supply train on its way to Detroit and captured dispatches to and from Hull.[64] Brock later gained a good deal of insight into the situation at Detroit and Hull's state of mind from reading his enemy's correspondence.

But from mid-July until mid-August it appeared that western Upper Canada might fall to the Americans. St George reported large numbers of local militiamen returning to their homes and some even deserting to the enemy. Militia forces in the Western and London districts refused to march with British troops against Hull, and the Natives on the Grand River declared for neutrality.[65] Brock had to allow half his militia force along the Niagara to return to their farms. He was also prevented by his political duties at York from taking military action against Hull. It was at this time that he showed his finest quality as a leader, simply by not giving way to despair. He expressed his determination clearly in his letter to Prevost of 29 July, in a comment often quoted: "Most of the people have lost all confidence – I however speak loud and look big."[66]

Brock was busy with the newly elected legislature, which began its first session on 27 July. Again he sought amendments to the Militia Act and the suspension of habeas corpus.[67] Although the representatives appeared willing to cooperate, Brock believed that he would not get the measures he sought; but if he imposed martial law, "I am told the whole armed force will disperse. Never was an officer placed in a more awkward predicament."[68] It is not surprising that, under all these pressures, the administrator did not appreciate the assembly's hesitation in giving him virtually unfettered authority. Anything that Brock might have said is unlikely to have changed the response of the majority of members.[69] Again the legislators refused to approve suspension of habeas corpus, but they did strengthen the Militia Act's provisions to ensure obedience to orders and voted £10,000 for the militia.[70] On 3 August the president met the Executive Council and described to its members a situation that could hardly have been gloomier. The American invaders threatened to advance farther into the Western District, where the militia was in a "perfect state of insubordination." Several persons in the London and Western districts had begun to negotiate with the enemy. Meanwhile, as Brock saw it, the assembly members were wasting time debating party issues. He sought the council's advice on the expediency of proroguing the house and proclaiming martial law. The next day the council unanimously recommended those actions.[71]

When it came to the matter of martial law, Brock was uncertain that his authority allowed him to impose it and, if it was put into effect, whether or not militia officers could sit on courts martial. Ever the cautious administrator, he sought Prevost's advice. The governor suggested that Brock had the authority to impose martial law, based on the king's commission, under the circumstances of an invasion of the province, but he was unwilling to authorize such a drastic measure. Instead, he advised the president to obtain the opinions of the "first law characters" of Upper Canada and then proceed as he judged best. In effect, this directive seemed to leave Brock on his own.[72] Eventually the governor sent him a warrant to strengthen his authority over courts martial, but Brock's success at Detroit made it unnecessary, as well as unwise, to resort to martial law.

While engaged with these concerns, Brock was also busy mobilizing troops and militia and crossing back and forth between York and Fort George. Finally, he set off for Amherstburg.[73] On his way, he visited the Mohawk village on the Grand River in search of Six Nations' support, but received a promise of only sixty warriors.[74] After a difficult and even perilous journey in small boats along the north shore of Lake Erie, he and his men arrived at Amherstburg on the night of 13 August. He met Tecumseh and the following day held a council with him and other Native leaders in order to gain their confidence and explain his plans.[75] The attack on Detroit on the 16th showed that he intended to waste no time.

When it came to actual combat in the War of 1812, Brock showed boldness, but his actions followed from his strategic vision and to a certain extent from his calculations. At Malden he rejected the advice of Procter and other officers not to attack. His crossing of the Detroit River on the morning of 16 August was bold, but even more dangerous was his advance on the fort. Yet it was not a thoughtless act. Batteries had been erected on the Canadian shore opposite Detroit, and those guns had been hitting the Americans within the fort, whose response was an inaccurate return fire. Brock explained to Sir George: "I crossed the river with the intention of waiting in a strong position the effect of our fire upon the Enemy's Camp, and in the hope of compelling him to meet us in the field. But receiving information upon landing that Colonel McArthur ... had left the Garrison three days before with a detachment of five hundred men, and hearing soon afterwards that his

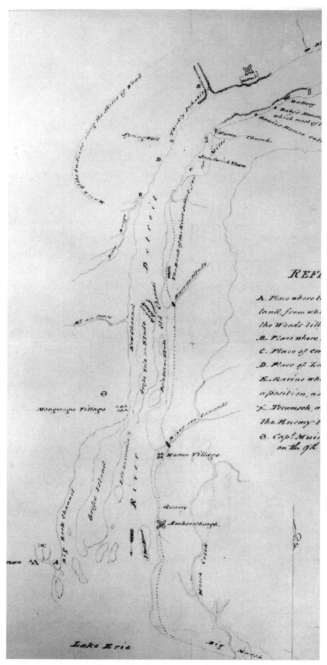

Map 6 The Detroit River, 1812
(courtesy of the William L. Clements Library, University of Michigan)

Cavalry had been seen that morning three miles in our rear, I decided on an immediate attack."[76] He knew a good deal about Hull's anxieties and the strength of his forces, and Hull's actions clearly indicated that he was excessively cautious. Given the information about McArthur, Brock could advance or withdraw, but he had come too far and committed too much simply to pull back.

The political and military gains from his success were enormous, namely, the surrender of Hull and his 2,000 regulars and militia, as well as the Michigan Territory. The expectation of such gains played a part in his decision, for it was neither reckless nor desperate. He had confidence in his men and knew that decisive measures were necessary. As he later told his brothers,

You will have heard of the complete success which attended the efforts I directed against Detroit ... Should the affair be viewed in England in the light it is here, I cannot fail of meeting reward, and escaping the horror of being placed high on a shelf, never to be taken down.

Some say that nothing could be more desperate than the measure; but I answer, that the state of the province admitted of nothing but desperate remedies ... It is, therefore, no wonder that envy should attribute to good fortune what, in justice to my own discernment, I must say, proceeded from a cool calculation of the *pours* and *contres*.[77]

Brock arrived back at Fort Erie on the evening of 23 August and was dismayed to learn that Prevost had ordered a ceasefire. Attack was still the best form of defence, he believed, and experience so far seemed to justify his view. But such plans had to be cancelled, and he therefore abandoned his intention to attack Sackets Harbor. This American naval base on Lake Ontario might have been an easy target, but it was not yet as important as it would become after Commodore Isaac Chauncey arrived in October and instituted a vigorous shipbuilding program. In the meantime, Lieutenant Melancthon T. Woolsey, the senior American naval officer on the Great Lakes, used Sackets as the base for his two small warships.[78] By allowing American vessels to come up the St Lawrence to Sackets, the truce enabled Woolsey to collect a little fleet. An attack such as Brock contemplated would have delayed rather than prevented the American naval build-up, but a successful raid would certainly have boosted morale in Upper Canada.

After the truce with the Americans ended on 8 September, Brock learned of increases in the enemy forces opposite, but also of discontent and desertion. He could make a successful attack, he believed, but restrained himself in accordance with Prevost's defensive strategy.[79] But this optimistic mood began to change, and by the third week he felt less confident. He was sufficiently worried to send Lieutenant-Colonel Robert Nichol on a mission to Prevost, perhaps to add weight to his complaint that he had too few troops to defend the Niagara frontier against an enemy attack which he expected at any moment because of increases in the American forces opposite and the belligerent mood of their militia.[80]

As summer turned to fall, tension continued to build along the Niagara River. The Americans erected batteries on commanding ground opposite Fort George and Queenston, and collected and constructed boats suitable for crossing. The American commander, Major-General Stephen Van Rensselaer of the New York State militia, received a steady stream of reinforcements, regulars, volunteers, and Native warriors.[81] By 12 October Van Rensselaer had at Lewiston 2,270 militia and 900 regulars and at Black Rock and Buffalo (villages about thirty miles to the south) 386 militia and 1,650 regulars.[82] This growing force was less formidable than it appeared, not least because of disagreements between Van Rensselaer and Brigadier-General Alexander Smyth, who commanded the regulars at Buffalo.

Brock strengthened his defences along the river while he tried to anticipate when and where his opponents might attack. From Fort George to Queenston, batteries were placed at points where they commanded the river and the American shore opposite. The most important for the coming battle were the 24-pounder carronade at Vrooman's Point (about a mile north of Queenston) and the 18-pounder in the redan above Queenston village. Arrangements were made for quick communication across the peninsula by means of beacons and cavalry riders.[83] To guard some thirty-five miles of river frontier, as well as parts of the Lake Ontario and Lake Erie waterfronts, the general had approximately 1,000 regulars and 600 militia, with a reserve of possibly 600 militia and Native warriors.[84] Regular artillerymen were so scarce that a volunteer corps of gunners was formed from infantrymen and militia.[85] Brock could not concentrate any large number of troops at one place, nor could they be marched from one end of the line to the other in much less than two days. His deployment of the bulk between Fort Erie and Chippawa and around Fort George indicates where he saw the greatest threat of invasion.

A day or two prior to 13 October he wrote copious instructions for the officers commanding the posts along the river.[86] In them he repeated his expectation that the principal attack would be delivered north of Fort Erie, but he warned his officers not to be lulled into a false sense of security, since he believed the enemy "more disposed to brave the impediments of nature ... in preference to the certainty of encountering British troops ready formed for his reception." This was

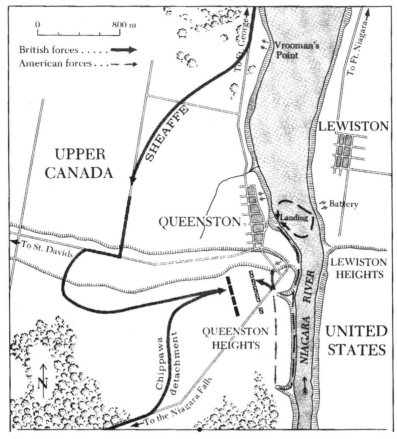

Map 7 The battle of Queenston Heights, October 1812
(reprinted, by permission, from Stanley, *The War of 1812*, 128)

prophetic utterance, which if Brock had realized its implications, might
have led to a very different result at Queenston Heights. By the evening
of 12 October the activity along the American side of the river convinced him that an invasion would soon be attempted. He consequently
wrote out orders "calling in the militia of the vicinity that same evening,
those more distant to follow with all alacrity." These dispatches he sent
off by riders of the Provincial Dragoons.[87] The same evening Brock
completed a letter to Prevost in which he expressed his conviction that
an attack was imminent, but at this time he thought it would come from
the lake side against Fort George.[88]

The invasion was launched in the pre-dawn hours of 13 October
from Lewiston across the river against Queenston, and all that is

needed here is a brief sketch of the battle to provide the framework for an analysis of Brock's generalship.[89] At Fort George, Brock was roused, probably by a messenger from Queenston. He hurriedly dressed and then mounted his horse; but still thinking that the greater American threat was to Fort George, he ordered only limited forces to move, while the remainder of the garrison was to stand ready to act in any direction when the enemy's intentions became known more definitely. Captain W. Holcroft with two guns and Norton with a party of Native warriors were to follow him.[90] The general hastened towards Queenston, soon followed by his ADCs, Captain John Glegg and Lieutenant-Colonel John Macdonell. If Brock stopped on that ride to Queenston, it was only for the briefest moment.

Once in the village, he quickly saw that a major assault was under way at Queenston, although he could not be sure that no other attacks were occurring.[91] Acting on what he did know, he dispatched orders to Sheaffe at Fort George to send the companies of the 41st Foot and of militia that were prepared to move and to turn all the fort's guns on the American batteries opposite. Brock hurried to the north end of the village, where he collected the light company of the 49th and perhaps some of the grenadier company. On his horse he led them southward at a run, telling them just before they reached the foot of the heights, "Take breath boys – you will need it in a few moments."[92] He then dismounted and led his men uphill. Most of the 49th grenadier company remained in the village to keep the Americans pinned down. If Captain James Dennis remained with his grenadier company and Captain John Williams was at the redan, that may explain why Brock, instead of one of these officers, led the charge.[93] His tall figure in a colourful uniform made him an obvious target. He was felled by a single shot and died almost immediately without time or strength to make a final dramatic pronouncement.[94]

This disaster ended the first counter-attack, but a second was soon attempted by Macdonell. After a fierce struggle the regulars and militia were repulsed with heavy losses, including Macdonell, who was severely wounded.[95] The regulars and militia then retreated to the other end of Queenston and subsequently to Vrooman's Point, where they waited for reinforcements. The troops left Brock's body in a house in Queenston; it remained until the afternoon, when it was taken to Fort George. The final battle, which ended in victory for the British, was fought in the afternoon under Sheaffe's leadership.

The historical explanation for Brock's motives in risking his life at the head of his troops by charging up the heights involves both rational motivation and an emotional response. When he saw American forces above the redan, Brock probably believed that he had no choice but to

launch an immediate counter-attack. He had provided for counteraction by artillery against the Americans around Fort Niagara and Black
Rock which would likely keep them off balance, but enemy control of
the heights would outflank his entire defensive line along the river.[96]
The extremities of Fort Erie and Fort George could hardly be held with
an American army between them and able to move by interior routes
towards Burlington Bay. If the Americans did advance, the British
would be forced out of the Niagara Peninsula and communications
with Procter's forces and Native allies would be severed. These may
have been Brock's thoughts as he fell back through the village. Meanwhile, the Americans on the heights were being reinforced, and he
knew that he could not quickly bring up more troops. Even if their
numbers were increased, however, the British, on the low ground,
would still be at a considerable disadvantage. Yet a flanking march
inland and then up the escarpment in order to gain higher ground
could easily be parried by the Americans. Such a manœuvre would also
require more manpower than Brock had at hand. At Detroit he had
advanced in the face of great danger, and perhaps he thought that it
could not be any riskier here. To take the chance of a swift counter-
attack fitted his principles of leadership.

Brock's career also demonstrated that he was capable of acting
impulsively in combat. In part, this was because he believed in decisive
action which by its very boldness might achieve success. Here, at dawn
on 13 October, he found himself in a situation that seemed to allow
no time for reflection or consultation. Moreover, he was the commanding officer of a province threatened by invasion at almost any
point on a long border. For the past seven weeks he had been prevented, by a truce, by orders from his commanding officer, and by
deficiencies in his forces, from launching a spoiling attack. During this
time the level of tension along the Niagara border had increased.[97] It
is therefore not hard to imagine Brock hoping, even yearning, for
action. As he had written to his brother Savery on 18 September, "You
will hear of some decided action in the course of a fortnight, or in all
probability we shall return to a state of tranquility. I say decisive,
because if I should be beaten the Province is inevitably gone, and
should I be victorious, I do not imagine the gentry from the other side
will be anxious to return to the charge ... I am quite anxious for this
state of warfare to end."[98] The opportunity arrived with Van Rensselaer's invasion.

Brock's uphill charge may be seen as the product of impulse combined with calculation. Also significant is the fact that he could not
have had more than five hours of sleep (and perhaps not uninter-
rupted) and probably little if anything to eat before galloping into

Queenston. A more rested commander might have acted differently. It also appears that neither Glegg nor Macdonell were with Brock when he made his decision, and they were therefore not available to lead it.[99] It is hard to imagine Brock behaving cautiously during a battle, given his combat record to 13 October 1812. What that record shows is that in his limited experience the tactic he seemed to prefer was a frontal assault led by himself. If he had taken time at Queenston to reflect, he might have responded differently. The outcome might have been both victory for his forces and the preservation of his own life.

As a civil administrator, Brock appears to have had little success in strengthening his authority at the expense of normal civil rights, but he did gain support for improving the militia. These changes helped to bolster the military effort, and it should not be assumed that his failure over habeas corpus and martial law impeded the province's defence. If the government had obtained stronger powers and had sought to apply them, this move might have provoked so much resistance as to undermine, rather than enhance, public authority. Brock's successors had varying luck in implementing measures like those he had wished for, and in Lower Canada Sir George met the same setback as Brock had, a fact which indicates that the Upper Canadians' response to their administrator was not unique or unusual. (In the United States, citizens in many places were as strongly opposed to wartime measures and appeals for military service. The phenomenon was not unique to British colonies.)

The civil secretary's letterbook and Brock's correspondence contain innumerable references to small administrative details which suggest his concern with order and efficiency. Nevertheless, an officer who worked closely with Brock later criticized his administration. Major Thomas Evans, his brigade major and subsequently also deputy adjutant general, wrote in January 1813 to Chief Justice William Dummer Powell, the most prominent legal and political leader in Upper Canada, that the militia and barrack departments and the commissariat were seriously inefficient. Although the fault lay with the heads of those departments, he believed that the ultimate responsibility belonged to Brock. Evans and Lieutenant-Colonel Christopher Myers, deputy quartermaster general, had informed Brock of the sorry state of those departments, but "it is a melancholy truth that everything that had for its object arrangement and method was obliged to be done by stealth. Poor General Brock's high spirit would never descend to particulars, trifles I may say in the abstract, but ultimately essentials."[100]

This is the only instance in the documents of such a criticism, but given Evans's position and experience, it cannot be ignored. Evans admitted, however, that his letter was written in defence of Sheaffe, who was then under fire from civilians and seemed to be losing the confidence of his regular officers.[101] There may be some truth in Evans's comments, but given the circumstances and the lack of similar criticism, his statements should not be accepted uncritically.

Although Brock's aides-de-camp may have been less significant than Prevost's, at least two of them deserve mention for what they suggest about Brock. His military ADC was Captain John B. Glegg, 49th Foot,[102] and his provincial aides were Major James Givins and Lieutenant-Colonel John Macdonell (Greenfield). Brock's choice of these latter two suggests a certain amount of calculation, for each man had a measure of influence with segments of the population in different parts of Upper Canada, Givins with Natives around York and Macdonell with Scots in Glengarry County. Each also had special knowledge and experience in his own sphere. Givins's career in government and military service in Upper Canada went back at least to 1775 and in the Indian Department to 1797. Brock appointed him an ADC, as well as a major in the militia, in August 1812. He was with Brock at Detroit, saw action at Queenston Heights, and continued to serve ably throughout the war.[103] Brock's choice of this ADC leaves no doubt that the general was concerned with the support of Native allies.

Macdonell came from a prominent Loyalist family, was related to other influential families of Glengarry County, and was acting as the upper province's attorney general when Brock named him his provincial ADC and a lieutenant-colonel in the militia. He was also a member of the House of Assembly. He accompanied Brock to Amherstburg and, along with Glegg, negotiated the surrender of Detroit. Brock commended his services in that action. Wounded at Queenston Heights on 13 October, Macdonell died on the 14th.[104]

By his biographers Brock is often depicted as a general without equal on the British side.[105] This perception can also be found in the writings on the war, except in a few accounts that criticize his generalship.[106] There are mild reservations about Brock in the writings of J.M. Hitsman (1965) and G.F.G. Stanley (1983), but they scarcely disturb the image of him as the heroic general whose loss was irreparable.[107] A.M.J. Hyatt (1961) suggests a degree of revisionism by criticizing Brock and praising Prevost. The latter's failings, he claims, "are not so numerous nor so glaring as Brock's," and he asserts that "the campaign in Upper Canada, despite Brock, was always under Prevost's control." Prevost thus appears as a strong commander who was forced to restrain the recklessness of his subordinate in Upper Canada. Carol Whitfield (1974) also offers a critical view of Brock because of his behaviour towards the civil authorities in Lower Canada before the war, his flawed strategic planning, and his "ill-considered" charge up Queenston Heights.[108] The most recent Canadian scholarly study of the war, by George Sheppard, finds fault with him in his political role but tends to reinforce the earlier perception of his military pre-eminence by referring to him as "a brilliant strategist."[109]

No other British commander from the war has been so frequently and publicly commemorated in place names and monuments, as well as in writings and speeches. An obvious reason for remembering Brock was his death while leading a charge against the enemy. Almost immediately, this behaviour was seen as heroic and his idealization began to blossom.[110] The dead general faced no competition for heroic stature, and Upper Canadians had no chance to become disillusioned with him as leader because at the time of his death they had not experienced military defeats, losses, destruction, shortages, and enemy occupation. In fact, they had seen the saving of the province apparently because of his generalship at Detroit and Queenston. Prevost made his own contribution to the heroic image as early as April 1813, when he wrote to the British colonial secretary about Brock's "eminent military talents," which he believed Sheaffe could not match. This was a critical comparison that was emerging before Sir Roger had lost the battle at York.[111] An indication of the attitude of Montreal fur traders may be seen in a letter from John McGillivray to Simon McTavish in which the former complained bitterly that the fruits of Brock's victory over Hull had been thrown away by the government.[112] In March 1813 the Upper Canadian assembly contributed by petitioning the Prince Regent to grant land to "his family," and only three months later Bathurst instructed Sheaffe to proceed with a grant.[113] The next year the assembly voted unanimously to contribute £500 towards a monument on Queenston Heights in memory of Brock, and in 1815 it would pass an act providing for the erection of a monument.[114]

Newspapers added to the chorus. The *York Gazette*, in its report of Brock's funeral, referred to "the last words of the dying Hero" and printed a lengthy poem, its title all in upper case: "TO GENERAL BROCK, A GARLAND."[115] A week later, reporting on the battle of Queenston Heights, the *Montreal Herald*, referred to "the severe loss of Major General Brock. That hero possessed the full confidence of every good man, and was the idol of Upper Canada." The *Quebec Mercury* combined the same kind of flattery, in both prose and poetry about Brock, with exultation in Britain's age of glory because of heroes such as Nelson, Moore, Abercromby, and Wellesley (later the Duke of Wellington)[116] – distinguished company indeed for Brock! These images found resonance in England, as the *Mercury* reported in June 1813, taking "From a Late London Paper" great praise for Brock's heroism. At the same time, the *Herald* praised Proctor and Vincent by referring to them as "SURVIVING BROCKS."[117] Could this phrase also have been a subtle criticism of Sheaffe, whose disgrace at York in April 1813 was so fresh?

One analyst of the glorification of Brock suggests that it can be explained by "the conduct of the colonists after 1812." What Sheppard means is that "the dismal display" of Upper Canadian militia participation during the first four months of the war was much better than the militia's "pitiful record" after Brock's death.[118] Under Brock, in other words, the Upper Canadian militia had responded to the call of duty and had contributed significantly to repulsing the enemy. Glorifying their leader reflected favourably on the troops. One limitation on this claim is the fact that the perception of Brock as a hero began before the "pitiful record" developed and came from sources outside the province which were unlikely to be influenced by the level of Upper Canadian militia participation. Aside from a particular or local interest in making a hero out of Brock, there was the general tendency of the age to seek heroes among naval and military men.[119] English-speaking Canadians had few of these, and in the upper province, they had no one with Brock's success and prestige. Other heroes would subsequently appear, for example, Tecumseh and, in Lower Canada, Salaberry, but these emerged after Brock's pre-eminence as *the* hero of the war had been firmly established.

A significant reason for his importance is the fact that he commanded at the outset of the war. Of the three years of warfare, the critical one was 1812, since the home country was then least able to provide aid to British North America. Defence of the Canadas rested upon the forces and matériel actually present. It was the skilful use of these by British officers that prevented American conquest; but even with incompetent generals and poorly trained and badly disciplined troops, the Americans came dangerously close to conquering Upper Canada.

Without Brock's energetic massing of forces at the western end of Lake Erie, there is a strong possibility that Hull would eventually have captured Fort Malden and Amherstburg. In the absence of Brock, it is difficult to see Tecumseh and his followers playing a major role under Procter. If Hull had advanced, he would have outflanked Canadian defences on the Niagara River and could possibly have reversed Roberts's victory at Michilimackinac. If this had occurred, it is hardly likely that Upper Canada west of York, or even as far east as Kingston, could have been kept out of American hands, for there were no defences or troop concentrations at Burlington Bay or York. The loss of Upper Canada in 1812 would have made the defence of Lower Canada extremely difficult, and perhaps impossible, in 1813. American morale would have been at its height – possibly great enough to overcome New England's reluctance to take part. The Americans could have concentrated their efforts on the key targets of Montreal and Quebec, and because of warfare in Europe, Britain would not have been able to provide the massive reinforcements of first-rate troops that would have been necessary to stop the invaders. Hence it can be argued that Brock's role affected the entire course of the war. The preservation of Upper Canada in 1812 was a sign that British sovereignty would continue. Of all the commanding generals who contributed to this situation during the war, Brock was the most significant.

CHAPTER FOUR

Prudence:
The Leadership of Major-General
Sir Roger Hale Sheaffe

… an insufficiency on the part of Major General Sir R.H.
Sheaffe to the arduous Task of defending Upper Canada.

Prevost to the Duke of York, 23 June 1813

On the first occasion that Roger Hale Sheaffe commanded forces in combat, he won an important battle. In fact, the victory at Queenston Heights was so highly regarded by the British government that it rewarded him with a baronetcy. Sir Roger had reached the height of his career, for he would never again win a battle, and less than a year afterwards he was recalled by the home government.

During his short command of Upper Canada, Sheaffe became the target of a good deal of criticism, particularly for his generalship at York when it was attacked by the Americans in April 1813. Modern scholarly writing offers both favourable and unfavourable judgments on him. He has been criticized for failing to lead boldly and decisively at York, but also praised for brave personal leadership and sensible judgment on that occasion and for his skilful conduct of the battle of Queenston Heights.[1] In a more general sense, he has been defended on the grounds that he was a competent, but unassuming general who was overshadowed by Brock.[2] Such contradictory and ambivalent opinions indicate the difficulties of arriving at a definitive conclusion about his capabilities and how he used the opportunities that became available to him to show his leadership.

Roger Hale Sheaffe was born in Boston on 15 July 1763, the third son in a family of eight children. His father died in 1771, leaving his widow in poor circumstances. She moved her family into a house owned by her father and apparently took in boarders.[3] Roger therefore came from a social and economic background much less favoured than that of the other generals in this study and much less common to

British officers of the period. He could hardly expect to advance without the aid of someone of prominence and wealth. His patron was to be Earl Percy, later the Duke of Northumberland,[4] who had boarded at the Sheaffe house. Percy sent Roger to serve in the Royal Navy when the lad was about ten years old. Soon afterwards, he enabled Sheaffe to attend Lochée's academy in England, the school at which Prevost was a student and at the same time.[5] He was thereby destined for a career in the army. On 1 May 1778 the earl purchased an ensigncy for Sheaffe in his own regiment, the 5th Foot. Sheaffe appears to have joined the regiment in 1779, and the next year the earl purchased the young man's lieutenancy.

Like Prevost's father, Percy was a prominent and distinguished general. He decided to launch this youth on a military career, and we do not know if young Roger wanted one or simply went along with Percy's decisions. But Sheaffe was put into the position of having to live up to the expectations of another. He also felt a duty to aid his family financially, and the opportunities to impress his patron and to help his family increased as he rose in rank. In Sheaffe's case, these responsibilities may have encouraged cautious behaviour. Brock also had a financial burden, which involved paying off a large debt and helping members of his family, but this obligation clearly did not dampen his impetuosity.[6] Rather, the different behaviour patterns of the two men arose from their characters. It was difficult for a soldier from an undistinguished family in the colonies to rise to high rank in the British army and even rarer for the son of a poor family. Sheaffe fitted both categories and could be in no doubt that his future advancement necessitated keeping the favour of his patron. Like the other generals in this study, in the eighteenth century Sheaffe was a junior officer learning his trade. When it came to the War of 1812, his generalship was similar to Prevost's, rather than to Brock's or Drummond's. Again, the explanation lies in these men's characters.

Between 1781 and 1787 Sheaffe served with the 5th Foot in Ireland. In July of the latter year he sailed with his regiment for Canada, where he remained until 1797. The 5th moved to Montreal in 1788 and served at Detroit and Fort Niagara before returning to Quebec in 1796, but very little is known about Sheaffe's activities during this decade.[7] His rise in rank was rapid, for in May 1795 he purchased a captaincy in the 5th Foot with funds provided by his patron, and in England in December two years later his majority in the 81st Foot.[8] On 22 March 1798 he obtained the rank of lieutenant-colonel in yet a different regiment, the 49th Foot, whose senior lieutenant-colonel was Isaac Brock. Sheaffe was with the 49th in the fighting in the Netherlands in 1799 and witnessed the attack on Copenhagen in 1801. He was not mentioned in reports on these engagements.[9] These were his first experiences of combat; his next would not occur until Queenston Heights.

The first significant notice of Sheaffe in the 49th appears in connection with two incidents which indicate that he had shortcomings as a regimental officer. The first case saw discontent among the men when Brock left the regiment in Jersey under Sheaffe's command. The second incident occurred in 1803 among the troops under his leadership along the Niagara River. The soldiers who planned to mutiny and desert seemed to focus their discontent on Sheaffe.[10]

Desertion by British troops, particularly from colonial outposts, was common. This incident, therefore, has been left in the obscurity it deserves, except by biographers of Brock. When the latter notice it, they usually place responsibility for the trouble on Sheaffe.[11] However, a recent biographer questions this interpretation, asserting that "Brock blamed the incident on Sheaffe, whom he claimed was too zealous and too much the disciplinarian. Several of the convicted men, however, produced statements praising Sheaffe for his humanity and leniency. Probably the isolation and loneliness of Fort George, coupled with a 'follow the rule-book' attitude by Sheaffe, ... created the atmosphere of desperation which induced the men to conspire."[12] Because Sheaffe was the commanding officer at Fort George, some blame would naturally fall on him. The prisoners complained about his "harsh and severe treatment" of them when on duty.[13] Brock attributed the major cause, not to Sheaffe, but to "the situation of the place, and ... the temptations which are perpetually offered to the unwary soldier" – in other words, to the proximity of the United States.[14] Yet Brock could not excuse Sheaffe entirely, for one of his faults was frequently reducing non-commissioned officers to the ranks; even worse was his conduct towards common soldiers:

His manner of addressing the men on the least irritation, must be allowed to be unfortunate, and to that failing must be attributed, in a great measure, the ill will which some men have expressed towards him. There is also another cause which ought not to be omitted.

Whenever the Command of the Regiment devolved by my absence on Colonel Sheaffe, he, unquestionably required more from the non-Commissioned Officers than I knew was useless to expect from them. He did not sufficiently study the character of the men and his ardent zeal made him seek with eagerness after perfection where it was not to be found – Serjeants, for trifling errors, were too often reduced, or for such faults, which, had he considered that they could be replaced only by men who were not likely to act with greater discretion, he would, however he might have lamented the necessity, have passed over by giving them a suitable admonition. He likewise perhaps was frequently tiresome in the exercise in the field, by which the men became disgusted with what they should have taken delight to practice.

Sheaffe conducted the prosecution in the men's court martial, and Brock expected that from this experience he might come to modify his behaviour, "correcting his present rude manner of speaking, and ... regulating his conduct to the times and place in which he may hereafter be engaged."

This letter hardly supports the claim that "Brock blamed the incident on Sheaffe." Nor is it quite accurate to attribute the plot to Fort George's "isolation and loneliness" and the excessive discipline imposed by Sheaffe. In terms of location, Fort George was not an isolated or lonely spot. Indeed, the problem may have been the opposite: namely, that the attractions of civilian life were too close and obvious, particularly across the international boundary. As for Sheaffe's being too strict in applying the rules, this may have been less a grievance than his harsh and contemptuous manner. Sheaffe may have modified his manner, for he did not again encounter this kind of conspiracy.

Other officers, however, were less willing to disregard his culpability. General Peter Hunter, lieutenant-governor of Upper Canada and commander of the forces in the Canadas, thought of showing open disapproval of the colonel's conduct, but Brock disagreed. He argued that Sheaffe's "imperfections proceed immediately from an error in judgment,"[15] and he believed that his junior was capable of reaching a better understanding of the rank and file. Sheaffe's career came close to a severe check, if not to its termination. Again with his habitual common sense and humaneness, Brock urged that this officer be dealt with frankly. If Hunter considered Sheaffe unworthy to continue as an officer, he should be told so and allowed to resign. On the other hand, if Brock's view of Sheaffe were accepted, then he should be treated with full confidence by his superiors. Sheaffe's career was saved, and that Brock influenced the decision is suggested by a pencil notation in the margin of Brock's letter: "The Lt. Governor has decided that on the opening of the navigation Lt. Colonel. Sheaffe is to proceed to York to take the command there." Brock warmly approved.[16]

Sheaffe served in the Canadas at different posts, obtaining the brevet rank of colonel in April 1808 and that of major-general on 4 June 1811.[17] By then he had sufficiently redeemed himself in the eyes of his superiors to be considered fit to succeed Brock in the event that the latter left for Europe. But Colonel Henry Torrens, military secretary to the commander-in-chief, hardly recommended this course enthusiastically, telling Prevost that, "as Major General Sheaffe is supposed to be on the spot and has strong Claims to Employment on the Staff, the Commander in Chief leaves it to your discretion to employ that officer in the room of Major General Brock."[18] By the time this letter arrived in Lower Canada in January 1812, Brock had made his decision to remain.

In 1811 Sheaffe was in command at Three Rivers.[19] In July 1812, when Prevost was looking for general officers to appoint to various commands, Sheaffe was available, and Prevost took it upon himself to appoint him temporarily to the staff of Upper Canada under Brock's command.[20] The appointment was tentative probably because Prevost could not know if a dispatch was on its way across the ocean ordering Sheaffe to take up a post elsewhere and possibly because Prevost had lingering doubts about the officer's capabilities. In this accidental way, Sheaffe undertook the command in which he would reach the height of his career. Although he had no experience of civil responsibilities before the war, he was no stranger to the political world of Upper Canada. Besides his years of service there, he had the advantage of a friendship, dating back to his childhood, with the influential William Dummer Powell, a leading member of the Executive Council.[21]

Of the five generals, Sheaffe had the least experience of command and, in common with Brock, the briefest exposure to combat. The evidence of his soldierly qualities is consequently too skimpy and that of his leadership abilities too ambivalent to enable judgments to be made. Sheaffe's knowledge of the art of war and his opinions on strategy are unknown, but it may be assumed that he was thoroughly professional because he had served in the army for over thirty years after his brief exposure to formal military education. Part of this outlook would have been an infantry officer's appreciation of the territory where fighting might take place. In this respect, Sheaffe's years of service in the Canadas may be significant. By 1811 he had spent nineteen years in the country, more time than any of the other generals, and he was more familiar with the critical areas of the Niagara Peninsula and York than were the others, except possibly Brock. Hence Prevost's opinion of Sheaffe's potential usefulness to Brock was soundly based, as far as the former's local knowledge was concerned. Sheaffe had never held a position that required him to express his opinions on strategies for the defence of the Canadas. What he thought will therefore have to be inferred from what he did.

On 18 August 1812, when Sheaffe arrived at Fort George to assume the command of the troops in the Niagara District, he found Brock off to Amherstburg on an expedition whose outcome was by no means certain.[22] He also learned of Prevost's truce with Dearborn and that a ceasefire was to be extended to the Niagara frontier.[23] This agreement allowed stores and reinforcements to be forwarded by both sides.[24] The American commander at Fort Niagara, Major-General Stephen Van Rensselaer, had already opened negotiations, and all that Sheaffe had to do was complete them. In so doing, he agreed to Van Rensselaer's demand, based on Dearborn's orders, that "men and supplies of ammunition" should not be sent past Fort Erie, meaning that neither side could reinforce the Detroit frontier.[25] Sheaffe explained to Prevost that he had acceded to the American stipulation because he had just learned of Brock's capture of Detroit and he knew that Van Rensselaer was unaware of it.[26] As well, Van Rensselaer had insisted that no agreement was possible which excluded that clause.[27]

Prevost had not intended to allow Sheaffe any discretion, and he replied that the terms conveyed in Baynes's letter "ought to have been considered as conclusive and binding not to be deviated from."[28] Fearing "embarrassment may ensue to His Majesty's Service in Upper Canada," he threatened to repudiate Sheaffe's arrangement. Although Prevost did not carry out his threat, he made it clear that he would not allow any latitude to Sheaffe, who had offered a reasonable explanation. The governor had not reacted in this manner or in such an acerbic tone to the initiatives of Brock and Captain Roberts.

Sheaffe remained on the Niagara frontier in September and October 1812.[29] Brock may have wanted the benefit of the officer's local knowledge in strengthening the frontier's defences, but it is also possible that he was unwilling to risk giving him a separate command. On the morning of 13 October, when Brock left Fort George to ride to Queenston, it is not clear what orders he left for Sheaffe. In his report on the battle, Sheaffe makes no mention of any instructions, an omission which suggests that Brock had left nothing written.[30] According to Brigade Major Thomas Evans, the Native warriors and regular artillery were "promptly despatched" to Queenston, presumably by Brock's order, but another account suggests that there was a delay. Captain John Norton related that Sheaffe told him to wait, but that almost immediately Evans instructed him to hurry to Queenston because it was in American possession.[31] A few regulars and militia still remained in the fort until scouts, sent out by Evans, returned to report the absence of any nearby American threat. The troops were then dispatched to Queenston. At this time, Sheaffe was in command at the fort, but in his later report he made no mention of these events or of his actions.

Once the news of Brock's death reached Fort George, Sheaffe's place was on the battlefield. His report does not mention the time at which he learned the news or when he rode towards Queenston. Brock was probably shot before 8 a.m., and it should not have taken more than an hour for the news to travel the six miles to Fort George. Norton saw the general riding past men marching towards Queenston. Sheaffe joined the forces gathered about two and a half miles north of the village at Durham's house. One militia officer put the time of his arrival there at just after 10 a.m.[32] It would take time for the troops and militiamen falling back from Queenston to gather at Durham's and for these units to be put into order.

Sheaffe methodically assembled his force of 700 to 800 men before marching them west nearly two miles and then south to climb the escarpment, intending to meet the invaders on equal ground.[33] On the heights above Queenston he formed his militia and regulars facing the Americans and waited until reinforcements from Chippawa joined them. In front, Iroquois warriors skirmished with the Americans to keep them at bay. The militiamen showed no signs of disorder or panic, even those without previous experience of combat.[34] Some time after 2 p.m., having received the reinforcements he expected, Sheaffe ordered the attack. His men fired a volley and then advanced with fixed bayonets while Norton's warriors swept around the American right to threaten them from the rear. This combination of the most effective battlefield tactics of Native warriors and European soldiers proved irresistible. Sheaffe put the successful termination of the battle at about 3 p.m.; other first-hand accounts place it later, from 3:15 to 5 p.m.[35]

Sheaffe benefited from an enemy force that was poorly organized, disciplined, and led. The Americans had the advantage of the heights from early morning, but made no use of it. They were unable to obtain reinforcements, in particular of New York State militia, and an orderly withdrawal was impossible. Sheaffe had the priceless advantage of time to prepare his forces because the Americans were unable to defeat or drive away the Native skirmishers. He was also fortunate that the Americans were unable to strike north from Queenston when he marched his troops away from the river road, in effect, leaving open the way to Fort George.[36] It is not clear whether he considered this possibility as he advanced against the heights.

Whatever the exact amount of credit he deserves for the victory, Sheaffe's leadership proved appropriate for the situation. His was the course of methodical professionalism, rather than brilliance or dash. He rallied the defenders, steadied them, and won by following the rules, rather than by giving way to impulse. Afterwards he was very thorough in praising the men for their service, mentioning not only regular and militia officers but also militia volunteers and Norton's warriors.[37]

By Brock's death Sheaffe had become commander of the forces and administrator of Upper Canada. He immediately proposed a truce to the Americans to allow each side to attend to its casualties and exchange prisoners. This reasonable action gave him time to become accustomed to his new responsibilities and to take stock of the military situation. The transfer of command from a well-known, much-admired, and even beloved commander to an untried, much less experienced one could not have been easy. Yet Sheaffe undertook his new roles with his customary professionalism.

The truce, moreover, fitted the non-aggressive policy that Prevost favoured. Yet when Sheaffe agreed to requests by Van Rensselaer and then by General Alexander Smyth to extend the ceasefire beyond three days, he found himself severely criticized by Prevost. The governor disagreed with Sheaffe's paroling the American militiamen and complained that Sheaffe had not obtained his consent to extend the armistice. Prevost may have thought that Sheaffe could have vigorously pursued the Americans after their defeat, even to the capture of Fort Niagara.[38] These views contradicted his own well-known opinion and orders for the defence of the Canadas. They also contrast with the behaviour that Prevost had urged on Brock. The governor, it seems, was unwilling to listen to Sheaffe, who carefully explained his reasons, or to depend on his judgment. Instead, Sheaffe was treated in a more high-handed and critical manner than any other general in Prevost's command.

During the term of the truce, Sheaffe continued to strengthen the Niagara frontier and its flanks along Lakes Erie and Ontario, for he rightly expected the Americans to try again. The new American commander, Brigadier-General Smyth, ended the ceasefire on 20 November and early on the 28th sent an invasion force across the Niagara River. It had been driven back before Sheaffe arrived on the spot, and in his report he claimed no credit for this success.[39] Smyth's second effort, on 1 December, did not even get across the river.

In spite of his successes, Sheaffe's image was becoming seriously tarnished. His prolongation of the truce was criticized as bringing no benefits to the defenders while displaying weakness towards the Americans.[40] After the American failure on 28 November, the commanding officer at Fort Erie, Lieutenant-Colonel Cecil Bisshopp, requested reinforcements. Sheaffe refused on the grounds that he could not commit any more men to the extremity of his defensive line. If Fort Erie came under attack by an overwhelming American force, Bisshopp was to consult his officers about a retreat, which course, Sheaffe advised, might be wisest. Bisshopp's officers responded with outrage over their commander's suggestion of retreat.[41] It was an extremely injudicious suggestion to advance even if it made tactical sense. Only an insecure commander would hint at retreat with the victories of 13 October and 28 November so recent, and only one lacking perception would put

himself in a position to be compared unfavourably to his heroic predecessor. It is not surprising that Sheaffe lost standing with regular officers, and this sentiment soon spread to militiamen, such as Captain
Andrew Gray (deputy quartermaster general) and Lieutenant-Colonel
Robert Nichol.[42] Civilian confidence in him ebbed, and some may even
have wondered about his loyalty. Before the end of 1812 it was therefore evident that Sheaffe would not be a decisive leader able to inspire
the pioneer community as Brock had, and the idealization of the latter
could proceed unhampered by competition.

Sheaffe's civil administration began on 20 October 1812, when he
met the Executive Council and took the oaths as its president.[43] One
of the immediate problems facing him was the neutral and pro-American sentiment among the population. To examine those who claimed
exemption from militia service on the grounds of being American citizens, he appointed boards at Niagara, Kingston, and York.[44] These
boards could decide if the claimants were to be issued passports that
would enable them to cross the border or were to be required to
remain in Upper Canada. There seem to be no figures on the number
who were sent to the United States or the number allowed to remain,
and it is possible that large numbers left the province illegally and
unrecorded.[45]

As the campaigning season ended, Sheaffe worked unceasingly to
correct the deficiencies of army departments, to supply the wants of
the militia, to improve their efficiency, and to obtain reinforcements
for Upper Canada.[46] One of his chief concerns was to ensure British
naval supremacy on the lakes when the shipping season reopened.
Captain Isaac Chauncey had virtually seized control of Lake Ontario
just before the winter freeze-up, and Sheaffe urged the fitting out of
additional warships at Kingston, York, and Amherstburg.[47] Over the
winter he also developed proposals to strengthen the militia, and these
would appear in the legislation he presented to the Upper Canadian
parliament.

In his opening speech to the legislature on 25 February 1813, he
congratulated the members on the successful defence of the province
in the previous year and praised Brock, the "loyal inhabitants," and the
militia.[48] He asked the assembly to vote money "to provide an Outfit"[49]
for the embodied militia, but made no other demand on its resources.
Finally, his report that "the most vigorous measures" were being pursued to strengthen the Provincial Marine may have allayed the Upper
Canadian concern that the Americans might gain mastery of the lakes.
Sheaffe prorogued the legislature on 13 March, having achieved virtually everything that he had requested. This accomplishment is not as
surprising as it might appear at first glance, since he sought measures

that directly benefited Upper Canadians without imposing new or particularly severe burdens on them. The passage of an act recognizing army bills as legal tender in Upper Canada made sense because the authorities were already using them. An act authorizing the lieutenant-governor to prohibit the export or distillation of grain meant that prices might be kept under control while the farmers would have no difficulty in selling everything they produced. Sheaffe asked for and was granted authority to pay in advance annuities to widows and children of militiamen killed, as well as to those disabled, and certain amendments in the militia law.

These amendments were Sheaffe's most significant measures, for they were intended to provide a larger and more efficient militia force.[50] His reforms replaced the flank companies with an incorporated militia to be made up of volunteers who would enlist for the duration of the war. To attract volunteers, a cash bounty was authorized; but Sheaffe considered the initial amount of eight dollars per man too low, and on his own he raised it to eighteen dollars and also offered land grants to all ranks at the end of their service.[51] Because of the immediate demands of warfare in 1813, as well as competition by recruiters of other units, only a start was made in recruiting the Volunteer Incorporated Militia.[52] By the end of the year, a battalion of some 300 men had been organized, and the unit would prove its military worth during the following year. While Sheaffe's goal of a force numbering 2,500 to 3,000 men may have been too ambitious, his idea was sound.[53]

He had more success with the legislature than did Brock, a different outcome that may be explained both by the optimism of his opening address and by the nature of his measures. Certainly, they dealt with wartime needs and met the wishes of Prevost, yet were not particularly controversial, restrictive, or burdensome. The sources do not indicate to what extent Sheaffe was responsible for this program and how much input came from members of the political elite such as Powell. That the general had his own sense of political realism may be seen in his decision to increase the bounty for the Incorporated Militia and apply for land grants for militiamen as well as in his refusal to impose martial law after his retreat from York.[54]

Sheaffe consistently declined to take risks in warfare. His refusal to cross the Niagara River after the battle of Queenston Heights was an example. Another was his rejection of Vincent's proposal to attack Fort Niagara. Even though he had estimates of the fort's garrison numbering only 200 men, he feared that there were not enough boats for the operation, and he also took shelter under Prevost's strategy of prudent defence.[55] Moreover, his conduct during the battle of York in April 1813 showed him again a brave, but cautious general.

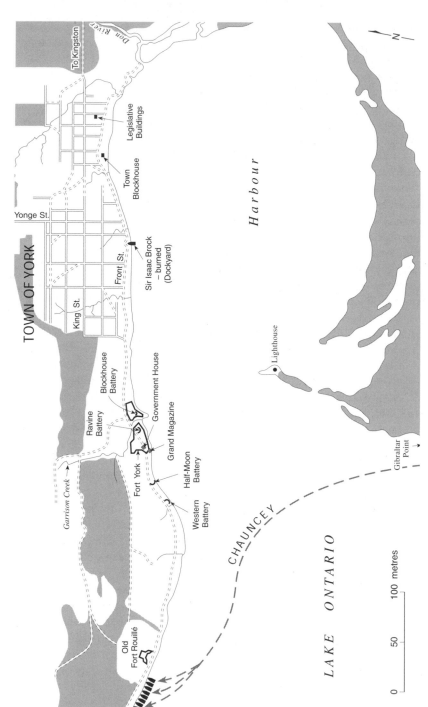

Map 8 The capture of York, April 1813 (adapted from Stanley, *The War of 1812*, 171)

The capital of Upper Canada was "a small backwoods settlement" with a population of perhaps 500.[56] The village had a blockhouse at its east end, but its principal defences were situated to the west, a mile and more away, and consisted of a blockhouse, batteries in four locations, the west wall of Fort York, and an unarmed earthwork. These defences had been strengthened under Brock's orders early in 1812, but still did not command the entrance to the harbour.[57] In 1813, even though the frigate *Sir Isaac Brock* was under construction in its shipyard, York was not important enough to warrant a large garrison. Official War Office returns reported rank-and-file strength there at 405 men on 25 March, no figures for April or May (nor for January and February), and 573 in June and July.[58]

On 26 April, when Chauncey's squadron was sighted, Sheaffe's force, numbering between 600 and 700 men, consisted of 350 militiamen, perhaps 50 Mississauga and Ojibwa warriors, and the remainder regulars.[59] The light company of the 8th Foot was east of York marching towards the town, but Sheaffe did not know its exact position. Approaching York was an American fleet of fourteen warships mounting eighty-three guns and carrying 1,750 regulars and volunteers. This effort under Dearborn, the commander of the armies of the Northeast and the Centre, was the first major American campaign of 1813. It was also one of the few occasions when the American army and navy cooperated effectively on Lake Ontario.[60] Dearborn planned to land his men west of Fort York early on the 27th, in an area of cleared fields, but their small boats were pushed further westward by strong winds. They arrived on a wooded shore that gave the defenders some cover but also increased the distance they had to march, their exposure to gunfire from Chauncey's warships, and the difficulties of forming a regular defensive line.[61]

Seeing the enemy's intentions, Sheaffe ordered the Native warriors and a company of regulars to meet the invaders at the shore, and he soon dispatched more troops as reinforcements.[62] Exposed to deadly fire from the American naval guns, the defenders were driven back towards York. The accidental explosion of a travelling gunpowder magazine killed or wounded 30 men, further lessening the defenders' strength and probably their morale. As the fighting retreat continued, Sheaffe decided to withdraw his regulars from what he saw as a losing battle. There is no evidence that he consulted with any of his officers or with militia leaders. Sheaffe gave orders for the detonation of the grand magazine and the burning of the *Brock*, naval supplies, and the Don River bridge in order to delay any American pursuit. The battle began at about 8 a.m. and ended about three hours later when the magazine blew up; the retreat seems to have begun at between 3 and

4 p.m.[63] Putting the preservation of his tiny army ahead of honourable death or capture, Sheaffe headed towards Kingston with his regulars and the shipwrights.

He had made a sound tactical decision, one proof being the American government's disappointment at the escape of Sheaffe's army. The American secretary of war, John Armstrong, wrote to Dearborn, "we cannot doubt but that in all cases in which a British commander is constrained to act defensively, his policy will be that adopted by Sheaffe – to prefer the preservation of his troops to that of his post, and thus carrying off the kernel leave us only the shell."[64] Sheaffe made a successful retreat to Kingston over bad roads rendered almost impassable by "heavy and copious rains" added to the spring thaw.

Unfortunately for him, the post that he was unable to defend was the provincial capital where there resided influential men already critical of his leadership. As a result of their experiences on 26 and 27 April, individuals such as Major William Allan (3rd York Militia), Captain Duncan Cameron (3rd York), William Chewett (commanding officer, 3rd York), Dr W.W. Baldwin (judge of the Surrogate Court), the Reverend John Strachan (chaplain to the York garrison), and the merchant Alexander Wood complained that Sheaffe had failed to provide clear and decisive leadership.[65] Even Sheaffe's friend W.D. Powell, in a letter to Vincent, may have added to this negative chorus by referring to the general's "entire abandonment of the civil government."[66] These attacks would finish Sheaffe's career in Upper Canada. With such a solid demonstration of non-confidence by many provincial leaders, the general could not be effective in his civil capacity, and this deficiency, more than any military shortcomings, made him a liability to Prevost.

In terms of generalship on 27 April, while Sheaffe led the defenders in his usual professional manner, what seems to have been absent was a clear plan of defence, even though earlier that month he had written that an American attack on York was "probable."[67] The kind of defence in depth that the American commanders, Chauncey and Colonel Alexander Macomb, had created for Sacket's Harbor might not have been possible for Sheaffe to develop at York, given the less-formidable terrain and the small numbers of his trained regulars, but the conflicting accounts by eyewitnesses suggest that not everyone clearly understood the general's role. There was an ambiguity about Sheaffe's control of the militia units which contrasted strikingly with his command at Queenston. Even Powell's favourable account of Sheaffe's generalship at York, where he gave orders "with his usual coolness," includes mention of disorder. This failing is also suggested in a militiaman's diary, while in contrast some Canadian and American accounts give the impression of an orderly defence.[68] As was typical with Sheaffe, his own report (dated 5 May at Kingston) was detailed, and he attempted to give credit to both units and individuals.

Lieutenant-Colonel John Harvey, who had arrived in Upper Canada in February and who, under Vincent, was commanding the forces from Chippawa to Fort George, criticized Sheaffe's decision to retreat eastward, writing in his journal that the general ought to have retreated westward because Fort George was closer than Kingston and his forces would have reinforced Vincent's.[69] This opinion disregards the fact that Sheaffe had been driven eastward by Dearborn's army and that the only way to get around the Americans would have been to march northward before turning west towards Burlington Bay. For the defeated general to have taken his greatly outnumbered, battle-weary troops through thick woods around the victorious enemy would have been very risky indeed. Furthermore, Chauncey's fleet controlled the western end of the lake and would have forced Sheaffe to take his little band by a route well inland from the lakeshore, thus of course entailing a more difficult and exhausting march. The size of Sheaffe's force must be estimated around 300 to 400 men, a useful, but hardly a significant addition to Vincent's strength of about 1,600.[70] A subordinate commander could have afforded to take the risk of being cut off from his base of supplies, Kingston, but not the officer commanding Upper Canada. While not heroic, Sheaffe's retreat to Kingston made strategic sense.

Whatever the reality of the events at York, what mattered was the perception of weakness at the head of affairs in Upper Canada. It was a impression that Prevost could not afford to have remain whether he considered Canadian, British, or American opinions. Furthermore, the responsibility for the loss of the provincial capital and the military stores there had to be pinned on someone.

Sheaffe remained at Kingston during the fighting in the Niagara Peninsula in May and June; command there was effectively exercised by Vincent.[71] But in the latter month, after the American invaders had been driven back to the river, Prevost removed Sheaffe from command of Upper Canada. The governor explained his decision thus to the Duke of York: "the support I have received from the General Officers in Command since the Death of Major General Sir Isaac Brock, I am sorry to say has not always corresponded with my expectations – circumstances indicating an insufficiency on the part of Major General Sir R.H. Sheaffe to the arduous Task of defending Upper Canada have induced me to place Major General De Rottenburg in the Military Command and civil administration of that province."[72] Sheaffe's fighting career had ended.

His remaining five months in the Canadas could not have been happy or satisfying, for Prevost displayed a total loss of confidence in him, placing him in command of the troops in the Montreal District. Since no fighting was occurring in the area, Sheaffe could win no glory and do no harm. Even so, only a month later, Prevost accused him of "indifference" in the discharge of his duties and demanded his "active support."[73] Indifference on Sheaffe's part would be understandable, considering the way that he had been treated, but he professed not to understand the basis of Prevost's charge, which indeed was never specified. When Prevost returned from Upper Canada in September, he removed Sheaffe from the Montreal command and gave him responsibility for the reserve.[74] Already, however, the governor was seeking Sheaffe's recall, and orders to that effect were sent in August from London. Sheaffe left in November, still expressing a high regard for Prevost.[75] Never again did he have the opportunity to lead troops in combat. His remaining years were spent in Britain; he was promoted by seniority to lieutenant-general in 1821 and to general in 1838. He died in Edinburgh on 17 July 1851.

Sheaffe's choice of aides-de-camp suggests that he was looking for administrative, rather than military abilities or influence in Upper Canada. His provincial ADC was his brother-in-law, Nathaniel Coffin, who was a surveyor, politician, and justice of the peace in the Montreal area. He did serve capably, however, at Queenston Heights and with Sheaffe at York in 1813.[76] Sheaffe's military ADC was Captain Robert R. Loring, who had been in the 49th Foot in Lower Canada before transferring to the 104th Foot.[77] His staff work impressed both Drummond and Sheaffe, and he served on Drummond's staff before the outbreak of war and again after December 1813. He was appointed Sheaffe's ADC on 29 October 1812 and was with him at York in 1813. Sheaffe's choices were safe men, but not ones likely to have close contact with military or civilian opinion in Upper Canada.

Sheaffe himself was competent, professional, and cautious, but these traits are to be expected of a trained officer with many years' experience and the benefit of personal contact with men of the quality of Simcoe, Brock, and even Prevost. He did have opportunities to demonstrate his leadership qualities, and he showed the traits mentioned above. But much more than these qualities is needed to achieve the status of a great or outstanding military leader. Sheaffe never demonstrated the imagination, self-confidence, brilliance, daring, and manipulation of circumstances of the exceptional leader in war.

Was he unfairly criticized by contemporaries, and has this treatment been characteristic of later historians? On the whole, the answer is yes. At Queenston Heights he demonstrated that he could plan, organize, and execute an effective counter-attack against the enemy, which had had plenty of time to entrench strongly. His approach was methodical because he intended to amass as much strength as possible to ensure a victory. He determined the time of his attack, and by then he had negated the American advantage of ground and gained the psychological advantage of the initiative. In answer to the criticism of his extension of the ceasefire after Queenston Heights, much can be said in its favour, for what the defenders most needed was time. That was more valuable to them than fighting for American territory or losing more men by attacking the enemy. The victories of 1812 had already achieved the important aims of winning Native support for the British, throwing the United States military effort off balance, preserving British territory, and changing Upper Canadian attitudes.

The most influential criticisms of Sheaffe followed the battle at York. Seven prominent residents signed a statement in which they claimed that during the invasion the general been indecisive, had failed to give clear orders, had stayed back from the battle line, and had abandoned the town prematurely.[78] The document was intended for Prevost in order to persuade him to recall Sheaffe. It contributed to his decision and has also influenced later historical assessments of Sheaffe. He seems not to have attempted a public defence of his generalship, but there is evidence that contradicts some of the criticisms. Contemporary accounts describe stiff resistance to the landing of the Americans, as well as to their advance towards York; moreover, Sheaffe did not begin his retreat until well after the battle had been lost, and it was an orderly withdrawal.[79] The suggestion has also been made that his critics were very concerned to divert attention away from their own shortcomings in the battle to defend York.[80] Carl Benn claims that the commander of the York militia and his officers contributed to the British defeat by failing to carry out Sheaffe's orders.[81] If this motive did fuel the protest, it was successful.

The belief of some that Sheaffe was pro-American may have arisen because of his family connections as well as from his conduct. His wife, Margaret, was a daughter of John Coffin of Quebec.[82] Both the Coffin and the Sheaffe families were Boston-based, and the general still had relatives in that city.[83] His mention of retreat in his reply to Bisshopp and his refusal to take up Vincent's proposal to attack Fort Niagara might indicate unwillingness to pursue warfare vigorously against the Americans. But to accept this conclusion would be to deny the skill Sheaffe demonstrated in leading his forces at Queenston and the bravery he displayed when under fire. His responses to Bisshopp and Vincent simply reflected his habitual prudence.

It was Sheaffe's misfortune that Prevost appears to have expected more of him than he did of other general officers, perhaps because the governor felt that he had taken a greater risk to his own prestige by appointing Sheaffe to Upper Canada than with the others. A glance at Prevost's criticisms of Sheaffe over the truce that he made in August 1812, his arrangements with Van Rensselaer and Smyth in October, and his performance when in command of Montreal, taken together with his removal of Sheaffe from Upper Canada, shows that the governor displayed less patience with Sheaffe and less understanding of his actions than he accorded the other commanders in this study.

The reasons for Sheaffe's dismissal from the Canadas appear extremely flimsy, particularly in view of the fact that there never was a court martial or inquiry into his conduct. If he had displayed any sign of cowardice or professional incompetence, there would no doubt have been an inquiry as there was for Proctor, Captain Barclay, and even Prevost. With Sheaffe's departure, the Canadas lost an able officer. He had had the misfortune to succeed a popular commander of the troops who spoke and acted heroically and died gloriously.[84] Before the end of 1812 a standard of British leadership for this war had been established – the Upper Canadian perception of Brock, a model already being embellished. If Sheaffe had been killed at the head of his troops defending York, he might have joined Brock in the emerging Upper Canadian pantheon of heroes. But that sort of leadership and fate would not have benefited the defence of the province.

CHAPTER FIVE

Detachment:
The Leadership of Major-General
Baron Francis de Rottenburg

He brought with him a very great name, so that we expected
he would do wonders – in fact, he did nothing.

William Hamilton Merritt

Baron Francis de Rottenburg was the oldest, and also the most experienced, of the generals, even though he began his military career three
years after Prevost and Sheaffe. Like Prevost, he was not of British
origin, but unlike him he did not come from a military family or background. Rottenburg, moreover, had a distinguished military career
before the War of 1812.

As officer commanding and administrator of Upper Canada, he
resembled Sheaffe in being a highly cautious professional. But the literature of the war is more favourable to him in usually mentioning only
that he succeeded Sheaffe in June 1813, appeared briefly in the Niagara Peninsula, returned to Kingston, and was succeeded by Drummond in December 1813; sometimes references also occur to his
imposition of martial law in eastern Upper Canada and to his position
as second-in-command to Prevost in the Plattsburgh expedition.[1] The
criticisms levelled against Sheaffe are not possible with Rottenburg, for
his usual portrayal as a shadowy and distant commander does not allow
judgments to be made about his success or failure. An exception
among historians is Stanley, for he applauds Rottenburg's leadership by
referring to his securing the position at Burlington Heights in early July
"against a possible *coup de main*." Otherwise, however, Stanley paints a
negative picture.[2] He implicitly criticizes Rottenburg for not supporting
Procter with troops and supplies, and sums up by saying, "the solid but
undistinguished Baron ... had exhibited few signs of brilliance, origi-
nality or forceful determination."

Francis de Rottenburg commanded at a time of greater strains and threats to Upper Canada's survival as a British colony than ever before in the war. During his tenure the Americans won two of their most significant victories of the war, Captain Oliver H. Perry's on Lake Erie and Major-General William Henry Harrison's at Moraviantown. These setbacks were only partly balanced by one of the most crucial of the British and Canadian victories, Crysler's Farm. The increasing strain on civilian morale probably pushed it to its lowest point; desertions from the militia increased, and spies and marauders acted more boldly. It cannot be said that Rottenburg coped successfully with these problems, but Prevost never rebuked him with anything like the severity he bestowed on Sheaffe, nor did Rottenburg receive among Upper Canadians the degree or extent of condemnation that descended on that unfortunate general.

Some explanation for the differences in treatment and for Rottenburg's very limited success in Upper Canada may be found in his background. He was born on 4 November 1757 in Danzig, Poland, into a merchant, or possibly noble, family.[3] No information has been found about his life before he entered the army of Louis XVI of France in 1782, in which he served until 1791.[4] Here the young man gained what appears to have been a sound military apprenticeship and an acquaintance with diplomacy, for he served for at least three years as an aide-de-camp to Baron de Salis, a French envoy to Naples. Rottenburg left the French army just before its transformation into a revolutionary citizen force. He then went to Poland, where he supported the nationalist and liberal cause against Russian rule. In the resulting armed revolt, he commanded an infantry battalion and was present at the final defeat of the Poles at Warsaw in November 1794.[5]

If Rottenburg wished to continue as a professional soldier, he would now have to look elsewhere for employment. His moves from one army to another were far from unusual in the eighteenth and nineteenth centuries, particularly for officers from central Europe. He joined the British army in 1795, becoming a major in Baron Carl von Hompesch's newly raised regiment of hussars. The next year he transferred to Hompesch's Fusiliers as a lieutenant-colonel, and in 1797 moved to the 5th battalion, 60th Foot, when the fusiliers were merged into that unit.[6] He served with the 5th battalion during the Irish rebellion of 1798 and afterwards in the West Indies, where he was present at the taking of the Dutch colony of Surinam in 1799.

It has been suggested that this unit was the first formation in the British army to be given rifles.[7] Rottenburg may well have introduced rifle-manned units to the British service, for he had an early and productive interest in the use of riflemen. The War Office in 1799 published his *Regulations for the Exercise of Riflemen and Light Infantry, and Instructions for their Conduct in the Field,* a translation from the original German of his year-old book. A second edition appeared in 1803, and Major-General John Moore, a proponent of light infantry, used the manual for his training program.[8] The fact that he was willing and able to produce such a work suggests that Rottenburg was well educated, observant, and dedicated to reform in the infantry. He had a concern probably greater than that of most British army officers for the thorough training of troops. He also had a reputation as an efficient instructor and a popular commanding officer.[9]

The government's confidence in Rottenburg is indicated by his appointment in 1808 to the command of the Light Brigade, which consisted of three regiments, and the next year he commanded a similar formation in an expedition to capture Antwerp. His brigade was part of the force that landed on Walcheren Island in July.[10] During that expedition he gained experience disembarking troops from ships under enemy fire, and his men subsequently skirmished with the French as they advanced across the island. Rottenburg probably remained on the island until the final British evacuation in December.

He was appointed to the forces in British North America on 25 April 1810, he was promoted major-general on 25 July, and he arrived at Quebec City to take command of its garrison in September.[11] No reasons for his move were spelled out, but the home government had a tradition of appointing non-Britons and officers fluent in French to important commands in Lower Canada.

The new major-general was a brave soldier, a capable leader of men, and an officer concerned about his duties and possessing some knowledge of the art of war. Compared to the other generals in this study, his combat experience with a variety of armies could not be matched, and only Drummond would equal his experience in the range of territories where he had served. Rottenburg had also had administrative experience with the British army and perhaps with others, although he had not held the high civil and military commands that Prevost had known. His administrative abilities seem to have been respected by his superiors. Governor Craig, for example, appointed him to head a board of officers to investigate hospital facilities and officers' quarters in Quebec City.[12]

In July 1812 Rottenburg was put in command of the Montreal District.[13] At the time, Prevost had a limited choice for such an appointment because he had already entrusted Quebec to Major-General George Glasgow of the Royal Artillery, and the only other general officer in Lower Canada was Duncan Darroch, who was a new brigadier-general.[14] Prevost may also have been demonstrating confidence in

Rottenburg, for Montreal's proximity to the U.S. border and its importance as the starting point for supplies and reinforcements going to Upper Canada made it a likely target for some kind of enemy thrust. There is a glimpse of Rottenburg as a stern disciplinarian in his inspection of the militia of the district. He publicly criticized battalions not in good state and stopped their officers' leaves, but praised the well-ordered ones.[15]

When Prevost made his two visits to Upper Canada in 1813, he left Rottenburg in command of the lower province.[16] Again, this appointment may have been the result of limited choice, for Glasgow was the only other general officer in Lower Canada; but there is no hint that Prevost doubted Rottenburg's fitness for the responsibility. No military action occurred during these periods to test his leadership in combat, but on one occasion he did indicate that he could be a decisive commander ready to grasp an opportunity to hit the enemy. As a result of the capture on the Richelieu River on 2 June of two of the largest American vessels from Lake Champlain, Rottenburg wrote secretly to Glasgow at Quebec on 5 June urging him to obtain Royal Navy personnel and attempt to destroy the American naval force on that lake.[17] He wanted Glasgow to act quickly, but the expedition did not take place until after Rottenburg had moved to Upper Canada. The order was given by Prevost, and he subsequently claimed credit for the idea.[18] As we have noted in chapter 2, the attack made between 29 July and 3 August was highly successful.

Once Prevost had decided to replace Sheaffe in Upper Canada, it is not surprising that he turned to Rottenburg. He was the senior general officer after Sheaffe, and the rules of the service required him to be considered first for a detached command. General Darroch at Kingston and the newly arrived Major-General Richard Stovin were junior to Rottenburg.[19] Moreover, neither of them had his experience of combat, military administration, and civil authority. Prevost may have feared that he was taking a risk in sending Rottenburg to Upper Canada, for he made an effort to justify his decision to the commander-in-chief: "except Sir John Sherbrooke, the Major General is the only General Officer of high character and established reputation serving in the Army in the North American Provinces to whom I could intrust this important duty, without embarrassing myself with it to the prejudice of the other possessions of His Majesty committed to my charge."[20]

When Rottenburg arrived in Upper Canada, the forces there were reorganized as the Right Division (those serving under Procter), the Centre Division (troops at Niagara and York), and the Left Division (troops at Kingston and downriver).[21] Rottenburg would hold the civil and military command of the upper province from 19 June to

12 December. Prevost remained in the province until September; thus Rottenburg was not in full control until then, and by 20 October he knew that he was to be replaced in Upper Canada by Lieutenant-General Gordon Drummond.[22] Ironically, in August the Duke of York had recalled Rottenburg and Sheaffe because Drummond was being sent to North America. Employment in Europe was hinted at for the two, but although Sheaffe returned to Britain, Rottenburg remained, being kept on by Prevost because of need, particularly after Vincent fell ill.[23] On 2 September he became colonel of Roll's Regiment.[24]

The new officer commanding was at Kingston on 19 June, and on the 21st he left for the Head of the Lake (Burlington Bay). He arrived at the headquarters of the Centre Division at Twelve Mile Creek (St Catharines) late on the 29th.[25] Prevost remained at Kingston, leaving Rottenburg to take what measures he thought necessary. One of his first communications indicates his defensive outlook, for he wrote to Procter on 1 July informing him of a plan to retreat if Yeo's fleet was destroyed, which would force Rottenburg to fall back to Kingston. The only feasible route for Procter would be northward, and Rottenburg had arranged with the North-West Company to provide on Lake Superior forty canoes to carry "one thousand men with their retinue and accoutrements" via the Ottawa River to Montreal.[26]

Rottenburg's initial response to the problem of defending Upper Canada was to prepare for the withdrawal of its regular forces and the abandonment of much of its territory. This reaction was not one of panic nor was it hasty, for he stated that he had made these arrangements "long ago." His main concern was to preserve the army rather than to protect people, an approach understandable in a professional soldier, particularly one who had no connection with the inhabitants over whom he presided. His plan, however, seemed to take no account of the difficulties that such a movement would face. Rottenburg did not specify how Procter was to move his force to Lake Superior and elude American pursuit. As well, there was no consideration of the effect of such a retreat on the morale of Native warriors and Upper Canadian militia. Nevertheless, Rottenburg's plan did not meet with the condemnation that had descended upon Sheaffe only seven months earlier when he had speculated about Bisshopp's possible retreat from Fort Erie.

Rottenburg was, however, also thinking of acting positively against the enemy. "There is a vast deal to be done in this Province," he wrote early in July, laying part of the blame on his predecessor's shortcomings.[27] His first harassing action was to send a party from the 8th Foot and Native warriors to recover medicines and surgical instruments buried near Fort George. Their close approach to the fort drew out an

American force and led to a clash between the Natives and the Americans on 8 July.[28] Such skirmishing, even if not directed to a specific objective, was beneficial to the morale of Rottenburg's forces and harmful to that of the Americans. Indeed, he believed that the Native warriors preferred action to idleness. For these reasons, and also to confine the Americans as much as possible to a limited area around Fort George, Rottenburg advanced his forces in a semicircle as close to the enemy lines as he dared, taking up this position by 17 July, before Prevost's orders to the same effect reached him.[29]

He even hoped for the soon arrival of Yeo's fleet, confident that a "well-combined attack on both sides of the river must lead to the capture of their army." Clearly, Rottenburg (not to mention Vincent) had sufficient information about the strength of the American position to obviate the need for the "general demonstration" that Prevost ordered on 24 August.[30] As well, he had pointed out the proper tactic of a combined naval and land attack to drive out the Americans.

He did not limit himself to acting against the Americans at Fort George, but decided also to raid their depot at Fort Schlosser, just above the falls. The complete success of this action on 5 July led the baron next to order an attempt against the important U.S. naval base of Black Rock.[31] This latter raid, carried out on 11 July, caused some damage but not enough to put the base out of action, and the attackers suffered heavier losses than their opponents.[32]

Rottenburg can hardly be blamed for the inadequate defences of York, which allowed the Americans to reoccupy it on 31 July. Prevost criticized him for removing a portion of the forces from the town in order to strengthen the position at Burlington Heights, but the heights was a more important strategic position than York. Because of the American naval superiority, it is not likely that additional forces at the capital could have prevented a successful American attack. At Burlington Bay, below the heights, the story was different. The Americans landed on the shore, but the presence of the reinforcements sent by Rottenburg made them decide to withdraw without attempting an assault on the heights.[33]

Where Rottenburg might be criticized for excessive caution was his refusal to send a sufficient number of troops to Procter to use in a proposed attack on Presque Isle (Erie), Pennsylvania. Captain R.H. Barclay, the Royal Navy commander on Lake Erie, and Procter had consulted about a combined assault on that vital American naval base, where a fleet was being rapidly constructed. Both believed that they had been promised a reinforcement from the 41st Foot, for without these men, Procter complained, he could not undertake the attack.[34] Although Rottenburg did send reinforcements to the Right Division,

they were apparently not in time or in sufficient numbers to suit Barclay and Procter.[35] He gave two reasons for not sending more men
sooner. Reinforcements were very slow in coming to him, and the
troops of the 41st Foot who did arrive were in wretched state, dressed
"in rags and without shoes."[36] Unless he chose to weaken his defences
along the Niagara or cease raiding across the river, he had sound reasons for telling Prevost, "It is not in my power directly to co-operate
with the Brigadier General."[37]

Although Rottenburg may have missed one of the rare opportunities
significantly to affect the course of the war, that is far from certain, and
one cannot expect him to have been a risk-taker to the same degree as
Brock or Vincent. He had been in command of Upper Canada for less
than a month and had nothing to gain professionally or personally by
taking a chance of weakening the Niagara frontier in hopes of obtaining a success at Presque Isle.[38] The movement of his troops towards
Fort George and the raids that he ordered across the river during July
in fact suggest that he preferred a strategy of small, low-risk successes,
something that suited his own situation as well as that of the forces he
had at hand. He docs seem to have been aware of the importance of
naval control of the lakes, but he and other army commanders could
hardly have anticipated that the situation on Lake Erie would be
changed so quickly by Captain Perry's small fleet, seemingly trapped
behind the sandbar at Presque Isle.

Rottenburg's initial reaction to Barclay's defeat on 10 September and
the critical situation facing Procter was one of calm. He did not see the
necessity for Procter to retreat immediately, although he admitted that
he might be unaware of other reasons that the latter might have. In
other words, Rottenburg did not accept that the destruction of the
British fleet had entirely changed the strategic situation. Consequently,
he proceeded to send an engineer officer to Long Point on Lake Erie
to undertake construction of the blockhouses recommended by
Procter, and he intended to dispatch Colonel John Murray to take
command there and call out the militia.[39]

The officer commanding in Upper Canada had also to be concerned
about the rest of the province. From late August until late September,
Yeo and Chauncey pursued one another around Lake Ontario, each
seeking a decisive action on his own terms. Rottenburg could not
always be sure of where the British fleet was, or of its condition or what
support it might be able to afford him.[40] At the end of September, he
observed American troops heading out onto the lake in batteaux from
the mouth of the Niagara River, and he had information that these
regulars were proceeding to Sackets Harbor "for the purpose of attacking Kingston."[41] Seeing the departure of 3,000 to 4,000 American

troops from Fort George, Rottenburg wasted no time embarking three regiments and then following them, leaving Vincent in command.[42] By the 14th he was at Kingston, having been "detained [at York] by indisposition."[43] Henceforth he commanded Upper Canada from the eastern end of the province. However, his movement of reinforcements to Kingston had wider consequences, convincing the American secretary of war to change the plan for the invasion and direct it at Montreal.[44]

These troop movements in October also cast light on relations between Prevost and Rottenburg. The former complained to Yeo about the capture of five British vessels out of a squadron of seven carrying two companies of De Watteville's Regiment from York to Kingston, and he wanted to know if Yeo had provided appropriate naval cover or if the fault lay elsewhere. Two days later Prevost's military secretary sent a letter to Rottenburg asking about the dispatch of the troops and arrangements for naval protection of the transports. Rottenburg coolly replied that he had issued the order and had also applied to Yeo "to afford these Vessels the necessary protection."[45] That was all he wrote – no lengthy explanation or any indication of embarrassment. He ended the letter almost curtly: "I have the honor to be Sir, Your most Obt. Servt., Francis de Rottenburg, M. General." At the same time, he explained why he had deviated from Prevost's orders "respecting the disposal of the squadron" and given Yeo instructions that superseded Prevost's. The baron had directed Yeo "to proceed with the squadron to the head of the lake for the purpose of affording all the aid in his power to the centre division of the army," which had just suffered its crushing defeat at Moraviantown.[46] There is no indication that Prevost faulted Rottenburg's decision or attempted to reprimand him in any way.

After Moraviantown, Vincent pulled his troops out of the Niagara Peninsula to concentrate on Burlington Heights. Expressing confidence in him, Rottenburg left him to decide on withdrawal to York.[47] By the 18th Rottenburg regarded Vincent's retreat to York as necessary rather than optional because he feared that the Americans would strike there before attacking Kingston and because Chauncey's fleet prevented him from reinforcing Vincent. By the 23rd, although Prevost wanted Vincent to retreat to Kingston, the commander of the forces was influenced by Rottenburg to agree that a "lightly equipped detachment" could be left at Burlington or Ancaster and that York ought to be held.[48] The situation facing Vincent and Rottenburg continued uncertain since the Americans still did not employ their naval and military strength against a Lake Ontario target. Realizing the difficulties of withdrawing the forces to eastern Upper Canada and sensing his enemy's hesitancy, by the beginning of November Rottenburg instructed Vincent to retain not only York but also Burlington Heights and Long Point on Lake Erie and even to attempt probing attacks against the American forces occupying the Niagara Peninsula.[49]

By the night of 5 November, Rottenburg knew that the American force from Sackets Harbor had passed Kingston on its way towards Montreal, thus ending the threat to Upper Canada. His final military decision for the province was to send Lieutenant-Colonel Joseph W. Morrison in pursuit of Wilkinson's invading army. In this case, the baron was putting into effect Prevost's earlier instructions, rather than taking an original decision.[50] By the time the two American armies, one under General Wade Hampton and the other under Wilkinson, withdrew to the United States, the campaigning season had ended. Rottenburg knew that he was to be replaced by Drummond, and decisions about how to defend Upper Canada ceased to be his concern.[51]

These movements between September and November suggest that Rottenburg would not be rushed into hasty decisions, particularly with regard to the abandonment of British territory. Withdrawal by Vincent to Kingston would have meant giving up most of Upper Canada, an outcome that would have had extremely serious consequences for Britain's Native allies and for loyal Upper Canadians. Vincent's army was far from being a defeated force, and Rottenburg seems to have been less apprehensive of American capabilities than was Prevost. Whatever his motives, Rottenburg's support for a delay in the withdrawal of forces denied the Americans an easy victory and left the defenders in a strategically strong position to take the offensive against the invaders.[52]

In December Rottenburg returned to Lower Canada, a move that did not represent a demotion or a criticism of him; indeed, the government's intention was to employ him "in Germany," which suggests confidence in him.[53] But he remained in the lower province and was subsequently given an important command in the defence of Montreal. In September 1814 he was put in charge of three brigades for Prevost's invasion of the United States. This appointment made him virtually second-in-command, but he played no conspicuous part in the battle at Plattsburgh. There is no reason to think that Rottenburg influenced Prevost's strategy in that invasion or his dealings with Captain Downie. (If – and it is a large "if" – Rottenburg did disagree with Prevost's actions, his training and experience would have made him obey orders to the best of his ability.) He was not subject to the criticism that descended on Prevost over Plattsburgh, nor did he join the chorus of critics. He remained in Lower Canada, where he commanded the troops and administered the government in Prevost's absence in Upper Canada. The following July he returned to England.[54]

During his period as administrator, Rottenburg preferred to leave non-military matters under civilian control as much as possible. Unlike the other administrators in this study, he did not meet the legislature but worked through a few advisers, the most influential of whom was W.D. Powell.[55] A proclamation of 21 May 1813 had called for parliament to meet on 1 July, but a week before, on the advice of the Executive Council, Rottenburg postponed the session, and he subsequently issued four further proclamations proroguing the meeting to later dates.[56] Civil government was, in consequence, carried on by appointed officials, for according to Powell, "the President has authorized the Council to deliberate any propositions supposed to be important without waiting for special reference in order to avoid delay in the execution of measures." He went on to assure Prevost "that under this arrangement there will be little display of weakness."[57]

In several matters that affected civil government, Rottenburg responded more strongly than Sheaffe. Faced with the growing lawlessness and disloyalty in the Niagara Peninsula after the fall of Fort George, he wanted to use courts martial to deal with suspected traitors, but he was unclear whether martial law was in force there. The uncertain response he received from Prevost included advice that he should consult his Executive Council, which in August recommended the suspension of habeas corpus and the declaration of martial law.[58] When asked his opinion by Rottenburg, Attorney General John Beverley Robinson thought the measures illegal, but gave his private advice to proceed because "the necessity must and will justify their adoption."[59]

Although Rottenburg acted autocratically, he was aware of and concerned about the sufferings of the population, for one of his first actions was to follow Sheaffe in forbidding the use of the new rye crop for distilling.[60] His concern is also indicated by his district general order of 29 July, which condemned the depredations of the troops and threatened drumhead courts martial against offenders.[61] But he was clearly high-handed when five days earlier he used his authority as military commander to declare the crops of harvestable grain on the farms of men who had fled to the United States to be government property.[62] In November Rottenburg took even stronger action when as administrator he imposed partial martial law in the Johnstown and Eastern districts in order to procure forage and provisions.[63] Although he was supported by Prevost and could cite precedents in Procter's district to force farmers to sell him supplies, he opened himself to criticism because he had not consulted the legislature. Moreover, the measure proved highly unpopular, even though local magistrates set the prices.[64]

Baron de Rottenburg was a competent, knowledgeable, and widely experienced officer when he came to Upper Canada. He was capable of grasping an opportunity, as he showed in June 1813 with regard to Lake Champlain, but much more often he was cautious. He was not unbending, for he changed his view about abandoning territory in Upper Canada from his initial willingness in July to see that happen to refusal by October. This shift suggests that he did learn from experience in the process of becoming acquainted with the forces defending the colony (and perhaps also its residents) as well as with those threatening it. While his strategic outlook remained traditional, he appeared less fearful about modifying it than did Prevost.

It should not be forgotten, however, that Rottenburg benefited from his enemy's weaknesses and inadequacies. American forces along the border from the Niagara River to Vermont suffered from desertion, widespread sickness, shortages, indiscipline among the troops, and careless commanding officers.[65] Canada's defenders also profited from faulty American strategy, as Secretary of War John Armstrong changed his original plan to strike first at Kingston, and from field commanders who failed to grasp the initiative or to keep it once they had gained it.[66] Furthermore, Chauncey did not exploit his advantages over Yeo or his naval victories in May and September to gain supremacy on Lake Ontario. His caution lessened American chances of conquest, whereas Yeo's bought the defenders time.[67]

At least three major dissimilarities between Rottenburg and Sheaffe may suggest explanations for the differences in Prevost's treatment of the two men, if not also the those in Upper Canadian attitudes and the generals' subsequent reputations. Rottenburg appeared on the Canadian scene as an aristocrat, a characteristic that gave him social standing at least equal to Prevost's. Moreover, he possessed a distinguished military reputation. Both these qualities would have made it difficult for Prevost to criticize or instruct him as he could and did with Sheaffe. The other side of this coin is that the baron did not need to prove himself militarily, nor would his personal reputation or career be advanced by bold action.

A second difference is that by the time Rottenburg came to Upper Canada, the people were well aware of the difficulties created by the war, and all the indications were that the struggle would continue for some time with little prospect of glorious or easy victories. There would thus be no reason to compare this new officer with the unrivalled Brock; nor was he tainted by failure, as was Sheaffe, or by lack of enterprise, as was Prevost.

Finally, Prevost, the son of a Swiss-born officer, could appreciate Rottenburg's situation as a central European refugee, displaced from his home and far from his family. Likewise, Rottenburg would have understood Prevost's father's situation. There is no trace of sycophancy in Rottenburg's correspondence with Prevost, for he did not depend upon him for advancement, career satisfaction, or fulfilment. After returning to England in 1815, he was promoted lieutenant-general by seniority and later knighted.

General de Rottenburg had no provincial aide-de-camp,[68] and his two military ADCs were young men who saw very little combat service in the war.[69] No discussion about these officers is necessary, for the information on them does not reveal how they were employed; nor does it throw light on Rottenburg's generalship.

CHAPTER SIX

Persistence:
The Leadership of Lieutenant-General
Sir Gordon Drummond

The War appears to be assuming a serious aspect.
J.B. Varnum to General J.B. Varnum, 24 July 1814

Gordon Drummond was the youngest of the general officers examined in this study and the last to enter military service: four years after Brock, seven after Rottenburg, and ten after Prevost and Sheaffe. Like Brock, Rottenburg, and Sheaffe, he did not come from a family with a military background; his father was deputy paymaster general to the forces in the Canadas, but this was not a military position. It is worth reviewing briefly the differences in experience between Drummond and the other generals. By June 1812 he had encountered more combat than Brock or Sheaffe, but less than Prevost and Rottenburg. Aside from his four-month stint in 1811 as commander of the forces in the Canadas, Drummond, unlike Prevost and Rottenburg, had not commanded a unit larger than a regiment. When in December 1813 he was appointed to the civil and military command of Upper Canada, he lacked any experience of civil government. Sheaffe also lacked such experience, but he did have an edge in his much longer acquaintance with the province, having served there for most of the decade between 1788 and 1797.

Given these circumstances, it is arguable that, in terms of achievements, Drummond is the most underrated of the five British commanders. During the first eight months of his tenure he rapidly achieved significant victories, beginning with the seizure of Fort Niagara and Lewiston, which was followed by destructive raids against Black Rock and Buffalo and, in 1814, by a raid on Oswego. He had considerable success in securing army and navy cooperation. He carried out a tour of inspection in the western part of Upper Canada and held his ground at Lundy's Lane on 25 July. In other words, during those first months in the province, Drummond led as dynamically and successfully as Brock had done in 1812. This positive image or perception of him seemed to change, however, from August to early November 1814, the weeks of his apparent least achievement as a commander and consequently the source for most of the criticism. Yet during those last three months, Drummond was active, determined, and far from unsuccessful.

The critical view needs to be reconsidered, for there are weaknesses in both the arguments and the use of evidence. Of the four officers who commanded in Upper Canada, Drummond is the most difficult to judge because by 1814 there had been great changes in the conditions of warfare and the civilian situation as compared with the previous two years. Drummond faced problems as great as, or even greater than, those encountered by the three previous commanders in the province. By 1814 the American government had increased the size and improved the training of its army, as well as appointing better commanders, particularly in the Niagara Peninsula. Drummond would face four of the most capable and experienced of the U.S. commanders: Major-General Jacob Brown, Brigadier-General Winfield Scott, Brigadier-General Edmund Gaines, and Major-General George Izard. The Americans also continued to dominate Lakes Erie and Huron until September and Ontario from mid-June until October, when Yeo's new three-decker HMS *St Lawrence* took to the lake. Drummond did not therefore have the convenience and security of naval superiority on the lakes that Brock had enjoyed, and he lacked the means of attacking American supply lines across Lake Erie to their troops in the Niagara Peninsula.

The Americans' control of Detroit from September 1813 and their freedom to raid throughout the Western District maintained their threat at least as far east as Burlington Heights. The Native pressure on Detroit and in the Ohio region had been eliminated; indeed, Native support of the British in southern Upper Canada was much reduced. In short, the possibility of an American conquest of the province was not less in 1814 than in the previous two years, while its war-sustaining resources had decreased. Food ran short in the contested stretches of the west as well as in the Niagara Peninsula; the refusal of farmers elsewhere to sell foodstuffs to the government suggests shortages there too. Even if the reason was merely the farmers' uncertainty about supply, rather than actual shortage, the effect was the same for those needing provisions and forage.[1] The strains on the population increased through demands for more fighting men (and from increased casualties caused more by disease than by fighting), more money, and the reduction of civil liberties. Civilians could hope for, but not expect, greater security; peace could remain only a dream throughout most of the year.

Fortunately for the defenders of British North America, the situation in Europe had changed fundamentally with Napoleon's defeat and exile to Elba. The British government was now free to send large reinforcements to its beleaguered colony – fourteen regiments by July. Equally significant, the troops were veterans of Wellington's campaigns and were led by battle-tested generals. Reinforcements were on their way, but it would be September before Drummond began to see them. Still, his forces in Upper Canada did increase from 6,600 in June to 9,700 in July, 10,800 in August, and 11,600 in September. Of these, there were 3,071 in the Niagara Peninsula in June and 4,080, 5,941, and 6,617 in each succeeding month.[2] But not all these troops in the peninsula were available for combat duties because Drummond had to keep garrisons in Forts Niagara and George and at Burlington Heights.

Both the British and American governments desired peace, and by the beginning of 1814 they were prepared to negotiate a settlement, although they were not willing to give up easily. The negotiations at Ghent dragged on for most of the year. The result of all these factors, paradoxically, was hard fighting, increased destruction of property, and heavier casualties than in previous comparable periods. Hence, while Drummond could expect his military strength to grow, he could not simply wait for that happy development. He could not spare his soldiers or Yeo his seamen; nor could the civilian population relax its efforts to sustain the war effort.

Drummond's father, Colin, was a younger son in the large family of John Drummond of Megginch, an estate in Perthshire, Scotland. In 1766 Colin had moved to Quebec, where he represented the London firm of Fludyer and Drummond and served as deputy paymaster general to the forces. Gordon's mother was Catherine Oliphant of Rossie.[3] The fifth and youngest son, he was born on 27 September 1772 at Quebec. His family returned to London in 1780 (four years after Colin's death), and Gordon was educated there. In 1807 he married Margaret Russell of Brancepeth Castle, and they would have three children, the first two of whom were born in Canada.[4]

Drummond entered the British army in Jamaica in 1789 as an ensign in the 1st Foot. He returned to England in autumn the following year.[5] His rise in rank was rapid, for he became a lieutenant in the 41st Foot in March 1791, a captain in January 1792, a major in the 8th Foot in February 1794, and its junior lieutenant-colonel in March. That year he first saw active service in the Netherlands campaign under the Duke of York. After a very difficult retreat through that country in January 1795, the regiment returned to England in May. Drummond was promoted colonel on 1 January 1798 and soon afterwards became senior lieutenant-colonel of his regiment.

After spending three years in England, Lieutenant-Colonel Drummond went with his regiment to Minorca, where in 1800 he became its commanding officer.[6] The following year he led the regiment in the campaign for the British reconquest of Egypt, where his men marched and fought under rugged desert conditions.[7] He next served in Gibraltar, and in 1804 he was appointed brigadier-general on staff duty in Britain. On 1 January of the following year he became major-general, and in May he went to Jamaica as second-in-command to Lieutenant-General Sir Eyre Coote. He arrived in the West Indies at about the same time as Prevost, resplendent with success, departed.

Drummond left Jamaica in August 1807, married, and remained in Scotland until May of the following year, when he sailed for Quebec to serve on the staff under Governor Craig.[8] In the Canadas Drummond, like Brock and Rottenburg, was concerned about accommodation and hospital facilities for the troops in Montreal.[9] Early in 1811 he requested permission to return to England for family reasons.[10] The request was granted at about the same time as he was promoted lieutenant-general in June, but in July Drummond, out of a sense of duty, offered to remain in North America because Craig had been forced by ill health to leave and his replacement had not yet arrived.[11] In fact, Drummond was commander of the forces from 9 June until 12 September, when Prevost reached Lower Canada.

Drummond then returned to Britain, where he spent time with his family before proceeding in November 1812 to Ireland and the command of a military district.[12] In August 1813 he learned that he had been appointed second-in-command to Prevost. He arrived at Quebec on 3 November and assumed responsibility for the troops on the south side of the St Lawrence, but Prevost soon made the decision to send him to Upper Canada to replace Rottenburg.[13] Meanwhile, on 7 November, the commander renamed the administrative districts of the British forces. The troops west of Kingston were to be called the Right Division and those east of the town the Centre Division, while further east were the Left Division and, distinct from it, the garrison of Quebec City.[14]

Drummond reached Kingston at the beginning of December, but he did not take command of Upper Canada until the 13th. He discussed with Rottenburg the civil and military affairs of the province and began to make decisions about the disposition of forces – decisions that indicated clearly his intention not only to hold on to the colony but also to advance from Burlington Heights against the invaders.[15] He issued orders for the Right and Centre divisions to concentrate and reverse the movement of units towards Lower Canada. Concluding that Lieutenant-Colonel Victor Fischer of De Watteville's Regiment did not possess the necessary qualities to command at Kingston in his absence,

Drummond ordered Rottenburg to remain there. Major-General Phineas Riall he dispatched to Burlington Heights to command the Right Division in place of Vincent.[16] Upper Canadians would soon realize that a man who believed in decision and action had taken over.

By the 12th Drummond was at York, where he had already examined the fortifications and issued orders for their completion and for changes in locations of a blockhouse and a battery.[17] While he was there, the American forces evacuated Fort George and committed what would become the unforgettable outrage of burning Newark. The recovery of the entire Canadian side of the Niagara River in a way so discreditable to the enemy was a promising inauguration of Drummond's tenure.[18] Whether or not he deserved any credit for the success, it could not fail to benefit him.

The contrast between the new commander and his predecessors was soon heightened by Drummond's aggressive moves against the American frontier. He wasted no time in transferring his headquarters to St David's and having boats brought in secrecy from Burlington Bay to Four Mile Creek and then overland to the Niagara River above Fort Niagara. Late at night on 18 December Colonel John Murray led some 500 regulars across the strong currents of the Niagara and by a surprise assault captured the fort entire with its garrison and stores.[19] As Drummond had planned, Riall crossed the next day with a force of regulars and Native warriors to assault Lewiston, where enemy guns were threatening Queenston. He easily gained control, for the Americans abandoned the post.[20] Scarcely two weeks after his arrival in the colony, Drummond had achieved a major advancement in its security with trifling casualties, and he was not finished. A comparison with Brock's success at Detroit would be entirely appropriate. Drummond moved his headquarters closer to Fort Erie, and after a brief delay caused by bad weather, he launched an assault against Black Rock and Buffalo on 30 December. A larger American force was driven back, the towns burnt, four vessels of the Lake Erie fleet destroyed, and many guns as well as other stores taken.[21] After this dramatic entrance to the scene of warfare in Upper Canada, Drummond placed the troops in winter quarters along the Niagara frontier.[22]

While he deserves much credit for energetic and successful leadership, the weaknesses of his opponents along the Niagara must also be recognized. Brigadier-General George McClure and his successor, Major-General Amos Hall, both militia officers, were far from competent and proved unable to bring order or instil confidence in the defending troops, who were all militia.[23] Once forced on the defensive, the Americans proved unable to recover as rapidly as Drummond could maintain his attack. His impression of American unwillingness and inability to stand up to British regulars seems to have been significantly shaped by the events of December 1813. Such experience was misleading because it was based on limited encounters, but it was justified until the battle of Chippawa.

During the winter Drummond made plans to recapture Detroit.[24] He consulted with Yeo and Colonel Nichol, who had local knowledge of the area, and he also waited for Prevost's approval.[25] Prevost agreed with the plan, but warned that he had no reinforcements to send, a response that would have ended the scheme if Drummond had not already done so. He wrote to Prevost on 3 February that he had abandoned the plan because he had learned that the ice was too thin to support a crossing.[26] This incident indicates Drummond's care to gather intelligence before acting and his ability to consider plans for other areas while engaged in warfare in one part of his line.

He intended to strengthen the defences of the colony in all their aspects, which meant much more than simply increasing the numbers of regular troops, although these were badly needed.[27] Sackets Harbor had long been a cause of concern for British commanders, and Drummond was no exception. In the early days after his arrival in Upper Canada, he was given information about Sackets, but he considered that he needed fuller and better knowledge before he could plan a strike.[28] As he gathered intelligence, he reported it to Prevost. Yet the idea of a raid on Sackets Harbor never received a high priority.[29] In part – and possibly this was the main reason – the plan foundered on Prevost's unwillingness to provide Drummond with more troops.[30] Drummond also believed that, when the shipping season opened in the spring, a more important role for Yeo's squadron would be the transportation of troops and supplies to the western end of Lake Ontario.[31]

In his role as president of the council, Drummond was the most successful of the four administrators in Upper Canada in obtaining parliament's approval for measures that strengthened the government's hand in prosecuting the war. During the session that lasted from mid-February to mid-March, he was given approval to suspend habeas corpus, to hold trials of suspected traitors in any district of Upper Canada, to confiscate the property of landowners who departed to the United States without permission, and to increase the embodied militia.[32] As a measure to conserve food supplies, Drummond requested a continuation of the prohibition on the distillation and export of grain, and the assembly agreed.[33] The legislators declared vacant the seats of Abraham Markle and Joseph Willcocks. What the assembly would not grant was authority to proclaim martial law in certain districts or across the province. Its dislike of that power was clearly indicated in the motion that it passed condemning Rottenburg's proclamation of martial law as "an arbitrary and unconstitutional measure,"[34] even though Drummond had already rescinded the proclamation. While the legislature was in session, he made a quick tour of inspection "as far as Delaware town on the River Thames and Long Point and vicinity on the shore of Lake Erie."[35] He reported to Prevost on the troops in that area and made recommendations for improving its defences, one being for more men.

When Drummond appeared before his parliament, he was already a dynamic and successful leader and might have been seen therefore as a worthy successor to Brock. This perception, along with his evident concern to ease the strains of warfare faced by the civilian population, may explain his political success. Many residents were holding back supplies because the government had not paid for goods and services provided earlier in the war – in fact, as far back as the summer of 1812.[36] Drummond suggested offering higher prices for supplies or paying in specie, but he encountered the frequent problem of a shortage of coin in Upper Canada.[37] Perhaps Upper Canadians were aware of his offer in January 1814 to the Loyal and Patriotic Society of a considerable sum of money to help relieve the distress of the residents of Newark and vicinity.[38]

It was the government demands for supplies that many found burdensome, and the resistance appeared to be strongest in eastern Upper Canada. Drummond was prepared to authorize martial law in the Midland and Newcastle districts, but he held off until he decided that he had no choice but to impose it on the entire colony, "so far as relates to the procuring of provisions and forage" for the troops.[39] Prevost approved, while at the same time criticizing Drummond for issuing the order as commander of the forces in Upper Canada instead of as administrator. Drummond hoped to lessen resistance by instructing his officers to apply the measure moderately, judiciously, and generously.[40] Near the end of April he sought the approval of the Executive Council for a prohibition of the export of "provisions" from the colony until 1 November, and the council readily agreed without asking for evidence of the need for such a measure.[41]

Despite Prevost's approval of martial law, Drummond was concerned that his assembly would pass a motion of censure against him, and he sought the sanction of the British government for his action.[42] Earl Bathurst sent an indecisive reply which suggested that he had doubts about the legality of Drummond's proclamation.[43] It was soon challenged by a farmer who sued a commissariat officer for trespass. Drummond sought the opinion of acting attorney general John Beverley Robinson; he replied in effect that Drummond's proclamation was not legal without the approval of the assembly. Robinson, however, delayed the farmer's suit until 1815 and induced other civil judges to reject similar suits.[44] The court awarded the farmer damages, with the result that the proclamation was struck down. But by then, with the war over, the issue could fade into legal history.

A negative portrayal of Drummond's attitudes towards and relations with the civilian population is presented by George Sheppard, and since this issue is an aspect of the general's leadership, it needs to be discussed briefly. Sheppard claims that Drummond was shocked by the high level of indifference among Upper Canadians towards supporting the war effort, a sentiment he discovered when he proposed to increase the Incorporated Militia by conscripting some 1,500 men. The assembly suggested that no more than 500 could be spared from farm work, and this reduction of his plan "angered" the general.[45] The evidence cited does not, however, indicate either shock or anger. For example, after the session had ended, Drummond reported to Bathurst, "I have the satisfaction to say that the best understanding subsisted between myself and the other branches [of the provincial parliament]."[46] He was pleased with the legislation that had been passed and in particular with the amendment of the militia law, which he expected to "produce about six hundred men" to be added to the 300 raised under the former act.[47] He regretted that there were not enough regular troops in Upper Canada to enable him to dispense with the militia role of "the yeomanry" so that they could look after their farms.[48] Neither shock nor anger is found in other letters to the colonial secretary written on 5 April and 3 July.[49] What Drummond was concerned about was not militia numbers but naval strength on Lake Ontario, supplies for the forces, and the constitutionality of his proclamation of martial law.

The general, in his closing address to the legislators, did not express dissatisfaction with their work as Brock had when he spoke at the assembly's final meeting in March 1812. Brock's criticism of the newly re-elected assembly in July that year and his condemnation of the Upper Canadian population in July and August have no equal in Drummond's correspondence with his superiors.[50] In July 1814 he thought that the Incorporated Militia along the Niagara frontier was "in an admirable state of discipline and efficiency." At times he may have been disappointed with the militia and civilian support for the war, but that was a frequent opinion of British officers in Upper Canada.[51] If he had been seriously angry or upset about the assembly's response or about civilian indifference, he surely would have reported his views in correspondence with his superiors.

Sheppard describes the assembly's address of 14 March to the Prince Regent as a protest directed against "the biased reports posted by British officers" because they had failed to give sufficient credit to the contributions and achievements of Upper Canada's militiamen. It was indeed a protest, but it clearly referred to one man, "the representative of Our Sovereign," because he had not "laid before Your Royal Highness a faithful account of our services and our sufferings."[52] What the assemblymen likely had in mind was the fate of militiamen held in the United States as prisoners of war. On 12 March the assembly had complained that "the Commander of the Forces in His Majesty's North American Dominions," in negotiations for the exchange of militia prisoners of war, had not given to Upper Canadian militiamen the same attention as he had to "our fellow subjects in Lower Canada." Drummond and his officers were not the target of this protest; rather, it was directed at Prevost.

All the administrators in Upper Canada had encountered the problem of treason, but only Drummond had to deal with the trial and sentencing of convicted traitors. When he arrived in the province and found that there were people being held on charges of rebellion, treason, or looting, he was anxious to bring them to trial as quickly as possible. The arrangements were left in the hands of Attorney General Robinson, and Drummond did not influence the course or outcome of the trials.[53] When they concluded on 21 June, fourteen men had been found guilty and one had pleaded guilty. All received the traditional sentence of death by hanging, drawing, and quartering, but the executions were delayed in order to allow appeals. Drummond was uncertain whether he had the power to pardon those guilty of high treason, commute the sentences, or banish the convicted traitors. In having the sentences carried out, he was concerned with the number of executions to sanction in order to create the maximum "salutary effect upon the People of this Province."[54] After conferring with his officials, he agreed to reprieve seven men, but eight would hang on 20 July.[55] For the remainder of 1814 he did not express serious concern about Upper Canadian traitors, a fact which suggests that the trials and hangings had an impact on public opinion.[56]

Drummond remained fully aware of the American naval threat on Lake Ontario and was happy to seize an opportunity to take action against the danger. Oswego, protected by a small fort and garrison, was an important port for the storage and transfer of naval supplies on their way from the Hudson River to Sackets Harbor. In April 1814, while considering a raid on Sackets but hesitating because of his need for reinforcements and heavy guns, Drummond suggested a strike at Oswego. He expected that this raid, if successful, would significantly delay enemy shipbuilding at Sackets.[57] The attack was carried out on 6 May, and a large quantity of supplies was secured and the barracks and fort burned. The success was limited, however, because the British failed to find some naval supplies and guns that the Americans had previously hidden. Yet this action, followed by Yeo's blockade along the shore to Sackets, would slow Chauncey's shipbuilding program.[58] The raid was also a demonstration of smooth cooperation between Drummond and Yeo and of an effective amphibious operation.

By the third week of June, informed by reports from Riall of enemy concentrations along the Niagara River, Drummond expected that front to be the scene of the Americans' principal attack, while they distracted British attention by manœuvres at Plattsburgh. (The newly appointed American commander, Major-General George Izard, was increasing his forces in the Lake Champlain valley, erecting fortifications at Plattsburgh, and concentrating his troops from that place north to the Canadian border.) The general's opinion seems to have been discounted at Prevost's headquarters,[59] but it is doubtful that Drummond received any comfort from being proven correct by events.

The major land actions of 1814 in Upper Canada began on 3 July with Brown's invasion of the Niagara Peninsula and his quick seizure of Fort Erie. News of the attack and of Riall's subsequent defeat at Chippawa reached Drummond in Kingston.[60] He sent what forces he had available and requested more from Prevost. In his reports to the governor, he praised the regular troops and militia under Riall, but criticized their Native allies. In fact, he consistently expressed a low opinion of Native warriors. He believed that the American success resulted, not from the quality of their fighting men or commanders, but from their overwhelming numbers at Chippawa. Riall had placed these at 6,000, whereas the actual figure was closer to 3,500 against somewhat fewer than 2,500 defenders.

By 13 July Drummond had made plans to go west himself, for the news from that front continued to be bad. The Americans had advanced to Queenston and were making preparations to assault the British-held forts.[61] Drummond acted boldly, stripping York of its few effectives in order to send them to Burlington Bay and hurrying the movement of units there from Kingston and from down the St Lawrence to Kingston.

Drummond finally reached York on the 22nd; from there he sent instructions to Riall about responding to General Brown's moves. These orders reveal Drummond's intention to take the offensive rather than await an American attack.[62] Based on information he had received from Riall, Drummond believed that the Americans were vulnerable to attack on the eastern bank of the Niagara River. Consequently he sent troops to Fort Niagara with instructions to Lieutenant-Colonel John Tucker to lead a sortie southward against Youngstown.[63] In conjunction with that movement, Riall was to divert American attention by advancing towards St David's, but he was to avoid being forced into a major action under unfavourable circumstances. Writing on Saturday the 23rd, Drummond proposed to cross the lake on Sunday and to have the attack from Fort Niagara take place "on Monday morning at daylight."

He reached Fort Niagara at daybreak on the 25th and learned that Brown had withdrawn his army from Queenston to Chippawa the previous day. Drummond in consequence ordered troop movements along the American bank against Lewiston, a supply depot, and along the Canadian side towards the falls. He accompanied the latter force, while ahead of him Riall proceeded along the Portage Road and arrived at its junction with Lundy's Lane late in the afternoon.[64] Brown, meanwhile, had decided that his riposte to these British moves ought to be a "motion towards Queenstown."[65] He assigned this duty to Winfield Scott, who led his 1st Brigade north on the Portage Road to arrive near Lundy's Lane between 6 and 6:30 p.m. When Riall learned of the advance of Scott's brigade, he feared that Brown's entire army was on the move, which would mean that he was greatly outnumbered. He ordered his troops to withdraw, arguably both a sensible decision and one conforming to his commander's instructions. But when Drummond encountered the retreating columns, he countermanded the order. In other words, he determined to keep the initiative by retaining possession of the high ground even if doing so brought about a battle against a larger force. He also demonstrated the skill of *coup d'œil*, for "One glance was enough to show Drummond that the terrain he could see from the top of the hill was a good defensive position."[66]

The general commanded his fighting men by riding to different parts of the field. Despite losing Riall early in the battle through wounds and then capture, and despite suffering a serious neck wound himself, he continued his personal direction. Drummond may not have anticipated a struggle as tough and prolonged as that which developed, because up to this time he had not fought against Brown and Scott and their well-trained and confident troops. He might have expected to encounter from his opponents weak leadership and poorly trained men, but when he met the opposite, he nevertheless demonstrated a cool head, physical courage, and the moral strength to accept casualties and the serious risks of a large-scale head-to-head clash with what he assumed was a bigger field army.[67]

Criticisms have been made of Drummond's generalship in this battle. In an early stage, for example, he realigned his infantry, leaving no troops in front of his artillery under Captain James Maclachlan, instead of protecting them with a line of skirmishers as was standard procedure.[68] The time of this move seems to have been after 8:45 p.m., when the darkness that was falling could have prevented Drummond from seeing the actual disposition of forces.[69] If that was the case, the most prudent course would have been to post a skirmish line. After the

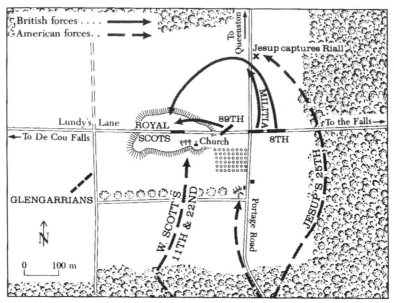

Initial phase – evening, 25 July

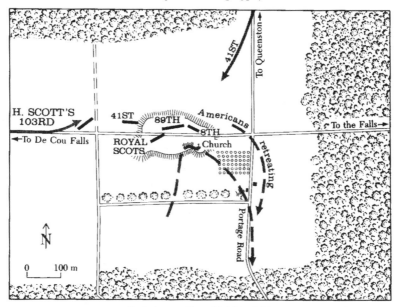

Final phase – after midnight, 26 July

Map 9   The battle of Lundy's Lane, July 1814
(reprinted, by permission, from Stanley, *The War of 1812*, 320)

Americans had gained control of the guns on the hilltop, it took Drummond nearly thirty minutes to organize a counter-attack, and he again failed to employ his skirmishers (or light infantry). He had six companies of them available, and they would normally have skirmished in advance of the attacking infantry line.

These shortcomings of the British commander at Lundy's Lane should not be seen in isolation from the failures of the opposing commanders, particularly Brown and Scott. At the beginning of the battle, the latter had placed his infantry regiments within range of Maclachlan's guns, so that his men suffered severely and even the American artillery and dragoons took casualties. The U.S. artillery was unable to reach the British guns because they were on higher ground; nor was musket fire effective. Later Brown and Brigadier-General Eleazar Ripley made exactly the same mistake attributed to Drummond of not using skirmishers to protect their artillery, although they were saved in part because they were alerted to the coming attack by the noise of the British advance. Perhaps the most serious tactical blunder by either side was Scott's attack with his 1st Brigade along Lundy's Lane, which brought his men between the contending armies and made them the target of fire from both. The failure to have the captured British guns removed to the security of the American lines may be considered the greatest error of all, for abandoning them meant that the American effort was simply wasted. Brown could have had them moved before he was forced by his wounds to hand over command to Ripley, who also failed to have the guns taken away. But Brown's responsibility for decisions remained, because at the Chippawa camp during the night and the next morning he continued to give orders to Ripley and other officers. It was still up to Brown to see that Ripley acted.[70]

In spite of the shortcomings of Drummond's generalship, it had an important element that remained constant, and that was his determination to hold the ground even if he did not command its summit and even with the certainty of suffering heavy casualties. His resolution was ruthless, but it meant that the side which apparently lost the battle gained its objective while the apparent winners made what would normally be described as a retreat. An American officer later wrote that just after "half-past 11 at night ... the enemy was compelled to retire, leaving us in quiet possession of the field of battle." This account contrasts with Le Couteur's assertion that "about midnight the whole of the American army had retired, while we kept the field."[71] The debate about Lundy's Lane, perhaps the most contentious land battle of the entire war, is not yet finished.

Lack of recent combat experience may partly explain Drummond's errors, for he had last participated in battle in 1801, while the American commanders all had more recent and more relevant experience. Mistakes could arise in the confusing conditions of darkness and from each side's uncertainty about its opponents' numbers and intentions.[72] Moreover, in a battle fought by men wearing similar uniforms and speaking the same language, confusion could not be avoided. On the British side, an additional factor was the weariness of the troops, particularly the regulars under Colonel Hercules Scott and the militia under Lieutenant-Colonel Christopher Hamilton, for these men had marched from the Twelve Mile Creek in the afternoon and had arrived at the battlefield already tired.

The battle at Lundy's Lane left both armies exhausted and their commanders badly wounded. Brown returned to Buffalo for medical care and remained there for more than a month. It was Ripley who decided to retreat to Fort Erie.[73] By contrast, in spite of his own severe wound, Drummond remained in control, and this without the assistance of his second-in-command. In a letter of 27 July to his wife he told her what had happened: "The ball entered just under my right ear and lodged in the back of my neck … The ball was cut out this morning, and I feel quite easy since. I lost a good deal of blood at the time but in other respects (with the exception of a little stiffness about the neck) I found no inconvenience from it and by tying two or three handkerchiefs round my neck, I was enabled to continue in the action." At the time of writing he was in bed, but he assured his wife that he was "suffering more from a severe cold and sore throat than the wound" and expected to be "on horseback the day after tomorrow."

Here was Drummond some thirty-six hours after the end of the battle (around midnight on 25 July), suffering from several ailments, but intending to be active soon and mentioning, "I have been interrupted a hundred times since I began this [letter]" – all the while supervising preparations for following the enemy towards Fort Erie. His letter was dated at Queenston, but a district general order of 26 July and a long dispatch to Prevost dated the 27th were both issued from "HQ Falls of Niagara."[74] It may be that Drummond had gone to Queenston, seven miles from Lundy's Lane, while his deputy adjutant general, Harvey, and other officers established a headquarters at the falls near the battle site. Wherever Drummond was located, he remained actively in command, probably holding discussions with his officers and dictating dispatches and orders. In other words, he could not and did not simply rest and recover.

By the next day, Norton and his Native scouts, along with a detachment of the 19th Light Dragoons, had made contact with a small party of Americans who had come out of Fort Erie under a white flag.[75] By the 29th Drummond's forces were following the enemy towards the fort, and on 1 August he transferred his headquarters "to Palmer's," halfway between Chippawa and the fort.[76] Does this lack of immediate, full-scale pursuit of the Americans prove a want of energy or enterprise in Drummond? Perhaps. But other factors besides the general's character should be considered. Two reasons that Stanley points out are the exhaustion of the troops and the need to replace losses and to obtain heavy guns and supplies.[77] Furthermore, the bridge over the Chippawa River, destroyed by the retreating Americans, had to be rebuilt before the army could cross. Finally, Drummond could not devote all his attention to Fort Erie because he had to ensure the security of the rest of the frontier, particularly his key defensive points (Forts George and Niagara) on the Lake Ontario shore. There still existed the threat of Chauncey's fleet, whose whereabouts, strength, and intentions Drummond did not know.[78] His concern about it was justified, for the fleet appeared off the mouth of the Niagara River on 5 August.[79]

To take no more than five days (including at least two spent in bed) to recover from a strenuous battle and a severe wound in order to organize a major forward movement does not seem excessive. In Norton's eyes, "Although suffering much from the effects of a severe wound – General Drummond was indefatigable."[80] Rather than a "desultory pursuit," Drummond's advance might be more accurately described as methodical and prudent.[81] It did not display the dash that he had shown in December 1813, and there is a strong possibility that in the heat of July his wound was more troublesome than he would admit. But he may also have assumed that the Americans would withdraw across the river to their own side. He knew that Brown and his most prominent brigadier-general, Scott, were both wounded, and Ripley seemed a less-aggressive opponent. Moreover, he may have assumed that there would be no good reason for the Americans to hold on to Fort Erie.

By 3 August he realized that the Americans were digging in and extending the fort's defences, so that he would require heavy guns to force them out.[82] The campaign became a siege operation, and Drummond's army was ill-prepared for this kind of warfare, a characteristic, it seems, of the British army.[83] What he lacked was sufficient heavy guns – mortars, in particular – and ammunition. Despite his urgent appeals to Yeo and Prevost for these and other supplies, they came slowly and in insufficient quantities. Near the middle of August, Drummond learned that the provisions available to the Right Division would last less than a month instead of until mid-October, as he had been told at Kingston.[84] Commissary officials were busy collecting supplies, but the only way that they could be sent effectively was by ship, and at the moment the American fleet dominated Lake Ontario. Consequently, supplies had been dispatched on batteaux, but these were too few, too slow, and too limited in carrying capacity to maintain the forces from York to the west, including Niagara.[85] The scarcity even touched him, for since there was no wine to celebrate his wedding anniversary, he and his friends were forced to drink Canadian whisky "out of one broken tea cup."[86] By mid-August at least, Drummond displayed no lack of drive in the face of the American army still strengthening Fort Erie's defences.[87]

An additional worry for him was the quality and well-being of his officers. He had lost his new second-in-command, Major-General Henry Conran, only a few days after he had jointed the Right Division.[88] Conran's replacement, Colonel Stuart of the 1st Foot, fell severely ill of ague the day after he arrived at headquarters, and at the same time Colonel Hercules Scott of the 103rd Foot, the next senior officer, sought permission to resign the command of his brigade.[89] Drummond's deputy adjutant general reported, "The Division is without a General Officer, for General Drummond through his exertions is evidently hurting his constitution & health, he suffers much from his wounds."[90] The general was an active commander, perhaps too active for his own good. (Fortunately, Harvey was both capable and energetic, even though he had suffered "a wound in the Eyebrow.")[91] Drummond also did not believe himself well served by the officer commanding the engineers, Captain Samuel Romilly, and when he became too ill to perform his duties, he was left with only junior and inexperienced officers in that department.[92] Another officer present at the time, Assistant Surgeon William Dunlop of the 89th Foot, complained of the lack of staff in the medical and commissariat departments.[93]

One way that Drummond had hoped to remedy shortages was to take from the enemy. Hence, after advancing close to Fort Erie on the 2nd, he had ordered a raid against depots in Black Rock and Buffalo.[94] That night 580 regulars drawn from four regiments crossed the river, but their assault failed, in large measure because of the erratic leadership of Tucker as well as the strong and organized American resistance.[95] The general's reaction to this setback seems excessively severe and his criticism misdirected. He commended the officers and laid entire blame for the failure on the troops' "misbehavior."[96] Perhaps his response demonstrates the accuracy of Harvey's concern.

The next aggressive move by Drummond depended on construction of siege batteries. Romilly selected the site of a battery, but Lieutenant G. Phillpotts supervised its construction between 4 and 12 August.[97] The battery was not a serious threat to Fort Erie, being at least a thousand yards from the target, beyond the effective range of the guns. The position also suffered enfilading fire from American batteries at Black Rock. Drummond contemplated storming those batteries, but recognizing that American resistance would be strong, and perhaps in view of the failure of the earlier raid, he never attempted the operation.[98] Instead, he undertook to weaken American naval support for Fort Erie by attacking three ships lying offshore, where their guns annoyed the British force and covered supply vessels. Under Drummond's orders, Captain Alexander Dobbs, of the Royal Navy, moved boats overland to the south shore of the lake. His force of seamen and marines then surprised the crews of two schooners, captured them, and floated them down to Chippawa. To follow up this successful raid, the general decided to assault Fort Erie.[99]

On the eve of the bombardment, Colonel Scott wrote to his brother a letter containing several criticisms of Drummond. The one of greatest relevance to this study is his accusation that at the battle of Lundy's Lane he "could not then or now observe the smallest appearance of generalship." The colonel continued, "I fear he [Drummond] has got his command, like many others, from the interest of friends, not from his own merit."[100] These comments are too brief to allow us to be sure of what Scott meant by generalship, in what ways Drummond had failed, or why Scott's confidence in his commander had been lost. It is possible that the two had quarrelled, as E.A. Cruikshank claims, and that Scott was simply expressing rancour. Commanders inevitably attract criticism; nor is it to be expected that each officer would get along with or would admire every other.

The battery began firing on American positions on 13 August. After two days of effort, Phillpotts admitted that the guns had done little damage to the fort.[101] Nevertheless, on the 15th Drummond launched the attack, even though conditions for it were not favourable. The scheme was complicated, to say the least, because it required three separate columns to make a coordinated assault at night against a strongly entrenched and alert army behind stout walls. These tasks would have been formidable for any army of the period, and Drummond's force, even though it included good veteran regular and militia units, was not qualified for this kind of operation.

The assault failed disastrously, partly the result of bad luck, but more because of the plan. Recent historical writing is in agreement about the principal reasons for the failure.[102] The preliminary artillery bombardment was inadequate, surprise was lacking, and the plan was too complicated. In addition, the Right Division lacked training or experience in this kind of warfare and lost the element of surprise, for when the

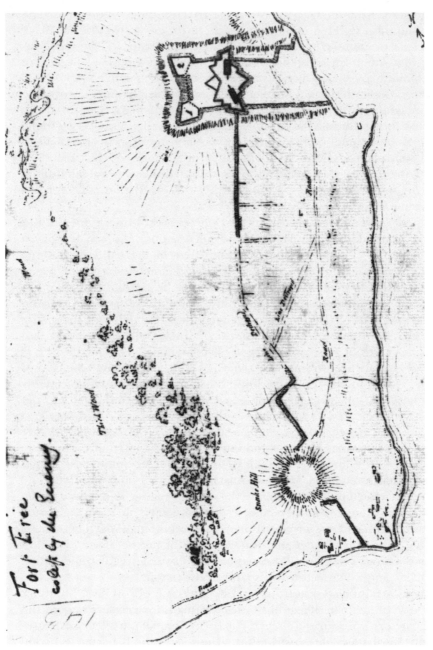

Map 10 The entrenchments at Fort Erie subsequent to the evacuation in November 1814 (NA, National Map Collection, 70956)

preliminary bombardment ceased, the Americans expected an attack and responded accordingly.[103] It is not difficult to understand the outbreak of panic during the darkness among soldiers in the right column, who came under well-directed American fire to which some could not reply because they had taken the flints out of their muskets.[104] Confusion and subsequently panic among soldiers in the centre and left columns is likewise understandable because from the outset of the attack they suffered heavy casualties, including their commanders.[105] The chief stroke of bad luck was the explosion of the magazine under the northeast bastion, which men of the centre column under Lieutenant-Colonel William Drummond had captured. As they battled fiercely to get into the fort, the ammunition below them exploded, causing appalling casualties.[106]

The British in Upper Canada had achieved a successful night attack against a fort in December 1813, but that was a simple operation compared with the attempt against Fort Erie. While there may have been extenuating circumstances for the failure of the latter, the commanding general cannot escape responsibility for it. Drummond and Harvey blamed the De Wattevilles, but bad execution does not justify a flawed plan. Drummond almost acknowledged as much when he wrote,

The failure of these most important attacks has been occasioned by circumstances which may be considered as almost justifying the momentary panic which they produced, and which introduced a degree of confusion into the columns which in the darkness of the night the utmost exertions of the officers were ineffectual in removing. The officers appear invariably to have behaved with the most perfect coolness and bravery, nor could anything exceed the steadiness and order with which the advance of Lieutenant-Colonel Fischer's brigade was made until, emerging from a thick wood, it found itself suddenly stopped by an *abbattis*, and within a heavy fire of musquetry and guns from behind a formidable entrenchment.[107]

The stiff American resistance at Lundy's Lane should have alerted Drummond to what he might expect from this army, particularly when it was defending a well-fortified position and had ample warning of the attack. A veteran of two years' warfare in Upper Canada, Sergeant James Commins of the 8th Foot, wrote in August 1815, "War was a new game to the Americans ... but I can assure you they improved by experience and before peace was concluded begun to be a formidable enemy."[108] Perhaps the commanding general was not well served by his commissariat and engineer officers, but the decision to attack or not rested with him. On this occasion, he was energetic and decisive when he should have been more cautious and painstaking.

Drummond decided that a second battery should be built, this time nearer the fort. Its construction took from 16 until 30 August, when it began to fire with somewhat more effect than the first. On 1 September his engineers started building a third battery, and they had it ready by the 6th. As well, the engineers were supervising construction of earth and timber works to protect and connect these batteries.[109] These breastworks and entrenchments, combined with obstructions of "*abattis*, brush, and felled timber," impressed Brigadier-General Peter Porter, commander of Brown's 3rd Brigade, when his troops undertook to capture them.[110]

In July Prevost had sent suggestions for Drummond's campaign, but had also stated that "much is left to Your discretion upon which I have the fullest reliance."[111] By September the situation in the Niagara Peninsula had changed considerably, and Drummond had no knowledge of Prevost's views on future strategy. This lack of information is surprising because Major-General Louis de Watteville had seen Prevost in Montreal on 10 August just before Watteville departed to join Drummond as his second-in-command.[112] The commander in Upper Canada wondered what to do about the siege of Fort Erie. Another attack, even if successful, would be pointless, he felt, because it would incur heavy casualties and would still allow the Americans to dominate Lake Erie and threaten the fort from their own side. A victory could thus leave Drummond weaker than before, with the extra burden of garrisoning Fort Erie. He could continue the investment in order to neutralize the Americans as an invading force, but if that was what Prevost wanted, fresh troops would be needed. Harvey believed that three more weeks in the fields and woods around the fort would see a dramatic increase in sickness among the troops. The resulting losses, he feared, would exceed those suffered from the attack on 15 August. Furthermore, the siege was becoming harder to sustain because the American means to fight were increasing while Drummond's were decreasing. Brown anticipated militia reinforcements and also knew of Izard's movement of regulars from Plattsburgh to Sackets Harbor.[113]

Bombardment continued, as well as skirmishing by parties sent out by both sides to probe the other's defences and alertness. The ground conditions facing Drummond worsened steadily. Referring to the period from 7 to 16 September, Phillpotts reported, "The weather during the whole of this time was very impossible, it was constantly raining." On the 21st Drummond complained that "torrents of rain" had fallen for the past thirteen days, and he described the plight of his men thus: "their present camp literally resembles a lake in the midst of a thick wood." This comment agrees with Dunlop's description of the British camp: "It was rather a bivouac than a camp, the troops sheltering themselves under some branches of trees that only collected the scattered drops of rain, and sent them down in a stream on the heads of the inhabitants [the troops] and as it rained incessantly for 2 months, neither clothes nor bedding could be kept dry."[114] Complaints of drenching rain, mud, and cold are plentiful in accounts from both sides.[115]

With no alternative plan, Drummond continued his partial encirclement. Early in September he knew of a large American militia reinforcement and seems to have hoped to see the enemy venture out of its fortifications to give battle.[116] Brown, for his part, thought of launching a sortie once the militia had been transported across the Niagara.[117] On the 17th the Americans sortied and succeeded in inflicting extensive damage to two batteries and heavy losses to the British, including wounding the inspecting field officer, Lieutenant-Colonel Thomas Pearson.[118] Two days later Drummond for the first time admitted to being less active and blamed it on his wound from Lundy's Lane. That may have been an influence, but it was only one of several on his decision about what to do next. His second-in-command, Watteville, on the 16th had strongly urged a withdrawal from Fort Erie.[119] As the appalling weather made the roads more and more unusable, American reinforcements arrived, and supplies dwindled, Drummond could see the siege becoming increasingly futile as well as difficult. On 21 September he informed Prevost that he was beginning a withdrawal towards Chippawa.[120]

Although abandoning the siege, he did not retire the entire distance to the Chippawa River. That is usually the way that the movement is described in the literature, and it conveys an impression that Drummond fled and somewhat cravenly took refuge behind a river barrier.[121] What happened was quite different. For a week or more he maintained outposts at Frenchman's Creek, about three or four miles from Fort Erie.[122] At the beginning of October, in consequence of the arrival of a considerable reinforcement on the American side (some 4,000 regulars from Sackets Harbor under Izard), Drummond withdrew more troops behind the Chippawa, but he still kept an "advance post" at Black Creek, approximately eight and a half miles from Chippawa and ten from Fort Erie, until at least 13 October, when the combined force under Brown and Izard moved against him. Meanwhile, the "greater part "of the Native warriors had left for their homes, but Norton came back with almost 100 men as soon as he heard of Izard's arrival and the prospect of a major clash.[123]

In an assessment of the siege, faults can be found in Drummond's conduct of the action. Regardless of these, it was important simply that he maintained the investment of the American position under conditions that were always difficult and getting worse. This stubborn action was valuable because it proved effective both in stopping an American invasion and in inflicting casualties.[124] It was never simply a passive or reactive siege. As long as there was ammunition, the British bombarded. One account refers to a period, beginning on 21 August, of "terrible fire ... of from 200 to 500 shots per day." The author, a retired American army engineer, also wrote that "the enemy was not idle, though their fire was suspended. They extended their intrenchment and constructed a new battery."[125]

While Drummond proved unable to capture Fort Erie, he certainly tied down large numbers of American troops in the position, with the result that they were not available to serve elsewhere.[126] In fact, the Americans shifted troops from the front facing Prevost to the Niagara, thus perpetuating their major strategic error of the war. Nor were these troops a threat to Upper Canada. Izard led some 4,000 men westward to Sackets Harbor, which he reached on 17 September. There he found no orders from Washington or any intention by Chauncey to attack an Upper Canadian port.[127] For lack of a better alternative, Izard decided to respond to a request from Brown for help. He moved slowly towards the Niagara River, reaching Lewiston on 5 October and Black Rock on the 9th, after which his division spent two days crossing. Between 13 and 15 October he moved north to Chippawa Creek, where he deployed in battle order across from Drummond's camp. An artillery duel provided the only action.[128]

It should also be noted that Drummond began this holding action at a time when Chauncey controlled Lake Ontario, and he maintained it until naval supremacy there shifted to Yeo. This change resulted from the launching at Kingston on 10 September of the *St Lawrence*, which could mount 110 guns. The vessel was not ready to sail until October, but rather than face the most powerful warship on Lake Ontario, Chauncey withdrew to Sackets Harbor. Drummond's army could now expect more men and supplies. On the 18th Yeo's squadron reached Niagara, but was unable to land the reinforcements until the 20th because of unfavourable winds.[129]

Izard made only one significant attempt against the British line: on 18 October he sent Brigadier-General D. Bissell to Cook's Mills on Lyons Creek, which joins the Chippawa about a mile and a half above its mouth. This force of 1,000 men was intended to capture supplies at the mill and outflank the British. Drummond reacted quickly, sending infantry from several regiments under Lieutenant-Colonel Myers. As the Americans seemed to be advancing, he ordered another force under Lieutenant-Colonel the Marquis of Tweeddale to support Myers. Drummond saw the enemy's move as a minor threat and not one requiring counteraction by large forces. His judgment of the situation and of the capabilities of his subordinate commanders was sound, for after a brief skirmish, both sides withdrew. The defenders' losses were considerably lighter than those of the attackers.[130]

On the 21st the Americans again confronted the British across the Chippawa, but at noon Izard ordered a withdrawal to Fort Erie. While Drummond had the advantage of a strong position on the Chippawa, his forces in that vicinity numbered only about 1,800; at Lundy's Lane and Niagara Falls there were a further 2,300.[131] Even when reinforced by Izard's division, the Americans were wary of tackling a tough, determined, and energetic opponent.[132] They still were left holding a patch of land of no importance.

Meanwhile, Brown and his division crossed the river, followed by Porter's militia. Izard changed his mind about wintering in Fort Erie and ordered its evacuation. The last troops departed between 1 and 5 November, after which the fort was blown up. Brown and Izard had no wish to face Drummond on Canadian territory at the head of fresher and more numerous troops.[133] Drummond had good reasons to avoid another futile and costly assault on Fort Erie, and his wait-and-see policy was strengthened by indications that the Americans were going to evacuate and destroy the fort.[134] After they did so, he returned to Kingston in early November.[135]

The end of American occupation of the Niagara Peninsula and of active campaigning in 1814 did not mean the conclusion of the war. Not knowing the progress of the peace negotiations, both sides expected fighting to resume in 1815 (skirmishing did occur in January). For a forthcoming campaign, Drummond was particularly interested in setting up a naval base on Lake Huron or Lake Erie or both. To that end, late in 1814 he ordered a road be cut from Lake Simcoe to Penetanguishene Bay on Lake Huron and took some steps to establish a naval depot at Turkey Point on Lake Erie; but news in February 1815 of the conclusion of peace curtailed both projects.[136]

As a lieutenant-general, Drummond was permitted four aides-de-camp, all of whom were capable men but without the influence or standing in Upper Canada of Brock's ADCs. Captain Colley L.L. Foster had a long record of administrative experience and was an aide-de-camp and military secretary in Jamaica at the same time that Drummond was there.[137] He subsequently served as Drummond's ADC in Ireland and accompanied him to Canada. In 1814 Drummond appointed him his military secretary and adjutant general of the Upper Canadian militia. He mentioned Foster for services at headquarters during the siege of Fort Erie.[138] Captain William Jervois, 57th Foot, had had a brief combat career and a longer administrative one before his appointment to

Drummond's staff in Ireland in 1813.[139] He arrived with the general in Upper Canada and was commended for his part in the attack on Buffalo in December.[140] Jervois also participated in action at Oswego and Lundy's Lane.[141] He carried Drummond's report to Prevost, who sent him with dispatches to London.[142] The ADC returned to the Canadas and remained until 1816, when Drummond departed.[143] Captain Robert R. Loring, 104th Foot, had been on Drummond's staff for a brief time in Ireland before the outbreak of war. After he ceased to be Sheaffe's ADC, he was appointed to Drummond's staff on 25 December 1813, and in February 1814 Drummond made him his private secretary. Loring was taken prisoner at Lundy's Lane, with the result that the general lost his services for the remainder of the war. When Loring returned to Quebec in April 1815, he was again appointed Drummond's private secretary, and he served in this position until Drummond returned to Britain.[144] He displaced Lieutenant William Nesfield, 89th, who had been appointed an extra ADC in September 1814 with effect from 25 July.[145]

Drummond's provincial ADC was Christopher A. Hagerman, the son of one of the first barristers in Upper Canada and a lawyer in training.[146] He enlisted in the militia and appears to have been a brave and useful officer, seeing combat service at Oswego and Fort Erie.[147] Hagerman was known to the rising elite of Upper Canada, but there is no evidence that he possessed political or social influence, and he certainly had nothing like the status of John Macdonell, Brock's ADC.

Gordon Drummond's generalship was characterized by aggressiveness and determination unequalled by his predecessors except Brock or by Prevost. His instinct was to take the risk – attack Fort Niagara, raid Black Rock, hold the high ground at Lundy's Lane, assault Fort Erie – rather than a cautious course, as Sheaffe did at Queenston Heights and York or as Rottenburg and Prevost did before Fort George. When Drummond was present, he held the initiative. It may appear that he lost it after 15 August, but a second glance suggests otherwise. Drummond maintained an active siege at least until 21 September, and his troops continued their skirmishing until 13 October. They subsequently repulsed an attack at Cook's Mills and stalemated a larger American force at the Chippawa. Brown tried to seize the initiative, but in spite of the successful sortie of 17 September, neither he nor Izard persisted in their aggressive efforts. Why not? The suffering their troops experienced from bad weather or combat was no worse than that felt by Drummond's forces. Most of the Americans instead had enjoyed a healthier diet and more weatherproof accommodation than their besiegers. The U.S. commanders made no mention of being affected by changing naval supremacy on Lake Ontario brought about by the launching of HMS *St Lawrence*. Indeed, the shift in naval dominance became significant for the Niagara front only when the British fleet arrived there on 18 October. Its appearance clearly meant the end of any opportunity for successful invasion during the rest of the 1814 campaign season. But for two months the American commanders had shown little initiative compared with Drummond.

The general demonstrated a strong understanding of the art of war in the measures that he undertook for fixed defences, as well as in his tactics and strategies. His determination to hold on to Forts George, Niagara, and Mississauga shows clearly that he appreciated their strategic value, as Brown and Chauncey certainly did also. Drummond thus understood the relationship between naval power on the lakes and successful defence on land. He was well aware and appreciative of the vital role that Royal Navy ships played.[148] Drummond took strong interest in erecting defences on Queenston Heights (Fort Drummond) and on the left bank of Chippawa Creek. His operational sense was demonstrated by his movement of troops southward on the U.S. side of the Niagara River just prior to Lundy's Lane, a manœuvre intended to relieve pressure on Fort George.

Drummond was nevertheless a fortunate commander – lucky in Napoleon's sense of the word. A further manifestation of his good fortune was sound health (unlike Sheaffe and Rottenburg) until he was wounded on 25 July 1814. By the 27th he was also suffering from a cold and sore throat, and these ailments were the first indications of any health problems. In September he mentioned being less active because of the lingering effects of his wound, but his first complaint of serious illness appears in a letter to Prevost on 23 October.[149] He grumbled that an old injury received before he came to North America, had worsened so much of late that he "continually" suffered "extreme distress," particularly when on horseback. Drummond requested permission to return to England after pointing out that the campaigning season had ended. That final comment suggests that he was sufficiently healthy to remain in Upper Canada as long as he did not have to engage in active combat. He added that he also had "important and urgent" private business that required his presence in England. In other words, it appears that his concern was to return home, and if his plea of poor health proved inadequate, he had another justification.

Accepting his plea of bad health, Prevost was prepared to request a replacement for Drummond; but after seeing him in person, wrote to London that Drummond wished to remain in his present command "as his health will be perfectly restored by the opening of the next Campaign."[150] It appears that Prevost did not regard Drummond's health problems as serious.[151] Perhaps they were not, for Drummond continued to serve in the Canadas for nineteen months longer. He took over as administrator and commander of the forces from Prevost on 4 April 1815, and his health seemed unimpaired when he sailed for home on 21 May the following year.[152]

For the most part, Prevost had had little reason to find fault with Drummond, yet their relations were not always smooth. While Drummond was in command of Upper Canada, he was mildly chided by Prevost over his repeal of martial law and strongly criticized about his movement of troops in early April 1814. He informed Prevost that he was transferring two companies of the 89th Foot from Cornwall to Fort Wellington, both on the St Lawrence River, to replace marines whom he had ordered up to Kingston. Prevost complained that Drummond's orders contradicted his own. The fault, he believed, lay with the bad advice Drummond was receiving from John Harvey, the deputy adjutant general for Upper Canada, and he instructed Drummond to restrain him. Prevost continued his complaint in terms that suggest he had a deeper grievance: "It has not escaped my observation that you sought my commands on an important subject (the partial operation of martial law,) on which I could only offer advice, as the power to do so comes from the commission under which you act as a governor; but on various other occasions affecting my responsibility you had not hesitated to act and afterwards report having done so, tho' nothing pressing attended the case."[153]

A commander-in-chief whose orders were countermanded by a subordinate would understandably be annoyed; an additional cause for Prevost's displeasure may have been the recent incursion into Canadian territory of Major-General James Wilkinson at the end of March and the continuing build-up of American forces just across the frontier. Prevost had to be concerned not only with the defence of the vital communication line to Upper Canada but also with the security of the lower province. His annoyance with Drummond did not last long, however, for eleven days later he assured the general that he had "perfect confidence" in him.[154]

In June the two men had a brief disagreement over Phineas Riall's abilities. Prevost apparently questioned Riall's qualifications to command on the Niagara frontier, but Drummond replied that he had no such doubts and he rejected any thought of removing Riall from his command.[155] A little over three months earlier, at Riall's request, Drummond had sent lengthy instructions to him about what actions to take in the event of an invasion. This letter did not indicate that Drummond believed Riall could not manage without his directions, for he concluded by expressing confidence in the officer's "tried zeal, activity and ability."[156] Drummond and Riall appear always to have worked well together, and there is little evidence of disagreements. The only one of any significance occurred in June, when Drummond reprimanded Riall for stopping the movement of some Native warriors from his sector to Kingston.[157] The commander appears not to have countermanded Riall's order, however.

Drummond's defence of his second-in-command is not surprising, for Riall's removal would have reflected negatively on Drummond himself. In any case, could Prevost have replaced Riall with a more capable or experienced officer? Riall had so far proved himself as able as any other major-general, and his experience included more exposure to combat and command than Brock or Sheaffe had had. Phineas Riall had joined the British army in 1794, had risen rapidly through the ranks, and had seen active service while commanding an infantry battalion in the West Indies in 1805, a brigade on Martinique in 1809, and forces of various sizes in the campaign on the American side of the Niagara in December 1813. He would come under criticism for his leadership at the battle of Chippawa, but in Prevost's eyes no officer emerged from that battle with credit.[158]

Modern historians tend to be reserved, if not critical, about Drummond. In the *Dictionary of Canadian Biography* he is generally praised and is described as "more aggressive and ruthless than either Sheaffe or Rottenburg." But because of his mistakes at the siege of Fort Erie, the author concludes that Drummond was "inferior to ... [General Jacob] Brown in both energy and skill."[159] In the standard work on the land campaigns of the war, Stanley avoids explicitly assessing Drummond, but is more critical than complimentary, for he rejects the general's explanation for the failure of the attack on Fort Erie, and the sole commendation he can manage is to suggest that Drummond was the only Canadian-born officer who displayed merit. Nor does the general fare better in two other comprehensive histories. Horsman accuses him of "lack of dynamic leadership" and a tendency to blame others for his failures, while Hitsman is only slightly less critical, giving no more praise than to say that Drummond "had good as well as bad days."[160]

More-specialized accounts continue this vein of finding more to criticize than to praise. In Donald Graves's study of Lundy's Lane, Drummond is shown to be tactically astute in his movement of forces on 25 July 1814 in order to threaten the supply line of Brown's army. However, his conduct of the battle is criticized, most particularly for his failure to use skirmishers ahead of his artillery, a mistake that Graves sees as a serious flaw in Drummond's generalship. The strongest criticisms are reserved for the general's report on that battle, for his slowness in following the enemy towards Fort Erie, and for the failure of his assault of 15 August against the fort. By October 1814 he was "Worn out," along with his Right Division.[161] This author attributes Drummond's shortcomings to the effects of his wound and, perhaps more important, to his inexperience of command in combat. George Sheppard's concern is not Drummond's generalship but his relationship with the civilian population. He argues that Drummond, like his three predecessors, received very limited support from the people of Upper Canada in the struggle against American invasion.[162] The image he leaves is one of an ineffectual civil administrator who evinced little understanding of the people he governed.

Earlier studies sometimes offered more-positive judgments. For instance, William Kingsford, writing in the 1890s, praised Drummond uncritically, while William Wood almost twenty years later was much more reserved.[163] Nearly two decades after that, Ernest Cruikshank spoke at the unveiling of a tablet in memory of Drummond and delivered a eulogy in which he suggested that the general deserved the title "saviour of Upper Canada" as much as Brock did. However, in reviewing Drummond's leadership, Cruikshank went no further than the battle of Lundy's Lane.[164] These few examples show that there have been differences of opinion among historians about Drummond, but the stronger tendency has been towards a downgrading of his abilities and achievements.

Yet the contrast between him and his two immediate predecessors could only be to his advantage. Drummond appears to have been a man of determination and decisive action, and a strong case can be made that he achieved notable successes until nearly the end of the war. In the areas of greatest concern to him, the Niagara Peninsula and Lake Ontario, he and his opponents reached stalemate, which meant, in effect, success for the defenders and their officer commanding. Under the circumstances of 1813 and 1814, the people of Upper Canada could hardly have expected the British government to send them a more capable military commander and civil governor. In terms of the leaders studied in this book, Drummond came closest to the ideal of leadership embodied by Brock.

CHAPTER SEVEN

Comparing Generals

When new raised troops are taken into action every thing
depends upon their officers.

Major David Campbell to his brother, 3 November 1812

Soon after joining the 49th Foot, Captain Isaac Brock encountered the
regiment's duellist, another captain reputed to be a dead shot. The
twenty-one-year-old Brock accepted a challenge, and when they came
to the chosen field, he drew out his handkerchief and insisted that, to
meet on equal terms, they fire across it rather than from twelve paces
apart. His opponent "positively declined."[1] As a young officer, Brock
chose a method of meeting danger that probably impressed his colleagues in the 49th, but this quality of leadership was not necessarily
the most suitable when he became commander of the forces in Upper
Canada. At Lundy's Lane "General Drummond, notwithstanding his
wound, was seen galloping from one Regiment to another, encouraging
the troops, and exciting them by his presence and example firmly to
Maintain ... the position of Lundy's Lane."[2] Personal leadership was his
model in that battle. Prevost demonstrated his heroic posture on one
occasion; that was during the raid on Sackets Harbor, when he
embarked in a canoe in order to reach shore and then coolly retreated
through "showers of grape" to the boats.[3] The absence of any accounts
of heroic, or foolhardy, conduct by Sheaffe and Rottenburg gives a hint
of their command style.

The major deficiencies and faults of British officers were described
in chapter 1, and a three-part classification was suggested with which
to judge generalship: the soldierly qualities and professional skills of a
commanding officer; knowledge of the "art of war"; and the ability to
exercise civil leadership. I now propose to compare the generals in this
study in terms of the eight failings listed in that chapter and at the

same time to touch on the first two classes of qualities. The third category will be left to later discussion.

The first fault was a failure to gather intelligence about the enemy and its territory. Such failure may be seen in the attack on Sackets Harbor, for which Prevost and Yeo were jointly responsible, and in Prevost's campaign against Plattsburgh. It is not clear that the joint army-naval expedition of July 1813 against American bases on Lake Champlain was founded upon intelligence. In August Sir George sought information about the American position centred on Fort George, but he never made good use of it. Occasionally, he had detailed knowledge about the enemy opposite: for example, in August 1814 about Izard's movement away from Plattsburgh and in October about Sackets Harbor. On the other hand, Brock's victory at Detroit resulted in large measure from the information that he had on his enemy's condition. He knew of the American fear of Native warriors, and his concern to have their support was demonstrated even before war broke out by his enquiry to Robert Dickson. We have a glimpse into one method of gaining intelligence from Brigade Major Evans's observations of American preparations during his crossing of the Niagara River on 12 October. Brock was anxious to have any scrap of information about his opponents, as Evans knew that he would be.

Perhaps the most daring example of an effort to gather intelligence was Drummond's personal undertaking to scout Sackets Harbor on 27 May 1814. He went to "the Squadron" blockading Sackets and then embarked in a canoe. In this craft he approached within about a mile and a half and obtained "a tolerable view of the Shipping and Harbour." Based on his first-hand observations, he made his plans, but had to cancel the undertaking because of Captain Stephen Popham's defeat at Sandy Creek. Sheaffe was particularly interested in information about Sackets Harbor.[4] There are a few references in the records to the British employment of informants[5] and to these officers' awareness of enemy activity of the same kind. It is almost superfluous to point out that all of the officers commanding Upper Canada kept a very close watch on their opponents along the Niagara River.

In this aspect of professional skill, high ranking must be given to Brock and Drummond and probably to Sheaffe and Rottenburg, but not to Prevost. He receives a low rating chiefly for his lack of knowledge of Sackets Harbor and at Plattsburgh, where he was unwilling to consult in person with Captain Downie. Meeting the captain either at Chazy, where Prevost could have seen the ships, or in the army commander's headquarters would have enabled Sir George to make a personal judgment of the naval officer's qualities and his force's capabilities. "Action without forethought or foreknowledge is foolhardy ... The essentials of action by the commander are *knowing* and *seeing*," writes Keegan,[6] and there is every indication that the commander-in-chief did not know his naval component, had little grasp of the geography of the battlefield, and seems not to have understood the mood of his army. In this specific shortcoming must also be included his failure to communicate his intentions clearly to the naval commander and to his brigade commanders.

The second fault was a lack of knowledge of history or theory, a criticism that cannot be directed at Brock or Rottenburg. With so little information concerning the education of Prevost, Sheaffe, and Drummond and none about their reading interests, any judgment on them in this regard must be very tentative. They made attempts on occasion to manœuvre their troops in order to hit the enemy's flanks, a tactic that was certainly current in European warfare.[7] Prevost tried such a move in his campaign against Plattsburgh, as did Drummond when he ordered Tucker to advance on Youngstown and Riall to move towards St David's earlier on the day that culminated in the battle of Lundy's Lane and in the assault against Fort Erie on 15 August. These manoeuvres did not produce victories, but such tactics were used successfully in battle at Queenston Heights when Sheaffe led and, for American generals, at the capture of Fort George and at Chippawa.

A third failing was a lack of planning. Prevost acted responsibly in 1811 and 1812 when preparing the Canadas for war, and he maintained a strong defensive stance for Lower Canada throughout. But he fell short in not planning in a number of instances: his raid with Yeo on Sackets Harbor, his campaign against Plattsburgh, and his failure to provide Drummond with direction or purpose for continuing the investment of Fort Erie. Brock put considerable effort into preparing Upper Canada's defences and followed a plan in his advance against Detroit. Sheaffe's leadership at Queenston Heights clearly indicated his professionalism, but it is unlikely that this particular movement had been planned because neither he nor Brock expected the Americans to seize the heights above the village. What is surprising is the absence of a clear plan for defending York in 1813, even though Sheaffe had anticipated the American attack only three weeks before it occurred. That Drummond relied heavily on planning can be seen in the actions which he commanded or intended or declined, namely, the assault on Fort Niagara and the follow-up ravaging of the American side, the proposed winter attack on Detroit, his advice to Riall in March 1814, the proposed raid on Sackets Harbor in April, the assault on Fort Erie, and his rejection of Prevost's proposal in February 1815 to seize the east bank of the Niagara River.

What is not found with Drummond is large-scale or long-range planning or the wider strategic thinking that was seen with Brock in 1812. Drummond did arrive at schemes, plans, and projects, but they were reactions to threats or the continuation or renewal of proposals previously made, rather than original ideas or part of a coherent plan of attack. With the American threat immediate and growing, he had no choice but to deal with it expeditiously. He had no leisure to devote to long-range strategic planning, nor was this something that Prevost expected of him.

In the sense of realizing that planning is a necessary art of war, all these commanders probably rank equally, but the case is more complex when we consider how they applied this professional skill. Four of the generals may be judged as roughly equal in their ability to make plans and carry them out, even if the upshot was not always victory on the field. The fifth commander, Prevost, probably should be placed in a lower rank.

Lack of understanding of the ordinary soldier was the fourth problem outlined in chapter 1. This was most evident in Sheaffe when he was a regimental officer against whom rank-and-file discontent was directed at least twice – in 1800 with the 49th Foot in Jersey and in 1803 by men of the same regiment at Fort George. After the mutineers on the latter occasion had been tried and executed at Quebec, Brock assembled the Fort George garrison, read them the news, and then spoke. "Since I have had the honour to wear the British uniform, I have never felt grief like this, as it pains me to the heart to think that any members of my regiment should have engaged in a conspiracy which has led to their being shot like so many dogs!"[8]

Speaking to the ordinary soldier in this way was not Sheaffe's style then or later, nor, evidently, was it that of Prevost, Rottenburg, or Drummond. In the British army a gap of understanding between officers and men would have been expected, but good generalship should not worsen this gap or make it a source of weakness to the force, as seems to have happened in Sheaffe's early career. Drummond may be faulted in this respect because he appeared too ready to criticize the rank and file for failures that were more the responsibility of higher command, and if he personally gave the order to the right column to remove the flints from their muskets for the assault on Fort Erie, doing so would seem to have been to mistrust the reliability of the men.[9] Of the five generals, Brock demonstrated more than usual insight into the men serving under him, judging by his expression of sympathy for them, the seemingly low level of desertions from garrisons under his command, and the soldiers' willingness to follow him unhesitatingly into mortal danger.[10] In ranking these commanders, there seems every reason to put him on a high level, while Sheaffe, Drummond, Rottenburg, and Prevost belong together on a lower grade.

Fifthly, insubordination, in the sense of wilful disregard of a lawful order or delay in putting a command into effect, cannot be found in

the case of the four officers commanding Upper Canada. Not surprisingly, there were disagreements between these commanders and
Sir George. The extent to which his subordinates would depart from
his intentions or take responsibility for acting on their own initiative is
a measure of both his and their capabilities as leaders. In other words,
a commander-in-chief who tried to prevent deviation from his orders
in the distant theatre of Upper Canada would be asking for frustration.
Such strict control would have been both unwise and unnecessary, and
the only commander in Upper Canada whom Prevost tried to control
in this manner was Sheaffe.

But there is another dimension to the relationship between the officers commanding the province and their superior, and it is worth touch-
ing on at this point because it relates to the connection between their
decision-making and Prevost's leadership. Sheaffe's replies to Prevost's
criticisms of his agreement with Van Rensselaer to extend the ceasefire
after Queenston Heights and of his leadership at York fell on deaf ears.
Nevertheless, even after he had been removed from the command in
Upper Canada and was subjected to further criticism, Sheaffe's responses
to Prevost were unfailingly courteous, as, for example, in July 1813,
when he described his "strong sense of obligation for the friendly frank-
ness with which you disclose the opinion which you have adopted" and
closed with "Your very devoted humble Servant."[11] Later letters to Prevost ended with "Your very faithful Servant" or "Your very devoted
faithful Servant."[12] This flattery indicates Sheaffe's feelings of insecu-
rity: under the most trying circumstances, he would write nothing dis-
agreeable to his superior.

In contrast is the brusqueness of Rottenburg's reply to Prevost when
he complained about the capture of two companies of De Watteville's
Regiment. The exchange between Prevost and Drummond over the
latter's failure to seek the former's advice in areas subject to Prevost's
jurisdiction is also enlightening about their relations. None of the other
commanders of the forces in Upper Canada received such a strong
reprimand, and to it may be added a greater variety of other complaints, including ones directed at his deputy adjutant general (Harvey)
and his second-in-command (Riall). Drummond made no apologies,
but simply justified his actions and refused to remove those two officers
from their positions. If Prevost was angry, it did not last long, and by
late October 1814 he was urging Drummond to remain in his command because he had done so well; moreover, the commander of the
forces would have had to send to England for a replacement. This
response raises the question of why Prevost could not find a general
officer in the Canadas capable of stepping into Drummond's shoes.

Prevost's responses to decisions of his commanders in Upper Canada
with which he disagreed prompts the suspicion that he was influenced

by the class origins of those men. For him to act this way would be understandable in terms of the social values to which all these generals subscribed, but it also raises the possibility that Prevost let class considerations influence his decisions on military matters. The removal of Sheaffe from Upper Canada can be explained on military and political grounds, but his gradual exclusion from further significant commands without concrete justification suggests the operation of motives kept unpublicized. Prevost may have had very good reasons, but since he did not reveal them, we are left with questions about his professional judgment.

To return to the list of deficiencies, the sixth and seventh were neglect of duty and being absent without leave. These faults cannot be charged to any of the generals in this study. Although in July 1813 Prevost accused Sheaffe of the "indifference with which you discharge the important Duties now committed to you," he provided no evidence, and Sheaffe's record suggests that such a charge was unwarranted.[13] Finally, there was a lack of interest in professional competence. For the five generals there is no evidence of this particular flaw. Indeed, quite the opposite applies in the cases of Rottenburg and Brock. In terms of ranking them, I see no reason not to put them all on the same level.

With regard to soldierly qualities and professional skills, some indication of the generals' abilities has already been given. What needs to be examined more closely is how appropriately any of these generals might be termed a "heroic type." This concept derives in part from the writings of the American sociologist Morris Janowitz, who more than thirty years ago projected a heroic-managerial model of military leadership to try to explain why some commanders acted with greater or lesser boldness or judgment than others.[14] His study tends to be directed towards the twentieth century and to American military experience, and though his sociological approach and leadership models are capable of wider application, they require too much adaptation to be useful in explaining the generalship of Prevost, Brock, Sheaffe, Rottenburg, and Drummond. While being aware of Janowitz's concepts and accepting their intellectual stimulation, I would subscribe to the scepticism expressed by Holmes – "I am concerned far less with the application of any particular model than I am with my own extrapolations from behaviour on the battlefields of history"[15] – and by Keegan, who writes, "I am an historian ... and am therefore free to believe that the generalship of one age and place may not at all resemble that of another."[16]

For the purposes of British generalship in the War of 1812, the heroic type may be described as an idealist, meaning an individual who believes that war has a glorious quality, that battle is a positive way to settle disputes, that heroism and glory matter, and that the sacrifice of life in combat is noble and worthwhile.[17] When combined with a powerful ambition to gain advancement, this outlook goes a long way to explain Brock's and Drummond's willingness to run great risks. They preferred action to waiting, manœuvring, or negotiating. Janowitz rightly points out that the combat role gives the military profession its distinctive character and outlook, a distinctiveness which the profession itself wants to maintain and which governments also support. The "operational logic of the military establishment," he writes, is supposed to be duty and honour rather than merely service to the public (as in government bureaucracy) or personal or corporate profit (as in a business).[18]

The evidence suggests that all these men believed in tradition and were strongly motivated by concepts of duty and honour. These concepts required a commanding officer to be present on the battlefield and visible to his men.[19] Brock's generalship at Detroit, Sheaffe's at York, Prevost's at Sackets Harbor, and Drummond's at Lundy's Lane met this expectation, but the clearest expression of its importance is seen in the court martial of Major-General Henry Procter.[20] Of the five charges preferred against him for his defeat at Moraviantown in 1813, the fifth was described as the most serious. It stated that Procter had not made the proper military dispositions for the anticipated battle with Harrison's pursuing army, that during the battle he had not made effective efforts "to rally or encourage" the fighting men, and, lastly, that he had "quitted the field soon after the action commenced, such conduct ... betraying great professional incapacity tending to the defeat and dishonour of His Majesty's arms, ... [and] being in violation of his duty, and unbecoming and disgraceful to his character as an officer." "Why," the prosecutor demanded," was he [the soldier] not animated by the example of his General; why when dismay fell upon him and he looked around for his Leader, did he look for him in vain"? Frequently, principal witnesses were asked if Procter had personally given the orders to the troops to fire or retreat, if he had tried to rally the men, and where he was during the course of the battle. The major-general more than once asserted that he was present on the battlefield, had tried to rally the men, and had not fled in panic, but had withdrawn at the point when he saw his troops ceasing to resist and simply in order to avoid being captured.

What seems to be missing from Janowitz's definition of the heroic type is the quality of ruthlessness which a successful commander must manifest towards his opponent in battle. Blumenson and Stokesbury, referring to Field-Marshal Bernard Montgomery's view, state, "The power to decide on an action, and the strength to see it through, are probably the most fundamental qualities of a great soldier."[21] In the War of 1812 the characteristic of robustness on the battlefield – the willingness to order troops to attack even if losses would be heavy, in order to attain the objective – was displayed by Brock at Detroit when he led his troops across open ground and at Queenston by his charge uphill. It was demonstrated by Drummond at Lundy's Lane and in the assault on Fort Erie. His reaction to his own troops' severe losses was to persist when on the defensive and to desist on the offensive only when defeat was certain. Prevost had displayed this quality in campaigns in St Lucia in 1803, Dominica in 1805, and Martinique in 1809, but it was conspicuously absent from his leadership at Sackets Harbor and at Plattsburgh. What Sheaffe showed at York during the American assault was bravery but not ruthlessness. In terms of the soldierly quality of being able to withstand the shock of combat, Brock and Drummond rank high, with Sheaffe close behind, followed by Prevost. Where Rottenburg fits is uncertain.

The contrasting model to the heroic may be designated the pragmatist, that is, an individual who believes that war can be avoided and ought to be as much as possible.[22] This type does not see any advantage to fighting battles, dying in action, or sacrificing large numbers of men to gain a temporary and uncertain advantage. Generalship in battle, therefore, should be cautious and calculating while also being visible in order to inspire the men's confidence and win the commander suitable recognition. Despite the risks run by Sheaffe at York and Prevost at Sackets Harbor, they both appear more pragmatic than heroic leaders, and so also does Rottenburg. But Brock also displayed characteristics of this type: for example, with his efforts before the war in trying to restrain Native peoples from attacking the Americans and at Detroit when he sought to win a bloodless victory. Drummond clearly does not belong in this category, for he preferred to seek battle rather than to settle for truces or accept coexistence.

More is known of what Prevost and Brock thought in terms of conducting war (rationally or otherwise), for they wrote about their strategies for defending the Canadas. When it came to applying strategic ideas, Prevost sought to make ceasefires with his opponents. These did not help to end the war and may have hampered the defence of the Canadas more than they assisted it because there is no evidence that they forestalled invasions, and the first one enabled the Americans to strengthen their defences. Yet when Sheaffe extended the truce that he had made with the enemy immediately after Queenston Heights, Prevost condemned it without explaining how it violated his strategic concepts. But he did encourage attacks on American naval bases and won a good deal of civilian support for the war effort.

Compared with Prevost's ideas of how to defend Upper Canada in a war with the United States, Brock's appear much sounder. He certainly showed more insight than his superior into how the Americans were likely to react to offensive moves and the use of Native warriors. The story about Brock's challenge to the 49th's duellist, even if largely apocryphal or merely distorted, does credit him with an ability that he demonstrated in 1811 and 1812, namely, understanding how his opponent would think. Of the attributes that separate a great commander from an ordinary one, write Blumenson and Stokesbury, "One of the most important ... is the ability to see the situation through the eyes of the enemy; Napoleon called this 'seeing the other side of the hill.'"[23] Prevost seems to have been conspicuously bereft of this talent.

When war and invasion came, Brock applied the strategy that he had previously proposed in writing, and it succeeded in unbalancing American efforts. This diversionary outcome lasted after his death in the form of repeated invasions of the Niagara Peninsula by the Americans which detracted from their efforts against more vital defensive sectors, particularly the St Lawrence River above Montreal. Furthermore, Brock displayed a flair for organizing and leading non-regular forces, and his tactics at Detroit showed his ability to improvise. Sheaffe and Drummond commanded both militia and Native fighting men, but did not win their affection as Brock had. Perhaps their aides-de-camp made a difference. Two of Brock's had influence because of their standing with civilians (Macdonell) and Natives (Givins). The other four generals had competent military ADCs, but only three had civilian (provincial) ones, and while these might have had connections in civil society, they lacked the authority of Macdonell.

What seems to follow from the discussion above is that Brock combined the heroic and pragmatic qualities more successfully than the other four generals. Yet that conclusion does not entirely explain his victory at Detroit, his posthumous fame, or his lack of success in persuading the assembly to grant the measures he sought.

The effect of combining civil and military leadership in the Canadas needs to be considered, particularly as it assisted or impeded the colony's defence. In the United States, civil leadership and military command were separate most of the time. When they were combined, the result might be disaster, as with William Hull and Stephen Van Rensselaer, or success, as with William Harrison. The British arrangement precluded militia-regular disputes over operations and authority, which on the American side in at least one case – Smyth's refusal to accept Van Rensselaer's authority – contributed to military defeat. Yet one scholarly examination of this combination reaches the conclusion that the civil authority dominated and checked the military function of the officers commanding Upper Canada.[24]

Sheaffe and Drummond appear to have been successful in their dealings with their legislatures, in the sense that they obtained most of the measures which they sought. Rottenburg does not have a record in this respect, for he did not meet his provincial parliament. Prevost's record was mixed; he succeeded in obtaining financial support and approval for changes to the militia law in 1812 and 1815 but not in 1813 and 1814. In 1813 he could not get assembly agreement for his authority to declare martial law if the need should ever arise. The governor did not raise this question again with the assembly; nor did he ever seek its approval to suspend habeas corpus. Sir George was unable to prevent the legislature's attempt to impeach Chief Justices Monk and Sewell and to appoint an agent to represent it in England. These were less indicators of the failure of Prevost's political leadership than of the persistence of long-standing personal and political animosities. It is no criticism of Prevost's leadership to agree with Fernand Ouellet's conclusion that "the War of 1812 failed to mobilize the entire population" of Lower Canada.[25]

It is Brock who appears the least successful in winning legislative support for his proposals, but it is important to note what was not supported and what was. In the final session of the fifth parliament, as well as in the initial session of the sixth, the members refused to approve an oath abjuring foreign powers and a suspension of habeas corpus. Despite Brock's feelings of frustration, these refusals are understandable, for they were not a rejection of British authority or an expression of disloyalty or unwillingness to defend Upper Canada. The refusal to restrict the rights of British subjects even when war threatened, as well as after it broke out, demonstrated something of what was worth defending in a British colony. There is no indication that the assembly majority expressed a political ideology, and if there was an organized opposition group under Joseph Willcocks, it was both rudimentary and not difficult to subvert, as is shown by the support its leader gave to Brock. Assemblymen were not unreasonable in wanting to maintain their civil freedoms while supporting concrete measures to defend their colony. Hence they approved amendments to the Militia Act and voted money for it. There is no evidence that what the assembly refused to grant to the administrator weakened Upper Canada's defence. As we know, Brock was able to include significant militia forces in his offensive actions (leading to the capture of Detroit) as well as in his defensive organization (along the Niagara River in September and October 1812).

Perhaps recognizing the futility of such requests, Sheaffe did not ask the assembly for suspension of habeas corpus or for authority to declare martial law. The situation had changed as 1814 opened, for Drummond obtained assembly agreement to suspend habeas corpus along with other measures designed to strengthen the government's hands in dealing with accused traitors. Perhaps it was the recent burning of Newark, in which Willcocks and his Canadian Volunteers had been so prominent, that softened the legislators' opposition to that particular limitation of their rights. Drummond never applied the suspension, thus raising the possibility that the assemblymen knew that their administrator would be very cautious about using such power. What seems to have determined the attitude towards martial law expressed by the parliaments of both Canadas and to suspension of habeas corpus by the assembly in Upper Canada was the degree of threat to the colony as perceived by the assemblymen themselves rather than on the basis of what their political masters told them.

There is no reason to believe that separating civil from military authority would have improved the supply situation. (It did not do so where such separation existed in the United States.) Nor is it clear that combining those authorities made collecting supplies easier. Brock and his successors could theoretically declare martial law under either their civil or their military powers, but this discretion did not make the decision any easier or assure either its legal foundations or its acceptance by the population. Brock and Sheaffe avoided imposing martial law, probably a valid decision because it is difficult to see how its imposition would have strengthened Upper Canada's defences. Rottenburg's imposition indicated that he put military considerations ahead of civil ones. His action was unpopular, as indicated by the assembly's condemnation; but for the army's requirements it was probably unavoidable.

In terms of civil leadership, Prevost, Sheaffe, and Drummond probably deserve high ranking, followed by Brock and with Rottenburg last. Brock has been placed lower than the others because, despite his skills in political negotiations and his patience, common sense, and popularity among civilians, he obtained less than he sought from the assembly when compared with the other three generals.

None of these generals challenged or changed the existing system of government from the top down, that is, one in which the popular element (represented in the elected assembly) was subordinated to the appointed elements. Successful generalship by Brock and Drummond may have enhanced the legitimacy of the system, while there is no indication that it suffered discredit from the failings of Sheaffe or Prevost. Thus the results of the leadership of the five generals continued into the post-war years.

A comparison of these commanding officers also requires consideration of their opponents. A case could be made that Brock faced fewer difficulties than his successors. He had complete control of Lakes

Ontario, Erie, and Huron, so that he could safely transport troops and supplies and also communicate easily with both superior and subordinate officers. This advantage ended late in 1812, and Sheaffe, Rottenburg, and Drummond saw control of the inland seas fluctuate between their side and the Americans. At times, these commanders could not be sure who was in control of Ontario, which was the crucial lake for the defenders of Upper Canada. Their strongholds of Fort George, Fort Niagara, Burlington Heights, York, and Kingston dotted its shoreline, and American domination of that lake would have made defence of these centres impossible for long, whereas the Americans' success on Erie in September 1813 and brief domination of Huron in August 1814 did not mean that they could conquer the upper province.

As for the American land forces, their regulars and militiamen suffered from a lack of training, discipline, and above all capable commanders.[26] But as part of the process of judging the British commanders, their capabilities need to be considered alongside those of their opponents. In Brock and Sheaffe the Americans faced commanders with little combat experience and none of leading large forces or an army made up of different regiments and of regulars and non-regulars (militia, Natives) and including a naval component. Many of the regulars, particularly in two principal regiments, the 41st and the 49th Foot, had not seen combat for a good many years, and the Upper Canadian militiamen had seen none.[27] The only experienced fighters in these generals' forces were the Native warriors who followed Tecumseh and possibly some of those from the Six Nations reserve and Caughnawaga. In short, the Americans did not face the best British and Canadian forces in 1812 or, with some exceptions, for most of 1813. American forces were capable of invading Upper Canada in 1812, but their leaders were not able to exploit this success. Nevertheless, judging from the responses of Prevost, Brock, and Sheaffe, even the limited American success appeared to be a serious threat to British rule over the Canadas. And it hardly needs to be said that poor-quality troops and incompetent leaders can inflict casualties. They may even kill first-class opponents such as Brock.

He was certainly aided by the incompetence of Hull and Stephen Van Rensselaer. So was Sheaffe at Queenston on 13 October, and later in the year by General Alexander Smyth's deficiencies. Prevost also encountered weak opponents except at Sackets Harbor and Plattsburgh (where his campaign was decided by the enemy navy not the army). Rottenburg faced some veteran American troops, but for the most part their leadership had not improved. It was Drummond who encountered truly effective opponents in the personnel of Brown's army in 1814, while in the background were the very competent Perry and Harrison. Did this difference in opponents mean that Drummond was a better general than his three predecessors in Upper Canada? Not necessarily. What it meant was an increase in the probability of defeat or of stalemate, rather than of clear-cut victory over the Americans and the surrender of entire armies. Drummond, because of his persistence, stymied rather than defeated the best of his enemies' troops and several of their best generals. Both he and his forces may deserve more credit for preserving Upper Canada than they are usually given in the literature.

Brock was the only commanding general who was killed at the head of troops in battle. But in terms of generalship, his death indicates absence of skill and care rather than the epitome of combat leadership. First, he should not have been leading a small force in a shock attack on one part of the battlefield. That is the job of subordinate officers – in this case, probably a captain's command.[28] The general's role is to stand back, assess the situation, and move his forces in the most effectual manner. In other words, Brock should have done precisely what Sheaffe did in the afternoon of 13 October or what Drummond did during the assault on Fort Erie. Secondly, Brock's death weakened the defence and might easily have led to confusion. His charge uphill had no effect on the battle, although his death may have strengthened the defenders' determination to drive the invaders back.[29] Even if he had succeeded in capturing the redan, that might not have turned the tide of battle, for enemy forces were above it in sufficient strength to hold their position. To remove the American threat would have required further uphill attacks, which would have been costly in terms of manpower whether or not they succeeded.

Yet Brock is remembered in relation to Queenston Heights far more than Sheaffe. The latter's leadership of the battle was brief and, in popular memory at least, far less dramatic than his predecessor's uphill charge. Sheaffe's and Rottenburg's terms in control of Upper Canada were short compared with Brock's and Drummond's, and the latter had the advantage of having commanded at Lundy's Lane, which Upper Canadians remembered as a victory. Neither Sheaffe nor Rottenburg seem to have won civilian affection as did Brock. Perhaps Drummond did not win it either (although there is evidence that he tried), but his military record was seen as successful, culminating in the American evacuation of Fort Erie, and he was associated with the heroic Sir James Yeo.[30]

In terms of actual success in combat, there seems little point in attempting to rank Brock, Sheaffe, and Drummond. Given his failure at Queenston Heights, Brock could be compared with Prevost at Sackets Harbor or could be placed on a level with Drummond and Sheaffe.

He had success at Detroit but not at Queenston, whereas Sheaffe won there but not at York. Drummond's gain of Fort Niagara, along with his stalling of Brown's invasion, was counterbalanced by his failure to capture Fort Erie. His record, however, of seizing an American fort (Niagara) and blocking invasion during the terrible summer and autumn of 1814 did as much – and arguably, did more – for the defence of British rule in Upper Canada than even Brock's victory at Detroit. Prevost's lack of success on the battlefield is obvious, and his presence at the raid on Sackets Harbor probably made no difference to the outcome. Rottenburg cannot be judged except in terms of his watch on Fort George, which witnessed no more than a number of skirmishes.

A summary ranking of these generals could be made on the basis of their suggested placements in all the categories listed above. This attempt would probably result in Brock and Drummond in the first rank, followed by Sheaffe and Prevost and lastly by Rottenburg. But do these suggestions indicate how any particular general would have performed in a different role? In other words, Brock or Drummond, as commander of the forces and governor of British North America, would have faced challenges that might have overwhelmed them to such an extent that they would have fallen short of Prevost's performance. Or, under such daunting circumstances, they might have risen to greater heights of achievement. It is difficult to see Sheaffe mastering the challenges of higher command more effectively than Prevost did. And where would Rottenburg fit? Speculation may be interesting and may raise many thought-provoking questions, yet "what might have been" contributes little to understanding the past.

A final question relates to the overall significance of this war and its British generals. Did any of these commanders truly influence the course of the war or the final peace settlement? Brock and Sheaffe did so in 1812 by stopping American invasions of Upper Canada, and, I suggest, these victories gave a lasting direction to subsequent American campaigns. If the invasions by Hull or Van Rensselaer had succeeded (or even that by General Smyth), it is quite possible that, with large sections of Upper Canada in enemy hands, Prevost would have limited his support to the colony by sending fewer troops, lessening the naval commitment, or abandoning the province west of Kingston. Drummond influenced the course of the war by capturing Fort Niagara and then devastating the enemy's Niagara shoreline. British possession of this fortress, as well as of Forts George and Mississauga, served to confine the scope of Brown's invasion and forced him to depend on naval support to carry out his mission fully. Drummond certainly benefited from British naval activity and American inactivity on Lake Ontario.

Lake Erie was a different matter altogether. He faced a greater threat from that lake than had Brock or Sheaffe, or than Prevost ever encountered with respect to the St Lawrence River. The factors of naval inferiority on Lake Erie and of uncertainty on Ontario should be considered when assessing Drummond's generalship. Prevost's ill conduct of the campaign against Plattsburgh influenced the peace negotiations in Ghent, although it is not certain that his capture of that base would have made any substantial difference to the treaty's terms. When the negotiators decided to bring an end to the fighting, it was European events and politics that counted far more than successes or failures of British, Canadian, and Native forces in North America.[31]

Chronology of the War of 1812

1811	
7 November	Battle of Tippecanoe

1812	
21 April	Conditional repeal of orders-in-council
18 June	United States declares war on Great Britain
23 June	British government repeals orders-in-council
24 June	Napoleon invades Russia
12 July	Brigadier-General William Hull invades Upper Canada
17 July	Captain Charles Roberts captures Michilimackinac
16 August	Brock and Tecumseh capture Detroit
20 August	USS *Constitution* captures HMS *Guerrière*
16 September	Americans attack British convoy on the St Lawrence River
21 September	American raid against Gananoque
4 October	Unsuccessful British raid against Ogdensburg
13 October	Battle of Queenston Heights and Brock's death
18 October	USS *Wasp* captures HMS *Frolic* but is captured by HMS *Poictiers*
19 October	Napoleon's army begins its retreat from Moscow
22 October	Americans attack Saint-Régis, Upper Canada
25 October	USS *United States* captures HMS *Macedonian*
10 November	Commodore Isaac Chauncey gains control of Lake Ontario
20 November	Major-General Henry Dearborn invades Lower Canada
28–30 November	Brigadier-General Alexander Smyth attempts to invade across the Niagara River
18 December	French army leaves Russian territory
29 December	USS *Constitution* captures HMS *Java*

1813

9 January	British declaration of war on the United States
22 February	Lieutenant-Colonel George Macdonell raids Ogdensburg
24 February	USS *Hornet* sinks HMS *Peacock*
27 April	Dearborn's forces occupy York
1–9 May	General Henry Procter's unsuccessful siege of Fort Meigs
25–27 May	Dearborn captures Fort George and General John Vincent retreats ultimately to Burlington Heights
29 May	British forces raid Sackets Harbor
1 June	HMS *Shannon* captures USS *Chesapeake*
6 June	Battle of Stoney Creek
22 June	Laura Secord's walk to Beaver Dam
24 June	Battle of Beaver Dam
26–28 July	Procter's forces fail to capture Fort Meigs
31 July	Americans again occupy York; Captain Robert Barclay lifts blockade of Presque Isle
1–4 August	Captain Oliver Perry takes his fleet out of Presque Isle
8 August	During the night, USS *Hamilton* and *Scourge* sink in Lake Ontario off Twelve Mile Creek
3 September	USS *Enterprise* captures HMS *Boxer*
10 September	Perry defeats Barclay in the battle of Lake Erie
27 September	Procter begins retreat from Fort Malden
5 October	Battle of the Thames (Moraviantown) and death of Tecumseh
7 October	Wellington invades France from Spain
25 October	Battle of Châteauguay
11 November	Battle of Crysler's Farm
10 December	Brigadier-General George McClure's forces burn Newark and retreat to Fort Niagara
19 December	British capture Fort Niagara and burn Lewiston
29 December	British forces burn Black Rock and Buffalo

1814

January	Russian and allied troops invade France; American delegates sail for Europe to open peace negotiations
30 March	Major-General James Wilkinson is defeated at Lacolle
31 March	The allies capture Paris
11 April	Napoleon abdicates
29 April	USS *Peacock* captures HMS *Epervier*
6 May	British raid Oswego; American forces capture Prairie du Chien and the British recapture it on 20 July
23 May–21 June	Treason trials at Ancaster, Upper Canada

2–5 June	William Clark, governor of Missouri Territory, takes possession of Prairie du Chien and begins to build Fort Shelby
3 July	Major-General Jacob Brown invades Upper Canada and captures Fort Erie
5 July	Battle of Chippawa
11 July	British invade Maine
19 July	American troops burn St David's, Upper Canada; British regain control of Prairie du Chien
25 July	Battle of Lundy's Lane
4–5 August	Lieutenant-Colonel George Croghan's attack on Michilimackinac fails
15 August	Lieutenant-General Gordon Drummond's assault on Fort Erie fails
19–25 August	British forces raid U.S. east coast, capture Washington, and burn public buildings
1 September	British seize part of eastern Maine; Prevost invades United States and reaches Plattsburgh on the 6TH; USS *Wasp* sinks HMS *Avon*
3–5 September	British capture USS *Tigress* and *Scorpion* on Lake Huron
11 September	Captain Thomas Macdonough defeats Captain George Downie in Plattsburgh Bay and Prevost retreats
12–15 September	British attack on Baltimore
17 September	Successful American sortie from Fort Erie against Drummond's batteries
5 November	Americans blow up Fort Erie and withdraw
10 December	British troops land near mouth of Mississippi River
24 December	Treaty of Ghent signed

1815
8 January	Battle of New Orleans
23 March	USS *Hornet* captures HMS *Penguin* in last naval action of the war.

The Military Careers of British and American Officers in the War of 1812

It may be useful to compare the dates of entry into military service, careers, and ages of the five British generals in this study with those of their chief American opponents.

1772 HENRY DEARBORN, age 19, was elected captain of a militia company; in 1775 his company was incorporated into the Revolutionary army, and he saw considerable active service. In 1812, as the senior major-general of the army, he was put in command of the northeast front by President Madison. Dearborn had trained as a physician.

1775 WILLIAM HULL, age 22, joined Revolutionary army as a militia captain and saw a good deal of combat service. In 1812 he accepted a commission as brigadier-general and command of the northwest army. He had trained as a lawyer.

1776 JAMES WILKINSON, age 19, was commissioned captain in the Revolutionary army. In 1813 he was commissioned major-general. As a young man he had studied medicine.

1779 PREVOST, age 12
      SHEAFFE, age 16

1780 or 1781 WADE HAMPTON, age 29 or 30, joined the Revolutionary army and by 1809 was a brigadier-general; he was appointed major-general in 1813. Hampton was a farmer with little formal education.

1782 DE ROTTENBURG, age 25

1785 BROCK, age 16

1786 STEPHEN VAN RENSSELAER, age 22, was commissioned major in New York State militia and rose to the rank of major-general. He was a well-educated politician and wealthy landowner.

1789   DRUMMOND, age 17

1791   WILLIAM HARRISON, age 18, joined the army as an ensign and resigned in 1798. He served as governor of Indiana in 1800–13 and commander of the mixed militia and regular force at the battle of Tippecanoe. Harrison was commissioned brigadier-general in the army in 1812 and major-general the following year. Later he would become ninth president of United States.

1792   SOLOMON VAN RENSSELAER, age 18, joined the army as cornet of cavalry; he was discharged in 1800. He returned to the army in 1812 as aide-de-camp to Major-General Stephen Van Rensselaer.

1794   GEORGE IZARD, age 18, after a military education in Europe, was commissioned second lieutenant in the army. He resigned in 1803, but returned in 1812 with a brigadier-general's commission.

1807   WINFIELD SCOTT, age 21, enlisted in the militia cavalry. In 1808 he was commissioned a captain of light artillery in the army. He had trained as a lawyer.

1808   ALEXANDER SMYTH, age 43, was commissioned a militia colonel. He was commissioned a brigadier-general in the army 1812. He had trained as a lawyer.

1809   JACOB BROWN, age 34, was given a militia command. In 1813 he was gazetted a brigadier-general in the regular army and shortly afterwards, major-general. He had no military education or training.

1812   ELEAZAR RIPLEY, age 30, entered army with a lieutenant-colonel's commission. He had trained as a lawyer.

NOTE: The main sources of information on the American commanders were *Dictionary of American Biography*; Gordon, *A Compilation of Registers of the Army of the United States from 1815 to 1837*; Peterson, *The Military Heroes of the War of 1812*; and Skelton, "High Army Leadership in the Era of the War of 1812."

Correspondence between
the Commander of the Forces and
Captain Downie

Major-General F.P. Robinson, commander, 1st Brigade, Chazy, to Captain Downie, 5 September 1811:

I am directed by His Excellency the Commander of the Forces to inform you of my arrival at this place, with Three Regiments of the First Brigade and request you will inform me in what way I can most usefully co-operate with you. (Adm. 1/5450, 185)

Lieutenant-General George Prevost, headquarters, Plattsburgh, to Captain Downie, commanding ships on the Richelieu, Wednesday, 7 a.m., 7 September:

The Enemy's force in the Bay consist [*sic*] of a Ship, inferior to the Confiance, a Brig – a large Schooner, a Sloop and seven or eight Gun Boats.

When the Gun boats are manned the remaining craft appear to have but few men left on board. – If you feel that the Vessels under your Command are equal to a contest with those I have described, you will find the present moment offers many advantages which may not again occur.

As my ulterior movements depend on your decision, you will have the goodness to favor me with it, with all possible promptitude.

P.S. In the event of your coming forward immediately, you will furnish conveyance for the two 8 Inch Mortars ordered from Isle aux Noix with their Stores, provided you can do so without delaying the sailing of your Squadron. (Adm. 1/5450, 187)

G. Downie, HMS *Confiance* off Ash Island, to Prevost at Plattsburgh, 7 September:

I have the honor of Your Excellency's letter of this Morning.

I am aware of the Comparative force of the Enemy, and am thus far on my way to find the Enemy; Conceiving that the moment I can put this Ship into State for Action I shall be able to meet them.

The Confiance is at this moment in such a state as to require at least a day or two to make her efficient before the Enemy; but with all the exertion I can make it will probably be that time at least, before I can get her up to Chazy, where I shall be happy to receive any further communication from Your Excellency. (CO 42/158, 201)

Prevost, headquarters, Plattsburgh, to Downie, at Point Au Fer, 8 September:

I have just received your reply to my Communication of yesterday.

As it is of the highest importance the Ship, Vessels and Gun Boats under your Command should commence a co-operation with the division of the Army now occupying Plattsburgh, I have sent my Aid de Camp Major Coore with this Letter, in order that you may obtain from him correct information of the disposition made by the Enemy of his Naval force in the Bay.

I only wait for your arrival to proceed against General McCombe's last position on the South bank of the Saranac. Your share in the operation in the first instance will be to destroy or to Capture the Enemy's Squadron, if it should wait for a Contest, and afterwards Co-operate with this division of the Army, but if it should run away and get out of your reach, we must meet here to consult on Ulterior Movements. (CO 42/158, 202)

Downie, HMS *Confiance*, Point Au Fer, to Prevost, Plattsburgh, 8 September:

I have the honor of Your Excellency's Letter of this day, to which I have to state that I am advancing with Squadron to Chazy as fast as the wind and weather will allow.

In the letter I did myself the Honor to address to you yesterday, I stated to you that this Ship is not ready. She is not ready now, and, until she is ready, it is my duty not to hazard the Squadron before an Enemy who will be superior in Force.

I purpose anchoring at Chazy until I am enabled to move which I trust will be very shortly, it depending upon my Guns being ready. (CO 42/158, 203)

Prevost, headquarters, Plattsburgh, to Downie, 9 September:

In consequence of your communication of yesterdays [*sic*] date, I have postponed moving on the Enemy's position on the South bank of the Saranac, until your Squadron is in a state of preparation to co-operate with the division of the Army.

I need not dwell with you on the Evils resulting to both Services from delay, as I am well convinced you have done everything in Your Power to accelerate the Armament and Equipment of Your Squadron, and I am also satisfied nothing will prevent its coming off Plattsburgh, the moment it is practicable.

I am happy to inform you that I find from Deserters who have come over from the Enemy that the American Fleet is insufficiently manned, and that a few days ago, after the arrival of the New Brig they sent on Shore for the Prisoners of all descriptions in charge of the Provost to make up a Crew for that Vessel.

Captain Watson of the Provincial Cavalry is directed to remain at little Chazy until you are preparing to get under-weigh, when he is instantly to return to this place with the intelligence. (CO 42/158, 204)

Downie, HMS *Confiance* off Little Chazy, to Prevost at Plattsburgh, 9 September:

I have the Honour to communicate to Your Excellency that it is my intention to Weigh and proceed from this Anchorage about Midnight, in the Expectation of rounding into the Bay of Plattsburgh about dawn of day, and commence an immediate attack upon the Enemy, if they should be found Anchored in a position that will offer a chance of success. I rely on any assistance you can afford the Squadron.

In manning the Flotilla & Ships, finding we are many short, I have made application to the Officer Commanding at Chazy for a Company of the 39th Regiment.

I have the honour of Your Excellency's letter of this morning, to which the preceding is a full answer. (CO 42/158, 205)

Prevost, headquarters, Plattsburgh, to Downie, 10 September:

I received at twelve last night your letter acquainting me with your determination to get under weigh about that time, in expectation of rounding Cumberland Head at dawn of day. In consequence the Troops have been held in readiness since 6 o'clock this morning to storm the Enemy's Works at nearly the same moment as the Naval Action should commence in the Bay.

I ascribe the disappointment I have experienced to the unfortunate change of wind, & shall rejoice to learn that my reasonable expectations have been frustrated by no other cause. (CO 42/158, 206)

NOTE: Correspondence found in *SBD* 3: pt 1, 379–83, 466–7; originals in NA, MG 12, Adm. 1/5450, and MG 11, CO 42/158.

Prevost's Reports to Earl Bathurst

Prevost, headquarters, Plattsburgh, to Bathurst, Downing Street, 11 September 1814:

Upon the arrival of the Reinforcements from the Garronne I lost no time in assembling three Brigades on the Frontier of Lower Canada extending from the River Richelieu to the St. Lawrence and in forming them into a Division under the command of Major general de Rottenburg for the purpose of carrying into effect His Royal Highness the Prince Regents [*sic*] commands which had been conveyed to me by Your Lordship in Your Dispatch of the 3rd June last.

As the Troops concentrated and approached the Line of Separation between this Province and the United States, the American Army abandoned its entrenched Camp on the River Chazy at Champlain, a position I immediately seized & occupied in force on the 3rd Inst., the following day the whole of the left Division advanced to the Village of Chazy without meeting the least opposition from the Enemy.

On the 5th it halted within Eight Miles of this place having surmounted the difficulties created by the obstructions in the Road from the felling of Trees and the removal of Bridges. The next day the Division moved upon Plattsburgh in two Columns on parallel Roads – The Right Column led by Major Genl Power's Brigade supported by four Companies of Light Infantry and a demi Brigade under Major Genl Robinson – The Left by Major Genl Brisbanes [*sic*] Brigade.

The Enemy's Militia supported by his Regulars attempted to impede the Advance of the Right Column but they were driven before it from all their positions and the Column entered Plattsburgh – This rapid movement having reversed the strong position taken up by the Enemy at dead Creek it was precipitately abandoned by him and his Gunboats alone left to defend the Ford and to prevent our restoring the Bridges which had been imperfectly destroyed, an inconvenience soon surmounted.

Here I found the Enemy in the occupation of an Elevated Ridge of Land on the South Branch of the Saranac crowned with three Strong Redoubts and other Field Works, and Block Houses armed with heavy Ordnance, with their Flotilla at Anchor, out of Gun Shot from Shore, consisting of a Ship, a Brig, a Schooner, a Sloop and Ten Gun Boats.

I immediately communicated this circumstance to Captain Downie who had been recently appointed to command the Vessels on Lake Champlain, consisting of a Ship, a Brig, two Sloops and Twelve Gun Boats, and requested his co-operation and in the mean time Batteries were constructed for the Guns brought from the Rear.

On the Morning of the 11th our Flotilla was seen over the Isthmus which joins Cumberland Head with the Mainland, Steering for Plattsburgh Bay, I immediately ordered that part of the Brigade under Major General Robinson which had been brought forward consisting of four Light Infantry Companies – 3rd Battn 27th And 76th Regts and Major Genl Power's Brigade, consisting of the 3rd, 5th – 1st Battn 27th And 58th Regts to force the Ford of the Saranac and advance provided with scaling Ladders to escalade the Enemy's Works upon the Heights, this force was placed under the Command of M. General Robinson – The Batteries opened their fire the instant the Ships Engaged.

It is now with deep concern I inform Your Lordship that notwithstanding the intrepid Valor with which Captain Downie led his Flotilla into Action my most sanguine hopes of complete success were not long after blasted by a combination, as it appeared to us, of unfortunate events to which Naval Warfare is peculiarly exposed – Scarcely had His Majesty's Troops forced a passage across the Saranac and ascended the Heights on which stand the Enemy's works when I had the extreme Mortification to hear the Shouts of Victory from the Enemy's Works in consequence of the British Flag being lowered on board the Confiance and Linnet, and to see our Gun Boats seeking their safety in flight. – This unlooked for Event depriving me of the Co-operation of the Fleet without which the further Prosecution of the Service was become impracticable, I did not hesitate to arrest the course of the Troops advancing to the attack, because the most complete success would have been unavailing, and the possession of the Enemy's Works offered no advantage to compensate for the loss we must have sustained in acquiring Possession of them.

I have ordered the Batteries to be dismantled the Guns withdrawn, and the Baggage with the wounded Men who can be removed, to be sent to the rear in order that the Troops may return to Chazy tomorrow, and on the following day to Champlain, where I propose to halt until I have ascertained the use the Enemy propose making of the Naval ascendancy they have acquired on Lake Champlain.

I have the honor to transmit herewith returns of the Loss sustained by the Left Division of this Army in its advance to Plattsburgh and in forcing a passage across the River Saranac. (CO 42/157, 187–9)

Prevost, Montreal, to Bathurst, 22 September:

Private
My Lord

In my Dispatch from Plattsburgh of the 11th Inst. I reported to Your Lordship the unfortunate event which induced me to withdraw the troops with which I had advanced into the Enemy's Territory – My reasons for that measure I can more fully explain to Your Lordship in a private communication than it might be proper to do in a public letter.

Your Lordship must have been aware from my previous despatches that no Offensive Operations could be carried on within the Enemy's Territory for the destruction of his Naval Establishments without Naval Support. Having ascertained that our Flotilla in the Richelieu was in every respect equal to the Enemy's, & having received from its Commander the assurance not only of his readiness, but of his ability to co-operate with the Army, I did not hesitate in advancing to Plattsburgh, & Confidently relying upon the successful exertions of the Squadron, I made my arrangements for the assault of the Enemy's Works, the moment it should appear.

The disastrous and unlooked for result of the Naval Contest by depriving me of the only means by which I could avail myself of any advantage I might gain, rendered a perseverance in the attack of the Enemy's position highly imprudent, as well as hazardous.

From the state of the roads Each days [sic] delay at Plattsburgh made my retreat more difficult.

The Enemy's Militia was raising En Masse around me, desertion encreasing [sic] & the Supply of Provisions Scanty.

Excluded from the advantage of water conveyance, & that by roads passing through Woods & over Swamps becoming, from the State of the weather as well as from the obstructions made by the Enemy nearly impassable.

Under the circumstances I had to determine whether I should consider my own Fame by gratifying the Ardor of the Troops in persevering in the Attack, or consult the more substantial interests of my Country by withdrawing the Army which was yet uncrippled for the security of these Provinces.

The most ample success on shore after the loss of the Flotilla could not have justified the sacrifice I must have made to obtain it.

Had I failed, & such an event was possible after the American Army had been cheered by the sight of a Naval Victory, the destruction of a great part of my Troops must have been the consequence, & with the remainder I should have had to make a precipitate and embarrassed retreat, one very different from that which I have made.

These are considerations, which without doubt will have their own due weight with Your Lordship, & induce you, I trust, to view the measures I have adopted, as those best calculated to promote, as well, the honor of His Majesty's Arms, as the safety of this part of his Dominions.

I herewith transmit a Comparative state of the force of the two Squadrons, in order that Your Lordship may be satisfied with my reasons for not discouraging a Naval Contest, in which if all had done their duty I might have had a very different report to make.

Enclosure

Comparative State of the Flotilla's [*sic*] on Lake Champlain on the 11th Septr. 1814.

English	Guns	American	Guns
Ship Confiance	36	Ship Saratoga	26
Brig Linnet	18	Brig Surprise	20
Sloop Chub	10	Schooner Thunderer	16
Sloop	10	Sloop Preble	7
Gun Boats 12 Carrying	16	Gun Boats 10 Carrying	14
Total	90		83

(CO 42/157, 209–12)

NOTE: Reports in *SBD*, 3: pt 1, 350–3, 364–6; originals in NA, MG 11, CO 42/157.

Abbreviations Used in the Sources

ADC aide-de-camp

AO Archives of Ontario

BECHS Buffalo and Erie County Historical Society

CHR *Canadian Historical Review*

CO Colonial Office

DCB *Dictionary of Canadian Biography*

DGO district general order

DHC *Documentary History of the Campaigns upon the Niagara Frontier*

DNB *Dictionary of National Biography*

DO district order

DRIC *Documents Relating to the Invasion of Canada*

GO general order

JSAHR *Journal of the Society for Army Historical Research*

MG manuscript group

MGO militia general order

MHR *Michigan Historical Review*

NA National Archives of Canada

NHS Niagara Historical Society

OH Ontario Historical Society, *Papers and Records*; subsequently *Ontario History*

PBHS *Publications of the Buffalo Historical Society*

PRO Public Record Office, London

RG record group

SBD *Select British Documents of the Canadian War of 1812*

TRL Toronto Reference Library

WO War Office

Notes

PREFACE

1 William Thomas designed the existing Brock monument; for a description of the memorial, including its architectural aspects, see G. McArthur and A. Szamosi, *William Thomas, Architect, 1799–1860* (Archives of Canadian Art, Guelph, Ont.: Ampersand Printing, 1996), 93–9.

2 Information gathered by Professor Carl Wolff of the History Department, Brock University. For the inscription see Brenton, *Some Account*, appendix 34.

3 Hitsman, *Incredible War*, 24.

4 On Sherbrooke see *DCB*, 6: 712–16, and Stanley, *War of 1812*, chap. 13.

5 Stanley, *War of 1812*, is the best recent history; see especially 222, 239–40, 344–50, 403–4. See also Graves, *Battle of Lundy's Lane*, especially chap. 14. Whitehorne, *While Washington Burned*, 76–7, 90–2, offers a few comments.

6 On Procter see *DCB*, 6: 616–18; on Vincent, 7: 888–9; on Riall, 7: 744–6; on Harvey, 8: 374–84.

7 On Baynes see chapter 2 below; on Beckwith, *DCB*, 6: 38–9.

8 Two studies provide excellent starting points for Native perspectives and leadership: Allen, *His Majesty's Indian Allies*; and Richard White, *The Middle Ground: Indians, Empires and Republics in the Great Lakes Region, 1650–1815* (New York: Cambridge University Press, 1991).

9 *British Military History*, 163; see also 170: "No one has attempted a major study ... of the attitudes of officers to the service and to their profession, let alone of their larger world view."

INTRODUCTION

1 Mahon, *War of 1812*, viii. This introduction is based principally on secondary sources, in particular Mahon; Stanley, *War of 1812*; *Naval War of*

1812, vols. 1 and 2; and Turner, *War of 1812*. Hickey, *War of 1812*, was of limited use.

2 Adams, *History of the United States of America*, 3: 224; Hickey, *War of 1812*, 255.

3 Weigley, *History of the United States Army*, 115, 120–1, 566; Mahon, *War of 1812*, 4, 9, 27, 32, 100n, 332–5; Stanley, *War of 1812*, 63–4. See also chapter 2 below.

4 I want to thank Jim Burant, chief of Art Acquisition at the National Archives of Canada, for providing information about the painter and the engraver.

CHAPTER ONE

1 Goodspeed, *British Campaigns in the Peninsula*, 75, 97, 129, 208, 213, 219. Michael Glover, in *Wellington as Military Commander*, 28, is critical of the army's performance up to 1808; on its commanding officers see chaps 1 and 10. See also *Wellington at War*, 246n, 265–6, 311, 312n. Sherwig, *Guineas and Gunpowder*, introd.

2 Goodspeed, *British Campaigns in the Peninsula*, 71–3, 138, 164, 206, 212, 214–17; Fuller, *Conduct of War*, 57–8; M. Glover, *Wellington*, 75, 83, 87–9, 93–4, 105–7, 114, 181, 248–9; R.F. Delderfield, *Imperial Sunset. The Fall of Napoleon, 1813–14* (London: Hodder & Stoughton, 1969).

3 M. Glover, *Wellington*, 205. See also George Bell, *Rough Notes of an Old Soldier during Fifty Years' Service* (2 vols., London: Day & Sons, 1867), 1: 165; cited by Rothenberg, *Art of Warfare*, 173–4; also Bruce, *Purchase System*, 76.

4 M. Glover, *Wellington*, 205; immediately afterwards Glover writes, "The hope was not realised."

5 Brett-James, *Life in Wellington's Army*, 257n, 253, 257.

6 For these officers see M. Glover, *Wellington*, 126 (General John Murray), 205, 210, 225, 227 (General J. Slade), 224 (Lieutenant-Colonel Barton); for examples of inadequate commanders superior to Wellington, see 65–8 (Lieutenant-General Sir Harry Burrard, Lieutenant-General Sir Hew Dalrymple).

7 Bruce, *Purchase System*, 76–82, 167; see also Preston, Wise, and Werner, *Men in Arms*, 201; Luvaas, *Education of an Army*, 3–5; M. Glover, *Wellington*, chap. 10.

8 R. Glover, *Peninsular Preparation*, 194; de Watteville, *British Soldier*, 179, 181–2. A slightly more favourable view of the officers is presented by John Houlding, in *Fit for Service*, chap. 9, and by S.G.P. Ward, in *Wellington's Headquarters*, chap. 4.

9 M. Glover, *Wellington*, 214.

10 R. Glover, *Peninsular preparation*, chap. 7; de Watteville, *British Soldier*, chap. 9; Rothenberg, *Art of Warfare*, 13, 179; *Makers of Modern Strategy*, 55, 97; Spiers, *Army and Society*, 26–7, 60–3; Whitfield, *Tommy Atkins*, 74,

also 43–57 (on alcohol) and 59–71 (on desertion); Farwell, *For Queen and Country*, 179–80 (on neglect of medical needs).

11 Rothenberg, *Art of Warfare*, 174. Brett-James, *Life in Wellington's Army*, 269–70, cites a letter from Wellington to Lord Bathurst of 2 July 1813 in which he states, "We have in the service the scum of the earth as common soldiers." By contrast, the soldiers of the American army, according to J.C.A. Stagg, were "men of largely respectable social status" (see "Enlisted men in the United States Army," 615–45).

12 Spiers, *Army and Society*, 52–5; on 14 he presents evidence that officers also were not well remunerated. See also Anderson, *Life of ... H.R.H. Edward, Duke of Kent*, 154–6; R. Glover, *Peninsular Preparation*, 174–8 and chap. 9; Luvaas, 3–4, 54–5.

13 Rothenberg, *Art of Warfare*, 87–8. Army regulations stipulated twelve wives per company on foreign garrison service, ten wives per company on domestic service, and six wives per company on foreign active service; the last applied to North America. I appreciate Don Graves's comments on this point. David Owen, in *Fort Erie (1764–1823)*, 10–15, by describing barrack life in Fort Erie, gives an idea of the lives of the rank and file in British North America. On 15–17 he describes the officers' quarters, which point up the contrast.

14 This paragraph relies heavily on Spiers, *Army and Society*, 60–3, 87–8. See also de Watteville, *British Soldier*, 116–21; Wellington's comment of 28 November 1812 in Brett-James, *Life in Wellington's Army*, 254; Whitfield, *Tommy Atkins*, 72–93; M. Glover, *Wellington*, 243–5; and Anderson, *Life of ... Edward, Duke of Kent*, 14–16.

15 Spiers, *Army and Society*, 26–7, 87, particularly the opinion of John Shipp, which he cites. See also de Watteville, *British Soldier*, 116–19; and R. Glover, *Peninsular Preparation*, chap. 7.

16 According to John Houlding, two-thirds of commissions in the British army were held by purchase; see *Fit for Service*, 100–5. See also Bruce, *Purchase System*, 42–6, 53–5, 167–8.

17 M. Glover, "Purchase of Commissions." Glover writes that his "analysis of promotions during the Peninsular War, shows that purchase accounted for only two in 10 of all promotions, that regimental seniority dictated seven out of 10 (without money passing) and the remaining 10 per cent were decided by what could loosely be described as patronage." Also relevant are Spiers, *Army and Society*, chap. 1; Bruce, *Purchase System*, chaps 1 and 2; R. Glover, *Peninsular Preparation*, chap. 6; McGuffie, "Significance of Military Rank," 207–24. Hansen, "War of 1812," 39, writes that the American army's system of promotion by seniority also created leadership problems.

18 Rothenberg, *Art of Warfare*, 174, 176. This is a principal theme in Spiers, *Army and Society*. See also Harris, *Canadian Brass*, 3–7. For a less-critical view, see Ward, *Wellington's Headquarters*, 62–5.

19 Bruce, *Purchase System*, 79, citing *Report of the Commissioners appointed to Inquire into the System of Purchase and Sale of Commissions* (1857), 18 (2267): 3377; see also 68–70, 80–2. Also Luvaas, *Education of an Army*, 4, 43–4, 55–7.

20 M. Glover, *Wellington*, 14. See also R. Glover, *Peninsular Preparation*, 14–29; Rogers, *Wellington's Army*, 82–3.

21 Farwell, *For Queen and Country*, 18 gives a total of thirteen departments. Whitfield, *Tommy Atkins*, 8–40, writes that the number ranged from five to thirteen, but she identifies eleven departments or officials. Besides these two sources, this section draws upon R. Glover, *Peninsula Preparation*, 15–45; M. Glover, *Wellington*, chap. 1; and Ward, *Wellington's Headquarters*, chap. 1.

22 "Horse-Guards, a public building situated in Parliament street Westminster, which is so called from a guard having been originally mounted there by the Horse-Guards" (Charles James's contemporary definition, cited in Whitfield, *Tommy Atkins*, 8). There was no commander-in-chief between 1783 and 1793. For the period of most concern to this study, the commanders-in-chief were Frederick Augustus, Duke of York (1795–1809 and 1811–27) and David Dundas (1809–11). See Ward, *Wellington's Headquarters*, 10–13, 16–19.

23 Whitfield, *Tommy Atkins*, 29.

24 M. Glover, *Wellington*, 232: "The Royal Artillery represented the only large body of professionally trained officers in the Peninsular Army." On the competence of these officers, see 234–5. See also Ward, *Wellington's Headquarters*, 6–9. The number of artillery and engineer officers was not large: in 1812 there were 837 "commissioned men" in the Royal Artillery, 65 in the Royal Artillery Drivers, and 221 Royal Engineers. The total of all commissioned officers in the British army was just under 11,000. See McGuffie, "Significance of Military rank," 216–17.

25 R. Glover, *Peninsular Preparation*, 90; for technological improvements, see chaps 2, 3, and 4.

26 He held this post again from 1811 to 1827; Preston, Wise, and Werner, *Men in Arms*, 191. See also Bruce, *Purchase System*, 167–8. Glover, in *Wellington*, 16, praises the duke as "an excellent administrator and a clear-headed and conscientious staff officer … [who] made the army into an efficient fighting machine"; see also 28–32. Also Thoumine, *Scientific Soldier*, 39–40.

27 R. Glover, *Peninsular Preparation*, 153. See also Bruce, *Purchase System*, 42–3, 46, 53, 167–8.

28 R. Glover, *Peninsular Preparation*, 121–2. He gives the example of Adjutant General Fawcett writing to Major-General Ainslie in July 1795.

29 R. Glover, *Peninsular Preparation*, 122; see also 142. Also Holmes, *Firing Line*, 28, chap. 2.

30 R. Glover, *Peninsular Preparation*, 125–9, 141–2; Falls, *Art of War*, 39; de Watteville, *British Soldier*, 95; Preston, Wise, and Werner, *Men in Arms*, 182; Rogers, *Wellington's Army*, 30–4, 39–40.

31 Examples of officers being dismissed ("superseded being absent without leave") may be found in NA, RG 8, I, C series, v. 1170, 248–56, GO of 17 June 1813, referring to Lieutenant Crooke of the 99th Foot and Lieutenant Carter of the 100th Foot; v. 1171, 181–85, GO of 7 February 1814, Ensign F. Johnson of the 89th Foot.

32 R. Glover, *Peninsular Preparation*, 151–2, chap. 7, 194–210. A college for officer training opened on 4 May 1799 and received its royal warrant in 1801; see Thoumine, *Scientific Soldier*, chaps 6, 8, and Ward, *Wellington's Headquarters*, 24–7. In the United States, West Point had been founded in 1802, and its influence on the army's officer corps was just beginning to be felt; see Skelton, "High Army Leadership," 259–60.

33 M. Glover, *Wellington*, 29.

34 R. Glover, *Peninsular Preparation*, 43.

35 M. Glover, *Wellington*, 251–2.

36 R. Glover, *Peninsular Preparation*, 43–4, 126, 139–40, 142, 167. Another example of the Duke of York's efforts to increase the capabilities of the British army was his establishment in 1800 of a training camp for riflemen under Lieutenant-Colonel William Stewart and Colonel Coote Manningham; see *Peninsular Preparation*, 130–1, 159.

37 Thoumine, *Scientific Soldier*, 67–102.

38 R. Glover, *Peninsular Preparation*, 44, 83, 128–9, 194–5, Falls, *Art of War*, 28–30; Houlding, *Fit for Service*, chap. 9.

39 Rogers, *British Army of the Eighteenth Century*, 70, 74; R. Glover, *Peninsular Preparation*, 119–22, 128–9, 139. For criticisms of Dundas's manual, see Luvaas, *Education of an Army*, 45–6, 45n10.

40 Houlding, *Fit for Service*, 234–7. There were several editions. The one I have consulted was published in Quebec City by John Neilson, probably in 1804, and has inserted after the title-page a circular issued by Adjutant General Sir Henry Calvert dated 25 May 1807.

41 R. Glover, *Peninsular Preparation*, 92, 118; Houlding, *Fit for Service*, 236–47. *Principles* was revised in 1792, and according to Houlding, this version survived "as the foundation of British infantry drill down to the Crimean War."

42 R. Glover, *Peninsular Preparation*, 23, 37–39, 109, 118–19, 185; Thoumine, *Scientific Soldier*, chap. 8.

43 Cited in R. Glover, *Peninsular Preparation*, 160.

44 Ibid., 161.

45 Hansen, "War of 1812," 36–7, provides one of the most recent expressions.

46 Cited in Rogers, *Wellington's Army*, 105; see also Blumenson and Stokesbury, *Masters of the Art of Command*, 143–6.

47 Wavell, *Generals and Generalship.* 5; Liddell Hart, "What is Military Genius?" 60, presents a slightly different version of this remark: "that calm courage in the midst of tumult, that security of soul in danger, which the English call a cool head."

48 Wavell, *Generals and Generalship,* 6–7; see also Burne, *Art of War on Land,* 7–8, 224; Falls, *Art of War,* 14–15.

49 On Wellington see Brett-James, *Life in Wellington's Army,* 246, 265–6, 266n, 311, 312n. Horatio Nelson should be included in this group. See Wavell, *Generals and Generalship,* 4–5, 9, 12, 15; Keegan, *Mask of Command,* 99–100, 114–6, 152–4, 329–31.

50 Holmes, *Firing Line,* 322, citing "Ensign John Colborne, later Field-Marshal Lord Seaton."

51 Wavell, *Generals and Generalship,* 2; Sixsmith, *British Generalship,* 26, 225, 227, 253; M. Glover, *Wellington,* 211; Holmes, *Firing Line,* chap. 4, 28, 340–1.

52 Rothenberg, *Art of Warfare,* 133, 82.

53 Holmes, in *Firing Line,* 348, writes that in the "horse and musket period" the percentage of officer casualties was usually greater than their proportion of the forces engaged; he provides figures. See also M. Glover, *Wellington,* chap. 10; Keegan, *Mask of Command,* 114–6.

54 Fuller, *Conduct of War,* 52; Liddell Hart, "What Is Military Genius?" 59–61; M. Glover, *Wellington,* 126–7, 130–1, 137, 211; Wavell, *Generals and Generalship,* 6, 8, 12, 18; Falls, *Art of War,* 14, 221; Sixsmith, *British Generalship,* 9, 26–8, 227, 236, 269–70, 292; Blumenson and Stokesbury, *Masters of the Art of Command,* 348–51.

55 Hart, "What Is Military Genius?" 60. See also Fuller, *Generalship,* 29, 70–2, 77; Burne, *Art of War on Land,* 145, 224; Sixsmith, *British Generalship,* 148–9.

56 See Fuller, *Generalship,* 31; Sixsmith, *British Generalship,* 93, 97, 110–12, 156, 227; R. Glover, *Peninsular Preparation,* 162–3; Blumenson and Stokesbury, *Masters of the Art of Command,* 2–3, 139–46; Rogers, *British Army,* 106; Luvaas, *Education of an Army,* 27–8, citing Major-General Sir William Napier.

57 R. Glover, *Peninsular Preparation,* 162–63. See also M. Glover, *Wellington,* 251–2; Carroll and Baxter, *American Military Tradition,* 44–5, 51–2.

58 Fuller, *Conduct of War,* 45–6.

59 Brett-James, *Life in Wellington's Army,* 169–70; see also 198–9, 200–1, 211–12, 212n, 223–3, 252–5, 257–8, 257n, 290–1; also Hitsman, *Incredible War,* 219–20, citing Lieutenant William Grattan on the Duke of Wellington; Goodspeed, *British Campaigns,* 63, 97, 129, 170. Napoleon's expressed views about the treatment of soldiers did not always coincide with his actions. For some of his opinions see Fuller, *Conduct of War,* 46–7.

60 Cited in *Taking Command*, 194. On Wellington see M. Glover, *Wellington*, 251–2.

61 Cited in Rogers, *British Army*, 105. On Marlborough see Rogers, 116–23; Wavell, *Generals and Generalship*, 14–15; Chandler, *Art of Warfare*, 133.

62 Fuller, *Generalship*, 21; Preston, Wise, and Werner, *Men in Arms*, 182; Wavell, *Generals and Generalship*, 13–19. *Taking Command*, chap. 13, as well as elsewhere, presents a modern American interpretation of discipline and military leadership; see especially the discussion on 179–80.

63 Graves, *Red Coats & Grey Jackets*, 51–4; Hansen, "War of 1812," 2, 36–7.

64 Fuller, *Generalship*, 50; Fuller discusses the age factor on 31–2, 48–52, 62–6, 87–9. See also Ward, *Wellington's Headquarters*, 62; Sixsmith, *British Generalship*, 30; Wavell, *Generals and Generalship*, 5–6.

65 Hitsman, *Incredible War*, 239, 255. Hitsman says of this source, "the book was badly written and citing the wrong issue of the *Quarterly Review* was merely one factual error which did not help its case" (239). See also Lucas, *Canadian War of 1812*, 110, and Peter Burrough's opinion in *DCB*, 5: 697.

66 It is unfortunate that Hyatt's thesis has not been published. Sutherland's is titled "The Civil Administration of Sir George Prevost, 1811–1815: A Study in Conciliation." It can be seen that neither is a biography or a full study of Prevost's career.

CHAPTER TWO

1 *DCB*, 5: 693–5; *DNB*, 16: 320–1; Everest, *War of 1812*, 199–201; Mahon, *War of 1812*, 15–7, 328.

2 Stanley, *War of 1812*, 214–15, 226, 348–51, 416; Hitsman, *Incredible War*, 220–1, 228, 231; Hitsman, "Sir George Prevost's Conduct," 34, 38–9, 42. Robert Christie, in *Military and Naval Operations in the Canadas* (1818), hesitated to criticize Prevost's conduct of the campaign, but in his later work, published in 1849, he was less reluctant; see his *History of the Late Province of Lower Canada*, 2: 112–14, 215–16, 242–5. The early and harsh published strictures appeared as letters from Samuel Gale and Veritas in the *Montreal Herald*, both subsequently turned into pamphlets, and in 1822 an article in the *Quarterly Review* of London.

3 Hyatt, "Defence of Upper Canada in 1812," 31, 93–5, 116–18, 122. See also Everest, *War of 1812*, 114–16.

4 On Prevost's father, Major General Augustine Prevost, see *DNB*, 16: 320; Brenton, *Some Account*, 4–5.

5 Brenton, *Some Account*, 5–6; *DCB*, 5: 693–8; *DNB*, 16: 320–1. On Lewis Lochée's Military Academy see Houlding, *Fit for Service*, 220 and n151, 253–4.

6 Suggested by Peter Burroughs in *DCB*, 5: 693.

7 See Duffy, *Soldiers, Sugar, and Seapower.*

8 Cited in Brenton, *Some Account,* appendix 5, 17–18.

9 Cited in ibid., 8 and appendices 6 and 7; see also Fortescue, *History of the British Army,* 5: 182–4.

10 Brenton, *Some Account,* 9–10 and appendices 9, 10, 11; Fortescue, *History of the British Army,* 5: 245–8.

11 While in England, Prevost caused Charles-Michel de Salaberry some difficulties with his recruiting efforts. See Anderson, *Life of ... Edward, Duke of Kent.* The correspondence is extensive: see 104–7, 114–15, 118–20, 144.

12 Brenton, *Some Account,* 9–11 and appendix 17; Fortescue, *History of the British Army,* 7: 12–17.

13 *DCB,* 5: 693–4; Brenton, *Some Account,* 7–11 and appendices 12, 13, 14, 15, 18, 19, 20.

14 Hyatt, "Defence of Upper Canada in 1812," 16–17; *SBD,* 1: 165–6.

15 On Craig see *DCB,* 5: 205–14. For Mountain see *DCB,* 6: 523–9. Members of the English-speaking minority who influenced Craig included John Young (*DCB,* 5: 877–83), John Richardson (*DCB,* 6: 639–47), Stephen Sewell (*DCB,* 6: 700–3), Jonathan Sewell (d. 1839), and Herman W. Ryland (d. 1838).

16 On Bédard, see *DCB,* 6: 41–9; Ouellet, *Economic and Social History of Quebec,* 234–6; Sutherland, "Civil Administration," chaps 1 and 2; *Canadian State Trials,* 1: 324–31, 336–41, 348–9, 416–17.

17 For details of Prevost's measures see Hitsman, *Incredible War,* 27–8; Ouellet, *Economic and Social History of Quebec,* 235–7; and Sutherland, "Civil Administration," chaps 1 and 4. For the politicians concerned see *DCB,* 5: 648–52 (J.-A. Panet); 6: 68–70 (François Blanchet); 80–3 (Louis Bourdages); 585–6 (J.-B. Planté); 750–1 (Jean-Thomas Taschereau); 7: 503–5 (Joseph Le Vasseur Borgia); 9: 806–17 (Denis-Benjamin Viger). On Bishop Plessis see *DCB,* 6: 586–99; *Canadian State Trials,* 1: 349–51, 355.

18 For conflicting views see Ouellet, 237–42, and Sutherland, "Civil Administration," chapter 2 and 134, 152–3, 159. See also Guitard, *Militia of the Battle of Châteauguay,* 16; Allen, "The Bisshopp Papers," 23–4, 19 October 1812.

19 *SBD,* 1: 166–7. R. Christie, *Memoirs,* 36, gives the date of 26 September for Prevost's visit to the Montreal District and nearby forts, while Hitsman, *Incredible War,* 28, places it in October.

20 NA, RG 8, v.1218, 308, Prevost to Liverpool, 15 July 1812; Tupper, *Life and Correspondence,* 132–3, Baynes to Brock, 12 December 1811. The corps was placed on the army establishment in October 1812; see Hitsman, *Incredible War,* 33–4, 111.

21 Hitsman, *Incredible War,* 35–6; *SBD,* 3: 651–7 and 1: 339; Lépine, *Officiers de milice du Bas-Canada,* 13–14, 31–2. On Salaberry see *DCB,* 6: 341–5, and Wohler, *Charles de Salaberry.*

22 NA, MG 24, G 45, v.3, 1766–69, Salaberry to Governor General, 27 October 1812; v.2, 1008–11, Salaberry to his father, 26 October. Salaberry gives the figure of 300.

23 NA, MG 24, G 45, v.2, 1112–15, Salaberry to his father, 13 November 1812. Difficulties over Salaberry's rank continued throughout the war. It was not until 25 March 1813 that he received the rank of lieutenant-colonel of the Voltigeurs and not until July 1814 that that rank in the army was confirmed. See DCB, 6: 342.

24 R. Christie, *Memoirs*, 37–40; Brenton, *Some Account*, 19–20.

25 Wallot, "Émeute à Lachine," 112–37, 202–32; *Canadian State Trials*, 1: 351–5; Sutherland, "Civil Administration," 33–4.

26 Wallot, "Émeute à Lachine," 213–32; Ouellet, *Economic and Social History of Quebec*, 231–4, 241–2; R. Christie, *Memoirs*, 41–4. The text of the act is given in SBD, 1: 210–26.

27 Hyatt, "Defence of Upper Canada," 20–2, 29; Hitsman, *Incredible War*, 246–7.

28 Hitsman, *Safeguarding Canada*, 82; Hyatt, "Defence of Upper Canada," 20–2, 24, 27, 29, 31. TRL, Baldwin Room, Prevost Military Papers, letterbooks 1, 2, and 3. Prevost's correspondence with Sherbrooke demonstrates his wider responsibilities and concerns.

29 Cited in Hitsman, *Incredible War*, 246–7. Lord Liverpool was secretary until June, when Bathurst took over the office. See also DHC, 3: 120, Prevost to Brock, 10 July 1812.

30 NA, RG 8, v.1218, 308. See also DHC, 3: 120–1, Prevost to Brock, 10 July; 114, Baynes to Brock, 8 July; and 113, Prevost to Brock, 7 July.

31 Bell, *A Short Essay on Military First Principles* (London, 1770), cited in *George Washington's Opponents*, 66–7; see also xxvl, 53–4, 57, 65–7, 184–5. Also Rothenburg, *Art of Warfare*, 13, 147–8; Ward, *Wellington's Headquarters*, 66–7, 132.

32 *George Washington's Opponents*, introduction and the chapters on these men. Howe was commander-in-chief in America from 1775 to 1778, Clinton from 1778 to 1782, and Carleton from 1782 to 1783. On Carleton see also DCB, 5: 140–55.

33 *George Washington's Opponents*, 53, quotes Sir William Howe in 1779: "The most essential duty I had to perform was not wantonly to commit his majesty's troops where the object was inadequate. I knew well that any considerable loss sustained by the army could not speedily, nor easily, be repaired."

34 SBD, 1: 292–3, Brock to Prevost, 6 February 1812; 355, same to same, 12 July; NA, RG 8, v.1218, 308–12, Prevost to Liverpool, 15 July; v.1219, 16, Prevost to Bathurst, 17 August; DHC, 3: 154–5, Prevost to Brock, 31 July; 167–9, same to same, 12 August; DCB, 7: 888–9, on Vincent.

35 NA, MG 13, WO 17, 1516, 5, 66, 81, 95, 109. Here are the monthly totals of rank and file at Fort George out of the total in Canada: in January, 932 out of 5,047; in June, 921 out of 5,720; in July, 898 out of 6,456; in August, 898 out of 7,570; in September, 890 out of 7,556. These numbers did not change significantly during the remainder of 1812. The returns were always dated on the 25th of the month. The figures exclude officers, sergeants, and drummers, and these categories could add one-eighth to the total number; see M. Glover, *Wellington*, 20.

36 *DHC*, 3: 113–15, Prevost to Brock, 7 July 1812, and Baynes to Brock, 8 July; Hitsman, *Incredible War*, 54–6.

37 *SBD*, 1: 428, Baynes to Roberts, 25 June 1812.

38 *DHC*, 3: 120–1, Prevost to Brock, 10 July 1812; NA, RG 8, v.1218, 308–9, Prevost to Liverpool, 15 July. For other measures taken to bolster Lower Canada's defences, see proclamations and orders in *Montreal Herald*, 4 July; Stanley, *War of 1812*, 76–9.

39 *SBD*, 1: 406, Prevost to Brock, 31 July 1812; 232, Bathurst to Prevost, 10 August; NA, MG 24, A 1, 48–53, Prevost to Brock, 2 August, "Private and Confidential." Prevost credited the British minister to the United States, Augustus J. Foster, with suggesting both the negotiation of a truce and a strictly defensive posture towards the that country. See *DHC*, 3: 169, Dearborn to Major-General Amos Hall or Commanding Officer on the Niagara Frontier, 8 August; 172, Baynes to Brock, 13 August; 181, Secretary of War to Dearborn, 15 August; Everest, *War of 1812*, 58–61. For a Canadian view of American military preparations, see *Montreal Herald*, 8 August. The adjutant general's job was to relieve his commanding officer of detailed work. He was the general's chief administrator, but in this war he might be called upon to assume combat responsibilities. See Hitsman, *Incredible War*, 29; Ward, *Wellington's Headquarters*, chap. 2.

40 Hitsman, in *Incredible War*, 78 and 80–2, 95, sees advantages, as does Horsman, in *War of 1812*, 42–3. Disadvantages are stressed by Tupper, *Life and Correspondence*, 285, 294–7, and Lucas, *Canadian War of 1812*, 40. In the 1820s Major General Sir James Carmichael-Smyth judged this armistice as proper, without any significant military disadvantages; see his *Precis of the Wars in Canada*, 141–2.

41 Hitsman, *Incredible War*, 95; see also *Naval War of 1812*, 1: 305, Lieutenant Melancthon T. Woolsey to Secretary of the Navy Hamilton, 5 September 1812.

42 Wilder, *Battle of Sackett's Harbour*, chaps. 1 and 2, provides historical background on Sackets Harbor and its development as a naval base.

43 *DHC*, 3: 168–9.

44 *DHC*, 3: 242–3, 7 September 1812; 260, Prevost to Brock, 14 September; 299, Brock to Prevost, 28 September.

45 Returns for rank and file indicate Prevost's concentration of manpower in Lower Canada. See NA, MG 13, WO 17, 1516, 109 (25 September 1812), 125 (25 October), 140 (25 November), 155 (December). For the weakness of his American opponents opposite see Everest, *War of 1812*, 61–6.

46 NA, MG 12, Adm. 1, Secret Letters, v.4358, John B. Warren to John W. Croker, 5 October 1812. On Warren see DCB, 6: 802–3, and Mahon, *War of 1812*, 54–5, 222–3.

47 Hitsman, *Incredible War*, 53, 98–9; DHC, 4: 138–9, Prevost to Brock, 19 October 1812.

48 NA, RG 8, v.1171, 216–18, GO, Adjutant General's Office, Quebec, 19 March 1814. The captain's name is not clear, but there can be no doubt that it was Bowie; see 1022, 92–4, Hercules Scott to Drummond, 7 April 1814; also Irving, *Officers of the British Forces*, 6. For another instance when Prevost stressed the role of officers, see DHC, 9: 277–8, Prevost to Drummond, 4 April 1814. On Wellington's view see M. Glover, *Wellington*, 245.

49 R. Christie, *Memoirs*, 68–70; Hitsman, *Incredible War*, 112–13; *Canadian State Trials*, 1: 358–66.

50 Hitsman, *Incredible War*, 164–6. Guitard, *Militia of the Battle of Châteauguay*. For Salaberry's complaints about Prevost's general order see NA, MG 24, G 45, v.3, 1125–7, Salaberry to his father, 19 December 1813; 1041–3, same to same, 1 February 1814. He was still grumbling about credit for Châteauguay in 1815; see 1082–4, same to same, 2 April 1815.

51 Hitsman, *Incredible War*, 110, 130; SBD, 2: 88, 359; 3: 661–2, 675–6, 694. The Corps of Provincial Royal Artillery Drivers was established on 11 January 1813 and disbanded in March 1815. It was attached to the Royal Artillery in order to reduce that unit's need to hire civilian drivers; see Irving, *Officers of the British Forces*, 113. Sheaffe followed Prevost's example in raising a similar corps in Upper Canada; see PBHS, 17: 339–40, Sheaffe to Colonel Baynes, 9 February 1813.

52 George R.J. Macdonell ("Red George") will be found in DCB, 9: 484–5. He received his brevet commission as lieutenant-colonel on 8 February 1813.

53 Hitsman, *Incredible War*, 118–19; SBD, 1: 52–3; 2: 13–24; AO, Journal of a Staff Officer (MS 842), 5–6.

54 DHC, 5: 83, Prevost to Earl Bathurst, secretary for war and the colonies, 27 February 1813; see also other correspondence, ibid., 74–82.

55 Hitsman, *Incredible War*, 120; for the correspondence that he cites, see SBD, 2: 13–24. See also AO, Journal of a Staff Officer (MS 842), 6, where Harvey claimed that he wrote Prevost's general order; also Raudzens, "'Red George' Macdonell," 201. Stanley, *War of 1812*, 228–33, makes no comment on Prevost's claim.

56 *DHC*, 5: 104–7, Bathurst to Prevost, 12 March 1813; 222, Yeo to Hon. J.W. Croker, 5 May; 232, Prevost to Bathurst, 18 May; *DCB*, 5: 874–7; Hitsman, *Incredible War*, 106–7. See also F.C. Drake, "Commodore Sir James Lucas Yeo and Governor General George Prevost: A Study in Command Relations, 1813–14," in *New Interpretations in Naval History*, 156–71.

57 Wilder, *Battle of Sackett's Harbour*. Patrick Wilder kindly allowed me to read the manuscript of his book before its publication. It and conversations with him have helped to increase my understanding of this battle.

58 Yeo commanded six warships, two gunboats, and thirty-three batteaux, but different figures are given for the number of troops. Lieutenant-Colonel E.B. Brenton, Prevost's provincial ADC and civil secretary, who was present at the action, gave a range of "700 or 800 men"; see *DHC*, 5: 279–82, Brenton to Captain N. Freer, 30 May 1813. Also at the scene, Lieutenant John Le Couteur gave the figure of 870 (*Merry Hearts*, 117), which is the same number reported in the diary of another participant, Captain Jacques Viger, reprinted in *Waterdown Daily Times*, 28 May 1963. (I want to thank Donald Graves for drawing this source to my attention.) Graves gives a total of 895 officers and men; see "Attack on Sackets Harbour," 2, 13; Wilder, *Battle of Sackett's Harbour*, 72–4. Over half the force consisted of men recruited in British North America, but many of the troops had not yet seen action.

59 Baynes's military service had begun in 1783 (at age twelve or thirteen) when he joined the 82nd Foot. He served in Barbados, Tobago, Martinique, the Cape of Good Hope, the East Indies, Gibraltar, Malta, Naples, England, and Nova Scotia. During most of these years from 1794 he acted as aide-de-camp to General James (later Sir James) H. Craig and so may have seen little action. When Craig assumed the governorship of British North America in 1807, Baynes came as adjutant general. In 1813 he was colonel of the Glengarry Light Infantry Fencibles and adjutant general in North America; the following year he was made major-general. (Most of this information was provided by Stuart Sutherland.)

60 *Naval War of 1812*. 2: 467, Commodore Isaac Chauncey to Lieutenant Wolcott Chauncey, 20 May 1813; 473–7, Brigadier-General Jacob Brown to Secretary of War Armstrong, 1 June 1813; Wilder, *Battle of Sackett's Harbour*, 65, 75, 80–2, 155–6.

61 *DHC*, 5: 276, Baynes to Prevost, 30 May 1813; 280, Brenton to Freer, 30 May. Hitsman, *Incredible War*, 131–4, suggests that Prevost took an active part in deciding to postpone the attack and that Yeo disagreed. This interpretation is supported by Midshipman David Wingfield's evidence; see NA, MG 24, F 18.

62 According to Le Couteur, early on the morning of the 28th, Major William Drummond of the 104th Foot had his men in batteaux heading for the landing place, but they were ordered by Prevost to return to the

ships (*Merry Hearts*, 115; also 117). See also *DHC*, 5: 292–4, Prevost to Bathurst, 1 June 1813. *SBD*, 2: 123–7, Baynes to Prevost, 30 May, offers a very similar explanation.

63 Viger, "Diary"; Le Couteur, *Merry Hearts*, 117; Wilder, *Battle of Sackett's Harbour*, 109–10; Brenton, *Some Account*, 84–6; NA, MG 24, F 18. *DHC*, 5: 279–8, Brenton to Freer, 30 May, 1813, describes the retreat as beginning when British troops were driven back by fierce Americann fire.

64 Viger stated that the bugle calls had been changed, which is probably why he did not understand that call until told its meaning by a soldier of the Glengarry regiment; see Wilder, *Battle of Sackett's Harbour*, 110–11. On the other hand, Le Couteur knew what the bugle signal meant; see his *Merry Hearts*, 117. See also Commins, "War on the Canadian Frontier," 203–4.

65 Chauncey wasted no time sailing from Niagara back to Sackets as soon as he learned that Yeo's fleet was off that port. See *DHC*, 5: 267, Dearborn writing from Fort George to Secretary of War, 24 May 1813; *Naval War of 1812*, 2: 473–7, Brown to Armstrong, 1 June 1813; Wilder, *Battle of Sackett's Harbour*, 111–25.

66 In Brenton's view, although the raid did not achieve total success, it did divert American attention away from their campaign in the Niagara Peninsula against General Vincent's army by drawing away Chauncey's squadron; see NA, MG 23, G 11, v.5, 2968–73, Brenton to J.S. Sewell, 1 June. Wilder, in *Battle of Sackett's Harbour*, 123, considers that "Prevost's repulse constituted a serious defeat"; but in terms of naval ascendancy on Lake Ontario, it was a successful "British pre-emptive strike" (154).

67 *Naval War of 1812*, 2: 477–8, Chauncey to Secretary of the Navy Jones, 2 June 1813; 478–9, Captain Richard Smith to Lieutenant-Colonel Commanding Franklin Wharton, 11 June, complaining that his men had "lost all their clothing camp utensils etc." and much other public property had been destroyed. The sloop *General Pike* was launched on 12 June. See also Wilder, *Battle of Sackett's Harbour*, 128–9, 140.

68 *DHC*, 5: 279–82, Brenton to Freer, 30 May 1813.

69 *SBD*, 2: 130–2, Prevost to Bathurst, 1 June 1813; Viger, "Diary." Graves states that Baynes turned over command to Prevost; see "Attack on Sackets Harbour," 8. See also NA, MG 24, F 18; according to Midshipman David Wingfield's account, Prevost denied giving the order to retreat. Le Couteur's opinion was that "It was a scandalously managed affair" (*Merry Hearts*, 144). TRL, Baldwin Room, Hagerman, Journal of Events in the War of 1812, 13–17, presents a critical eye witness's account. See also James Richardson, "Reminiscences," 16–18. Major General Carmichael-Smyth's later judgment was that the plan failed because the forces employed were not large enough to ensure success; see his *Precis of the Wars in Canada*, 173, 193.

70 The principal American commanders were Lieutenant-Colonel Electus Backus, Major Jacint Laval, and Major Thomas Aspinwall. On them and Sackets' defences, see Wilder, *Battle of Sackett's Harbour*, chaps 8, 9, 10. Wilder proves that Brigadier-General Jacob Brown, the local militia commander, was not in overall command of the defenders; nor was he particularly bold in confronting the invaders.

71 *DHC*, 6: 249–51, Prevost to Bathurst, 18 July 1813; 298–300, same to same, 1 August; *SBD*, 2: 229–38; Everest, *War of 1812*, 114–21; *Naval War of 1812*, 2: 512–20, 603–6.

72 NA, RG 8, v.229, 28, His Excellency's Route to Kingston, March 1813; v.1203, 1/2 I, 157–61, GO, Montreal, 27 September: *DHC*,7: 61–2, Captain Noah Freer to Procter, St Davids, [25 August].

73 R. Christie, *Memoirs*, 78, 83; *DHC*, 7: 87, T.G. Ridout to T. Ridout, 30 August 1813; 205–8, Prevost to Bathurst, 8 October; *John Strachan Letter Book*, 47–8, 50–1, Strachan to Dr James Brown, 30 October.

74 *DHC*,7: 62–6, Prevost to Bathurst, 25 August 1813; 56, GO, 24 August; 52–4, GO, 23 August. See also NA, MG 23, G 11, v.5, 2082–5, Colonel Plenderleath to Jonathan Sewell, 3 September. Rank-and-file strength in the Niagara Peninsula (Queenston, Four Mile Creek, and St David's) was reported on 25 August as 3,201; see NA, MG 13, WO 17, 1517, 110.

75 Rottenburg already possessed this information from a reconnaissance on 31 July; see *DHC*, 6: 297, Rottenburg to Captain Freer, 1 August 1813. Le Couteur was sent on such missions by Rottenburg and garnered considerable information; see his *Merry Hearts*, 133–5 (10, 11, 26 September). Information could also have been gained from American deserters; see, for example, *DHC*, 7: 97–8, Harvey to Yeo, 4 September, with two depositions enclosed.

76 *DHC*, 7: 50, Yeo to Prevost, 22 August 1813. Chauncey went into Sackets on 13 August.

77 *DHC*, 7: 87, Thomas G. Ridout to Thomas Ridout, St Davids, 30 August 1813; 90–1, *Buffalo Gazette*, 31 August; NA, MG 23, G 11, v.5, 2082–5, Plenderleath to Sewell, 3 September; T. Malcomson, "September 1813."

78 *DHC*, 7: 148–9, Prevost to Yeo, 19 September 1813.

79 *DHC*, 7: 87, Thomas G. Ridout to Thomas Ridout, 30 August 1813: "By what I can learn Sir George's presence here is very little sought."

80 NA, MG 23, G 11, v.5, 2082–5, Plenderleath to Sewell, 3 September; Le Couteur, *Merry Hearts*, 131.

81 *DHC*, 5: 40–1, Prevost to Bathurst, 15 January 1813; 59–60, Prevost to Bathurst, 8 February; 124–7, Prevost to Bathurst, 19 March; 158–60, Prevost to Bathurst, 21 April; 292–3, Prevost to Bathurst, 1 June; 6: 52–3, Prevost to Bathurst, 6 June; 138–9, Prevost to Sir John Warren, 24 June; 255–6, Prevost to Bathurst, 20 July; 7: 130–1, Prevost to Bathurst,

15 September; 8: 111, Prevost to Bathurst, 31 October; 136–7, Prevost to
Bathurst, 4 November; TRL, Baldwin Room, Prevost Military Papers, letterbook 2, Sherbrooke to Prevost, 23 March; Prevost to Sherbrooke,
20 April; Warren to Prevost, 24 August; Warren to Prevost, 21 September; Prevost to Warren, 13 November; Rear Admiral Griffiths to Prevost,
7 December.

82 Hitsman, *Incredible War*, 108, 117, 121, 128–30, 135, 151, 171. The
troops sent upriver included six companies of the 104th Foot who had
marched overland from New Brunswick along the route that Prevost had
earlier had investigated.

83 NA, MG 13, WO 17, 1517, 80, 94, 110, 126, 142, 158. In September the
excess in Upper Canada was only about 90 men, and until August about
half the forces in the upper province were at Kingston.

84 *DHC*, 5: 134–6, Prevost to Sheaffe, 27 March 1813; see also 233, Prevost
to Bathurst, 18 May; 6: 101, Prevost to Procter, 20 June; 8: 89–90, Rottenburg to Prevost, 23 October; NA, RG 8, I, v.679, 264, Rottenburg to
Prevost, 20 July.

85 NA, RG 8, v.1221, 154–5, Prevost to Rottenburg, 31 July 1813.

86 NA, RG 8, v.1221, 154–5, Prevost to Rottenburg, 31 July 1813; *DHC*, 7:
128, Prevost to Yeo, 14 September; 148–9, Prevost to Yeo, 19 September; see also 50, Yeo to Prevost, 22 August; 6: 249–51, Prevost to
Bathurst, 18 July; 298–300, Prevost to Bathurst, 1 August; 7: 130–1,
Prevost to Bathurst, 15 September; 160–2, Prevost to Bathurst,
22 September.

87 The garrisons in the area of Montreal or southern Lower Canada were
Chambly, William Henry (now Sorel), Laprairie, Lacadie, Blairfindie
(Blainfindy), St John's, St Philip (now Saint-Philippe), Lake St Francis
(now Lac Saint-François), and Coteau du Lac. Prevost shifted units to
these posts late in 1812, and the following year he sent the bulk of reinforcements to them.

88 *DHC*, 6: 299, Prevost to Bathurst, 1 August 1813; 7: 162, same to same,
22 September; 207–8, same to same, 8 October; 8: 117, Rottenburg to
Vincent, 1 November; TRL, Baldwin Room, Prevost Military Papers,
letterbook 2, Prevost to Sherbrooke, 20 April; Prevost to Warren,
24 June.

89 Hitsman, *Incredible War*, 137, 172; *SBD*, 3, pt 2: 608.

90 Ouellet, *Economic and Social History of Quebec*, 236–7; R. Christie, *Memoirs*,
115–19; *Documents Relating to the Constitutional History of Canada*, 2: 443–
61, 462–4, Prevost to Bathurst, 18 March; 464–5, Bathurst to Prevost,
12 July; 465–8, Prevost to Bathurst, 4 September. For expressions of
hostility towards Prevost from the English minority, see NA, MG 23,
G 11, v.5, 2149–52, Chief Justice James Monk to Chief Justice Jonathan

Sewell, 30 and 31 January 1814; 2217–19, John Richardson to Sewell, 24 February.

91 The assembly approved seventeen "Heads of Impeachment" against Sewell and eight against Monk. Both were charged with attempting to subvert the constitution of Lower Canada and to usurp the powers of the legislature. Sewell was also condemned for giving bad advice to Craig, while Monk was censured for improper and illegal use of his judicial power. See *Documents Relating to the Constitutional History of Canada*, 2: 445–56; further proceedings and correspondence will be found on 458–68. See also R. Christie, *Memoirs*, 115–19, 148–50. On Monk see DCB, 6: 511–5; on Sewell, DCB, 7: 782–92. The proceedings were instigated by James Stuart; see DCB, 8: 842–5. See also DCB, 6: 643–4.

92 *Canadian State Trials*, 1: 450–86.

93 DHC, 9: 137–40, Drummond to Prevost, 21 January 1814; 143, same to same, 23 January. Hitsman, *Incredible War*, 177, attributes the suggestion to Drummond and Yeo.

94 DHC, 9: 153–5, Prevost to Drummond, 29 January 1814.

95 DHC, 9: 171–2, Prevost to Drummond, 8 February 1814.

96 DHC, 9: 163–4, Drummond to Prevost, 3 February 1814; 192, Drummond to Prevost, 19 February. Yeo agreed with Drummond; see 170–1, Yeo to Prevost, 8 February; see also 175, Military secretary to Drummond, 12 February.

97 DHC, 9: 165–6, Military Secretary to Drummond, 4 February 1814; 247, Drummond to Prevost, 22 March.

98 DHC, 9: 282, Drummond to Prevost, 5 April 1814. Prevost agreed to Drummond's requests to shift units; see 282, Prevost to Drummond, 6 April.

99 NA, MG 13, WO 17, 1518, 29, 57, 75, 93.

100 DHC, 9: 305–6, Prevost to Drummond, 23 April 1814; 311, Drummond to Prevost, 27 April; 313, Drummond to Prevost, 28 April. Hitsman, *Incredible War*, 184, attributes the proposal to Drummond in a letter of 26 April. Drummond claimed credit in a letter to Bathurst; see DHC, 1: 24, 3 July.

101 DHC, 9: 319, Prevost to Drummond.

102 DHC, 9: 323–4, Drummond to Prevost, 3 May 1814; 350–1, Prevost to Drummond, 7 May; SBD, 3, pt 1: 61–3, Yeo to J.W. Croker, First Secretary to the Admiralty, 9 May; NA, MG 24, A 41, 113, Drummond to Prevost, 10 May; 120–1, Drummond to Prevost, 19 May.

103 See Prevost's GO of 12 May describing the attack on Oswego; DHC, 9: 344–6.

104 DHC, 9: 274–5, Drummond to Prevost, 2 April 1814; 291–2, Yeo to Prevost, 13 April.

105 *DHC*, 9: 315–17, Prevost to Baynes, 29 April 1814; see also 287, Monroe to Colonel N. Pinkney, 11 April; 308, Brigadier General A. Macomb to Prevost, n.d.; 322, Baynes to Pinkney, 1 May; 322–3, Baynes to Prevost, 1 May; 323, Baynes to Pinkney, 1 May; 326–7, Baynes to Prevost, 3 May.

106 *DHC*, 9: 318–19, Prevost to Drummond, 30 April 1814.

107 Hitsman, *Incredible War*, 176–7; NA, RG 8, v.684, 76–8, Bathurst to Prevost, 11 July 1814.

108 *DHC*, 2: 245–6, Prevost to Bathurst, 11 October 1814; see also 239–40, Prevost to Bathurst, 4 October; 441, Colonel Baynes to Drummond, 26 August.

109 NA, MG 13, WO 17, 1518, 131, 155; troop returns were August, 27, 145 (15,450 in Lower Canada), and September, 26,045 (approximately 14,400 in Lower Canada).

110 NA, CO 43, v.23, 296–301, "Secret"; Hitsman, *Incredible War*, 249–51.

111 Heinrichs, "Battle of Plattsburg," 44–8; Everest, *War of 1812*, 166.

112 NA, CO 43, v.23, 296–301, Bathurst to Prevost, 3 June 1814.

113 *SBD*, 3, pt 1: 411, 469, testimony from Captain Pring's court martial; see other correspondence, 378–9. There is a good discussion of the battle of Plattsburgh, particularly its naval aspects, in Everest, *War of 1812*, chap. 11.

114 *SBD*, 3, pt 1: 378–9, Downie to Captain Upton, 1 September 1814.

115 *SBD*, 3, pt 1: 379, Downie to Prevost, 7 September 1814; 379–80, Prevost to Downie, 8 September; 382, Downie to Prevost, 9 September; 468–75, Lieutenant Robertson's Statement. Brenton, *Some Account*, 141–2, mentions that Prevost and Downie met on 5 September, when Downie said that the flotilla would be ready to cooperate with the army in less than forty-eight hours.

116 Stanley, *War of 1812*, 343–4; Stickney, "Logistics and Communications," 172–7; Mahon, *War of 1812*, 319–21.

117 *SBD*, 3, pt 1: 353–60, Major-General Macomb to the American secretary at war, 15 September 1814. Duke University, Special Collections Library, Diary of John Lang, 155–6, refers to rain on 3 September and gives the lengths of each day's march, which added up to a total of fifty-seven miles. For references to bad road conditions see McCord Museum, War of 1812 Papers, folder 8, M17930, Pliny Moore to Mrs Moore, 14 September; NA, RG 8, v.1203, 1/2 L, 199, GO [15 September]. Everest, *War of 1812*, chap. 10, gives details of Prevost's invasion, including numbers of troops.

118 *SBD*, 3, pt 1: 350–3, Prevost to Bathurst, 11 September 1814; 368–9, Captain Pring to Yeo, 12 September; 465, Baynes to Downie, 4 September; 397, Captain J.S. Sinclair to Baynes, 20 March 1815; Brenton, *Some Account*, 141–3.

119 *SBD*, 3, pt 1: 356–8, Macomb to Secretary at War, 15 September 1814; 351, Prevost to Bathurst, 11 September; Everest, *War of 1812*, 175.

120 *SBD*, 3, pt 1: 356, 358, Macomb to secretary at war, 15 September 1814.

121 Brenton, *Some Account*, 143–4; NA, MG 24, F 21, part 1, "General Robinson's Letter on the Affair at Plattsburgh, 1814," 1–2.

122 "Robinson's Letter" indicates that Prevost changed his intention from an immediate attack on the 6th to waiting for the naval squadron to cooperate, a suggestion that Robinson had made; see NA, MG 24, f 21, part 1, 1–2. Major General Carmichael-Smyth in the 1820s thought that this delay was "a very great error." See his *Precis of the Wars in Canada*, 189; also 191–4. Even if Robinson had suggested the delay, the decision lay with Sir George.

123 Hitsman, *Incredible War*, 224–5; Fortescue, *History of the British Army*, 10: 130; Everest, *War of 1812*, 175–6.

124 In section 9, "Duties of General and Staff Officers," 47–8 (see chap. 8 below). See also Jarvis, *Three Centuries of Robinsons*, 106–7. NA, RG 8, I, v.685, 184–91, contains reports of three deserters from American infantry regiments at Plattsburgh, which indicate some of the detailed information that was being made available to Prevost.

125 *SBD*, 3, pt 1: 441–2, 463, Captain Pring's statement at the naval court martial. R. Christie, in *Military and Naval Operations*, 207–8, wrote that Prevost and Downie had not settled on a signal, so that the army commander saw no such meaning in the scaling of the guns.

126 *SBD*, 3, pt 1: 369, 398, 495, 359. Pring said the engagement began at 8 a.m., while John S. Sinclair said, shortly after 8 a.m., Lieutenant William Hicks 8.30 a.m, and Macomb 9 a.m. See also NA, MG 24, F 21, pt 1; Robinson's account suggests that it was after 9 a.m. The secondary sources give different times. Characteristically, no times are given in Prevost's reports.

127 NA, MG 24, F 21, pt 1, "Robinson's Letter," 5; Stanley, *War of 1812*, 348.

128 *SBD*, 3, pt 1: 382, Downie to Prevost, 9 September 1814; NA, MG 24, F 21, pt 1, "Robinson's Letter," 6.

129 Brydon's opinion cited in *SBD*, 3, pt 1: 414, 462–3, and Pring's views at 463–4; see also 368, Pring to Yeo, 12 September; 441–2.

130 Robertson's opinions cited in *SBD*, 3, pt 1: 438–41, 468–75; see also 383–4, his letter to Pring, 15 September 1814.

131 His reports might be contrasted with those of Baynes about the raid on Sackets Harbor (29 May 1813) in *SBD*, 2: 123–7; Drummond on Chippawa, 3, pt 1: 112–13, and on Lundy's Lane, 144–51; and the GO, 27 October 1813, about the battle at Chateauguay, 2: 388–90. Prevost tended to be vaguer than others in his reports; for example, see *DHC*, 7: 62–6, Prevost to Bathurst, 25 August 1813.

132 *SBD*, 3, pt 1: 351.

133 *SBD*, 3, pt 1: 365–6, Prevost to Bathurst, 22 September 1814, 369, Andrew Cochrane to Gordon, 20 September; Brenton, *Some Account*, 167–70.

134 NA, MG 24, F 21, pt 1, "Robinson's Letter," 1, 6. R. Christie, in *Military and Naval Operations*, 204–6, justifies the speed of the retreat in terms of the rapid growth of American forces threatening Prevost's army, yet asserts that the British experienced little molestation during the two-day retreat. See also Everest, *War of 1812*, 187–90; Mahon, *War of 1812*, 327–8.

135 Fortescue, *History of the British Army*, 10: 128. For his treatment of the battle of the Nivelle, see vol. 9, chap. 13. Major General Carmichael-Smyth concentrated his criticism on Prevost's delay; see his *Precis of the Wars in Canada*, 189, 191–2. See also Heinrichs, "Battle of Plattsburg," 56.

136 Fortescue, *History of the British Army*, 9: 321. Heinrichs, "Battle of Plattsburg," 45, 56, also criticizes Prevost's lack of understanding of naval-army cooperation.

137 For critical newspaper opinion see the *Montreal Herald,* 17, 24 September, 5, 26 November 1814. Much less critical was the *Quebec Mercury*, 20 and 27 September. For a discussion on the authorship of the critical letters, see Kingsford, *History of Canada*, 9: 9–12, 29.

138 Cited in Hitsman, *Incredible War*, 235, 231; *DCB*, 5: 697.

139 The complete text of the court martial of Captain Pring and the officers and men on Lake Champlain is given in *SBD*, 3, pt 1: 400–98. For the original document see NA, MG 12, Adm. 1, v.5445.

140 NA, RG 8, v.1710, 20, J.A. Oldham [deputy judge advocate general] to Captain Freer, 27 December 1815; MG 24, B 3, v.4, Thomas Amyot to H.W. Ryland, 9 January 1816; TRL, Baldwin Room, Prevost Military Papers. Dropsy was given as the immediate cause of death.

141 Queen's University Archives, Cartwright Family Papers, John Kirby Papers, 2254, box 1, folder 1, W. Leitman [?] to John Kirby, 24 September 1815, commenting on the effect of the publication of "Veritas Letters"; Sutherland, "Civil Administration," 140–8.

142 NA, MG 24, G 45, v.3, 1125–7, 19 December 1813. The effects of Prevost's bad relations with Salaberry in England in 1806 and 1807 probably continued to be felt. Besides, Salaberry was very friendly with Baron de Rottenburg. See correspondence in Anderson, *Life of … the Duke of Kent*, 102–3, 104–5, 149–50, 192–5, 209–18, 240–1.

143 Wohler, *Charles de Salaberry*, chaps. 8 and 9. The Upper Canadian Legislative Council also voted its thanks. See NA, MG 24, G 45, v.3, 1037–9, Salaberry to his father, 31 January 1814; 1041–3, same to same, 1 February; R. Christie, *History of … Lower Canada*, 152–3.

144 NA, MG 24, G 45, v.3, 1029–31, Salaberry to his father, 8 July 1813.

145 *SBD*, 3, pt 1: 17–21, GO, 9 May 1814; Irving, *Officers of the British Forces*, 133; Hitsman, *Incredible War*, 179–80; Lépine, *Officiers de milice*, 16, 34.

146 Although Salaberry had actively sought the position of inspecting field officer of militia, he expressed no appreciation of Sir George's action. Perhaps the reason is that he knew of Prevost's criticisms of him in a confidential report. See *DCB*, 6: 343; NA, MG 24, G 45, v.3, 1064–5, Salaberry to his father, 21 March 1814. The Prevost-Salaberry acquaintance went back at least to 1794, when both men were in the 60th Foot. See Anderson, *Life of ... Edward, Duke of Kent...*, 28–31, 47–8, 62–3, 66, 107–8.

147 *SBD*, 2: 77–8, Commission appointing Sir James L. Yeo, commander of the naval forces on the lakes of Canada, 19 March 1813; 76–7, John W. Croker to Yeo, 19 March; Hitsman, *Incredible War*, 106–7.

148 Hitsman, *Incredible War*, 106–7; F.C. Drake, "Commodore Sir James Lucas Yeo and Governor General George Prevost: A Study in Command Relations, 1813–14," in *New Interpretations in Naval History*, 157–8.

149 *DHC*, 7: 61–2, Captain Noah Freer to Procter, undated (probably 25 August 1813). R. Malcomson, "Barclay Correspondence," 31.

150 *DHC*, 7: 49–50, Prevost to Procter, 22 August 1813; 128, Prevost to Yeo, 14 September; 148–9, Prevost to Yeo, 19 September; NA, MG 12, Adm. 1, v.5445, 29, Prevost to Procter, 8 September.

151 *DHC*, 7: 130–1, Prevost (headquarters, Kingston) to Bathurst, 15 September 1813; 50, Yeo to Prevost, 22 August; T. Malcomson, "September 1813;" 304–5.

152 *DHC*, 7: 160–2, Prevost to Bathurst, 22 September 1813. Prevost also criticized Yeo's role; see NA, RG 8, I, v.1221, 164–5, Prevost to Rottenburg, 21 September.

153 *DHC*, 8: 180, Yeo to Warren, 14 November 1813. Antal, in "Myths and Facts Concerning General Procter," 256–7, argues that neither Procter nor Barclay should be blamed for the latter's defeat because they agreed on the decision to fight Perry's fleet. He sees Prevost and Rottenburg as looking for a scapegoat for their own failures.

154 NA, RG 8, v.1221, 182–3, Prevost to Yeo, 12 October 1813; 183, Freer to Rottenburg, 14 October; v.680, 229, Rottenburg to Military Secretary, 17 October; *DHC*, 8: 60–1, Rottenburg to Prevost, 14 October.

155 TRL, Baldwin Room, Prevost Military Papers, letterbook 2, 129, Prevost to Admiral Warren, 24 June 1813; 89–91, Warren to Prevost, 24 August; 93–4, same to same, 21 September; 97–9, Prevost to Warren, 13 November.

156 *DHC*, 9: 197–8, Yeo to Sir Sidney Beckwith, 26 February 1814; 199, Yeo to Prevost, 28 February; 1: 179–80, Prevost to Bathurst, 27 August; 239–40, Prevost to Bathurst, 4 October; 259–60, Prevost to Bathurst, 18 October.

157 Lucas, *Canadian War of 1812*, 190–1.

158 Sir Robert S. Milnes was lieutenant-governor of Lower Canada from 1797 to 1798 and administrator from 1799 to 1805; see DCB, 7: 613–16. In his diary, Lieutenant Lang related the circumstances leading to Captain Milnes's death; see Duke University, Diary of John Lang, 86–7. See also R. Christie, *Memoirs*, 88–9.

159 On all these officers see Irving, *Officers of the British Forces*. For McDouall see DCB, 7: 556–7.

160 For this suggestion and much of the evidence on which it is based, I want to thank Stuart Sutherland.

161 His father was René-Amable Boucher de Boucherville, and their seigneury was Boucherville. Pierre married Marguerite-Émilie, daughter of Clément Sabrevois de Bleury, who was a major in the militia. (I want to thank Luc Lépine for this information.)

162 See Irving, *Officers of the British Forces*. For Brenton see DCB, 7: 104–5. "Percival" is the spelling used by Irving, but Marjory Whitelaw corrects that to "Perceval" in *The Dalhousie Journals* (Ottawa: Oberon Press, 1981), 2: 187n13; see also 27, 115. Perceval sat in the Legislative Council from 1818 until his death in 1829 and for a time in the Executive Council. For most of the information on these men, I am indebted to Stuart Sutherland. Stanley, *War of 1812*, 417, erroneously names four militia officers as provincial aides-de-camp of the governor-in-chief. In fact, John Macdonell was Brock's provincial ADC, Nathaniel Coffin was Sheaffe's, and Christopher Hagerman was Drummond's, while Allan McLean was ADC to none of these commanders.

163 Besides Plattsburgh, there are the following examples: his reactions to the captures of Michilimackinac and Detroit and his caution over the proposal to attack Ogdensburg. See TRL, Baldwin Room, Prevost Military Papers, letterbook 3, Prevost to Sherbrooke, 15 July and 27 August 1814; Sutherland, "Civil Administration," 35–6, 144.

164 Hitsman, *Incredible War*, 231, and "Sir George Prevost's Conduct"; Fortescue, *History of the British Army*, 10: 134–5.

165 For two examples see NA, MG 24, J 48, John William Whittaker, 9–12, John Rolph to John William Wittaker, 3 January 1814; and AO, Strachan Letterbooks (MS 35), 10: 122–3, Strachan to Colonel Harvey, 31 March 1814. See also Sutherland, "Civil Administration," 25–6, 32, 40, 139, 151, 154–9.

CHAPTER THREE

1 Turner, "Career of Isaac Brock," 83; DHC, 3: 21–5, Major General Brock to Sir George Prevost, 2 December 1811. NA, MG 13, WO 17, 1516, 66, lists 921 rank and file at Fort George on 25 June 1812. The addition of officers, sergeants, drummers, and possibly other units at Kingston,

Amherstburg, and Fort St Joseph's would raise the total to over 1,000. See also p. 81, which shows that by 25 July the total in Upper Canada had reached 1,381. Major General Sir James Carmichael-Smyth gives a figure of 1,500 in Upper Canada distributed among Kingston, York, the Niagara frontier, Amherstburg, and St Joseph's Island; see his *Precis of the Wars in Canada*, 138.

2 For example, see *Montreal Herald*, 24 October 1812; *Quebec Mercury*, 3 and 10 November. See also *DCB*, 5: 114.

3 Tupper, *Life and Correspondence*, 3. Tupper placed his family in the "upper ranks" of island society. See also *DCB*, 5: 109–15.

4 NA, MG 24, E 1–4, Extract from the Baptismal Register of the Town Church, St Peter-Port, Guernsey; NA, MG 11, CO 42/353, 218–19, Savery Brock to Earl Bathurst, 28 November 1812; Tupper, *Life and Correspondence*, 1–4. I have also made use of my "Career of Isaac Brock," 18.

5 John died in 1801 while a brevet lieutenant-colonel in the 81st Foot, Ferdinand died in 1779 while a lieutenant in the 60th Foot, and Savery served as paymaster of the 49th Foot and later ADC to Sir John Moore before settling down to married life in Guernsey. On Savery see Tupper, *Life and Correspondence*, 22–3; on Daniel see also 418, 463–72. D.E. Graves, editor of Le Couteur's *Merry Hearts*, 5–6, remarks on the connections of the Brocks and other families on the Channel Islands and the frequency with which their sons followed military careers.

6 See Tupper, *Life and Correspondence*, 419.

7 Ibid., 4–5: "Having entered the army at so early an age, he happily felt sensible of his deficiencies of education; and for a long period he devoted his leisure mornings to study, locking the door of his room until one o'clock, to prevent intrusion."

8 Tupper, *Life and Correspondence*, 4–6. On Brock's ambition see, for example, ibid., 104–5, Major General Vesey to Major General Brock, 10 June 1811.

9 Ibid., 5; *DCB*, 5: 110. On the 49th Regiment of Foot see Petre, *Royal Berkshire Regiment*, vol. 1, particularly chaps 4–6.

10 Tupper, *Life and Correspondence*, 4–5. On the dangers to health from service in the West Indies see Duffy, *Soldiers, Sugar, and Seapower*, epilogue; Thoumine, *Scientific Soldier*, 53–4.

11 26 November 1799; cited in Tupper, *Life and Correspondence*, 13. For the campaign of 1799 in North Holland see Bunbury, *Narratives of Some Passages*, 2–56, and Piechowiak, "Anglo-Russian Expedition," 182–95. The *Annual Register, 1799*, 108–19, provides details of the action but without special mention of the 49th Foot or of Brock. I want to thank Don Graves for supplying me with a copy.

12 Cited in Tupper, *Life and Correspondence*, 72–4; Whitfield, *Battle of Queenston Heights*, 25–6.

13 Tupper, *Life and Correspondence*, 6, 18. Emsley, *British Society and the French Wars*, 85–9, refers to civilian disorders in 1799 and 1800 throughout England and reports made to the government of possible troop involvement. Thoumine, *Scientific Soldier*, 56, reports a similar incident of troops cheering their commanding officer and being rebuked. It happened in 1797 in the 7th Light Dragoons when the senior colonel, Lord Paget, made a brief visit to the regiment, which had been experiencing strict discipline under the young lieutenant-colonel John Gaspard Le Marchant. Paget reprimanded the men for their display of indiscipline.

14 The incident is recounted in DCB, 5: 110–11, and Tupper, *Life and Correspondence*, 25–6. These versions have Brock hurrying across the lake from York to catch the deserters, an account that is not supported by contemporary documents. See NA, RG 8, v.922, 86–7, Sheaffe to ———, 13 Aug 1803; 71–2, Thomas Cartwright to ———, 24 August. See also Turner, "Career of Isaac Brock," 28–33.

15 Turner, "Career of Isaac Brock," 70–1. For the documents see NA, RG 8, v.1214 (no. 11), 195–7, Brock to Adjutant General, 18 March 1807, plus enclosure.

16 Turner, "Career of Isaac Brock," 61; DCB, 5: 111. In his correspondence during this period, Brock referred to himself as colonel.

17 *Naval War of 1812*, 1: 26–34; Turner, "Career of Isaac Brock," 39–43.

18 DCB, 5: 111. For details of Brock's activities see that source or Turner, "Career of Isaac Brock," 40–3, 61–72, and the references cited there.

19 See DCB, 5: 214–15 on John Craigie. He was dismissed by Governor Craig and died bankrupt.

20 Turner, "Career of Isaac Brock," 45–8.

21 4 October 1810 cited in Tupper, *Life and Correspondence*, 82–3; see also 81–2, Brock to his brothers, 13 September.

22 NA, RG 8, v.1706, 64, GO, 20 June 1811.

23 SBD, 1: 166–7, GO, 14 September 1811. See also Turner, "Career of Isaac Brock," 103–5.

24 The literature on the topics of this paragraph is, to say the least, extensive. A good place to start is G.M. Craig, *Upper Canada: The Formative Years, 1784–1841* (Toronto: McClelland and Stewart, 1963). Patronage advanced careers, for example, that of John Strachan, and its lack held back or ended them, as in the cases of Judge Robert Thorpe and Joseph Willcocks. For a quick survey relevant to Brock's civil role see Sheppard, *Plunder, Profit, and Paroles*, chap. 2, where there are also several references to other recent writings. R.L. Fraser's biography of Robert Nichol in the DCB, 6: 539–46, is most informative.

25 Turner, "Career of Isaac Brock," 40–8, 57–60. See also Tupper, *Life and Correspondence*, 60–6, 74–8.

26 The fifth parliament, elected in 1808, contained fewer government appointees and more members willing to criticize government actions than any previous assembly. See Johnson, *Becoming Prominent*, 121–9, 131–2.

27 On Willcocks see *DCB*, 5: 854–9.

28 *DHC*, 3: 21–5, Brock to Prevost, 2 December 1811 (Cruikshank misdates the letter to 1812).

29 *DHC*, 3: 21–5, 2 December 1811, Brock to Prevost; see 1–18 for the Militia Act of 1808. Brock thought that the militia might be strengthened by enlarging its basic unit, the company; see Gray, *Soldiers of the King*, 11–19, 25–9.

30 Sheppard, *Plunder, Profit, and Paroles*, 46, chooses not to mention Brock's reasons, but attributes this policy to a desire to keep weapons out of residents' hands because of doubts about their loyalty. Brock did express doubts about the reliability of the militia as a military force, but no direct connection between that sentiment and this policy is proved. Sheppard's only documentary citation, a letter that Brock wrote to Liverpool on 23 March, more than three months after he made the suggestion, does not support the claim. See also Turner, "Career of Isaac Brock," 149, 152.

31 Tupper, *Life and Correspondence*, 87–9, 92–4, Brock to Irving, 10 January and 19 February 1811; 256–9. Brock's interest in education extended to his soldiers. James Fitzgibbon's account of how he was educated gave the credit to Brock and some of his officers, but it is clear that Brock was the central inspiration. See TRL, Baldwin Room, William Allan Papers (S123), Inventory of the Effects of Sir Isaac Brock, sold at York, November 1812. This document lists the books in Brock's possession at the time of his death. A few titles will indicate the range and depth of his interests: *Life of Condé*, Voltaire, *Siècle de Louis XIV*; *King of Prussia's Tactics*; Comte de Guibert, *Œuvres militaires* (5 vols.); *Reglement de l'infantrie*, *Expedition to Holland*; and *Reflexions sur les principes militaires*. Perhaps Brock's reading influenced his tactics against the Americans; for example, de Guibert's emphasis on mobility was something that he put into practice.

32 *DHC*, 3: 21–5, Brock to Prevost, 2 December 1811.

33 Turner, "Career of Isaac Brock," 112–3.

34 Turner, "Career of Isaac Brock," 113; NA, CO 42/136, Gore to Craig, 5 January 1808, enclosed with Craig to Castlereigh, 15 July.

35 In his letter of 2 December, Brock referred to an American army near the Wabash River; he expected that once its mission against the Natives was completed, "a large portion of the regulars" would be sent to strengthen Detroit. He was sending Lieutenant-Colonel St George to take command of Fort Malden.

36 Gray, *Soldiers of the King*, 183–5, describes the Royal Provincial Artillery Drivers, or Car Brigade, and lists its personnel; see 182–3 for the cavalry.)

37 *DHC*, 3: 21–5, Brock to Prevost, 2 December 1811; 26–7, Prevost to Brock, 24 December; 28–9, "Memorandum to be submitted to His Excellency, the Governor-in-Chief, by Desire of Major General Brock," [no date]; see also 38–41, Brock to Baynes, 12 February.

38 NA, RG 8, v.728, 77, Captain Gray to Prevost, 29 January, 1812; 86, Gray, "Report on the Marine Establishment of Upper Canada," 24 February; v.1168, 94, GO, Quebec, 15 February; Upper Canada Sundries, v.15, 5975–6, Prevost to Brock, 14 February. Andrew Gray, captain in the Nova Scotia Fencibles and acting deputy quater master general from January 1812 to October, was killed at Sackets Harbor in May 1813.

39 See Turner, "Career of Isaac Brock," 122–3, where numerous references will be found.

40 *DHC*, 3: 45–6, Colonel Baynes to Brock, 10 March 1812; 51, Prevost to Brock, 31 March.

41 NA, RG 8, v.256, 209, "Confidential Communication transmitted to Mr. Robert Dickson," 27 February 1812; 211, Dickson's answer, dated 18 June, received at Fort George on 14 July; 229, both enclosed in J.B. Glegg to Baynes, 11 November. On Dickson see *DCB*, 6: 209–11.

42 Norton, *Journal*, 287–9.

43 Upper Canada, Journals of the Legislative Assembly, 1812, 1–97; Brock's opening address is on 4–5. For the dates of the fifth and sixth assemblies and the names of their members see *Legislators and Legislatures of Ontario*, 1: vi, 31–42.

44 *DHC*, 3, 38–41, Brock to Colonel Baynes, 12 February 1812. The oath was defeated in a house of twenty members by the deciding vote of the chairman, while suspension of habeas corpus was defeated "by a very trifling majority."

45 *DHC*, 3: 43–4, Brock to Prevost, 25 February 1812. Sheppard, *Plunder, Profit, and Paroles*, 43, stresses the authoritarian intent of Brock's proposal and cites this letter, including a passage that does not appear in it. See also Graves, "Joseph Willcocks and the Canadian Volunteers," 22–30.

46 Upper Canada, Journals of the Legislative Assembly, 1812, 97. See also NA, MG 11, CO 42/352, 7–9, Brock to Liverpool, 23 March 1812; *DHC*, 3: 65–6, Prevost to Brock, 27 May. The governor agreed with Brock's complaint but suggested that in the event of war, if the legislature took no action, the act would continue in force.

47 Upper Canada, Journal of the Legislative Assembly, 1812, 44, 49.

48 Turner, "Career of Isaac Brock," 145–8; NA, RG 8, v.676, 103–8, Brock to Prevost, 22 April 1812; 112–4, Brock to Prevost, 16 May. The act may be found in *DHC*, 4: 5–11. Each battalion was to have two flank companies.

Each company, up to a maximum of one hundred strong, was to be made up of volunteers or, if insufficient men volunteered, of men under age forty chosen by ballot. These companies were to train for up to six days a month, drilling that would have been much more intensive than that undergone by the sedentary militia. Brock expected an initial enrolment of 700 men, but hoped eventually to raise the total to 1,800 or more, with the possibility that this number would be increased as these men were replaced by new recruits at regular intervals. The act provided for the replacement of one-third of the men in a flank company after six months of service, a second third after seven months, and the final third after eight months. Sheppard, *Plunder, Profit, and Paroles*, 43–5, gives a figure of 13,000 for the total of Upper Canada's militia. He assumes a difference of view between Brock and most Upper Canadian males towards service in the flank companies. The "recruitment difficulties" that he refers to were not evident at this time. See also Gray, *Soldiers of the King*, 27, 29–31 (for figures see 32–4); also Crooks, "Recollections," 12–3.

49 Turner, "Career of Isaac Brock," 145–6; *Kingston Gazette*, 19 May 1812. Tupper, *Life and Correspondence*, 163–5, Brock to Lieutenant-Colonel Nichol, 8 April, is an example of the kind of letter sent to militia commanding officers. See also G.F.G. Stanley, "The Contribution of the Canadian Militia," in *After Tippecanoe*, 31–2.

50 *DCB*, 6: 539–46; Turner, "Career of Isaac Brock," 132–6; *DHC*, 8: 247–53, Memorial from Lieutenant-Colonel Robert Nichol to Earl Bathurst, 24 September 1817; Upper Canada, Journal of the Legislative Assembly, 1812. On Nichol see *DCB*, 6: 539–46.

51 Brock had been in Lower Canada when Governor Craig had tried to suppress anti-government critics by jailing members of the assembly and suppressing the newspaper *Le Canadien*. The brigadier-general endorsed Craig's action. See Turner, "Career of Isaac Brock," 57–61; Greenwood, *Legacies of Fear*, 202–9, chap. 11.

52 Graves, "Joseph Willcocks," 16–8, 23–4; *DCB*, 5: 854–9; Turner, "Career of Isaac Brock," 137–8; Sheppard, *Plunder, Profit, and Paroles*, 30, 48; *Canadian State Trials*, 1: 418–23.

53 Dinner by invitation with Brock may have softened Willcocks's animosity. The dinner is mentioned in Edgar, *Ten Years of Upper Canada*, 116, Thomas Ridout to his father, 23 May 1812. See also *DCB*, 5: 858; *DHC*, 3: 243. Willcocks was reputed to have influence among the Six Nations. For his report on his mission see *DRIC*, 209–12, Willcocks to Lieutenant-Colonel John Macdonell, 1 September 1812; Graves, "Joseph Willcocks," 27–9. See also Sheppard, *Plunder, Profit, and Paroles*, 85–6; Turner, "Career of Isaac Brock," 138. Crooks, "Recollections," 20, mentions "Joe Wilcox" at the battle of Queenston Heights. See also Windsor Public Library John

Stodgell Collection (MS 24 1/13), series 1, Askin Documents, unit 13, Charles Askin to John Askin, 12 November 1812.

54 Another critic of Gore, Dr William Warren Baldwin, also expressed his respect for Brock by suggesting that the latter did not want to follow Gore's "system." See Turner, "Career of Isaac Brock," 138–9; DCB, 5: 521. During the assembly's session, members had requested an extension of the sitting beyond the date set for prorogation (3 March). Brock readily agreed, a move that may have contributed to the respect towards him. See Upper Canada, Journal of the Legislative Assembly, 1812, 71–3, 75, 88–9. In June a general election resulted in a considerable change in the composition of the assembly. Of twenty-five members, only seven had been in the previous house, and the number of government supporters had grown considerably. Willcocks was the only leading opponent re-elected. See Edgar, Ten Years of Upper Canada, 129–31, George Ridout to his brother Thomas, 25 June 1812. Half the members held government offices; see Johnson, Becoming Prominent, 20, 129. For members' names see Legislators and Legislatures of Ontario, 1: 31–42.

55 The declaration of war was known at Albany, New York, by the 23rd, in Montreal on the 24th, in Quebec by the 25th, at Niagara at least by the 27th, and at Black Rock, New York, the same day. See DHC, 3: 69–77, for the relevant correspondence. Colonel Philetus Swift wrote from Black Rock to New York's governor Thompkins on 27 June that he believed the British knew of the declaration two days earlier. The news was known at York by the 27th, but at least two days earlier there had been public expectation of imminent war with the United States. See Edgar, Ten Years of Upper Canada, 129–31, George Ridout to his brother Thomas, York, 25 June 1812. Sheppard, in Plunder, Profit, and Paroles, 47, suggests that Brock knew on 24 June and that he deliberately did not inform the public or the militiamen who had been called out. An indication of their alleged lack of knowledge was that the militiamen did not bring blankets or extra equipment with them. His sources appear to be M. Smith, A Geographical View of the Province of Upper Canada ... (3rd ed., rev.; Trenton, NJ, 1813), 81–2, and John Richardson, Richardson's War of 1812, 11. The latter makes no reference to a delay in the public's being informed of the declaration of war, nor is there evidence for this claim in Smith. What the documents indicate is that Brock learned of the declaration at York on the 26th; that same evening he crossed by boat to Fort George. A district general order issued at Niagara on 27 June, which included a call up of some of the 1st Lincoln Militia in fact did recommend that they bring blankets with them. See Turner, "Career of Isaac Brock," 161–2; DHC, 3: 76–7, 93–5, Brock to Prevost, 3 July. See also DHC, 3: 119–20, MGO, 10 July, as an example of Brock's solicitude for his troops. Also Robinson, Life of Sir John Beverley Robinson, 30. Six days later, when Brock

wrote to Prevost, he complained of his forces' lack of "Blankets, haver-
sacks and kettles" as well as tents. He often expressed concern for his
soldiers' comforts, making it likely that, if the men needed to bring
necessities, he would have reminded them. In any case, the absence of
that sort of advice to militiamen called up is not a firm basis for a claim
that Brock attempted to suppress information.

56 DRIC, 53–4, Captain Roberts to Brock, 12 July 1812; 65–6, Roberts to
Brock, 17 July (two letters); 67–9, Hanks to Hull, 4 August.

57 SBD, 1: 303–4, Prevost to Liverpool, 18 May 1812. On Charles Roberts
see DCB, 5: 713–14.

58 NA, RG 8, v.676, 115–18, Brock to Prevost, 3 July 1812.

59 Ibid., 156, Roberts to Brock, 12 July 1812.

60 NA, RG 8, v.688A, 65, Baynes to Roberts, 25 June 1812.

61 DRIC, 65, Roberts to Baynes, 17 July 1812.

62 DRIC, 66, Roberts to Brock 17 July 1812; 100–3, Roberts to Glegg,
29 July; 214–17, Observations by Toussaint Pothier on Michilimackinac,
8 September.

63 DRIC, 35, Secretary of War to Hull, 18 June 1812, informed Hull of the
declaration of war; see also 37, Secretary of war to Hull, 24 June. On
26 June Hull wrote that he had received the secretary's letter of 18 June,
but on 7 July he denied knowing about the state of war before he
loaded and sent off the vessel. The correspondence is in DRIC, 38–9,
43–4.

64 DRIC, 135–6, Procter to Brock, 11 August 1812; Hitsman, *Incredible War*,
61–72. The first ambush was on 5 August. A less-successful one was carried out on 11 August.

65 As a result of their refusal and his fears that Natives might commit atroc-
ities if the British were forced to withdraw from Upper Canada, Brock
advocated displacement of the Natives from the Grand River reserve
when the government's position was strong enough to enable it to take
such drastic action. See Turner, "Career of Isaac Brock," appendix G. At
this same period, the American militia commanders on the Niagara frontier were plagued by militia desertions. See BECHS, A. Conger Goodyear,
War of 1812 MSS, box 1, v.3, Major-General Amos Hall letterbook, General Orders, 31 July 1812, to Brigadier-Generals Burnett and Ray.

66 DHC, 3: 153, Brock to Colonel Baynes.

67 SBD, 1: 389–9, Brock to Prevost, 28 July 1812. Here will be found also
the replies of the House of Assembly and the Legislative Council.

68 NA, RG 8, v.676, 217–18; see also 236–8, Brock to Prevost, 29 July; also
Graves, "Joseph Willcocks," 26–9.

69 Sheppard, *Plunder, Profit, and Paroles*, 52–3, claims that by "lying to the
Assembly" Brock "undercut his case for wider powers." This interpretation
seems to suggest that a different speech by him could have persuaded the

members to vote for the suspension of habeas corpus. The claim that Brock was "unnerved" by events is not clearly supported by the evidence.

70 Sheppard, *Plunder, Profit, and Paroles*, 60, claims that the amendments "created a host of newly exempt occupations." All the exemptions and even more are found in the Militia Act of 1808, clauses 26 and 27. See *DHC*, 3: 3–18; Gray, *Soldiers of the King*, 31.

71 *DHC*, 3: 162–3; Turner, "Career of Isaac Brock," 141–2. The situation concerning the militia in eastern Upper Canada was better, although there were still some problems. See AO, Alexander Fraser Papers, series 1, box 1, Colonel Lethbridge to Brock, 10 August 1812 (MU 1063).

72 Turner, "Career of Isaac Brock," 142–3 and appendix E; *DHC*, 3: 164, Brock to Prevost, 4 August 1812; NA, MG 24, E 1–4, 54–64, Prevost to Brock, 12 August; 65–71, same to same, 30 August. Weekes, "War of 1812," 150, seems to suggest, incorrectly, that Brock employed martial law. The correspondence does not support Sheppard's claim, in *Plunder, Profits, and Parole*, 55, that Brock "considered declaring martial law on his own authority."

73 *DHC*, 3: 76–7, DGO, 27 June 1812; Robinson, *Life of Sir John Beverley Robinson*, 30; "Career of Isaac Brock," 178–9. Brock departed York on the night of 5 August.

74 AO, F.B. Tupper Papers (MS 496), W. Claus to ———, 15 October 1812; Alexander Fraser Papers, series 1, box 1, John Norton to Captain Glegg, 11 August (MU 1063). The following correspondence in the Fraser Papers makes clear the various pressures on the Six Nations and the dissension among them over what action to take: M. Elliott to Colonel Claus, 26 July; Norton to Glegg, 11 August; W.I. Kerr to Glegg, 17 August. See also Norton, *Journal*, 295–9.

75 For the relevant correspondence see *DRIC*, 118–23, 130–1, 141–3, 156–60.

76 *DRIC*, 156–60, Brock to Prevost, 17 August 1812; Norton, *Journal*, 300–1.

77 NA, MG 11, CO 42/353, 226, 3 September 1812; Robinson, *Life of Sir John Beverley Robinson*, 46–51.

78 *Naval War of 1812*, 1: 273, 295, 305. Woolsey's vessels were the gunboat *Julia* and the brig *Oneida*. See chapter 3 above.

79 *DHC*, 3: 258–9, Brock to Prevost, 13 September 1812; 4: 24–5, Chief Justice Scott to Colonel Talbot, 12 September.

80 NA, RG 8, v.677, 90, Brock to Prevost, 18 September 1812; Crooks, "Recollections"; *DHC*, 8: 247–53, Memorial of Lieutenant-Colonel Robert Nichol to Lord Bathurst, 24 September 1814; W.H. Merritt, in *Campaigns of 1812–14*, 6.

81 *DHC*, 3: 295–6, Major-General Dearborn to Van Rensselaer, 26 September 1812; 301–2, *Buffalo Gazette*, 29 September; 4, 28, Brigadier-General Smyth to Van Rensselaer, 2 October; 30–1, Dearborn to Van Rensselaer,

4 October; 39, *Buffalo Gazette*, 6 October; 41–2, Van Rensselaer to Dearborn, 8 October; 42, John Lovett to Joseph Alexander, 8 October. On Stephen Van Rensselaer and his cousin Solomon see *Defended Border*, 24n3; on Alexander Smyth, 26n9. Van Rensselaer, *Narrative of the Affair of Queenstown*, is informative about American preparations and the weaknesses of their forces including their leadership.

82 *DHC*, 4: 68; 95–103, Chrystie to General T.H. Cushing, 22 February 1813.

83 A system of beacons was established from Lake Erie to Queenston and thence inland to Pelham Heights by which messages could be sent during the daytime by means of coloured balls or flags or at night-time by burning wood in a basket hung on a pole. *SBD*, 1: 266–9, provides a description from 1809 of this telegraph system. BECHS, A. Conger Goodyear, War of 1812 MSS, box 2, v.7, Nicholas Gray to General Van Rensselaer, 31 August 1812, refers to "the Combustible telegraph" on the Canadian side of the Niagara River. Pennsylvania State Archives, MG 6, Jacob Miller Diary, 27, 16 October 1812, mentions a black flag "hoisted at the Telegraph" on the Canadian shore opposite Black Rock. A militia dragoon was to be ready at Fort George by 12 noon daily to carry mail to Fort Erie.

84 Returns to the War Office show rank-and-file strength (excluding drummers, sergeants, and officers) of 890 at Fort George on 25 September and the same on 25 October; see NA, MG 13, WO 17, 1516, 109, 125. The only other Upper Canadian location reported on was Kingston, which had rank-and-file strength of 1,141 in September and 652 in October. See also *DHC*, 4: 108–14, Major Thomas Evans to ———, 15 October 1812; Cruikshank, *Battle of Queenston Heights*, 20–1; Norton, *Journal*, 302; *SBD*, 3, pt 2, 557, W.H. Merritt, "Journal of Events"; James Dennis, "Memorial to Sir Gordon Drummond, 20 March 1815," in "Records of Niagara," 51.

85 *DHC*, 4: 108–14, Major Thomas Evans to ———, 15 October 1812; Cruikshank, *Battle of Queenston Heights*, 20–1; Norton, *Journal*, 302; *SBD*, 3, pt 2: 557; W.H. Merritt, "Journal of Events"; James Dennis, "Memorial to Sir Gordon Drummond, 20 March 1815," in "Records of Niagara," 51; Gray, *Soldiers of the King*, 157–8, 160.

86 NA, MG 24, A 1, 92–6. The document begins without preamble and on the back is written: "1812 – Instructions sent to Officers commanding forts by Major General Brock some days prior to the attack on Queenston." (I want to thank Douglas Hendry for this point of information.) Tupper, *Life and Correspondence*, 328, quotes a few lines.

87 *SBD*, 1: 617–25, Evans, 15 October 1812 to ———. Upon a report of mutiny among the 49th Foot at Queenston, Brock had sent Brigade Major Evans to investigate. Evans crossed the river under a flag of truce

to negotiate an exchange of prisoners and was alarmed by what he saw and heard. He hurried back to Fort George and convinced Brock to prepare for immediate invasion.

88 NA, RG 8, v.677, 11 October 1812, with the last paragraph dated 12 October. Tupper, in *Life and Correspondence*, 328, believes that this was Brock's final writing.

89 To produce as accurate an account as possible, I have based it primarily upon eyewitness reports. While there are many good secondary accounts, they are distorted by being filtered through their authors' eyes. The secondary works I refer to are James, *Full and Correct Account*; Christie, *Military and Naval Operations*; Thompson, *History of the Late War*; John Richardson, *Richardson's War*; Symons, *Battle of Queenston Heights*; Cruikshank, *Battle of Queenston Heights*; Hitsman, *Incredible War*; Whitfield, *Battle of Queenston Heights*; R. Malcomson, *Battle of Queenston Heights*; Stanley, *War of 1812*. Even with the abundance of written evidence, I would agree with the comment of American major David Campbell, who wrote that no correct account could be provided because of the confusion of the battle on 13 October; see Duke University, Campbell Family Papers, Campbell to his brother, 3 November 1812.

90 *DHC*, 4: 108–14, Major Thomas Evans to ———, 15 October, 1812. Norton, in his *Journal*, 304, says Sheaffe gave him this order. See the discussion in chapter 5. On Holcroft see Irving, *Officers of the British Forces*, 21. His service in the artillery went back at least to 1798.

91 Brock arrived in Queenston between 6:30 and 7 a.m. See Crooks, "Recollections," 16. Crooks heard that Brock had left Fort George for Queenston at "break of day." If this was true, the time would have been shortly after 6 a.m., and a swift horse would certainly have carried him the six miles to Queenston by 7 o'clock. W.H. Merritt, in *Campaigns of 1812–14*, 10, does not specify when Brock departed from Fort George, but reports that he arrived at Queenston as "The morning was breaking"; but Merritt was not an eyewitness. No eyewitness states that Brock went to the redan and ordered down its guard, although he may have ridden to the south end of the village in order to survey the scene. See *DHC*, 5: 12, Letter from Brown's Point [Lieutenant John Beverley Robinson]. *Letters of 1812 from Dominion Archives*, C. Askin to J. Askin, 14 October, says Askin heard that Brock was at the redan.

92 *DHC*, 4: 116–7, Narrative of Volunteer G.S. Jarvis, 49th Regiment. He was a gentleman volunteer in the 49th Foot. This is the source that reports Brock being on horseback.

93 American troops were at that time above the redan, and some accounts claimed that they made their way up a fisherman's path that Brock, or Sheaffe, had failed to guard. The only contemporary account that makes this claim is that of Major Evans, who obtained his information from an

officer who was not present at Queenston until later in the day. See *DHC*, 4: 112, Evans to ———, 15 October 1812. All other eyewitness accounts, including those of American officers who participated, do not mention a fisherman's path or a difficult climb from the riverside to a point above the redan. Relevant correspondence is in *DHC*, 4: 98–9, 118–20, 155; Van Rensselaer, *Narrative of the Affair of Queenstown*, 26; Crooks, "Recollections," 23–4; BECHS, A. Conger Goodyear, War of 1812 MSS, box 2, v.7, Colonel H.B. Armstrong to Henry B. Dawson, 6 March 1860. My research also included a wide survey of secondary literature.

94 *DHC*, 4: 114–16, Extract of a letter from Upper Canada, dated at Brown's Point, 15 October. Lieutenant Archibald McLean, who wrote this letter, mentioned that Captain Williams was at the redan; see *DHC*, 4: 116–7, Narrative of Jarvis. He was an eyewitness to Brock's charge up the hill and to his death. He describes Brock dying without uttering any final words. It is not known when Jarvis wrote this narrative, but the exactness of some details, such as Brock's falling on his left side after being shot, suggests that his recollections were clear. I want to thank Michael Power for his observations on this and other points.

95 *DHC*, 4: 116–17, Narrative of Jarvis; 114–16, Extract of a letter from Upper Canada [Lieutenant Archibald McLean], dated Brown's Point, 15 October; 88–9, Glegg to William Dummer Powell, 14 October, 112–13, Major Thomas Evans to ———, 15 October 1812. Evans says Captain Williams led.

96 Pennsylvania State Archives, MG 6, Diary of Jacob Miller, 24–5, entries for 12 and 13 October, reports British cannonading of Black Rock that caused both damage and casualties.

97 An indication of rising tension was shooting by sentries across the river. See *DHC*, 3: 273–4, Major-General Van Rensselaer to Brock, 17 September 1812; 274, Brock to Van Rensselaer, 17 September; 283, Van Rensselaer to Brock, 20 September; 288–9, J. Lovett to J. Alexander, 22 September. See also Van Rensselaer, *Narrative of the Affair at Queenstown*, 23, appendix 2, 57, 73–5.

98 Tupper, *Life and Correspondence*, 315–16, Brock to Savery Brock, 18 September 1812. See also NA, RG 8, v.677, 90, Brock to Prevost, 18 September.

99 James Dennis, "Memorial to Sir Gordon Drummond," in "Records of Niagara," 50–3, states that Brock was unaccompanied. *DHC*, 4: 116–17, Narrative of Jarvis, says that Glegg and Macdonell were present; see also 83, Glegg to William Brock, 14 October, and 88–9, Glegg to William Dummer Powell, 14 October. In these two letters Glegg does not mention accompanying Brock.

100 *DHC*, 5: 29–30, Evans to Hon. W.D. Powell, 6 January 1813. On Evans see *DCB*, 9: 245–6. The brigade major acted as a chief of staff for his

commanding officer. Sheppard, in *Plunder, Profits, and Paroles*, 69–70, refers to this criticism and cites as additional evidence a letter from Prevost to Sheaffe of 27 March 1813; he assumes that the governor had made a visit to Upper Canada in 1812. Prevost's first visit, however, was made in February and March of 1813, so that his criticisms of deficiencies in pay and supplies for the militia more likely apply to the period of Sheaffe's command than to that of Brock's. See *DHC*, 5: 134–6.

101 See chapter 5 below. See also Turner, "Career of Isaac Brock," 275–9.

102 Glegg joined the 49th in 1797, and he was present in the same actions as Brock in 1799 and 1801. He also had previously been an ADC and had attended the Royal Military College between 1803 and 1805. Brock chose him as an ADC in 1810. He served at Detroit and for this action was breveted major on 8 October, and Sheaffe praised his services at Queenston Heights. See *The Royal Military Calendar* ... (3rd ed.; London, 1820), 5, 205–6. I want to thank Stuart Sutherland for providing me with this and other references, along with information relating to Glegg. After Brock's death, Glegg sought to become an aide to Prevost, who agreed, but there is no record of his taking up the post. He acted briefly as ADC to Sheaffe before serving as major of brigade to Sheaffe, Rottenburg, Vincent, and Drummond. See NA, RG 8, v.1220, 8, Prevost to Sheaffe, 21 October 1812; v.1220, 8, Prevost to Sheaffe, 21 October 1812; MG 13, WO 17/1517, passim, and 17/1518, passim; RG 8, v.12031/2M, 42, GO, 14 July 1814. Other useful sources are PRO, WO 25/759, and Irving, *Officers of the British Forces*. Glegg retired with the rank of lieutenant-colonel.

103 *DCB*, 7: 347–8. His dates were c.1759–1846. In 1797 he was appointed assistant superintendent of Indian affairs for the Home District, and he continued as a prominent official of the Indian Department until his retirement in 1837.

104 Called "Greenfield" after his birthplace in Scotland in order to distinguish him from the many other Macdonells named "John." See *DCB*, 5: 520–3. The authors of this biography attribute Macdonell's appointment principally to the influence of W.D. Powell.

105 A reader can easily gain a sense of biographers' attitudes towards Brock by a perusal of the titles and chapter headings of the following books: Eayrs, *Sir Isaac Brock*; Edgar, *General Brock*; D.J. Goodspeed, *The Good Soldier* ... (Toronto, 1964); W.K. Lamb, *The Hero of Upper Canada* (Toronto, 1962); W.R. Nursey, *The Story of Isaac Brock* (4th ed., rev. and enlarged; Toronto, 1923); D.B. Read, *The Life and Times of Major-General Sir Isaac Brock* (Toronto, 1894); Tupper, *Life and Correspondence*.

106 References in two of the best-known histories of the war are Hannay, *History of the War of 1812*, 26, 36, 84; and Lucas, *The Canadian War of 1812*, 18, 27, 35, 40, 52, 54–6, 92, 256. Horsman, in *War of 1812*, sees Brock

as the "best general" on the British side. *DCB*, 5: 111–14, contains C.P. Stacey's very favourable biography of Brock.

107 Hitsman, *Incredible War*, 16, 54, 72–3, 38, 64, 90; see also 17–18, 74–6, 78, 81, 87–8; Stanley, *War of 1812*, 79, 126–7, 131, 403.

108 Hyatt, "Defence of Upper Canada," 116, 123; see also 114–15, 122, 127, 132. In *Battle of Queenston Heights*, 24, 27, 30, Whitfield's criticisms of Brock's "strategic planning" are basically those made by Hyatt. Yet she also praises him for his leadership, tenacity, and military success; see 10, 18–19, 22–7.

109 Sheppard, *Plunder, Profit, and Paroles.* Most of Sheppard's comments occur in chapter 3. On Brock's strategic brilliance see 14–15.

110 See Walden, "Isaac Brock, Man and Myth"; *DHC*, 4: 146–7, Lieutenant G. Ridout to his brother, 21 October 1812. Duke University, Campbell Family Papers, David Campbell to his brother, 13 October, provides an American viewpoint. See also W.H. Merritt, in *Campaigns of 1812–14*, 8; Tupper, *Life and Correspondence*, 335–7, 446; Edgar, *General Brock*, 307–8.

111 *DHC*, 5: 159, 21 April 1813.

112 *DHC*, 6: 17–22, 7 June 1813. This letter may have been sent also to Earl Bathurst. On McTavish see *DCB*, 7: 561–2. McTavish, McGillivray and Company dominated the fur trade out of Montreal.

113 Tupper, *Life and Correspondence*, 449–50 (the petition was passed 6 March); *DHC*, 6: 58–9, Bathurst to Sheaffe, 8 June.

114 Upper Canada, Journals of the Legislative Assembly, 1814, 159, 14 March; AO, Gordon Drummond Letterbook (MU 8190), 201, Robert Loring to William Jarvis (secretary of the Province of Upper Canada), 16 March 1815; Tupper, *Life and Correspondence*, 450–1.

115 *York Gazette*, 17 October 1812. This paper also printed a short poem. The *Montreal Herald*, 24 October, had already begun to refer to Brock in heroic terms. In its account of the capture of Detroit, the *Herald* praised the officers, men, and Brock as "willing, at the risk of their lives, to gather laurels to adorn his brow." See also *Kingston Gazette*, 24 October.

116 *Quebec Mercury*, 10 November 1812, 352; 22 June 1813, 197. See also Walden, "Isaac Brock," chap. 3.

117 *Montreal Herald*, 5 June 1813; upper case in the original. See also 29 May.

118 Sheppard, *Plunder, Profit, and Paroles*, 67. This interpretation appeared earlier in Walden's thesis. *John Askin Papers*, 2: 735–9, Charles Askin to [his father] John Askin, 11 December 1812, written at Queenston, refers to Brock's popularity with the militia. See Gray, *Soldiers of the King*, 19–25, 39–46, for a more positive interpretation of the militia's role.

119 See Walden, "Isaac Brock," for a discussion of this tendency and for readings. Hero-worship is seen as one of the attributes of the Romantic age; on that subject see Jacques Barzun, *Berlioz and the Romantic Century* (2 vols.; Boston: Little, Brown and Company, 1950).

CHAPTER FOUR

1 For critical views see Stanley, *War of 1812*, 172–4; Hitsman, *Incredible War,* 124, 126, 137; and *The Town of York*, xc-xci, where Firth cites *SBD*, 1: 56. Views favourable to Sheaffe are given by Humphries, "The Capture of York" (reprinted in *Defended Border,* 251–70); Whitfield, *Battle of Queenston Heights*, 34; and Benn, *Historic Fort York*, 62–4; and on Queenston Heights by Hitsman, *Incredible War,* 90. Sheppard, *Plunder, Profit, and Paroles,* 76–8, 148, seems to agree with Benn.

2 Whitfield, *Battle of Queenston Heights*, 31–7 and appendices A, B, and C.

3 *DCB*, 8: 793; Whitfield, *Battle of Queenston Heights*, 31; Sabine, *Biographical Sketches*, 2: 284.

4 *DNB*, 15: 865–7 (Hugh Percy, 1742–1817, second Duke of Northumberland "of the third creation"); Sabine, *Biographical Sketches*, 2: 285. Sheaffe's friendship with the duke continued during his career in Canada; see NA, MG 23, D 2, Sheaffe to Winslow, 6 May 1812; Sheaffe to "My Dear Friend," 12 November 1813.

5 According to W.D. Powell, who referred to the school as a military academy and "the only school of that description in England, except that of Woolwich"; see NA, MG 23, H 1, 4, 3, 117. See also *DHC*, 5: 35–9, Notes on the Conduct of Major-General R.H. Sheaffe and Major-General Vincent.

6 Tupper, *Life and Correspondence*, 110–16. The financial problem arose in June 1811 out of a business failure in England which left Brock with a debt of £3,000 to pay, and he also offered to help reduce his brother Savery's debt.

7 *DCB*, 8: 793; Sabine, *Biographical Sketches*, 2: 286–7. The only significant event involving Sheaffe occurred in 1794, when Lieutenant-Governor Simcoe sent him to protest to the Americans about settling at Sodus Bay on the south shore of Lake Ontario. The relevant correspondence is in *The Correspondence of Lieutenant Governor John Graves Simcoe*, edited by E.A. Cruikshank (5 vols; Toronto: Ontario Historical Society, 1923–3l), 2: 364, 366, 382, 385, 393–4; 3: 16–17, 27–8, 85, 133.

8 Sabine, *Biographical Sketches*, 2: 285, citing a letter from Sheaffe's brother-in-law, Captain Molesworth, to Mrs Sheaffe, his mother. See also NA, RG 8, v.15, 52–3, W. Windham to Lord Dorchester, 2 June 1795, enclosing a list of promotions.

9 Petre, *Royal Berkshire Regiment*, 1: 68–73, 77–81.

10 See the discussion in chapter 3. References are Tupper, *Life and Correspondence*, 18; Edgar, *General Brock*, 22; NA, RG 8, v.922, 83–4, Brock to [Major Green], 16 August 1803.

11 Tupper, *Life and Correspondence*, 27–33, 430–2; Edgar, *General Brock*, 62–4; Goodspeed, *British Campaigns*, 30–8. See also Petre, *Royal Berkshire Regiment*, 1: 83–5.

12 Whitfield, *Battle of Queenston Heights*, 32, 48–9.

13 NA, RG 8, v.922, 77–9, Brock to Green, 17 August 1803.

14 NA, RG 8, v.923, 12–16, Brock to Lieutenant-Colonel Green, 8 February 1804. The quotations that follow are from this letter. See also Allen, "Bisshopp Papers," 25, Bisshopp to Kate (his sister), 21 March 1813, for later evidence of this problem.

15 NA, RG 8, v.923, 12–16, Brock to Green, 8 February 1804.

16 Ibid.

17 NA, MG 30, D 1, 27, 753; DCB, 8: 793.

18 Tupper, *Life and Correspondence*, 116–17, Lieutenant-Colonel Torrens to Brock, 17 October 1811; 140–1, Prevost to Brock, 22 January 1812 and Baynes to Brock, 23 January; NA, RG 8, v.30, 105–6, Torrens to Prevost, 18 October 1811. Compare this last letter with NA, RG 8, v.550, 84, Torrens to Drummond, 27 August.

19 NA, RG 8, v.550, 50–2, Edward Sills to Sheaffe, 9 May, and several other letters. In possession of Baroness Strange at Megginch Castle, Scotland, is an "Extra Warrant Book" (49th Regiment) which refers to Sheaffe at Three Rivers as "Lt. Colonel commanding and Colonel" (3, 24 June 1811).

20 NA, RG 8, v.334, N. Freer to Major-General Glasgow, 23 July 1812; v.1218, 312, Prevost to Liverpool, 15 July; v.1219, 16, Prevost to Bathurst, 17 August.

21 Robinson, *Life of Sir John Beverley Robinson*, 54; Whitfield, *Battle of Queenston Heights*, 35. The *York Gazette*, 24 October 1812, described Sheaffe as "intimately acquainted with our local situation."

22 DHC, 3: 191, Sheaffe to Major-General Van Rensselaer, 19 August 1812; 201, Sheaffe to Prevost, 22 August.

23 DHC, 3: 169, Major-General Dearborn to Major-General A. Hall or commanding officer on the Niagara Frontier, 8 August 1812. Sheaffe passed through Montreal between 3 and 5 August, apparently before it was known there that Prevost in Quebec City was sending Colonel Baynes to negotiate the truce. See NA, RG 8, v.677, 8–9, John Vincent to Baynes, 4 August.

24 DHC, 3: 172, Baynes to Brock, 13 August 1812.

25 DHC, 3: 184, John Lovett to Joseph Alexander, 17 August 1812; 189, Van Rensselaer to Dearborn, 18 August, and same to Lieutenant Colonel Myers.

26 DHC, 3: 201–2, Sheaffe to Prevost, 22 August 1812.

27 DHC, 3: 197, Van Rensselaer to Sheaffe, 20 August 1812; 197–8, "Articles of Agreement for an Armistice."

28 NA, RG 8, v.1218, 377, Prevost to Brock, 30 August 1812; Hitsman, *Incredible War*, 77–81.

29 *DHC*, 3: 234, Brock to his brothers, 13 September 1812; 237, Sheaffe to
   Major-General Van Rensselaer, 5 September; 238–9, Van Rensselaer to
   Major-General Dearborn, 5 September; 241, John Lovett to Joseph Alex-
   ander, 6 September; 240, Regimental Orders, Lieutenant-Colonel
   Chewett, Commanding 3rd York Militia, 5 September; 4: 28, DGO,
   2 October.

30 *DHC*, 4: 71–3, Sheaffe to Prevost, 13 October 1812. For what others
   present at the fort wrote, see 88–9, Major J.B. Glegg to Justice W.D. Powell, 14 October; 108–14, Major Thomas Evans to ————, 15 October;
   77–9, William Woodruff to David Thorburn, 29 July 1840. AO, F.B.
   Tupper Papers (MS 496), Isaac Todd to [one of Brock's brothers], 2
   November, claims that "though he [Brock] fell early in the last affair yet
   he had arranged everything."

31 Norton, *Journal*, cxvi–cxvii, 304–5.

32 Robinson, *Life of Sir John Beverley Robinson*, 37, [J.B. Robinson], Brown's
   Point, 14 October 1812; *DHC*, 4: 77–9, W. Woodruff to David Thorburn,
   29 July 1840; W.H. Merritt, in *Campaigns of 1812–14*, 8–9. Merritt does
   not give a time for Sheaffe's arrival at Durham's house.

33 *DHC*, 4: 95–103, Lieutenant-Colonel John Chrystie to General Thomas H.
   Cushing, 22 February 1813. From the heights above Queenston Chrystie
   saw Sheaffe's advance at about 11 a.m. The distance by road from the
   waterfront of present-day Queenston to the marker of "Sheaffe's path" is
   1.4 miles. Sheaffe started about 2.5 miles north of Queenston to swing
   westward. If we assume that this was his route, the total distance his men
   might have marched after leaving the river road until the reached the
   top of the escarpment would have been between 4 and 6 miles. Crooks,
   "Recollections," 18, puts the "old road" up the escarpment "about two
   miles west of Queenston."

34 Crooks, "Recollections," 18–19, describes shot from an American gun
   above Lewiston flying over them as they lay on the ground.

35 *DHC*, 4: 71–3, Sheaffe to Prevost, 13 October 1812; 100–2, Chrystie to
   Cushing, 22 February 1813. For other start times see 90–5, Colonel
   Mead's Statement, 18 November (about 3:30 p.m.); 79–82, Van Rensselaer to Hon. William Eustis, 14 October (4:30 p.m.); 85–8, John Lovett
   to Joseph Alexander, 14 October 1812 (5 p.m.); 5: 9–10, Lieutenant
   Patrick McDonogh to his sister, 16 October (4 to 5 p.m.). Robinson,
   Life of Sir John Beverley Robinson, 34, [J.B. Robinson], Brown's Point,
   14 October, puts the start of the attack on the Americans at "About
   three o'clock." See also BECHS, War of 1812 Papers (Boo–15), box 1,
   folder 1, David Willson to Allan Stewart, 9 November. Willson, who was
   taken prisoner in this battle, put the start time at about 4 p.m. W.H.
   Merritt, in *Campaigns of 1812–14*, 9, claims that Sheaffe's forces waited

an hour for the 41st to arrive from Chippawa, but he does not give a start time.

36 Van Rensselaer, *Narrative of the Affair of Queenstown*, 37–8.

37 *DHC*, 4: 71–3, Sheaffe to Prevost, 13 October 1812; 175–6, Sheaffe to Prevost, 3 November. James Crooks claimed that the militia in the battle on the heights were not given clear orders, and he also criticized other aspects of Sheaffe's conduct on 13 October. See his "Recollections," 19, 22–3. See also W.H. Merritt, in *Campaigns of 1812–14*, 8–9. Merritt was present among the forces under Sheaffe, and his account suggests that the men knew exactly what they were supposed to do. John Richardson, who served with the 41st, thought that that regiment did not receive all the credit it deserved. See his *Major Richardson's Major-General Sir Isaac Brock.*

38 NA, RG 8, V.1220, 10–2, Prevost to Sheaffe, 27 October 1812; *DHC*, 4: 186, Sheaffe to Prevost, 8 November; 5, 159, Prevost to Bathurst, 21 April 1813; Whitfield, *Battle of Queenston Heights*, 34; W.H. Merritt, in *Campaigns of 1812–14*, 10–1. Merritt, writing in 1814, criticized the failure to seize Fort Niagara and the truce because they left the militiamen feeling unneeded and many went home.

39 *PBHS*, 17: 310–11, Sheaffe to Prevost, 19 November 1812. *DHC*, 4: 251–7, includes Sheaffe's report of 30 November to Prevost and Lieutenant-Colonel Cecil Bisshopp's report of 1 December to Sheaffe. See also Stanley, *War of 1812*, 135–7. For the official American report see *DHC*, 4: 260–3, Colonel Wm. H. Winder to Brigadier General Alexander Smyth, 7 December 1812. This differs in some details from the letter in Winder, *Statement of Occurrences*, 3–6, which was printed in connection with a dispute about events on that frontier in November and December 1812.

40 *SBD*, 1: 609–10, 625–7; 3, pt 2: 563–4, Merritt's Journal. See Thomas Talbot's complaint in *The Talbot Papers*, edited with an introduction by J.H. Coyne (Ottawa: Royal Society of Canada, 1908–09), 170. See also *DCB*, 8: 794; Windsor Public Library, John Stodgell Collection (MS 24 I/13), series I, Askin Documents, unit 12, Charles Askin to John Askin, 12 November 1812.

41 AO, F.B. Tupper Papers (MS 496), Letters, 16 December 1812; *DHC*, 5: 35–9; 45, Sheaffe to Hon. W.D. Powell, 20 January 1813; Turner, "Career of Isaac Brock," 275–8. See also *John Askin Papers*, 2: 735–9, Charles Askin to John Askin, Queenston, 11 December 1812. According to Charles Askin, the militiamen had very high regard for Lieutenant-Colonel Bisshopp; it is therefore likely that his critical attitude towards Sheaffe would influence the civilians' viewpoint. On Bisshopp see *DCB*, 5: 82–3.

42 *DHC*, 4: 327, Lieutenant-Colonel Nichol to Thomas Talbot, 18 December 1812; Crooks, "Recollections," 22.

43 *DHC*, 4: 142, Sheaffe to Bathurst, 20 October 1812.

44 *DHC*, 4: 188–9, Proclamation dated 9 November 1812; 5: 28–9, Sheaffe to Powell, 6 January 1813; *PBHS*, 17: 314–15, Captain Loring to Colonel Claus, T. Dickson, J. Edwards [n.d.]. In *Defended Border*, 210–2, Cruikshank quotes Michael Smith's description of militia resisters north and east of York.

45 Graves, "Joseph Willcocks," 31–4, concludes that these boards did not solve the problem, and indeed, because of Sheaffe's policy, "a large part of the population of Upper Canada had received notice that they were regarded officially as being of doubtful loyalty."

46 *DHC*, 4: 174, MDO, 1 November 1812; 178, DGO, 3 November; 211–12, MGO, 14 November; 322–3, Sheaffe to Prevost, 16 December; 5: 30–1, Sheaffe to ———, 7 January 1813; 29–30, Major Thomas Evans to Hon. W.D. Powell, 6 January.

47 *DHC*, 4: 186, Sheaffe to Prevost, 8 November 1812; 229, Sheaffe to Prevost, 23 November; 322–3, Sheaffe to Prevost, 16 December; 272–5, Captain A. Gray to Prevost, 3 December; 297–8, Sheaffe to Prevost, 11 December; 330–2, Prevost to Gray, 19 December; NA, RG 8, C, v.688E, 3–4, Report of a Committee of the Executive Council, 17 November; "Records of Niagara," 59–61, Charles Askin to his father, 18 November; 63, Sheaffe's reply to the Executive Council; 63–5, Prevost to Sheaffe, 1 January 1813.

48 See *DHC*, 5: 90–9, for Sheaffe's speeches and the replies of the two houses. For his closing speech and the results of the session see ibid., 113–5, and Gourlay, *Statistical Account*, 2: 255–8. Altogether eleven acts were passed.

49 Whatever Sheaffe meant by this term, it was put into effect in the form of the bounty; see *DHC*, 5: 111–12, Sheaffe to Prevost, 13 March 1813; 127–8, Sheaffe to Bathurst, 20 March. Clothing for the Upper Canadian militia was forwarded to Kingston; see NA, RG 8, v.12031/2H, 188–92, GO, Kingston, 30 June.

50 In January 1813 Prevost had indicated his approval of Sheaffe's proposals to improve the militia. See *PBHS*, 17: 331–2, Sheaffe to Prevost, 6 January; NA, RG 8, v.1220, 118–19, Prevost to Sheaffe, 21 January. Stanley, "Contribution of the Canadian Militia," in *After Tippecanoe*, 36–7, attributes the initial idea to Brock. See also Gray, *Soldiers of the King*, 21–3, 31.

51 *DHC*, 5: 111–12, Sheaffe to Prevost, 13 March 1813; 124, Sheaffe to Prevost, 18 March; 127–8, Sheaffe to Bathurst, 20 March; 151–2, Regulations for Incorporated Militia; 6: 214, Bathurst to Sheaffe, 10 July.

52 *PBHS*, 17: 369, Sheaffe to Baynes, 7 April 1813. For an indication of competition for manpower, see *DHC*, 5: 137–9, A Sketch of the Campaign of 1812 ... by W. Hamilton Merritt. See also Stanley, "Contribution of the Canadian Militia," in *After Tippecanoe*, 37.

53 Sheppard, in *Plunder, Profit, and Paroles*, 70–1, 73–5, regards the effort to raise a large force of incorporated militia as a failure. He has the same opinion about General Drummond's efforts in 1814; see 94–5. His opinion that the low recruitment figures prove lack of popular support for the war should be recognized as only one possible explanation. Stanley, "Contribution of the Canadian Militia," in *After Tippecanoe*, 41–2, presents a more positive view of that battalion's role. See also Gray, *Soldiers of the King*, 43–6, 187–94; Hitsman, *Incredible War*, 110–11.

54 Prevost authorized the use of martial law because Sheaffe's troops on their march to Kingston had frequently encountered unfriendly attitudes among the population. See DHC, 8: 228–9, "A Lover of Justice" to Major-General de Rottenburg, n.d.

55 PBHS, 17: 361–2, Sheaffe to Prevost, n.d. [March 1813]; BECHS, A. Conger Goodyear, War of 1812 MSS, box 1, folder 3, Sheaffe to Prevost, 5 April. See also DHC, 5: 134–6, Prevost to Sheaffe, 27 March.

56 Benn, *Historic Fort York*, 40; see also 34, 44–5, 52; also DHC, 5: 175, "An Account of the Capture of York" (manuscript in the handwriting of W.D. Powell).

57 *Town of York*, 77–8, Bruyères' "Report Relative to the Present State of York Upper Canada," n.d.

58 NA, MG 13, WO 17, 1517, 4, 20, 36, 51, 65, 80, 94; *Town of York*, 288–9, Bruyères to Prevost, 28 January 1813. This letter reports a dispute between officers about where to establish the navy yard and build a ship, and makes clear that this difference of opinion delayed the operation. Bruyères thought that York was much less defensible than Kingston, a view that may suggest why the capital's garrison of regulars was so small.

59 DHC, 5: 175, "An Account of the Capture of York." Benn, *Historic Fort York*, 50, gives the total British strength at 700–750, which appears high. He also mentions a unit of the 49th being present, but the only reference to that regiment in the documents is in DHC, 5: 215–16, "Return of Killed, Wounded, Prisoners and Missing of the Troops at York under the Command of Major-General Sir Roger Hale Sheaffe, on the 27th ultimo," Kingston, 10 May, 1813, signed by Richard Leonard, acting deputy assistant adjutant general, and Edward Baynes, adjutant general, North America. The 49th was not mentioned in accounts of the fighting. Norton, *Journal*, 318–19, states that there were "sixty Missisagas and Chippawas" at York.

60 Hansen, "War of 1812," 21–2, 36–7. A significant reason for difficulties of cooperation arose from the attitude of Chauncey, the naval commander.

61 DHC, 5: 166–8, General Dearborn to the Secretary of War, 28 April 1813; 170–1, Dearborn to Governor Tompkins, 28 April; 169–70, Commodore Chauncey to the Secretary of the Navy, 28 April; 179–82, Lieutenant

Fraser's account; *Town of York*, 303–6, Colonel Cromwell Pearce's account.

62 Accounts differ on whether the initial resistance was made only by Native warriors or included militia and regulars. Sheaffe reported that "Major Givins and his small band of Indians" opposed the landing for a short time alone before being supported by regulars, but the other eyewitness accounts by Canadian militiamen and American officers report the presence of regulars (some mention militia) in the opposing force. See DHC, 5: 187–9, Sheaffe to Prevost, 5 May, 1813 (this official report is in NA, RG 8, I, v.678, 195). Benn, *Historic Fort York*, 51–8, follows Sheaffe on this point. For the other accounts see DHC, 5: 176, 179–83, 193–4, 205–6, 208, 214; *Town of York*, 279–80, 292–3, 304, 328–9; Norton, *Journal*, 320.

63 For times see DHC, 5: 207–10, P. Finan's Journal; 213–5, Letter from U.S. officer, 9 May 1813, in the *United States Gazette*; *Town of York*, 303–6, Colonel Cromwell Pearce's Account. Sheaffe's claim that "the contest ... was maintained for nearly eight hours" was, to say the least, an exaggeration; see DHC, 5: 187–8, Sheaffe to Prevost, 5 May. Stanley, *War of 1812*, 173, puts the time of the explosion after 12 noon.

64 DHC, 5: 147, 15 May 1813. On the road conditions see 210, P. Finan's Journal. Stanley, *War of 1812*, 178, mentions the retreat taking fourteen days, but in fact Sheaffe reported from Kingston on the eighth day after the battle.

65 These men were prominent in several areas not only in the life of York life but also in Upper Canadian society. See *Town of York*, xci; also 294–6, Strachan to Dr James Brown, 26 April 1813; 311, Mrs Powell to W.D. Powell, 12 May, and 312, 6 June; *John Strachan Letter Book*, 37, Strachan to Hon. John Richardson, 10 May. Strachan suggested that Prevost might "think it necessary to recall general Sheaffe." The following have biographies in the DCB: Allan (8: 4–13), Baldwin (7: 35–44), Chewett (7: 175–6), Strachan (9: 751–66).

66 DHC, 5: 174–5, n.d.

67 *Town of York*, 291, Sheaffe to Bathurst, 5 April 1813. Hitsman, *Incredible War*, 123, mentions earlier warnings of the American threat to York.

68 DHC, 5: 175–7, for Powell's account; *Town of York*, 279–80, for extracts from E. Playter's diary. For the accounts that suggest orderly defence see *Town of York*, 207–10, 303–4, 328–9; and DHC, 5: 179–82, 213–5.

69 AO, Journal of a Staff Officer (MS842), 10–12.

70 See note 59 for official reports of rank-and-file strength. If the regulars' effective strength was towards the higher figure (573), deductions must be made for losses suffered as a result of the battle. Information on these is fragmentary, but they appear to have been over 100 men. DHC, 5: 164–6, "Terms of Capitulation," made at York, reported that 2 regulars and 4 Royal Artillerymen (among others) were taken prisoner; 215,

Memo by Lieutenant Colonel Glegg, reported 104 casualties for the 8th
Foot; 215–6, "A Return of Killed, Wounded, Prisoners and Missing of the
Troops at York," reported casualties ranging from 134 to 153. In addition to these casualties, more men would have been lost to various
causes during a march of such difficulty. Another method of arriving at
an approximate figure is to start with the total force available to Sheaffe
and deduct the losses. If the larger figure of 700 is accepted, the "Terms
of Capitulation" report of 264 militia prisoners, 6 regulars, and 22 men
from other services leaves about 500 men unaccounted for. Deducting
the casualties given in the various reports above leaves fewer than
400 survivors. For official reports on rank-and-file strength on the Niagara see NA, MG 13, WO 17, 1517, 51, 65; slightly higher figures are
given in DHC, 5: 164.

71 *Montreal Herald*, 5 June 1813, 3, report on the American capture of Fort
George; 19 June, 3, Prevost's proclamation of 14 June and a general
order of 11 June.

72 NA, RG 8, v.1220, 23 June, 1813; DHC, 6: 139, Prevost to Bathurst,
24 June.

73 NA, RG 8, v.1170, 229–31, GO, 6 June 1813; 266–8, GO, 18 June; v.1221,
106, Prevost to Sheaffe, 22 July, and v.229, 136–7, Sheaffe's reply,
25 July.

74 NA, RG 8, v.1694, 56, GO, 27 September 1813; Stanley, *War of 1812*,
250–1.

75 NA, RG 8, v.679, 382–7, Commander-in-Chief Frederick, Duke of York, to
Prevost, 10 August 1813; v.230, 28–9, H. Torrens to Prevost, 14 August;
v.230, 88–90, Sheaffe to Prevost, 13 November.

76 DCB, 7: 199–200. Coffin remained in Upper Canada after Sheaffe's
departure and served in the militia, first as deputy adjutant general and
then as adjutant general until 1837.

77 DCB, 7: 517–18. Other sources consulted were NA, RG 8, I, v.1168, 260,
GO, Quebec, 13 September 1812, and 339, 29 October; v.1220, 12, Prevost to Sheaffe, 27 October; v.12031/2, 216, GO, Montreal, 29 January
1814; v.684, 235–45, Drummond to Prevost, 27 July 1814; WO 25/765,
Half-pay officers' forms, 1828, L. I want to thank Stuart Sutherland for
providing this last source.

78 DHC, 5: 192–203, "MS. Carefully Preserved by the Late Colonel William
Allan...," signed by Chewett, Allan, Cameron, Samuel Smith, Strachan,
Woods, and W.W. Baldwin. The chief critics were Strachan and Allan.
See *Town of York*, 311, Mrs Powell to W.D. Powell, 12 May 1813, and
note 54, which refers to documents published in DHC, 5: 192–203.

79 DHC, 5: 169–70, Chauncey to secretary of the Navy, 28 April; 179–82,
Lieutenant Fraser's Account; 213–15, Letter from U.S. officer; 207–11, P.
Finan's Journal; *Town of York*, 303–6, Colonel Cromwell Pearce's Account;

294–5, Strachan to Brown, 26 April. Strachan mentions meeting wounded British soldiers at about 7 a.m. If that time is correct, it means that they had resisted the initial landing. See also *Town of York*, 328–9, John Beikie to Miles Macdonell, 19 March 1814.

80 Humphries, "The Capture of York," in *Defended Border*, 251–70; Whitfield, *Battle of Queenston Heights*, 34; Benn, *Historic Fort York*, 62–4; Sheppard, *Plunder, Profit, and Paroles*, 76–8, 148.

81 Benn, *Historic Fort York*, 51–4, 64. The militia commander was Lieutenant-Colonel William Chewett; see DCB, 7: 174–6.

82 DCB, 8: 793; Thompson, *History of the Late War*, 102.

83 DHC, 3: 184. John Lovett wrote from Lewiston to Joseph Alexander, 17 August 1812, "Major General Sheaffe, formerly of Boston (brother of Nancy Sheaffe, tell my wife) is now commanding at Fort George." Major Lovett was General Van Rensselaer's aide and private secretary, and Alexander was a friend in Albany.

84 W.H. Merritt, in *Campaigns of 1812–14*, 9–10.

CHAPTER FIVE

1 R. Christie, *History of the Late Province of Lower Canada*, 2: 75, 87–9, 117–19, 137; Kingsford, *History of Canada*, 8: 339–47; Hannay, *History of the War of 1812*, 179, 203; Lucas, *Canadian War of 1812*, 105, 123, Horsman, *War of 1812*, 134; Hitsman, *Incredible War*, 147, 162, 167, 172. D.B. Read deals with Rottenburg, but offers no evaluation of him; see *Lieutenant-Governors of Upper Canada*, 89–90. In the most recent study, Rottenburg is mentioned in connection with martial law in eastern Upper Canada, and no attempt is made to assess him as the military and civil leader of the colony; see Sheppard, *Plunder, Profit, and Paroles*, 117, 156, 158.

2 Stanley, *War of 1812*, 156–7, 197, 201, 203–4, 206, 214–15, 344. The quotations are found on 197 and 344. Stanley is echoing Rottenburg's own words in his letter of 7 July 1813 to Prevost; see DHC, 6: 199–200.

3 DCB, 6: 660–2. There were many difficulties in obtaining accurate and complete information because of the dramatic boundary changes, frequent wars, and destruction of historical records in that part of Europe, all of which explain the vagueness about his early years. Information from Polish sources indicate that his father was a merchant in Danzig, whereas documents from French archives suggest that his father was a nobleman in that city. This matter is still being researched.

4 In NA, MG 24, F 78, there is a commission from Louis XVI of France dated 1 September 1785 appointing Rottenburg second lieutenant of the Count de La Marck's Regiment d'Infanterie d'Allemand. His diplomatic experience is mentioned in a letter to the author from the Archives de l'Armée de Terre, Vincennes, France, 11 January 1995.

5 Butler and Hare, *Annals of the King's Royal Rifle Corps*, 2: 12.

6 N.W. Wallace, *A Regimental Chronicle and List of Officers of the 60th, or the King's Royal Rifle Corps* (London, 1879), 291. Butler and Hare, *Annals of the King's Royal Rifle Corps*, 2: 12–13, gives the date of his commission to the rank of lieutenant-colonel in the 60th Foot as 30 December 1797. Hompesch's Fusiliers were raised in 1796 by Ferdinand, brother of Baron Carl. As the various foreign regiments in the British service were depleted by casualties and disease, the remaining manpower was drafted into the 60th Regiment. Rottenburg and six others from Hompesch's Fusiliers transferred to the 5th battalion, 60th Foot. In September 1813 he was listed as colonel of Roll's Regiment, another of the foreign units raised in the 1790s. Baron de Roll had been an officer in the Swiss Guard. His regiment was disbanded in summer 1816. On the complex subject, see Atkinson, "Foreign Regiments in the British Army."

7 "Notes, Questions and Replies," *Journal of the Society for Army Historical Research*, 10, no. 40 (October 1931): 237; Strachan, *European Armies and the Conduct of War*, 28, 56.

8 Rogers, *Wellington's Army*, 30–2, 40.

9 NA, MG 24, F 78, Address from the inhabitants of Halifax, 6 November 1805, to "Colonel Barron [*sic*] De Rottenburg Commanding the fifth Battalion of H M's Sixtieth Regiment," praises him and his troops for their conduct and relations with the townspeople.

10 Christie, "Walcheren Expedition," 255–8, 263–7, 270–2; Bond, *Grand Expedition*, 87–8, 128, 130–3, 167.

11 He was first appointed to British North America in April 1808 but remained in Britain until 1810. See NA, RG 8, v.226, 50, Lieutenant-Colonel Gordon to General Sir James Craig, 9 May 1808; v.227, 18, Gordon to Craig, 25 March 1809; v.227, 86, Lieutenant-Colonel H. Torrens to Craig, 20 April 1810; *Quebec Gazette*, 6 September 1810; *Army List*.

12 NA, RG 8, v.550, 15–24, Lieutenant-Colonel William Thornton to Major-General de Rottenburg, 25 February 1811.

13 NA, RG 8, v.1168, 191, GO, 6 July 1812; v.688A, 105, E. Baynes to ———, 10 July; Stanley, *War of 1812*, 76–8.

14 On Glasgow see *DCB*, 5: 346–7, and Irving, *Officers of the British Forces*, 2, 9, 21, 261. On Darroch see Irving, *Officers of the British Forces*, 9. In October 1813 Darroch was transferred to Nova Scotia.

15 NA, RG 8, v.677, 240–2, Rottenburg to Prevost, 9 December 1812; v.677, 248–51, Rottenburg to Prevost, 14 December.

16 The periods were 25 February to 19 March and 12 May to 13 June. See Irving, *Officers of the British Forces*, NA, RG 8, v.1170, 102, GO, 20 February 1813; v.12031/2H, 23, GO, 12 May. These orders indicate that Rottenburg would exercise both civil and military authority.

17 NA, RG 8, v.679, 64–5, Rottenburg to Glasgow, "Secret and Confidential," 5 June 1813; 66–9, Glasgow to Rottenburg, 7 June; Hitsman, *Incredible War*, 136–7, 144–5; Stanley, *War of 1812*, 240–3. See also *Naval War of 1812*. 2: 488–92.

18 *DHC*, 6: 298–301, Prevost to Bathurst, 1 August 1813.

19 On Stovin see Irving, *Officers of the British Forces*, 9; NA, RG 8, v.1170, 229–31, GO, 6 June 1813; v.266, GO, 18 June. Mahon, in *War of 1812*, 223, writes that Stovin was acting "'informally as chief of staff to Prevost at Montreal."

20 NA, RG 8, v.1220, 408–10, Prevost to HRH, Duke of York, 23 June 1813. Since Sherbrooke was in command of Nova Scotia, he was unavailable for this appointment. In *DHC*, 6: 174, Captain W.H. Merritt commented on Rottenburg's "very great name."

21 NA, RG 8, v.12031/2H, 128, GO, 15 June 1813. This organization was revised in October in consequence of Procter's defeat at Moraviantown (see below). See also NA, RG 8, v.1221, 210–1, Prevost to Colonel Torrens, 25 October.

22 NA, RG 8, v.1221, 188, Freer to Rottenburg, 16 October 1813; v.680, Rottenburg to Military Secretary, 20 October.

23 NA, RG 8, v.679, 382–7, Duke of York to Prevost, 10 August 1813; v.230, 28–9, Torrens to Prevost, 14 August; v.1221, 188, Freer to Rottenburg, 16 October.

24 NA, RG 8, v.1221, 188, Freer to Rottenburg, 16 October 1813. Freer suggested that Rottenburg would be employed in Germany. See also NA, RG 8, v.1227, 50, Prevost to Torrens, 19 May 1814; *Army List*.

25 *DHC*, 6: 97, GO, Kingston, 19 June 1813; 139, Prevost to Bathurst, 24 June; 163, Captain James P. Fulton to Prevost, 30 June.

26 NA, RG 8, v.679, 218, Rottenburg to Brigadier-General Procter, 1 July 1813.

27 *DHC*, 6: 199–200, Rottenburg to Prevost, 7 July 1813. He criticized Sheaffe for neglecting the roads.

28 NA, RG 8, v.679, 210, Rottenburg to Prevost, 9 July 1813; *DHC*, 6: 207–9, Colonel Claus to Harvey, 9 July; 208–11, notes by Captain W.H. Merritt; *John Askin Papers*, 2: 763–8, Charles Askin to John Askin, 8 and 19 July. Norton, *Journal*, 333–6.

29 NA, RG 8, v.679, 264, Rottenburg to Prevost, 20 July 1813. Lieutenant-Colonel Harvey, the newly arrived deputy adjutant general, claimed that this bold advance resulted from a plan he proposed to the Rottenburg; see AO, Journal of a Staff Officer (MS 842), 38–9. Prevost encouraged Rottenburg to cooperate with Yeo in attacking the Americans along the Niagara frontier, but at the same time he advised him that if he, Rottenburg, was forced to retreat to Burlington Heights, he should retire "with the fierceness and deliberation of the Lion and without leaving to the

Enemy any Trophy of any kind." See NA, RG 8, v.1221, 154–5, Prevost to Rottenburg, 30 and 31 July.

30 *DHC*, 6: 297, Rottenburg to Freer, 1 August, 1813, where he reported on the American force (about 3,000 strong) and strong entrenchments. See also NA, RG 8, v.679, 264, Rottenburg to Prevost, 20 July.

31 NA, RG 8, v.679, 210, Rottenburg to Prevost, 9 July 1813; Hitsman, *Incredible War,* 147; *DHC*, 6: 184–5, Lieutenant-Colonel Thomas Clark to Harvey, 5 July.

32 British and Canadian reports claimed the destruction of the navy yard and a large schooner, but such damage is not mentioned in American reports. *DHC*, 6: 217–19, Clark to Harvey, 12 July 1813, includes "Returns of casualties, ordnance destroyed and captured, and stores captured"; see also 240–1, two general orders, 15 July. The American militia general, Peter B. Porter, praised the Natives' role in defending Black Rock and expected to see them employed more often for the American side; *DHC*, 6: 223–5, Porter to Dearborn, 13 July. See also *DHC*, 8: 4–5, Captain Perry to the secretary of the Navy, 15 July; BECHS, A. Conger Goodyear, War of 1812 MSS, box 2, vol.5, Narrative of the Battle of Black Rock, 11 July 1813. Among the casualties was the leader of the raid, Lieutenant-Colonel Cecil Bisshopp, the kind of capable and popular young officer whom Rottenburg could ill afford to lose. See *John Askin Papers,* 2: 763–8, Charles Askin to John Askin, 8 and 19 July; Allen, "Bisshopp Papers," 26–9, letter, 20 July. On Bisshopp see *DCB*, 5: 82–3. See also *DHC*, 6: 214–15, Memo, "Confidential," J. Harvey, lieutenant-colonel, to Lieutenant-Colonel Nichol," 10 July; AO Journal of a Staff Officer (MS 842), 40–1. In Harvey's opinion, the severe casualties, including Bisshopp's wounds, resulted from his "imprudence, in remaining too long on the enemy's shore."

33 NA, RG 8, v.1221, 29–30, Freer to Rottenburg, 5 August 1813; v.679, 414, Rottenburg to Military Secretary, 11 August; *Naval War of 1812,* 2: 528–9, Commodore Isaac Chauncey to Secretary of the Navy Jones, 4 August; *DHC*, 6: 295, Colonel F. Battersby to Colonel Baynes, 31 July; 297, Rottenburg to Freer, 1 August; 305–6, Colonel Winfield Scott to Brigadier-General Boyd, 3 August; AO, Journal of a Staff Officer (MS 842), 42–3.

34 *DHC*, 6: 160–1, Procter to Captain McDouall, 29 June 1813; 243, Barclay to Prevost, 16 July; 181–2, Procter to McDouall, 4 July; 182–3, Procter to Prevost, 4 July; NA, RG 8, v.679, 220, Procter to Prevost, 11 July.

35 A rough estimate of the rank-and-file strength of Procter's Right Division may be gained from the official figures: 25 June, 819 on board the *Queen Charlotte;* 25 July, 784 near Fort Meigs; 25 August, 831 at Sandwich (or Amherstburg); 25 September, 831 at Sandwich plus 549 at Turkey Point, just east of Long Point; and 25 October, 1,074 at Barton

(near Burlington) and 543 at Long Point. See NA, MG 13, WO 17, 1517, 80, 94, 110, 126, 142; Carmichael-Smyth, *Precis of the Wars in Canada*, 153.

36 NA, RG 8, v.679, 210, Rottenburg to Prevost, 9 July 1813; DHC, 6: 232–3, Rottenburg to Baynes, 14 July; 159, GO (issued at Kingston), 28 June. Cruikshank, *Drummond's Winter Campaign*, 4, 6–7, describes "The wretched state" of Rottenburg's army in the Niagara Peninsula.

37 NA, RG 8, v.679, 210, Rottenburg to Prevost, 9 July 1813.

38 He appears to have been ill in July, and the state of his health may also have influenced his judgment. See DHC, 6: 297, Rottenburg to Freer, 1 August 1813.

39 DHC, 7: 120–1, Procter to Rottenburg, 12 September 1813; 141–2, Harvey to Procter, 17 September; NA, RG 8, v.680, 78, Rottenburg to Commander of the Forces, 17 September.

40 T. Malcomson, "September 1813," 299–313. For correspondence see DHC, 7: 140–1, Rottenburg to Prevost, 17 September 1813 (two letters).

41 DHC, 7: 179–80, Rottenburg to Prevost, 30 September 1813; Le Couteur, *Merry Hearts*, 135 (28 September), 147–8. By the 30th Rottenburg knew that Yeo's ships were ready to come to challenge Chauncey.

42 DHC, 7: 192, Rottenburg to Prevost, 3 October 1813; 187–8, General Wilkinson to Secretary of War, 2 October. Wilkinson reported that he was taking about 3,500 men to Sackets. See also ibid., 202–3, Major-General Darroch to Prevost, 7 October; AO, Journal of a Staff Officer (MS 842), 47–51. Harvey claimed that he had persuaded Rottenburg to send reinforcements to Kingston, and he gave the figure of 1,000. Le Couteur, *Merry Hearts*, 135–6, 1 October, indicates that the order to move out was given with little warning to the troops. Kearsley, "Memoirs," 8, presents the Americans' perspective, including their fear that the British might attack the fort.

43 AO, Journal of a Staff Officer (MS 842), 50.

44 DHC, 8: 70–1, Secretary of War to Major-General Wade Hampton, 16 October 1813; 71, Major-General Lewis to Mrs Livingston, 16 October; 81–2, Secretary of War to Major-General Wilkinson, 19 October; 104–7, Chauncey to Secretary of the Navy, 30 October.

45 NA, RG 8, v.1221, 182–3, 12 October 1813; 183, N. Freer to Rottenburg, 14 October; v.680, 229, Rottenburg to Military Secretary, 17 October; DHC, 7: 209–11, Chaucey to the Secretary of the Navy, 8 October.

46 DHC, 8: 60–1, Rottenburg to Prevost, 14 October 1813, written from Kingston.

47 DHC, 8: 68–9, Rottenburg to Prevost, 16 October 1813; 47–50, Colonel Winfield Scott to General Wilkinson, 11 October; 50–1, Vincent to Rottenburg, 11 October; AO, Strachan Correspondence (MS 35), Major Glegg to Rev. John Strachan, 11 October. On the condition of Vincent's

forces see Cruikshank, *Drummond's Winter Campaign*, 8–9. Antal, "Myths and Facts Concerning General Procter," 25–60, criticizes Rottenburg and Prevost for avoiding the blame for the Thames River campaign.

48 *DHC*, 8: 78–80, Rottenburg to Prevost, 18 October 1813; 88–9, Rottenburg to Vincent, 23 October; NA, RG 8, v.680, 269–72, Rottenburg to Commander of the Forces, 23 October. According to a young militia officer, Vincent complained that Rottenburg was away from the Niagara district at a critical time; see *DHC*, 8: 57–8, Thomas G. Ridout to Thomas Ridout, 14 October. It was at this time that Prevost revamped the organization of the forces that he had established in June. See NA, RG 8, v.1221, 210–1, Prevost to Colonel Torrens, 25 October.

49 *DHC*, 8: 102, Rottenburg to Prevost, 30 October 1813; 117–18, Rottenburg to Vincent, 1 November; 110–11, John F. Bacon to Governor Tompkins, 31 October; 114–15, General McClure to Tompkins, 1 November; 116–17, Harrison to Tompkins, 1 November; 151, Rottenburg to Prevost, 11 November; *Naval War of 1812*, 2: 599–600, Chauncey to Secretary of the Navy, 21 November.

50 NA, RG 8, v.1221, 179–80, Prevost to Rottenburg, 12 October 1813; 182–3, Prevost to Yeo, 12 October; AO, Journal of a Staff Officer (MS 842), 52–3. Harvey claims that Rottenburg took his advice to detach a corps to harass the Americans. On 9 or 10 November Rottenburg may have ordered Morrison to break off his pursuit and return to Kingston, but the colonel fortunately disobeyed the order, and Prevost later countermanded it. It is unclear why Rottenburg would issue such a command.

51 NA, RG 8, v.1221, 188, Freer to Rottenburg, 16 October 1813; v.680, Rottenburg to Military Secretary, 20 October; *DHC*, 8: 143–4, Lieutenant Edward MacMahon to Hon. W.D. Powell, 8 November.

52 Stanley, *War of 1812*, 214–15, suggests that as late as October Rottenburg continued to support abandonment of Upper Canada west of Kingston. The documentary evidence indicates otherwise. See also Cruikshank, *Drummond's Winter Campaign*, 8–9.

53 NA, RG 8, v.1227, 50, Prevost to Torrens, 19 May 1814; v.227, 179–80, Torrens to Prevost, October.

54 NA, RG 8, v.12031/2L, 240, GO, 6 October 1814; *Montreal Herald*, 15 October and 5 November. On 14 December Torrens sent orders for Rottenburg's recall; see NA, RG 8, v.227, 213, Torrens to Prevost.

55 *DHC*, 8: 192–3, Memo in Powell's handwriting enclosed in Prevost to Powell, 18 November 1813. Powell was particularly influential because he was consulted and kept informed by Prevost and by others. See ibid., 8: 59–60, Glegg to Powell, 14 October; 143–4, MacMahon to Powell, 8 November; 6: 189–90, MGO, 6 July; 191, Prevost to Powell, 6 July.

56 Upper Canada, Journals of the Legislative Assembly, 1814, 101–2. Rottenburg tried to prepare for the British government a collection of acts

passed by the provincial legislature. See *SBD*, 2: 219–20, Rottenburg to Lord Bathurst, 25 October 1813.

57 NA, RG 8, v.679, 148–50, Powell to Prevost, 28 June 1813.

58 Graves, "'The Best Means,'" 16–18; W.M. Weekes in *Defended Border*, 198–200. The council also recommended that Rottenburg station a body of troops at York to apprehend suspected traitors, and he put this suggestion into effect. See Cruikshank, "Record of the Services of Canadian Regiments," 42–3; *DHC*, 6: 232–3, Rottenburg to Baynes, 14 July 1813; Cruikshank, "Study of Disaffection," 213–15.

59 Cruikshank, "John Beverley Robinson," 200–1. The letter was dated 20 August 1813. See also Brode, *Sir John Beverley Robinson*, 21–2.

60 NA, RG 8, v.679, 148–50, Powell to Prevost, 28 June 1813.

61 *DHC*, 6: 291, DGO, 29 July 1813. By "drumhead court martial" Rottenburg meant an immediate court martial in the field. Even militiamen helped themselves to the produce of local farms. See ibid., 7: 153–4, Thomas G. Ridout writing from Four Mile Creek to Thomas Ridout, 21 September.

62 *DHC*, 6: 268–9, DGO, 24 July 1813; NA, RG 5, A 1, v.16, 6662–3, 28 August 1813; Graves, "Joseph Willcocks," 46–7. Rottenburg was advised that he could not take this action in his civil capacity; see *Canadian State Trials*, 1: 384–7.

63 *DHC*, 8: 226, 22 November 1813. W.M. Weekes in *Defended Border*, 198–200.

64 *Canadian State Trials*, 1: 383–4 and n23; Romney and Wright point to evidence that Procter imposed martial law only in the Michigan Territory. See also AO, Solomon Jones Papers (MS 520), S. Sherwood to Solomon Jones, 11 February 1814; *DHC*, 8: 226–9, House of Assembly, 19 February 1814, and two notes in Powell's handwriting; 9: 279–80, Drummond to Earl Bathurst, 5 April; *Documents Relating to the Constitutional History of Canada*, 435; Graves, "'The Best Means,'" 19–20.

65 Clements Library, War of 1812 Papers, box 3, Noah Morrison (writing from Buffalo) to his brother and sister, 18 July 1813; Robert Troup (writing from Geneva) to Abraham Van Vechten, 10 November; Alexander Neef (writing from Plattsburg) to Andrew W. Bell, 20 December. The ranks of these letter-writers ranged from private to colonel. AO, Military Records, (MU 2036), #6, 1813, Letters, A.H. Sinclair, Master Commandant Arthur Sinclair to Brigadier-General J.H. Cocke, 4 July; *DHC*, 6: 240, Brigadier-General Boyd to the Secretary of War, 15 July.

66 Hitsman, *Incredible War*, 122–3, 160–2, 166–70. Examples of such field commanders would be Generals William A. Winder, John Chandler, Wade Hampton, Henry Dearborn, and his sucessors, John Boyd and James Wilkinson. Even Harrison's victory over Procter was limited in its effects. See BECHS, Diary of Colonel G. McFeeley (M81–1), 65–70, 86–

90; War of 1812 Papers (B00–15), box 1, folder 4, Peter B. Porter, 16 October 1816; *DHC*, 6: 282–5, General Peter B. Porter to Governor Tompkins, 27 July 1813; 293–4, same to General Boyd, 31 July.

67 See T. Malcomson, "September 1813."

68 In 1810 he appointed Charles Michel de Salaberry as his aide-de-camp, an appointment that presumably ceased when Salaberry was chosen to raise the Voltigeurs Canadiens. See Anderson, *Life of … Edward, Duke of Kent*, 192–5.

69 The first appointed was Captain Thomas Crosse, 8th Foot, who seems to have arrived in Lower Canada in 1811 from Nova Scotia. The information on him comes from many sources: PRO, WO, 27/102, pt 1, Inspection return of 8th Foot at Quebec, 13 June 1811; 108, Monthly returns of the 8th Foot; 259, Monthly returns; 274, Monthly returns; 1517, Returns of the British forces in the Canadian command; 133, Inspection Returns; NA, RG 8, v.19, 222, Promotions since 5 August 1813 in British North American command; v.1218, 223, Names of officers recommended for the Quartermaster General's Office, 27 April 1812; v.1220, 390, Prevost to Torrens, 10 June 1813; *Army List*, 1826; *Blackwood's Edinburgh Magazine* 18 (1825): 648; *Historical Record of the King's Liverpool Regiment* (2nd ed., London, 1883), 217, 228, 241.

The second ADC was Lieutenant John Lang, 19th Light Dragoons, who arrived in Quebec City from Ireland in May 1813. The information on him comes from NA, RG 8, v.12031/2 M, 125, GO, 13 August 1814; PRO, WO, 27/257, Monthly returns, 10th–25th Dragoons; 272, Monthly returns, 10th–25th Dragoons; 133, Inspection returns (1815); 25/765 (1828); *Army List*, 1812, 101; 1815, 134. Lang's diary is held in the Special Collections Library, Duke University, Durham, NC. (Much of the information on these two officers was provided by Stuart Sutherland.)

CHAPTER SIX

1 *SBD*, 3: 94, Drummond to Prevost, 14 March 1814.

2 NA, MG 13, WO 17, 1518, 93, 111, 131, 155.

3 *DCB*, 8: 236; Letter from Hon. Mrs Drummond.

4 *DCB*, 8: 236: Letter from Hon. Mrs Drummond; *Army List*.

5 Perhaps because of bad health, as suggested by his brother Robert in his diary entry of December 1790; see Megginch Castle, Diary of Robert Drummond (by permission of Baroness Strange of Megginch).

6 *A Military History of Perthshire, 1660–1902*, edited by the Marchioness of Tullibardine (2 vols.; Perth, 1908), 2: 487–8.

7 Megginch Castle, Diary of Robert Drummond, entry for 1801. Drummond is not mentioned in the three major contemporary accounts of the campaign in Egypt: Bunbury, *Narratives of Some Passages*; Walsh, *Jour-*

nal of the Late Campaign in Egypt; and Wilson, *History of the British Expedition to Egypt.*

8 Megginch Castle, Diary of Robert Drummond, entries for 1807 and 1808.

9 NA, RG 8, v.289, 6, Drummond to Lieutenant-Colonel Thornton, 17 May 1810; 52–3, same to same, 22 July.

10 NA, RG 8, v.30, 14, Drummond to Sir James H. Craig, 27 February 1811; 24, Torrens to Craig, 18 June.

11 NA, RG 8, v.550, 84, Torrens to Drummond, 27 August 1811; Megginch Castle, Extra Warrant Book, 49th Regiment, 17. On the staff in Canada see NA, RG 8, v.1706, 32, Return of the general and staff officers at present serving at Canada, Quebec, 25 June; 64, GO, 20 June.

12 Megginch Castle, Diary of Robert Drummond, entries for 1811, 1812, and 1813.

13 Ibid., August 1813; *SBD*, 2: 438–9, GO, La Chine, 11 November.

14 NA, RG 8, v.1221, 210–11, Prevost to Colonel Torrens, 25 October 1813; *SBD*, 2: 437, GO, Montreal, 7 November. *DHC*, 8: 192–3, Prevost to Hon. W.D. Powell, 18 November.

15 NA, MG 24, A 41, 3–5, Drummond to Prevost, Kingston, 6 December 1813; TRL, Baldwin Room, Hagerman, "Journal."

16 *DCB*, 7: 744–6; Hitsman, *Incredible War,* 172.

17 *DHC*, 8: 272–3, Drummond to Prevost, York, 12 December 1813.

18 Cruikshank, *Drummond's Winter Campaign,* 12–16; Stray, "Canadian Volunteers Burn Old Niagara."

19 *DHC*, 9: 3–4, Harvey to Murray, 17 December 1813; 6–8, Drummond to Prevost, 18 December; 11, Drummond to Prevost, 19 December; 11–13, Murray to Drummond, 19 December; 21–3, Drummond to Prevost, 20 December. Captain John Norton crossed with Murray's force but without Native warriors; see Norton, *Journal,* 344–5. His account and the official reports indicate that militia and Natives did not accompany the initial attack as Stanley, in *War of 1812,* 219, claims. Murray's casualties were 6 killed and 5 wounded, while the Americans lost 422, including 65 killed.

20 *DHC*, 9: 14, Riall to Drummond, 19 December 1813; 14–15, GO, 19 December; 23–4, Drummond to Prevost, 20 December. Riall reported no casualties.

21 *DHC*, 9: 35–8, Drummond to Prevost, 22 December 1813; 51–2, Drummond to Prevost, 26 December; 60–1, DGO, 28 December. Drummond added a personal touch by mentioning that he had "personally served" in each of the corps employed for the attack; see ibid., 61–3, Harvey to Riall, 29 December; also 67, Drummond to Prevost, 30 December; 70–2, plus enclosures, 73–4, Riall to Drummond, 1 January 1814. Riall reported the destruction of three vessels. See also Cruikshank, *Drummond's Winter Campaign,* 22, 25–9.

22 *DHC*, 9: 74–6, Drummond to Prevost, 2 January 1814.

23 *DHC*, 9: 47–8, Governor Tompkins to Major-General Hall, 25 December
   1813; 63–4, Hall to Brigadier-General McClure, 29 December; 54–5,
   Hall to Governor Tompkins, 26 December; 65–6, GO, Buffalo, 29
   December; 77, extract from the *New York Evening Post*, 11 January 1814;
   83, extract from the *Manlius Times*, 4 January; Cruikshank, *Drummond's
   Winter Campaign*, 9–10, 16–17, 24; Mahon, *War of 1812*, 189–91.

24 *DHC*, 9: 35–8, Drummond to Prevost, 22 December 1813.

25 *DHC*, 9: 51, Drummond to Prevost, 26 December 1813; 137–40, Drummond to Prevost, 21 January 1814.

26 *DHC*, 9: 163–4, Drummond to Prevost, 3 February 1814; 191–2, Drummond to Prevost, 19 February; 170, Yeo to Prevost, 8 February.

27 *DHC*, 9: 132, Drummond to Prevost, 19 January l814; 219–20, Military
   secretary to Drummond, 7 March; 227–8, Drummond to Prevost,
   11 March.

28 *DHC*, 9: 100, Rottenburg to Military Secretary, 7 January 1814; 132,
   Drummond to Prevost, 19 January.

29 *DHC*, 9: 166–7, Drummond to Prevost, 5 February 1814; NA, RG 8, v.683,
   1–6, Drummond to Prevost, 2 April; *DHC*, 9: 285, Harvey to Yeo, 9 April;
   305–6, Prevost to Drummond, 23 April; 313–14, Drummond to Prevost,
   28 April.

30 NA, RG 8, v.683, 57–60, Drummond to Prevost, 27 April 1814; 61–4,
   same to same, 28 April; *DHC*, 9: 318–19, Prevost to Drummond, 30 April;
   350–1, same to same, 7 May.

31 NA, RG 8, v.683, 1–6, Drummond to Prevost, 2 April, 1814; *DHC*, 9: 284–
   6, Lieutenant Colonel Harvey to Sir James Yeo, 9 April.

32 *DHC*, 9: 232–4, Third Session of the Sixth Provincial Parliament of Upper
   Canada; see also 236, Drummond to Prevost, 14 March 1814; 259–61,
   Drummond to Bathurst, 20 March. For the official report see Upper
   Canada, Journals of the Legislative Assembly, 1814, 101–64, and Upper
   Canada, Journals of the Legislative Council, 433–57. See also Stanley,
   War of 1812, 301–2. The next (fourth) session was held in 1815 between
   1 February and 14 March. See also *Canadian State Trials*, 1: 388–9,
   665–9.

33 Upper Canada, Journals of the Legislative Assembly, 1814, 108, and
   Upper Canada, Journals of the Legislative Council, 435, 455; *DHC*, 9:
   235, Proclamation, 14 March 1814, signed Wm Jarvis, Secretary; 236,
   Drummond to Prevost, 14 March; Stickney, "Logistics and Communications," 65–71.

34 *Documents Relating to the Constitutional History of Canada*, 435. This motion
   does not appear in the official record of the House of Assembly. The
   editors of *Documents*, Doughty and McArthur, 436 n2, state that Drummond repealed Rottenburg's proclamation on 25 January. See also *DHC*,

9: 234, *Kingston Gazette*, 22 March 1814, quoting a letter dated at York, 22 February; 242–3, Prevost to Drummond, 19 March; 279–80, Drummond to Bathurst, 5 April.

35 DHC, 9: 208–9, Drummond to Prevost, 5 March 1814.

36 In January 1814 residents were still waiting for the government to pay expenses dating back to May 1813, and unsatisfied pay lists in the Indian Department went back even further. See NA, MG 24, A 41, 36–7, Drummond to Prevost, 27 January 1814; 178, Drummond to Freer, 21 January; DHC, 9: 208–9, Drummond to Prevost, 5 March; W.M. Weekes in *Defended Border*, 200–4. See also DHC, 9: 237, Colonel Robert Young to Riall, 14 March 1814; 238, Riall to Drummond, 15 March. These letters about the condition of the 8th Foot, who had long been unpaid, show that this problem was not limited to the civilian population. For the same problem in Wellington's forces during the Peninsular War, see Ward, *Wellington's Headquarters*, 92–6.

37 NA, MG 24, A 41, 61, Drummond to Prevost, 4 March 1814; 46–8, Drummond to Prevost, 8 February.

38 DHC, 2: 321–3, Report of a Meeting of the Loyal and Patriotic Society, 22 December 1814. Drummond donated his share of the prize money from the capture of Fort Niagara along with an additional £200. The report of his offer was made in December, but it is hardly likely that it had been kept secret for the entire year.

39 DHC, 9: 236, Drummond to Prevost, 14 March 1814; 255–6, Drummond to Prevost, 24 March; 242–3, Prevost to Drummond, 19 March; 268–9, Prevost to Drummond, 31 March; 277, Prevost to Drummond, 2 April; 292–3, Proclamation of martial law, 12 April; W.M. Weekes in *Defended Border*, 202.

40 DHC, 9: 279–80, Drummond to Earl Bathurst, 5 April 1814; 302, Prevost to Drummond, 20 April. See also Kingsford, *History of Canada*, 8: 468. For an example of the law's application, see *Town of York*, 330–1, Minutes of the general quarter sessions of the peace, Home District.

41 AO, Drummond Letterbook (MU 8191), 17, Loring to John Small (Clerk of the Executive Council), 21 April 1814; 171–8, Loring to J.B. Robinson, 21 April; DHC, 9: 312, Copy of proceedings of a committee of the Executive Council on the 27th of April; 308–9, Proclamation, 26 April. NA, RG 8, v.683, 52–6, Drummond to Prevost, 26 April, reporting on the heavy consumption of flour, provides some evidence of the need for an export ban. See also Gourlay, *Statistical Account*, 2: 259–62.

42 DHC, 9: 279–80, Drummond to Earl Bathurst, 5 April 1814; 302, Prevost to Drummond, 20 April; 1, 24, Drummond to Lord Bathurst, 3 July.

43 NA, RG 8, v.685, 115–16, Bathurst to Prevost, 23 August 1814. Graves, in "The Best Means," 27, thinks that Bathurst was definitely questioning the legality of Drummond's proclamation.

44 *Documents Relating to the Constitutional History of Canada*, 437–9, Robinson to Loring, 2 June and 28 June 1814; W.M. Weekes in *Defended Border*, 203–4; Brode, *Sir John Beverley Robinson*, 19–20. Civilians started law suits against army and militia officers, much to General Drummond's annoyance. See AO, Drummond Letterbook (MU 8191), 80–1, 97, 104.

45 Sheppard, *Plunder, Profit, and Paroles*, 94–5. Sheppard gives the date of 14 February for Drummond's opening address when it was actually 15 February. See also Gray, *Soldiers of the King*, 24–5, 32.

46 DHC, 9: 259–61, 20 March 1814 (Sheppard, *Plunder, Profit, and Paroles*, 95n94, incorrectly cites p.250); see also DHC, 9: 189–90, Drummond to Prevost, 19 February. Sheppard, 98–9, refers to the assembly's angry response to Drummond's request for an increase in the embodied militia. On 16 February the assembly responded that it would "most cheerfully co-operate" in measures to improve the militia's condition and to embody more of the militia population. This reply appears to be doubtful evidence of anger. See Upper Canada, Journals of the Legislative Assembly, 1814, 106.

47 The sources that Sheppard cites do not indicate that Drummond sought to conscript men into the militia or that the additional number he wanted was as large as 1,500. See Upper Canada, Journals of the Legislative Assembly, 1814, 104, and Upper Canada, Journals of the Legislative Council, 434. Drummond asked the legislature to authorize "embodying" no more than "one-third of the corps" for up to one year. See W.M. Weekes in *Defended Border*, 204; Gray, *Soldiers of the King*, 32, 44, 190.

48 Sheppard, *Plunder, Profit, and Paroles*, 95, suggests that Drummond thought of dispensing with the militia because of his annoyance with the assembly. Another possible explanation is that he wished to alleviate the burdens imposed on the residents by warfare. See NA, MG 24, A 41, 33–5, Drummond to Prevost, 26 January, in which Drummond suggested that a corps of waggoners be created to lessen demands on farmers for transport. See also NA, MG 24, A 41, 87, Drummond to Prevost, 29 March, in which Drummond reported that, owing to the capture of American waggons, he would have less need of civilian ones. It also possible that he preferred to have regulars when it came to fighting.

49 DHC, 9: 279–80; 1,24; Upper Canada, Journals of the Legislative Assembly, 1814, 147, 159. Despite the privations and increasing costs of the war, the members unanimously voted to spent 100 guineas on a presentation sword to Colonel John Murray, 100th Foot, 50 guineas on one for Captain James Kerby, Incorporated Militia, and £500 for a monument on Queenston Heights to Brock.

50 Turner, "Career of Isaac Brock," 173–7. The best-known expression appears in Brock's letter of 29 July to Prevost: "Most of the people have

lost all confidence – I however speak loud and look big." Brock also had
doubts about the reliability of the population. See chapter 3 above.

51 NA, MG 24, A 41, 172–4, Drummond to Prevost, 16 July 1814. Drummond at Kingston, referring to Riall's forces on the Niagara frontier,
wrote that "little reliance can be placed on the numbers of the Militia."
For examples when he approved of militiamen working on their own or
other people's farms, see NA, RG 8, v.684, 200–2, Drummond to Prevost, 24 July, enclosing letter from Thos. Ridout to Robert R. Loring,
23 July; v.685, 288–90, Harvey to Major-General de Watteville, 24 September; 291–2, Harvey to Peter Turquand, deputy commissary general,
25 September. See also Gray, *Soldiers of the King*, 24–5, 190–4.

52 Sheppard, *Plunder, Profit, and Paroles*, 99; Upper Canada, Journals of the
Legislative Assembly, 1814, 157–8; 148. See also AO, Drummond Letterbook (MU 8191), 159–60, McMahon to D'Arcy Boulton, 2 February 1815.

53 AO, Drummond Letterbook (MU 8191), 4, Loring to Robinson, 5 April
1814; Stanley, *War of 1812*, 286–7. Most of the prisoners came from the
London District, but the trials could not be held there because of the
American threat. In order to have a secure site close to that district, the
Union Hotel at Ancaster, near the army base at Burlington Heights, was
chosen. *Cuesta*, spring 1981, 30–1, reproduces a picture of the building.
See also W.W. Riddell, "The Ancaster 'Bloody Assize' of 1814," in
Defended Border, 241–50; Sheppard, *Plunder, Profit, and Paroles*, 165–9.
Sheppard sees Robinson as anxious to hold the trials and gain convic-
tions in order to advance his career. He claims that the attorney general
was unhappy with the Ancaster location, whereas Brode asserts that Robinson insisted on holding the trials there although Drummond preferred York. See Brode, *Sir John Beverley Robinson*, 22–5.

54 AO, Drummond Letterbook (MU 8191), 77, R.R. Loring to Colonel
Scott, 28 June 1814; 78, Loring to Hon. the Chief Justice, 28 June; 87,
Loring to Robinson, 5 July; *Canadian State Trials*; 1: 387–93.

55 AO, Drummond Letterbook (MU 8191), 87–9, Drummond to Robinson,
5 July 1814; 93–4, Drummond to Chief Justice, 9 July; NA, RG 8, v.1219,
249–50, Prevost to Earl Bathurst, 14 July, enclosing Drummond to
Prevost, 11 July; Kingsford, *History of Canada*, 8: 470–1; *Canadian State
Trials*, 1: 393–5.

56 For criminal proceedings and sequestration of forfeited estates subsequent to the Ancaster trials, see *Canadian State Trials*, 1: 395–6, 667–8.

57 The background and account is taken from Stanley, *War of 1812*, 303–5,
and Mahon, *War of 1812*, 262–3. See also NA, RG 8, v.683, 57–60, Drummond to Prevost, 27 April 1814; 61–4, Drummond to Prevost, 28 April;
93–6, Drummond to Prevost, 3 May; DHC, 9: 350–1, Prevost to Drummond, 7 May. On the raid see NA, RG 8, v.683, 105–12, Drummond to
Prevost, 7 May, and various reports; DHC, 9: 337–46.

58 Drummond and Yeo continued until June to correspond about the possibility of attacking Sackets; see *DHC*, 1: 18–20, Yeo to Drummond, 3 June 1814; Drummond to Yeo, 6 June; see also 24, Drummond to Bathurst, 3 July. This correspondence indicates that Drummond agreed with Yeo's decision to lift the blockade of Sackets.

59 NA, RG 8, v.683, 286–92, Drummond to Prevost, 21 June 1814. At the bottom of the last page is written in pencil, "Very much obliged to Genl. D for his opinion – unfortunately for him it is not founded on fact as not one Soldier intended for U C has been prevented moving forward by the Enemy's ———." This comment may be related to Drummond's lament that he had no troops to replace the 8th (King's) Regiment at Chippawa, which was suffering severely from fever according to Staff Surgeon O'Maley; his report was enclosed in ibid., 293–7, Drummond to Prevost, 21 June. For the state and movement of American forces see Everest, *War of 1812*, 155–6.

60 *DHC*, 1: 31–3, Riall to Drummond, 6 July 1814; NA, RG 8, v.684, 44–50, Drummond to Prevost, 9 July; 57–64, Drummond to Prevost, 10 July (two letters), 72, Drummond to Prevost, 11 July.

61 NA, RG 8, v.684, 66–8, Drummond to Prevost, 11 July 1814; 85–93, Drummond to Prevost, 13 July (two letters); 101–4, Drummond to Prevost, 15 July; v.388, 146–51, Riall to Drummond, 12 July.

62 NA, RG 8, v.684, 164–6, General Stovin to Prevost, 21 July 1814; *DHC*, 1: 82–4, Harvey to Riall, 23 July; 84–5, Harvey to Tucker, 23 July; 85–6, Drummond to Prevost, 23 July.

63 The purpose was to destroy American batteries that threatened Fort George. Graves, *Battle of Lundy's Lane*, 84–5, points out that Riall's report of batteries at Youngstown was erroneous.

64 NA, RG 8, v.684, 235–45, Drummond to Prevost, 27 July 1814; Graves, *Battle of Lundy's Lane*, chap. 6. The times are given in that chapter.

65 *SBD*, 3, pt 1: 157–64, Brown to the American secretary at War, n.d. Brown had fallen back to Chippawa because Chauncey's fleet had not arrived at the Niagara River, and he needed to resupply. He was not retreating from Drummond's advance.

66 Graves, *Battle of Lundy's Lane*, 101, 127. The American assessment was the same.

67 NA, RG 8, v.684, 235–45, Drummond to Prevost, 27 July 1814; Graves, *Battle of Lundy's Lane*, 101.

68 Graves, *Battle of Lundy's Lane*, 123–4; other criticisms on 130, 140, and 144. Graves is also extremely critical of Drummond's report on the battle; see 182–4. For shortcomings of the American leadership see 113–15, 145, 151–2.

69 Graves, *Battle of Lundy's Lane*, 124, At about 8:30 p.m. Brown found it difficult to distinguish troops because of the growing darkness, smoke, and shade cast by trees in the moonlight. See also ibid., 114.

70 Graves, in *Battle of Lundy's Lane*, 149, writes that "Brown never considered removing the captured artillery ... Perhaps he forgot about it in the heat of the action." Later, on 160–2, he describes the confusion among American officers about who was in command, what the orders were regarding the guns, and who was to carry them out. For Brown's later actions see ibid., 166–7. See also appendix D.

71 *DHC*, 1: 110–12, Extract of a letter from an officer of the 11th Regiment to his friend in Burlington, Vt, dated at Buffalo, 2 August 1814. See also ibid., 108, Copy of a letter from an officer in the army to his friend in Alexandria, dated at Fort Erie, UC, 28 July, which admits that about midnight the American army "retired to Chippewa." Le Couteur, *Merry Hearts*, 175; Commins, "War on the Canadian Frontier," 208–9; and NA, MG 19, A 39, present participants' evidence of an American withdrawal. See also Graves, *Battle of Lundy's Lane*, chap. 11 and appendix D. Graves makes a persuasive case that the battle was an American victory. Also Whitehorne, *While Washington Burned*, 37.

72 Even in the daytime, visibility in a battle could be severely limited. Holmes, *Firing Line*, 63, refers to the experience of Captain Cavalié Mercer "commanding a battery at Waterloo, ... in the very forefront of the battle. But he saw little of it. 'What was passing to the right and left of us I know no more than the man in the moon ... The smoke confined our vision to a very small compass, so that my battle was restricted to the two squares [of infantry] and my own battery.'"

73 BECHS, War of 1812 Papers (BOO-15), box 1, folder 3, E.L. Allen to Lieutenant Colonel John Brick, 28 July 1814. Ripley's command lasted until 2 September. Some of the American troops feared they might be attacked. See *Soldiers of 1814*, 75, "The Narrative of Alexander McMullen."

74 NA, RG 8, v.684, 233–4, 235; MG 24 A 41, 188, Drummond to Prevost, 31 August 1814. See Graves, *Battle of Lundy's Lane*, chap. 13, for his view on Drummond's location.

75 Norton, *Journal*, 358–60. Graves, *Battle of Lundy's Lane*, 183, places the British farther away from Fort Erie than the documentary evidence suggests. According to Lieutenant Le Couteur, "Cavalry, Indians and light troops" followed the Americans on the 26th; see his *Merry Hearts*, 176.

76 *DHC*, 1: 113, Colonel H. Scott to his sister, Falls of Niagara, 30 July; 115–16, Drummond to Prevost, 31 July; 116–18, Drummond to Prevost, 4 August; NA, RG 8, v.231, DGO, HQ Falls, 1 August; MG 24, F 23, v.1, Campaign of 1814 in Upper Canada by Captain Gaugreben, 13–4; Le Couteur, *Merry Hearts*, 179. Graves, *Battle of Lundy's Lane*, 188, dates Drummond's arrival at Palmer's to 2 August.

77 Stanley, *War of 1812*, 325. Drummond approached Fort Erie before 4 August, as stated by Stanley. See also Le Couteur, *Merry Hearts*, 179.

78 *DHC*, 1: 115–16, Drummond to Prevost, 31 July 1814.

79 AO, Journal of a Staff Officer (MS 842), 72, Harvey to Colonel Stewart, 6 August 1814. Graves, *Battle of Lundy's Lane*, 187, seems to place the arrival of the American fleet several days earlier.

80 Norton, *Journal*, 360.

81 Graves, *Battle of Lundy's Lane*, 188; on 187 Graves claims that Drummond "did not push very hard towards this [Fort Erie] objective." See also 206.

82 *DHC*, 1: 116–18, Drummond to Prevost, 4 August 1814; NA, RG 8, v.231, DGO, HQ Falls, 1 August. On 4 August Drummond ordered that an "additional half Gill of Spirits shall be issued to the troops actively in the Field," a standard practice when troops faced extra work. See NA, MG 24, F 112, Diary of General Orders; Regimental Order Book, the 6th Foot, DGO, 4 August.

83 Stickney, "Logistics and Communication," 57, 65–73, 141–50, 154–7. M. Glover, in *Wellington*, chap. 8, agrees.

84 NA, RG 8, v.1219, 274–5, Drummond to Prevost, 18 August 1814; *DHC*, 1: 183–6, Drummond to Prevost, 21 August.

85 *DHC*, 1: 180–3, Robinson to Prevost, 27 August 1814, and Drummond to Yeo, 18 August; 186–7, Drummond to Prevost, 24 August; NA, RG 8, v.1219, 274–5, Drummond to Prevost, 18 August; AO, Journal of a Staff Officer (MS 842), 111–15, Harvey to Baynes, 5 September; AO, Drummond Letterbook (MU 8191), 112–13, McMahon to John Small, 14 September; Stickney, "Logistics and Communications," 65, 72–3, 144–7, 223–4; *Snake Hill*, 42, 50–1.

86 Stacey, "Upper Canada at War," 41, Captain R.E. Armstrong to General Hugh Swayne, 1 September 1814. Armstrong, of the Nova Scotia Fencibles, probably heard the story from Drummond's ADC, Captain Jervois.

87 On American defensive works see Cullum, *Campaigns of the War of 1812–15*, chap. 6, on Major David B. Douglass; *Snake Hill*, 36–8, 42–3; White-horne, *While Washington Burned*, 42–50.

88 AO, Journal of a Staff Officer (MS 842), 72, Harvey to Colonel Stewart, 6 August 1814. Major-General Stovin had earlier complained that the "junior" Major-General Conran had been given command of the Right Division instead of himself. See NA, RG 8, v.684, 105–110, Stovin to Drummond, enclosed in Drummond to Prevost, both 16 July.

89 *DHC*, 1: 132–4, Drummond to Prevost, 12 August 1814. At this same time Colonel Scott complained about Riall's leadership in the battle of Chippawa and also his lack of confidence in General Drummond. See NA, MG 24, F 15, H. Scott to "My dear James" [his brother], 12 August.

90 AO, Journal of a Staff Officer (MS 842), 73–4, Harvey to Colonel Baynes (adjutant general), 6 August 1814; 102–5, Drummond to Prevost, 24 August; 108–10; Le Couteur, *Merry Hearts*, 179.

91 *Quebec Mercury*, 23 August 1814, 270.

92 The engineer officers were Lieutenants Philpott and Portlock. See *DHC*,
   1: 132–4, Drummond to Prevost, 12 August 1814; AO, Journal of a Staff
   Officer (MS 842), 108–10, Drummond to Prevost, 2 September; Dunlop, *Tiger Dunlop's Upper Canada*, 40–2. Back in March, Riall had complained about an engineer officer, Lieutenant Frederic de Gaugreben,
   who was "head of the department here" (Niagara frontier). See *DHC*, 9:
   238, Riall to Drummond, 15 March; 245–6, Drummond to Prevost,
   21 March. Drummond reported that he had ordered Lieutenant Phillpotts to replace Gaugreben, who was suffering from "severe sore eyes."
   Gaugreben retained an animosity to Drummond after the end of the
   war. See NA, MG 24, F 23, v.1, 53–4, Gaugreben to Colonel Nicholls,
   23 August 1816.
93 Dunlop, *Tiger Dunlop's Upper Canada*, 34.
94 *DHC*, 1: 116–21, Drummond to Prevost, 4 August, with enclosures; 121–
   2, Major Morgan to Brown, 5 August. This encounter was known as the
   battle of Black Rock.
95 Le Couteur, *Merry Hearts*, 183–4; *DHC*; 1: 121–2, Morgan to Brown,
   5 August 1814. See also Stanley, *War of 1812*, 325–6.
96 *SBD*, 3, pt 1: 167–78, Drummond to Prevost, 4 August, 1814, enclosing
   DGO of 1 August, Harvey to Major-General Conran, 2 August, and
   Tucker to Conran, 4 August; AO, Journal of a Staff Officer (MS 842),
   70–1, Morning DGO, 5 August. This order contains the severe criticism
   of the rank and file, along with the command to officers to "punish with
   death ... any man under his Command who may be found guilty of misbehavior before the enemy." Graves, *Battle of Lundy's Lane*, 190–1,
   accuses Drummond of overreacting, but if he did so, it was a short-lived
   response. The order may have been suppressed, but not before it
   became known elsewhere in Upper Canada. See Stacey, "Upper Canada
   at War," 41.
97 PRO, WO 55, v.860, 135–44, Journal of Lieut. G. Phillpotts, 1–4. For subsequent batteries see 5–10. This journal presents a stark picture of the
   difficulties of besieging Fort Erie. (I wish to thank David Owen for drawing this source to my attention and for sharing with me his own extensive knowledge of Fort Erie and its surroundings.) *Snake Hill*, 42,
   provides different numbers of guns. The source for these figures is not
   given. See also AO, Journal of a Staff Officer (MS 842), 108–10, Drummond to Prevost, 2 September; Le Couteur, *Merry Hearts*, 184–6.
98 *DHC*, 1: 188–9, Drummond to Prevost, 27 August 1814. See also Stanley's criticisms in *War of 1812*, 326, 330. He cites Colonel Hercules Scott
   and Dr Dunlop, who were both present at the time. See also Graves,
   Battle of Lundy's Lane, 192.
99 *DHC*, 1: 132–4, Drummond to Prevost, 12 August 1814; 134, Drummond to Prevost, 13 August; 135, Morning DGO, 13 August; 135–6,

Captain Alexander Dobbs, RN, to Sir James L. Yeo, 13 August; NA, PRO, WO 55, v.860, 135–44.

100 NA, MG 24, F 15, Scott to "My dear James," 12 August 1814; see also Cruikshank, "Drummond's Night Assault upon Fort Erie, August 15–16, 1814," in *Defended Border*, 155–6; Graves, *Battle of Lundy's Lane*, 126. Hercules Scott's force had covered nearly twenty miles on 25 July, part of it at double time, and so had arrived at the battlefield exhausted. This experience may have shaped the colonel's critical judgment of Drummond's generalship on that day.

101 Phillpotts stated that the range was "about 1100 yards"; see PRO, WO 55, v.860, 135–44. For other criticisms of the bombardment see Le Couteur, *Merry Hearts*, 189; Dunlop, *Tiger Dunlop's Upper Canada*, 40–2; NA, MG 24, F 15, H. Scott to his brother, 12 August 1814, and C. Young to James Scott, 20 December. Young was a surgeon in the 103rd Foot. Norton, however, had the impression that the Americans suffered more damage from British gunfire than his side felt from the American batteries. See Norton, *Journal*, 361–2.

102 Stanley, *War of 1812*, 326–30; Graves, *Battle of Lundy's Lane*, 193–6, and "William Drummond and the Battle of Fort Erie," 31–9; DHC, 1: 141–4, Drummond to Prevost, 15 August 1814. See also Owen, *Fort Erie (1764–1823)*, particularly 49–52. An earlier statement of many of the reasons for failure may be found in Dunlop, *Tiger Dunlop's Upper Canada*, 50–4. In 1801 Gordon Drummond had been colonel commanding the 8th Foot, which was part of the British force in Egypt when Colonel George Smith led the first battalion of the 20th Foot in an assault with unloaded muskets and bayonets fixed. This attack succeeded in capturing a French redoubt. See Bunbury, *Narratives of Some Passages*, 152. Was this precedent in his mind in August 1814?

103 Kearsley, "Memoirs," 12–14. Major Kearsley commanded the 4th Rifle Regiment at Fort Erie.

104 Le Couteur, *Merry Hearts*, 187, 192. Le Couteur criticized the removal of the soldier's flints. How many lacked flints is unclear because Fischer's column, before it attacked, received a counter-order from General Drummond, and so some may have inserted their flints. The ladders were made by the army's carpenters, presumably under the supervision of the engineers as suggested by Phillpotts; see PRO, WO 55, v.860, 135–44. See also "Assault on Fort Erie," 88–9.

105 Le Couteur, *Merry Hearts*, 189–92; DHC, 1: 139–41, Harvey to [Lieutenant Colonel Fischer], 14 August 1814; 141–4, Drummond to Prevost, 15 August; 144–5, Fischer to Harvey, 15 August.

106 DHC, 1: 141–4, Drummond to Prevost, 15 August; 152–6, Gaines to secretary of War, 23 August; 156–8, Ripley to Gaines, 17 August; 2: 434–5, Lt. Colonel. E.D. Wood to Ripley, 15 August; Whitehorne, *While Washington*

Burned, 61–6; Norton, *Journal,* 362–3; Commins, "War on the Canadian Frontier," 209–10.

107 *DHC,* 1: 141–4, 15 August. Prevost did not accept Drummond's criticism of the De Watteville Regiment; see U.S. National Archives, RG 125, reel 38, Prevost to Drummond, 26 August. (There are two letters, one mis-dated 15 August, which were intercepted by the Americans.) Dr Dunlop had a poor opinion of the reliability of De Watteville's Regiment (Dunlop, *Tiger Dunlop's Upper Canada,* 47), and so did Phillpotts (PRO, WO 55, v.860, 135–44), while Le Couteur claimed that they "behaved admirably" (Le Couteur, *Merry Hearts,* 192).

108 Commins, "War on the Canadian Frontier," 211. A report in the *Quebec Mercury,* 16 August 1814, 263, suggests that there was some expectation, based on reports from deserters, that the Americans in Fort Erie would "surrender without resistance" if attacked.

109 AO, Journal of a Staff Officer (MS 842), 105–8, Drummond to Prevost, 30 August; 108–10, Drummond to Prevost, 2 September; 116–20, Drummond to Prevost, 8 September; *Snake Hill,* 42, 50.

110 *DHC,* 1: 208–11, Brigadier-General Porter to Brown, 23 September 1814.

111 NA, RG 8, v.1219, Prevost to Drummond, 25 July, enclosed in Prevost to Earl Bathurst, 2 August; AO, Journal of a Staff Officer (MS 842), 111–15, Harvey to Baynes, 5 September; 115–16, same to same, 8 September.

112 NA, MG 24, F 96, De Watteville diary, 196.

113 NA, MG 24, F 22, Brown to Commodore Sinclair, 9 September 1814. Drummond was aware of these American reinforcements. See AO, Journal of a Staff Officer (MS 842), 115–16, Harvey to Baynes, 8 September; *DHC,* 1: 197, Brown to Izard, 10 September; 198, Brown to Izard, 11 September.

114 Dunlop, *Tiger Dunlop's Upper Canada,* 37. J. Douglas, *Medical Topography,* 7, 9–10, 12–14, gives a contemporary view of conditions and the health problems of the soldiers. Like Dunlop, Douglas was a surgeon with the army. See also AO, Journal of a Staff Officer (MS 842), 134–6, Drummond to Prevost, 21 September; PRO, WO 55, v.860, 135–44.

115 PRO, WO 55, v.860, 135–44; MG 24, F 23, v.1, Campaign ... by Capt. Gaugreben, 17. This engineer described the ground as low and moist, suggesting that natural drainage was poor. See also AO, Journal of a Staff Officer (MS 842), 120–2, Drummond to Prevost, 11 September; 123–6, Drummond to Prevost, 14 September; 134–6, Drummond to Prevost, 21 September; *Snake Hill,* 50–2.

116 AO, Journal of a Staff Officer (MS 842), 115–16, Harvey to Baynes, 8 September 1814.

117 NA, MG 24, F 22, Brown to Commodore Sinclair, 9 September 1814. Sinclair commanded American naval forces on Lake Erie.

118 Whitehorne, *While Washington Burned,* chap. 6.

119 NA, MG 24, F 96, De Watteville diary, 196.

120 AO, Journal of a Staff Officer (MS 842), 123–6, Drummond to Prevost, 14 September; 127–33, Drummond to Prevost, 19 September; 126–7, Drummond to Prevost, 17 September; 134–6, Drummond to Prevost, 21 September; *DHC*, 2: 288–90, Drummond to Prevost, 5 November; 224–5, Brown to Governor Thompkins, 20 September. This last letter mentions how much Brown appreciated the reinforcement of New York state militia. On the American sortie see PRO, WO 55, v.860, 135–44.

121 Stanley, *War of 1812*, 331; *DCB*, 8: 238; Whitehorne, *While Washington Burned*, 83–6; Graves, *Battle of Lundy's Lane*, 201–2.

122 *DHC*, 2: 235, Drummond to Prevost, 28 September; AO, Journal of a Staff Officer (MS 842), 142–4, Drummond to Prevost, 2 October; 147–50, Drummond to Prevost, 10 October; 153–4, Drummond to Prevost, 15 October. The British withdrawal behind the Chippawa seems to have been completed on 14 October. See NA, MG 24, F 96, De Watteville diary, 197–8; Dunlop, *Tiger Dunlop's Upper Canada*, 54–5.

123 Norton, *Journal*, 366.

124 Dunlop, *Tiger Dunlop's Upper Canada*, 46–7, regarded "this kind of warfare" as serving "no purpose." While it cost the British side casualties, these were also heavy among the Americans. See BECHS, A. Conger Goodyear, War of 1812 MSS (B00–11), v.15, General James Miller to Ruth (Mrs Miller), 19 September 1814. The siege may have been "frustrating and ineffectual" as Don Graves asserts in *Battle of Lundy's Lane*, 207, but it was not fruitless. For a colourful account of life under this bombardment, including several examples of horrible injuries suffered, see *Soldiers of 1814*, 40–5, "The Memoir of Drummer Jarvis Frary Hanks."

125 Cullum, *Campaigns*, 250. See also *DHC*, 1: 194–5, GO, 6 September 1814, and DGO, 7 September; BECHS, A. Conger Goodyear, War of 1812 MSS (B00–11), box 3, v.11, Major-General Benjamin Mooers to Governor Tompkins, 4 September.

126 General Peter B. Porter admitted as much in an address to the Militia of western New York, which appeared in the *Buffalo Gazette* on 30 August 1814; see *DHC*, 2: 436–7.

127 Stagg, in *Mr. Madison's War*, chap. 9, shows how bitter divisions among their political and military leaders prevented effective planning of campaigns and distracted American military forces in 1814. See also Hansen, "War of 1812," 37.

128 This account of American army movements is based upon *Snake Hill*. See also Whitehorne, *While Washington Burned*, 84–8. NA, MG 24, F 96, De Watteville diary, 197–8, seems to date the artillery exchange to 14 October.

129 *DHC*, 2: 243–4, Prevost to Drummond, 11 October, 259 Go, Prevost to
Bathurst, 18 October; AO, Journal of a Staff Officer (MS 842), 155–7,
Drummond to Prevost, 18 October. NA, RG 8, v.12031/2, 242, GO,
15 October, created a "Corps d'Armee" of the Right and Centre divisions and put it under Drummond's command.

130 AO, Journal of a Staff Officer (MS 842), 147–50, Drummond to Prevost,
10 October; 161–6, Drummond to Prevost, 23 October; NA, RG 8, v.686,
73–4, Morning DGO, 20 October; *DHC*, 2: 270–2, Brigadier-General Bissell to Izard, 22 October; NA, MG 24, F 96, De Watteville diary, 197–8;
Le Couteur, *Merry Hearts*, 276–8. Grain supplies, but not the mills, were
destroyed. The American losses were 13 killed and 53 wounded; the British were 1 killed and 35 wounded.

131 NA, MG 13, WO 17, 1518, 178; figures of 25 October, on which date the
rank and file in the Niagara Peninsula totalled 6,593.

132 Clements Library, University of Michigan, War of 1812 Papers, box 4, J.
McGavock to H. McGavock, camp near Buffalo, 23 November 1814. For
defences on the Chippawa see AO, Journal of a Staff Officer (MS 842),
142–4, Drummond to Prevost, 2 October; 150–2, Drummond to Prevost, 12 October.

133 *DHC*, 2: 254–6, Izard to Secretary of War, 16 October 1814; 274–5, same
to same, 23 October; 284–6, same to same, 2 November; NA, RG 8,
v.686, 121–9, Drummond to Prevost, 5 November; AO, Military Records
(MU 2036), #6, 1813, Letters, A.H. Sinclair. Sinclair, in a letter to Brigadier-General J.H. Cocke, 18 November, commented that Izard's withdrawal was wise in the face of "a superior force pressing upon him."

134 AO, Journal of a Staff Officer (MS 842), Harvey to Baynes, 5 September,
1814; *SBD*, 3, pt 1: 239–44, Drummond to Prevost, 5 November.

135 *DHC*, 2: 257–8, Drummond to Prevost, 18 October 1814; NA, RG 8, v.686,
68–9, Lt Colonel Harvey to Lt Colonel Myers, 18 October; 70–2, Lt Colonel Myers to Drummond, 19 October; 77–81, Drummond to Prevost, 20
October; 85–91, Drummond to Prevost, 23 October; *Montreal Herald*, 19
November. For the American reports see *DHC*, 2: 270–5; on Cook's Mills see
ibid., 303, Drummond to Captain Freer, Military Secretary, 12 November.

136 *DHC*, 2: 279–81, Drummond to Prevost, 30 October 1814 (Drummond
seems to confuse Lake Huron with Lake Erie). See also *SBD*, 3, pt 1:
237–9, Drummond to Yeo, 4 November 1814; 239–42, Drummond to
Prevost, 5 November; 245–8, same to same, 9 November. On the post-
ponement of the scheme see *DHC*, 2: 303–4, Drummond to Yeo,
13 November; 304–5, Yeo to Drummond, 14 November; 305–6, Drummond to Captain Noah Freer, 14 November. Also Dunlop, *Tiger Dunlop's
Upper Canada*, chap.4; NA, MG 24, F 96, De Watteville diary, 207. Watteville was dining with Drummond when they learned of the peace treaty.

137 *DCB*, 7: 316–17; NA, MG 24, A 41, 12, Drummond to Prevost, 20 December 1813; 29, Drummond to Prevost, 20 January 1814; RG 8, v.1171, 173–4, GO, Montreal, 29 January; AO, Foster Papers (MU 1057), Drummond's certificate appointing Foster adjutant general of the militia and lieutenant-colonel.

138 *DHC*, 1: 141–4, Drummond to Prevost, 15 August 1814; 204–6, Drummond to Prevost, 19 September. Foster continued his career in military administration after the war, and for three months in 1838 he was commander of the forces in Upper Canada.

139 Much of the information on Jervois comes from the Jervois correspondence, courtesy of James Jervois, London. See particularly Captain W. Jervois to his mother, 29 May 1811; Jervois to his sister, 12 June; Jervois to his sister, 11 June 1813. For Jervois's arrival in Canada, see Jervois to his mother, 4 November. The DCB files, the *Army List*, and the *Gentleman's Magazine* 2 (1862) also provided information.

140 *DHC*, 9: 70–2, Riall to Drummond, 1 January 1814; NA, RG 8, v.682, 1–4, Drummond to Prevost, 2 January. Prevost also credited Jervois with distinguished service in the attack on Fort Niagara. See ibid., v.1227, 59–60, Prevost to Field Marshall HRH the Duke of York, 20 May 1814; v.231, 121–6, Schedule of letters from Sir George Prevost, 20 May.

141 NA, RG 8, v.1219, 225, Drummond to Prevost, 7 May 1814. Drummond also praised the service of his provincial aide-de-camp, Hagerman. See also *DHC*, 9: 344–6, GO, 12 May, issued by Adjutant General Baynes.

142 NA, RG 8, v.684, 235–45, Drummond to Prevost, 27 July 1814; v.1224, 131–2, Prevost to Rear Adm. Otway, 9 August; v.685, 270, Duke of York to Prevost, 26 September.

143 Jervois correspondence, Jervois to sister, 12 May 1815; same to his mother, 1 March 1816. Jervois became a general in 1860, two years before his death. He and Drummond had become friends during the war and continued to correspond. See Jervois correspondence, Sir G. Drummond to Lt. Colonel W. Jervois, 23 February 1834; Drummond to General Jervois, 5 January 1855; Eliza, Lady Effingham (Drummond's daughter), to same, July 1856.

144 *DCB*, 7: 517–18; NA, RG 8, v.1203 1/2, 216, GO, 29 January 1814; *DHC*, 9: 191, GO, York, 19 February.

145 Information from DCB files; PRO, WO 27/107; and *DNB*. NA, RG 8, v.231, 157–8, Drummond to Prevost, 31 August 1814, mentioned that Drummond knew Nesfield's family. See also ibid., v.1203 1/2 M, 174, GO, 2 September. Stuart Sutherland suggests that Drummond's wife may have known the Nesfield family in England a connection that could explain why he received the appointment.

146 *DCB*, 7: 365–72. Drummond appointed him on 13 December 1813. Hagerman was admitted to the bar in 1815. See NA, RG 8, v.679, 332,

Rottenburg to Prevost, 5 August 1813; v.1221, 177, Freer to Rottenburg, 8 October.

147 NA, RG 8, v.1219, 255, Drummond to Prevost, 7 May 1814; *DHC*, 1: 204–6, Drummond to Prevost, 19 September. Hagerman served briefly as ADC to Lieutenant-Colonel Morrison.

148 *DHC*, 1: 132–4, Drummond to Prevost, 12 August, 1814; NA, RG 8, v.1219, 274–5, Drummond to Prevost, 18 August. On the importance of "Cordial Co-operation and good understanding with the Naval Branch of the Service," see RG 8, v.684, 111–13, Harvey to Major-General Stovin, 15 July; and AO, Drummond Letterbook (MU 8191), 175–7, Drummond to Prevost, 17 July; 196–7, Drummond to Freer, 29 September.

149 *DHC*, 2: 270, Drummond to Prevost, 23 October 1814. The autumn was considered an unhealthy season in Upper Canada; see J. Douglas, *Medical Topography*, 9–10.

150 NA, RG 8, v.1127, 150–1, Prevost to Major General Torrens, 20 December 1814; see also 136, Prevost to Torrens, 18 November.

151 NA, RG 8, v.1222, 218, Prevost to Drummond, 27 October 1814; 229–30, Prevost to Drummond, 18 November. Prevost denied Drummond's request to depart for England.

152 R. Christie, *Memoirs*, 148.

153 *DHC*, 9: 281–2, Drummond to Prevost, 5 April 1814; 286, Prevost to Drummond, 10 April.

154 *DHC*, 9: 303, Prevost to Drummond, 21 April 1814.

155 NA, RG 8, v.684, 12–18, Drummond to Prevost, 2 July 1814. Drummond refers to letters from Prevost of 27, 28, and 29 June which have not been located.

156 *DHC*, 1: 3–6, Harvey to Riall, "Most Secret and Confidential," 23 March 1814.

157 AO, Drummond Letterbook (MU 8191), 75–7, Loring to Riall, 25 June 1814. Drummond later mildly admonished Riall for forcing a Native raiding party to return horses they had captured near Lewiston, NY, warning that such action might cool the Natives' ardour for the British cause; see ibid., 89–90, Loring to Colonel Caldwell, 7 July; 90–1, Loring to Riall, 7 July. See NA, MG 24, A 41, 165, Drummond to Prevost, 7 July, for his report on the raid.

158 NA, RG 8, v.1224, 144–5, Prevost to Major-General Glasgow, 26 August 1814; Graves, *Red Coats & Grey Jackets*, 137–8.

159 *DCB*, 8: 236–9.

160 Stanley, *War of 1812*, 325–30, 404; Horsman, *War of 1812*, 182–4; also Hitsman, *Incredible War*, 241, where this comment also applies to Sheaffe and Riall; see also 202–3.

161 Graves, *Battle of Lundy's Lane*, 90–2, 101, 123–4, 130, 144, 182–4, 187, 190–5, 203 (quotation), 205–6.

162 Sheppard, *Plunder, Profit, and Paroles*, 94–9, 117, 131, 154–5.

163 Kingsford, *History of Canada*, 8: 521; Wood, in *Canada and Its Provinces*, 3: 251, 259–60.

164 Cruikshank, "An Address at the Ceremony of Unveiling a Tablet in the Parliament Buildings, Toronto, October 27, 1932," in *Defended Border*, 315–20.

CHAPTER SEVEN

1 Tupper, *Life and Correspondence*, 5.

2 NA, MG 19, A 39.

3 *DHC*, 5: 279–82, Brenton to Freer, 30 May 1813.

4 *PBHS*, 17: 315–16, Sheaffe to Prevost, 23 November 1812; 327–8, Sheaffe to Colonel Vincent, 1 January 1812 [i.e., 1813].

5 NA, RG 8, v.230, 31–3, Sheaffe to Brenton, 21 August 1813; v.684, 72, Drummond to Prevost, 11 July 1814; v.685, 204, Drummond to Captain Freer, 14 September; v.686, 100, Drummond to Freer, 25 October; MG 24, A 41, 50–1, Drummond to Freer, 14 February 1814; 115–16, Drummond to Prevost, 14 May; 122–3, Drummond to Prevost, 21 May; Clements Library, University of Michigan, Brisbane Papers, Prevost to Brisbane, 12 November 1814; same to same, 17 November; *SBD*, 3, pt 2: 850–6, "Secret Service" (contains various correspondence); R. Malcomson, "War on Lake Ontario," 6.

6 Keegan, *Mask of Command*, 325; see also 148–58, 326–9.

7 Carroll and Baxter, *American Military Tradition*, 26–34. For a general to be concerned about his army's flanks was nothing new at that time. See Keegan, *Mask of Command*, 116–17, 145–54.

8 Turner, "Career of Isaac Brock," 32; Tupper, *Life and Correspondence*, 348.

9 AO, Journal of a Staff Office (MS 842), 70–1, Morning DGO, 5 August 1814; *DHC*, 1: 141–4, Drummond to Prevost, 15 August 1814. Drummond was not alone in his criticisms of the men. See Lieutenant Colonel Harvey's comments in Journal of a Staff Officer, 75–6, Harvey to Colonel Baynes, 6 August; *DHC*, 1: 139–41, Harvey to [Lieutenant Colonel Fischer], 14 August; AO, Strachan Correspondence (MS 35), Harvey to "My Dear Sir," 17 August. Drummond also issued a counter-order to the soldiers to replace their flints.

10 See Keegan, *Mask of Command*, 316–19, on the importance of understanding "between commander and followers." See also John Richardson, *Major Richardson's Major-General Sir Isaac Brock*. Richardson in a letter of 1846 found fault with Brock for his general criticism of the officers of the 41st Foot, and he was particularly bitter at F.B. Tupper for publishing this letter in his *Life and Correspondence*.

11 NA, RG 8, v.229, 136–7, Sheaffe to Prevost, 25 July 1813.

12 NA, RG 8, v.230, 27, Sheaffe to "Dear Sir George," 12 August 1813;
v.680, 43–6, Sheaffe to Prevost, 9 September; v.230, 88–90, Sheaffe to
Prevost, 13 November.

13 NA, RG 8, v.1221, 106, Prevost to Sheaffe, 22 July 1813.

14 Janowitz gained recognition as an important analyser of the nature and
role of armed forces with his *Professional Soldier*. He has authored or co-
authored several other books. For an informative, yet succinct discussion
of this topic and of Janowitz's contributions, see Preston, "Military Education, Professionalism and Doctrine," 281–9. References to Janowitz will
be found in many works, including Holmes, *Firing Line*; Dixon, *On the
Psychology of Military Incompetence*; *New Dimensions in Military History*; Weigley, *History of the United States Army*; and *The Military and American Society:
Essays and Readings*, edited by S.E. Ambrose and J.A. Barber Jr (New
York: The Free Press, 1972).

15 Holmes, *Firing Line*, 341. Holmes discusses psychological models of military leadership, of which there are numerous examples. See chapter 8,
where he refers to the writings of John A. Adair. An interesting study is
Dixon, *On the Psychology of Military Incompetence*. I see no value in trying
to discuss all the possible models in this chapter.

16 Keegan, *Mask of Command*, 1; see also the introduction.

17 Janowitz, *Professional Soldier*, 21–2, defines the essence of the martial spirit
as the "uncritical willingness to face danger" and on 35 claims that the
heroic officer seeks "success in combat, regardless of his personal safety."
See also 265–7, 271–7.

18 Janowitz, *Professional Soldier*, 15, 32–6; see also 216–17, 271–7, along with
278n8, where Janowitz discusses personal values or orientation." Also
Holmes, *Firing Line*, 301.

19 See Keegan's description of Wellington's command style at Waterloo,
which fitted this expectation exactly, in *Mask of Command*, 99–100, 114,
116, 329–31. Edgerton, *Like Lions They Fought*, 175–9, makes the observation that British officers believed that "by showing indifference to danger
they were steadying their men," an attitude equally valid in the War of
1812. See also Holmes, *Firing Line*, chaps 4, 6.

20 The court martial was held in Montreal from December 1814 to January 1815; see NA, MG 13, WO 71, v.243, particularly 5, 17–18, 37–43, 57,
71–4, 77–8, 89–90, 95, 103–5, 333, 376–7, 408–24. For a sympathetic
treatment of Procter see Antal, "Myths and Facts Concerning General
Procter."

21 Blumenson and Stokesbury, *Masters of the Art of Command*, 2. See also
Bernard Montgomery, *The Path to Leadership* (London: Collins, 1962).

22 I use the term "pragmatist" rather than Janowitz's "managerial" type
because his definition would fit all the generals without making significant distinctions. Basically, he defines the managerial type as practical,

"concerned with the scientific and rational conduct of war," and retaining "effective links to civilian society." Officers of this kind consider themselves brave men prepared to face combat, but they are "mainly concerned with the most rational and economic ways of winning wars or avoiding them. They are less concerned with war as a way of life." See Janowitz, *Professional Soldier*, 21–2, 35; see also 8–15, 26–9, 265–7, 271–7, 278n8.

23 Blumenson and Stokesbury, *Masters of the Art of Command*, 3.

24 Graves, "'The Best Means,'" especially 28. Compare Whitehorne's opinion in *While Washington Burned*, ix.

25 Ouellet, *Economic and Social History of Quebec*, 242.

26 Skelton, "High Army Leadership," 265–70. See also Hansen, "War of 1812."

27 The 41st Foot had arrived in Canada in 1799 and the 49th in 1802, previous to which the latter had been in England without having seen action since 1799. See Stanley, *War of 1812*, 98; Petre, *Royal Berkshire Regiment*, 1: 76–82.

28 Walden, "Isaac Brock," 17, citing John Richardson. See also Blumenson and Stokesbury, *Masters of the Art of Command*, 6.

29 *DHC*, 4: 116, Narrative of Volunteer G.S. Jarvis, 49th Regiment, claims that the men of the regiment raised the cry "Revenge the General!" immediately before Colonel Macdonell led them in his unsuccessful charge. For W.H. Merritt's view see *Campaigns of 1812–14*, 8.

30 See, for example, *Quebec Mercury*, 1 November 1814, 346; *Montreal Herald*, 19 November 1814; 26 November, letter to the editor from "Citizen."

31 Hitsman, *Incredible War*, 234–5. Prime Minister Liverpool wrote to Lord Castlereagh on 18 November, "I think we have determined, ... not to continue the war for the purpose of obtaining, or securing any acquisition of territory. We have been led to this determination by the consideration of the unsatisfactory state of the negotiations at Vienna, and by that of the alarming situation of the interior of France." See also Stanley, *War of 1812*, 390–2.

Bibliography

ARCHIVAL SOURCES

Canada

ARCHIVES OF ONTARIO, TORONTO (AO)
Gordon Drummond Letterbook (MU 8191)
Colley L.L. Foster Papers (MU 1057)
Alexander Fraser Papers (MU 1063, series 1)
Givins Family Papers (MU 7253)
Solomon Jones Papers (MS 520)
Journal of a Staff Officer, Military Operations Upper Canada 1813, with Official Documents Annexed (Lieutenant-Colonel John Harvey; MS 842)
Military Records (MU 2036)
Sir David W. Smith Papers (MU 2826)
John Strachan Correspondence and Letterbooks (MS 35)
F.B. Tupper Papers (MS 496)
Isaac Wilson Diary (MS 199)

MCCORD MUSEUM OF CANADIAN HISTORY, MONTREAL
Cuthbert Family Papers
War of 1812 Papers

NATIONAL ARCHIVES OF CANADA, OTTAWA (NA)
MG 11, Public Record Office, London
    CO 42, Canada, Original Correspondence, 1700–1909
    CO 43, Canada, Entry Books, 1763–1873
    F 112, Charles K. Gardner Papers
    G 45, Famille de Salaberry Papers

J 48, John William Whittaker Papers

MG 12, Admiralty 1, Admiralty and Secretarial Papers, 1689–1913

MG 13, WO 17, Return of the General and Staff Officers at Present Serving in British North America (Monthly Returns)

    WO 71, v.243, Court Martial of Maj. Gen. H. Procter

MG 19, A 39, Duncan Clark Papers

MG 23, D 2, Edward Winslow Papers

    G 11, Sewell Correspondence

    H 1, John Graves Simcoe Papers

MG 24, A 1, Sir Isaac Brock Papers

    A 41, Drummond Letterbook

    B 3, v. 3, Ryland Papers

    E 1–4, Merritt Papers

    F 15, Scott Papers

    F 18, Memoir of Midshipman David Wingfield

    F 21, pt 1, William Henry Robinson, Letter on Plattsburgh

    F 22, Arthur Sinclair Papers

    F 23, v. 1, Gustavus Nicolls Papers

    F 78, Francis, Baron de Rottenburg, Papers

    F 96, De Watteville Papers

MG 30, D 1, Francis-Joseph Audet Papers

RG 5, A 1, Upper Canada Sundries

RG 8, I, C series, British Military and Naval Records

QUEEN'S UNIVERSITY ARCHIVES, KINGSTON
Cartwright Family Papers

TORONTO REFERENCE LIBRARY, BALDWIN ROOM (TRL)
William Allan Papers (5123)
C.A., Hagerman, Journal of Events in the War of 1812
Prevost Military Papers

UNITED CHURCH OF CANADA/VICTORIA UNIVERSITY ARCHIVES, TORONTO
Journal of Rev. George Ferguson (fonds 3122)

WINDSOR PUBLIC LIBRARY, WINDSOR, ONT.
John Stodgell Collection (MS 24 I/19)

United Kingdom

MEGGINCH CASTLE, ERROL, SCOTLAND
Diary of Robert Drummond Esqr., 1773–1817

Extra Warrant Book, 49th Regiment, Quebec

PRIVATE COLLECTION, LONDON
Jervois Correspondence

PUBLIC RECORD OFFICE, LONDON (PRO)
WO 25, Half-pay Officers, 1828, G
WO 27, Inspection Returns
WO 55, v. 860, 135–44, Journal of the Attack made upon Fort Erie by the Right
    Division of the British Army in Canada under the Command of Lieut. Genl.
    Drummond in the Months of August and September 1814; Lieut. G. Phill-
    potts, RE, to Capt. Romilly, RE

United States

BUFFALO AND ERIE COUNTY HISTORICAL SOCIETY,
BUFFALO, NY (BECHS)
A. Conger Goodyear, War of 1812 Manuscripts
Inventory of War of 1812 Microfilms
Manuscript Collection, War of 1812, Letterbook of Maj. Gen. Phineas Riall
War of 1812 Papers (BOO-15)

WILLIAM L. CLEMENTS LIBRARY, UNIVERSITY OF MICHIGAN,
ANN ARBOR
Sir Thomas Brisbane Papers
Jacob Brown Papers
David B. Douglass Papers, "Reminiscences of the Campaign of 1814"
Lucius D. Lyon Papers, Account of Major Kearsley
War of 1812 Collection, Bloomfield-Pike Letterbook
War of 1812 Papers

DUKE UNIVERSITY, DURHAM, NC
Campbell Family Papers, Correspondence, 1812–13
Diary of John Lang, Lieut. 19. Light Dragoons during War in Canada 1813

PENNSYLVANIA STATE ARCHIVES, HARRISBURG, PA
MG 6, Jacob Miller Diary
MG 6, John Witherow Jr Journal

NEWSPAPERS

Kingston Gazette
Montreal Herald

Quebec Gazette
Quebec Mercury
York Gazette

OTHER PUBLISHED SOURCES

NOTE: A few works of limited scope for this study are not listed in the bibliography; their publication details are given in the endnotes.

Adams, Henry. *History of the United States of America during the Administration of James Madison.* Vols. 3–4. New York: Boni, 1930

Addington, Larry H. *The Patterns of War since the Eighteenth Century.* Bloomington, Ind.: Indiana University Press, 1984

After Tippecanoe: Some Aspects of the War of 1812. Edited by Philip Mason. Toronto: Ryerson Press, 1963

Allen, Robert S. "The Bisshopp Papers during the War of 1812." *JSAHR* 61 (spring 1983): 22–9

– *His Majesty's Indian Allies: British Indian Policy in The Defence of Canada, 1774–1815.* Toronto: Dundurn Press, 1992

– "His Majesty's Indian Allies: Native Peoples, the British Crown and the War of 1812." *MHR*, 14 (fall 1988): 1–24

Altoff, G.T. "Oliver Hazard Perry and the Battle of Lake Erie." *MHR* 14 (fall 1988): 25–57

Anderson, William J. *The Life of F.M., H.R.H. Edward, Duke of Kent, Illustrated by His Correspondence with the De Salaberry Family, … from 1791 to 1841.* Ottawa/Toronto: Hunter Rose, 1870

Antal, S. "Myths and Facts Concerning General Procter." *OH* 79 (Sept. 1987): 251–62

[*Army List*]. *A List of All the Officers of the Army & Royal Marines on Full and Half Pay; with an Index and a Succession of Colonels.* London: War Office, 1814, 1815

"The Assault on Fort Erie; or, Two ways of Telling a Story." *United Service Journal,* pt 3 (Sept. 1841): 84–90

Atkinson, C.T. "Foreign Regiments in the British Army, 1793–1802." *JSAHR* 22 (1943–44): 2–14, 45–52, 107–15, 132–42, 187–97, 234–50, 265–76, 313–24

Barlow, W., and D.O. Powell. "A Physician's Journey through Western New York and Upper Canada in 1815." *Niagara Frontier* 25, no. 4 (1978): 85–95

Benn, Carl. *The Battle of York.* Belleville: Mika, 1984

– *Historic Fort York, 1793–1993.* Toronto: Natural Heritage/Natural History Inc., 1993

Berton, Pierre. *Flames Across the Border, 1813–1814.* Toronto: McClelland and Stewart, 1981

– *The Invasion of Canada, 1812–1813.* Toronto: McClelland and Stewart, 1980

Blumenson, Martin, and J.L. Stokesbury. *Masters of the Art of Command.* Boston: Houghton Mifflin Co., 1975

Bond, G.C. *The Grand Expedition: The British Invasion of Holland in 1809.* Athens, Ga: University of Georgia Press, 1979

Bonney, Catharina V., comp. *A Legacy of Historical Gleanings.* 2nd ed. Albany, NY: J. Munsell, 1875

Bowler, R.A. "Propaganda in Upper Canada: A Study of the Propaganda Directed at the People of Upper Canada during the War of 1812." MA thesis, Queen's University, 1964

Boylen, J.C. "Strategy of Brock Saves UC: Candid Comments of a U.S. Officer Who Crossed at Queenston." *OH* 58 (March 1966): 59–60

Brazer, M.C. "An Afterword to the Battle of Lake Erie." *Inland Seas* 33 (1977): 180–3

[Brenton, E.B.]. *Some Account of the Public Life of the late Lieutenant-General Sir George Prevost, Bart. ...* London: T. Cadell and T. Egerton, 1823

Brett-James, Anthony. *Life in Wellington's Army,* London: George Allen and Unwin, 1972

British Military History: A Supplement to Robin Higham's Guide to the Sources. Edited by Gerald Jordan. New York and London: Garland, 1988

Brode, Patrick. *Sir John Beverley Robinson, Bone and Sinew of the Compact.* Toronto: University of Toronto Press, 1984

Bruce, Anthony P.C. *The Purchase System in the British Army, 1660–1871.* London: Royal Historical Society, 1980

Buell, W.S. "Military Movements in Eastern Ontario during the War of 1812." *OH* 10 (1913): 60–71

Bunbury, Sir Henry. *Narrative of Some Passages in the Great War with France from 1799 to 1810.* London, 1854

Burne, Alfred H. *The Art of War on Land.* 2nd ed. London: Methuen, 1950

Burt, Alfred L. *The United States, Great Britain and British North America from the Revolution to the Establishment of Peace after the War of 1812.* New York, 1961

Butler, L.W.G., and S.W. Hare. *The Annals of the King's Royal Rifle Corps.* 5 vols. London, 1913–21

Calloway, Colin G. *Crown and Calumet: British-Indian Relations, 1763–1815.* Norman, Okla: University of Oklahoma Press, 1987

– "The End of an Era: British-Indian Relations in the Great Lakes Region after the War of 1812." *MHR* 12 (fall 1986): 1–20

Campaigns of 1812–14: Contemporary Narratives by Captain W.H. Merritt, Colonel William Claus, Lieut.-Colonel Matthew Elliott and Captain John Norton. Edited by E.A. Cruikshank. Niagara Historical Society, no. 9. [Niagara] 1902

Canada and Its Provinces: A History of the Canadian People and Their Institutions. General editors, Adam Shortt and Arthur G. Doughty. 23 vols. Toronto: T. & A. Constable, 1914

Canadian State Trials. Vol. 1. Edited by F. Murray Greenwood and Barry Wright. Toronto: Published for the Osgoode Society for Canadian Legal History by University of Toronto Press, 1996

The Capital Years: Niagara-on-the-Lake, 1792–1796. Edited by R. Merritt, N. Butler, and M. Power. Toronto: Dundurn Press, 1991

Carmichael-Smyth, Sir James, Bart. *Precis of the Wars in Canada, from 1755 to the Treaty of Ghent in 1814, with Military and Political Reflections.* Edited by Sir James Carmichael, Bart. London, 1862

Carroll, John M., and Colin F. Baxter, eds. *The American Military Tradition: From Colonial Times to the Present.* Wilmington, Del.: Scholarly Resources, 1993

– *The Causes of the War of 1812: National Honour or National Interest?* Edited by B. Perkins. New York, 1963

Chambers, E.J. *The Canadian Militia: A History of the Origin and Development of the Force.* Montreal: L.M. Fresco, 1907

Chandler, David G. *The Art of Warfare on Land.* London: Hamlyn, 1974

– *Atlas of Military Strategy, 1618–1878.* London: Arms and Armour, 1980

– *Dictionary of the Napoleonic Wars.* New York: Macmillan, 1979

Christie, Carl. "The Walcheren Expedition of 1809." PhD thesis, University of Dundee, 1975

Christie, Robert. *History of the Late Province of Lower Canada, Parliamentary and Political … Embracing a Period of Fifty Years.* 5 vols. Quebec: T. Cary, 1848–55

– *Memoirs of the Administration of the Colonial Government of Lower-Canada, by Sir James Henry Craig and Sir George Prevost, from the year 1807 until the year 1815 … Quebec, 1818*

– *The Military and Naval Operations in the Canadas, during the Late War with the United States … from the Year 1807 until the Year 1815.* Quebec, 1818 (another edition of the *Memoirs*)

Commins, James. "The War on the Canadian Frontier, 1812–14: Letters Written by Sergt. James Commins, 8th Foot." Edited by Norman C. Lord. *JSAHR* 18 (1939): 199–211

Craig, H. "The Loyal and Patriotic Society of Upper Canada and Its Still-Born Child – the 'Upper Canada Preserved' Medal." *OH* 52 (March 1960): 31–52

Crooks, A.D. "Recollections of the War of 1812. From a manuscript of the late Hon. James Crooks." Women's Canadian Historical Society of Toronto, *Transactions*, no. 13 (1913–14): 11–24

Crosswell, D.K.R. "The American Invasion of the Niagara Peninsula, 1814." MA thesis, Western Michigan University, 1979

– "A Near-Run Thing on the Niagara: The Battle of Lundy's Lane." In *Sharing Past & Future* (Toronto, 1988), 33–56

Cruikshank, E.A. *The Battle of Lundy's Lane …* 3rd ed. Welland: Printed at the Tribune Office, 1893

– *The Battle of Queenston Heights.* 2nd ed. Niagara Falls, 1891

– *Drummond's Winter Campaign 1813*. 2nd ed. Lundy's Lane Historical Society, 1900

– "From Isle aux Noix to Chateauguay: A Study of Military Operations on the Frontier of Lower Canada in 1812 and 1813." Royal Society of Canada, *Proceedings and Transactions*, 3rd ser., 7 (1913), sec. 2, 129–73; 8 (1914), sec. 2, 25–102

– "John Beverley Robinson and the Trials for Treason in 1814." *OH* 25 (1929): 191–219

– "Record of the Services of Canadian Regiments in the War of 1812 – XII: The York Militia." Canadian Military Institute, *Transactions* 16 (1908)

– *The Siege of Fort Erie, August 1st – September 23d, 1814*. Lundy's Lane Historical Society Publications. Welland, Ont., 1905

– "A Sketch of the Public Life and Services of Robert Nichol." *OH* 19 (1922): 6–79

– "A Study of Disaffection in Upper Canada." Royal Society of Canada, *Transactions*, 3d ser., 6 (1912): 55–65

Cullum, George W. *Campaigns of the War of 1812–15, against Great Britain, Sketched and Criticised; with Brief Biographies of the American Engineers*. New York: James Miller, 1879

Curzon, Sarah. *Laura Secord, the Heroine of 1812: A Drama and Other Poems*. Toronto: C.B. Robinson, 1887

The Defended Border: Upper Canada and the War of 1812. Edited by M. Zaslow. Toronto: Macmillan, 1964

de Watteville, Herman G. de. *The British Soldier, His Daily Life from Tudor to Modern Times*, London: J.M. Dent and Sons, 1954

Dictionary of American Biography. Edited by Allen Johnson. 11 vols. New York: Scribner, 1946–58

Dictionary of Canadian Biography. Volumes 5–8 (1800–70). Edited by Francess G. Halpenny. Toronto: University of Toronto Press, 1977–88

Dictionary of National Biography. 22 vols. New York: Oxford University Press, 1953

Dixon, Norman F. *On the Psychology of Military Incompetence*. London, 1976

Documentary History of the Campaigns upon the Niagara Frontier. Edited by E.A. Cruikshank. 9 vols. Welland: Lundy's Lane Historical Society, 1893–1906

Documents Relating to the Constitutional History of Canada, 1791–1818. Selected and edited with notes by A.G. Doughty and D.A. McArthur. Ottawa: Public Archives of Canada, 1914

Documents Relating to the Invasion of Canada and the Surrender of Detroit, 1812. Edited by E.A. Cruikshank. Publications of the Canadian Archives, no. 7. Ottawa, 1913.

Documents Relating to the Invasion of the Niagara Peninsula by the United States Army, Commanded by General Jacob Brown, in July and August, 1814. Edited by E.A. Cruikshank. Niagara-on-the-Lake: Niagara Advance County Printers, 1920

Douglas, John. *Medical Topography of Upper Canada.* Introduction by Charles G. Roland. Canton, Mass.: Science History Publications U.S.A., 1985

Douglas, W.A.B. "The Anatomy of Naval Incompetence: The Provincial Marine in Defence of Upper Canada before 1813." *OH* 71 (March 1979): 3–25

– *Gunfire on the Lakes: The Naval War of 1812–1814 on the Great Lakes and Lake Champlain.* Ottawa: Canadian War Museum, 1977

Duffy, Michael. "The British Army and the Caribbean Expeditions of the War against Revolutionary France, 1793–1801." *JSAHR* 52 (1984), 65–73

– *Soldiers, Sugar, and Seapower: The British Expeditions to the West Indies and the War against Revolutionary France.* Oxford: Clarendon Press, 1987

Dunlop, William. *Tiger Dunlop's Upper Canada, comprising Recollections of the American War 1812–1814 and Statistical Sketches of Upper Canada for the Use of Emigrants, by a Backwoodsman.* Introduction by C.F. Klinck. Toronto: McClelland & Stewart, 1967

Eayrs, Hugh. *Sir Isaac Brock.* Toronto: Macmillan, 1924

Edgar, Matilda. *General Brock.* Revised by E.A. Cruikshank. The Makers of Canada Series, vol. 4. Toronto: Oxford University Press, 1926

– *Ten Years of Upper Canada in Peace and War, 1805–1815; being the Ridout Letters with Annotations.* Toronto: William Briggs, 1890

Edgerton, R.B. *Like Lions They Fought: The Zulu War and the Last Black Empire in South Africa.* London: Ballantine Books, 1989

Elliott, C.W. *Winfield Scott: The Soldier and the Man.* New York: Macmillan, 1937

Emsley, Clive. *British Society and the French Wars, 1793–1815.* London: Macmillan, 1979

Ermatinger, E. *Life of Colonel Talbot & the Talbot Settlement.* New introduction by J.J. Talman. Belleville: Mika, 1972

Errington, Jane. "Friends and Foes – the Kingston Elite and the War of 1812: A Case Study in Ambivalence." *Journal of Canadian Studies* 20 (spring 1985): 58–79

Everest, A.S. *The War of 1812 in the Champlain Valley.* Syracuse, NY: Syracuse University Press, 1981

Falls, Cyril B. *The Art of War from the Age of Napoleon to the Present Day.* New York: Oxford University Press, 1961

Farwell, Byron. *For Queen and Country.* London: Allen Lane, 1981

Fitzgibbon, Mary A. *A Veteran of 1812: The Life of James Fitzgibbon.* Toronto: William Briggs, 1894

Fortescue, Sir John. *A History of the British Army.* 13 vols. London, 1911–20

Fredriksen, John C. *Officers of the War of 1812 with Portraits and Anecdotes. The United States Army Left Division Gallery of Honour.* Lewiston, NY: Edward Mellen Press, 1988

– "The War of 1812 in Northern New York: The Observations of Captain Rufus McIntire." *New York History* 68 (July 1987): 297–324

French, David. *The British Way in Warfare, 1688–2000.* London: Unwin Hyman, 1990

Frey, Sylvia. "Courts and Cats: British Military Justice in the 18th Century." *Military Affairs* 43 (1979): 5–11

Fuller, J.F.C. *The Conduct of War, 1789–1961: A Study of the Impact of the French, Industrial, and Russian Revolutions on War and Its Conduct.* London: Eyre and Spottiswoode, 1962

– *Generalship, Its Diseases and Their Cure: A Study of the Personal Factor in Command.* London: Faber & Faber, 1933

Gaugreben, Baron de. "Baron de Gaugreben's Memoir on the Defence of Upper Canada." Edited by H.R. Holmden. *CHR* 11 (March 1921): 58–68

General Regulations and Orders for the Army to 1st January 1816. A facsimile ed. London: Frederick Muller, 1970

George Washington's Generals. Edited by George Billias. New York: Morrow, 1964

George Washington's Opponents. Edited by George Billias. New York: Morrow, 1964

Glover, Michael. "The Purchase of Commissions: A Reappraisal." *JSAHR,* 58 (winter 1980): 223–35

– "Purchase, Patronage and Promotion in the Army at the Time of the Peninsular War." *Army Quarterly* 103 (1972–73): 211–15, 355–62

– *Wellington as Military Commander.* London: B.T. Batsford Ltd., 1968

Glover, Richard. *Peninsular Preparation: The Reform of the British Army, 1795–1809.* Cambridge: Cambridge University Press, 1963

Goodspeed, D.J. *The British Campaigns in the Peninsula, 1808–1814.* Ottawa: Queen's Printer, 1958

Gordon, William A. *A Compilation of Registers of the Army of the United States from 1815 to 1837.* Washington: James C. Dunn, 1837

Gourlay, Robert. *Statistical Account of Upper Canada.* 2 vols. 1822; reprint, New York: Johnson Reprint Corp., 1966

Graves, Donald E. "The Attack on Sackets Harbor, 29 May 1813: The British/ Canadian Side." Unpublished

– *The Battle of Lundy's Lane on the Niagara in 1814.* Baltimore, Md: The Nautical & Aviation Publishing Co., 1993

– "'The Best Means of Suppressing the Growing Evil': British Military Commanders and the Use of Martial Law in Upper Canada, 1812–1814." Paper presented to the Conference on Aid to the Civil Power, Acadia University, April 1991. Unpublished

– "The Canadian Volunteers, 1813–1815." *Journal of the Company of Military Historians* 31 (fall 1979): 113–17

– "Joseph Willcocks and the Canadian Volunteers: An Account of Political Disaffection in Upper Canada during the War of 1812." MA thesis, Carleton University, 1982

– *Red Coats & Grey Jackets: The Battle of Chippawa, 5 July, 1814.* Toronto: Dundurn Press, 1994

– "William Drummond and the Battle of Fort Erie." *Canadian Military History* 1 (autumn 1992): 31–9

Gray, William. *Soldiers of the King: The Upper Canadian Militia. 1812–1815.* Erin, Ont.: Boston Mills Press, 1995

Greenwood, F.M. *Legacies of Fear: The Impact of the French Revolution on the Politics of Law in Quebec/Lower Canada, 1789–1811.* Toronto: University of Toronto Press, 1993

Greer, Allan. *Peasant, Lord and Merchant: Rural Society in Three Quebec Parishes 1740–1840.* Toronto: University of Toronto Press, 1985

A Guide to the Sources of British Military History. Edited by Robin Higham. Berkeley and Los Angeles: University of California Press, 1971

A Guide to the Sources of United States Military History. Edited by Robin Higham. Hamden, Conn.: Archon Books, 1975

Guitard, Michelle. *The Militia of the Battle of Chateauguay: A Social History.* Ottawa: Parks Canada, 1983

Hannay, James. *History of the War of 1812 between Great Britain and the United States of America.* Toronto: Morang and Co., 1905

Hansen, D.K. "The War of 1812: 'A Lesson in Leadership.'" MMS thesis, U.S. Marine Corps, Command and Staff College, 1995–96

Harris, Stephen J. *Canadian Brass: The Making of a Professional Army, 1860–1939.* Toronto: University of Toronto Press, 1988

Heinrichs, W.H., Jr. "The Battle of Plattsburgh – the Losers." *American Neptune* 21 (Jan. 1961): 42–56

Hickey, Donald. *The War of 1812: A Forgotten Conflict.* Urbana and Chicago: University of Illinois Press, 1989

Hitsman, J.M. *The Incredible War of 1812: A Military History.* Toronto: University of Toronto Press, 1965

– *Safeguarding Canada, 1763–1871.* Toronto: University of Toronto Press, 1968

– "Sir George Prevost's Conduct of the Canadian War of 1812." CHA, *Report,* 1962, 34–43

Holmes, Richard. *Firing Line.* London: Jonathan Cape, 1985

Horsman, Reginald. *The Causes of the War of 1812.* Philadelphia: University of Pennsylvania Press, 1962

– *The War of 1812.* New York: Knopf, 1969

Houlding, J.A. *Fit for Service: The Training of the British Army, 1715–1795.* Oxford: Clarendon Press, 1981

Howison, John. *Sketches of Upper Canada, Domestic, Local, and Characteristic.* East Ardsley, Yorkshire: S.R. Publishers, 1965

Humphries, Charles W. "The Capture of York." *OH* 51 (winter 1959): 1–21

Hyatt, A.M.J. "The Defence of Upper Canada in 1812." MA thesis, Carleton University, 1961

Ingersoll, Charles J. *Historical Sketch of the Second War between the United States of America and Great Britain.* 3 vols. Philadelphia: Lea and Blanchard, 1845

Ingram, G. "The Story of Laura Secord Revisited." *OH* 57 (June 1965): 85–97

Irving, L.H. *Officers of the British Forces in Canada during the War of 1812–15.* Welland, Ont.: Welland Tribune, 1908

James, William. *A Full and Correct Account of the Military Occurrences of the Late War between Great Britain and the United States of America.* 2 vols. London: Printed for the author, 1818

Janowitz, Morris. *The Professional Soldier: A Social and Political Portrait.* New York: Free Press of Glencoe, 1961

Jarvis, Julia. *Three Centuries of Robinsons: The Story of a Family.* Toronto, 1967

Jenkins, John S. *The Generals of the Last War with Great Britain.* Auburn: Derby, Miller & Company, 1849

The John Askin Papers. Edited by Milo M. Quaife. 2 vols. Detroit: Detroit Library Commission, 1928–31

The John Strachan Letter Book, 1812–1834. Edited by G.W. Spragge. Toronto: Ontario Historical Society, 1946

Johnson, J.K. *Becoming Prominent: Regional Leadership in Upper Canada 1791–1841.* Montreal and Kingston: McGill-Queen's University Press, 1989

Kaye, J.W. "The Army and its Officers." *North British Review.* 12 (Feb. 1850): 499–531

Kearsley, Jonathan. "The Memoirs of Jonathan Kearsley: A Michigan Hero from the War of 1812." Edited by John C. Fredriksen. *Indiana Military History Journal* 10 (May 1985): 4–16

Keegan, John. *The Mask of Command.* London: Jonathan Cape, 1987

Kimball, Jeffrey. "Strategy on the Northern Frontier." PhD dissertation, University of Louisiana at Baton Rouge, 1969

Kingsford, William. *The History of Canada.* 10 vols. Toronto: Rowsell & Hutchison, 1887–98

Lauerma, Matti. "The End of a Planner: The Count de Guibert during 1787–90." *Turun Historiallinen Arkisto* 31 (1976): 285–307

– "The Influence of Antiquity upon French Military Literature in the 1700's." *Historiallinen Arkisto* 73 (1978): 103–9

– "The Life Work of Count de Guibert." *Historiallinen Arkisto,* 70 (1975): 142–58

Le Couteur, John. *Merry Hearts Make Light Days: The War of 1812 Journal of Lieutenant John Le Couteur, 104th Foot.* Edited by Donald E. Graves. Ottawa: Carleton University Press, 1993

Legislators and Legislatures of Ontario: A Reference Guide. Vol. 1: *1792–1866.* Compiled and edited by Debra Forman. Toronto: Legislative Library, 1984

Lépine, Luc. *Les officiers de milice du Bas-Canada 1812–1815 / Lower Canada's Militia Officers.* Montreal: Société généalogique canadienne-française, 1996

Letters of 1812 from Dominion Archives. Edited by E.A. Cruikshank. Niagara Historical Society, no. 23. [Niagara] 1911

Liddell Hart, B.H. "What is Military Genius?" *Canadian Army Journal* 12 (July 1959): 54–61

Lossing, Benson J. *The Pictorial Field-Book of the War of 1812.* New York: Harper, 1869

Lucas, C.P. *The Canadian War of 1812.* Oxford: Clarendon Press, 1906

Lucas, Robert. *The Robert Lucas Journal of the War of 1812 during the Campaign under General William Hull.* Edited by John C. Parish. Iowa City: State Historical Society of Iowa, 1906

Luvaas, Jay. *The Education of an Army: British Military Thought, 1815–1940.* Chicago: University of Chicago Press, 1964

Macdonell, J.A. *Sketches Illustrating the Early Settlement and History of Glengarry in Canada.* Montreal: Wm Foster, Brown and Co., 1893

MacEwan, William. "Excerpts from the Letters From Lieutenant and Adjutant William Macewen to His Wife, Canada, 1813–14." Edited by Arthur Brymner. n.p., n.d.

McGuffie, T.H. "The Significance of Military Rank in the British Army between 1790 and 1820." *Bulletin of the Institute of Historical Research* 30 (1957): 207–24

McKenzie, R. *Laura Secord: The Legend and the Lady.* Toronto: McClelland & Stewart, 1972

Mahan, A.T. *Sea Power in Its Relations to the War of 1812.* 2 vols. London, 1905

Mahon, John K. "British Command Decisions in the Northern Campaigns of the War of 1812." *CHR* 66 (Sept. 1965): 219–37

– *The War of 1812.* Gainesville, Fla: University of Florida Press, 1972

Makers of Modern Strategy: Military Thought from Machiavelli to Hitler. Edited by Edward M. Earle with the collaboration of G.A. Craig and F. Gilbert. Princeton, NJ: Princeton University Press, 1971

Malcomson, Robert. "The Barclay Correspondence: More from the Man Who Lost the Battle of Lake Erie." *Journal of Erie Studies* 20 (spring 1991): 18–35

– *The Battle of Queenston Heights.* Niagara-on-the-Lake: Friends of Fort George, 1994

– "War on Lake Ontario: A Costly Victory at Oswego, 1814." *Beaver* 75 (April/May 1995): 4–13

Malcomson, Tom. "September 1813: The Decidedly Indecisive Engagements between Chauncey and Yeo." *Inland Seas* 47 (winter 1991): 299–313

Martin, Sir Henry Byam. *Friendly Spies on the Northern Tour, 1815–1837: Sketches of Henry Byam Martin.* [Ottawa] Public Archives, 1981

Martin, J.D.P. "The Regiment de Watteville: Its Settlement and Service in Upper Canada." *OH* 52 (March 1960): 17–30

Morgan, Cecilia Louise. *Public Men and Virtuous Women: The Gendered Languages of Religion and Politics in Upper Canada, 1791–1850.* Toronto: University of Toronto Press, 1996

Morgan, H.J. *Sketches of Celebrated Canadians and Persons Connected with Canada.* Quebec: Hunter, Rose and Co., 1862

The Naval War of 1812. A Documentary History. Vol. 1: 1812; vol. 2: 1813. Edited by William S. Dudley. Washington, DC: Naval Historical Center, Department of the Navy, 1985–92

Neuburg, V.E. "The British Army in the Eighteenth Century." *JSAHR* 61 (1983): 39–47

New Cambridge Modern History. 14 vols. Cambridge: University Press, 1957–79

New Dimensions in Military History: An Anthology. Edited by R.F. Weigley. San Rafael, Calif., 1975

New Interpretations in Naval History: Selected Papers from the Eighth Naval History Symposium. Edited by William B. Cogar. Annapolis, Md: Naval Institute Press, 1989

Norton, John. *The Journal of Major John Norton, 1816.* Edited by C.F. Klinck and J.J. Talman. Toronto: Champlain Society, 1970

Ouellet, Fernand. *Economic and Social History of Quebec, 1760–1850: Structures and Conjonctures.* Translated under the auspices of the Institute of Canadian Studies. [Toronto]: Gage, 1983

– *Lower Canada 1791–1840: Social Change and Nationalism.* Translated and adapted by P. Claxton. Toronto: McClelland and Stewart, 1980

Owen, David. *Fort Erie (1764–1823): An Historical Guide.* Niagara Falls, Ont.: Niagara Parks Commission, 1986

Peterson, C.J. *The Military Heroes of the War of 1812; with a Narrative of the War.* 10th ed. Philadelphia: J.B. Smith, 1858

Petre, Francis L. *The Royal Berkshire Regiment (Princess Charlotte of Wales's) 49th/66th Foot.* 2 vols. Reading: The Regiment, 1925

Piechowiak, A.B. "The Anglo-Russian Expedition to Holland in 1799." *Slavonic and East European Review* 41 (1962–63): 182–9

Preston, R.A. "The Journals of Sir F.P. Robinson, G.C.B." *CHR* 37 (Dec. 1956): 352–5

– "Military Education, Professionalism and Doctrine." *Revue internationale d'histoire militaire / International Review of Military History* 54 (1982): 273–301

– S.F. Wise, and H.O. Werner. *Men in Arms: A History of Warfare and Its Interrelationships with Western Society.* Rev. ed. New York: Frederick A. Praeger, 1965

Raudzens, G. "'Red George' Macdonell, Military Saviour of Upper Canada?" *OH* 62 (Dec. 1970): 199–212

Read, D.B. *The Lieutenant-Governors of Upper Canada and Ontario, 1792–1899.* Toronto: Briggs, 1900

Recollections of the War of 1812. Three Eyewitnesses' Accounts. Toronto: Baxter, 1964

"Records of Niagara: A Collection of Contemporary Letters and Documents, 1812." Collected and edited by E.A. Cruikshank. Niagara Historical Society, *Transactions*, no. 43 (1934)

Reminiscences of the War of 1812–14; Being Portions of the Diary of a Captain of the "Voltigeurs Canadiens" while in Garrison at Kingston etc. Translated from the French by J.L. Hubert Neilson. Kingston, 1895

The Report of the Loyal and Patriotic Society of Upper Canada. Montreal: William
    Gray, 1817

Richardson, James. "Reminiscences of Lieut. James Richardson, Naval Officer
    during the War of 1812." Women's Canadian Historical Society of Toronto,
    Transactions, no. 15 (1915–16): 13–38

[Richardson, John]. *The Letters of Veritas, Re-Published from the Montreal Herald,
    Containing a Succinct Account of the Military Administration of Sir George Prevost,
    during his Command in the Canadas, Whereby it Will Appear Manifest, that the Merit
    of Preserving Them from Conquest, Belongs Not to Him.* Montreal, W. Gray, 1815

– *Major Richardson's Major General Sir Isaac Brock and the 41st Regiment.* Edited
    by T.B. Higginson. Burks Falls: Old Rectory Press, 1976

– *Richardson's War of 1812.* With notes and a life of the author by A.C. Cassel-
    man. Toronto: Historical Publishing Co., 1902

Riddell, W.R. "Joseph Willcocks: Sheriff, Member of Parliament, and Traitor."
    OH 24 (1928): 475–99

– *The Life of William Dummer Powell, First Judge at Detroit and Fifth Chief Justice of
    Upper Canada.* Lansing, Mich.: Michigan Historical Commission, 1924

Robinson, C.W. *The Life of Sir John Beverley Robinson.* Toronto: Morang and Co.,
    1904

Rogers, Hugh C.B. *The British Army of the Eighteenth Century.* New York: Allen and
    Unwin, 1977

– *Wellington's Army.* London: Ian Allan, 1979

Rothenberg, G.E. *The Art of Warfare in the Age of Napoleon.* Don Mills, Ont.:
    Fitzhenry and Whiteside, 1978

*The Royal Military Calendar, or Army Service and Commission Book, containing the
    Services and Progress of Promotions of the Generals, Lieutenant-Generals, Major-
    Generals, Colonels, Lieutenant-Colonels and Majors of the Army.* Edited by John
    Philippart. 3rd ed. 5 vols. London, 1820

Sabine, Lorenzo. *Biographical Sketches of Loyalists of the American Revolution, with
    an Historical Essay.* 2 vols. Port Washington, NY: Kennikat Press, 1966

Select British Documents of the Canadian War of 1812. Edited by William Wood.
    3 vols in 4. Toronto: Champlain Society, 1920–28

Sheppard, George. "'Deeds Speak': Militiamen, Medals and the Invented Tra-
    ditions of 1812." *OH* 83 (Sept. 1990): 207–392

– *Plunder, Profit, and Paroles: A Social History of the War of 1812 in Upper Canada.*
    Montreal and Kingston: McGill-Queen's Universtity Press, 1994

Sherwig, John M. *Guineas and Gunpowder: British Foreign Aid in the Wars with
    France, 1793–1815.* Cambridge, Mass.: Harvard University Press, 1969

Shipp, John. *Memoirs of the Extraordinary Military Career of John Shipp, Late a Lieut.
    in His Majesty's 87th Regiment.* London: T.F. Unwin, 1890

Sixsmith, E.K.G. *British Generalship in the Twentieth Century.* London: Arms &
    Armour Press, 1970

Skelton, William B. "High Army Leadership in the Era of the War of 1812: The Making and Remaking of the Officer Corps." *William and Mary Quarterly*, 3rd ser., 51 (April 1994): 253–74

Snake Hill: An Investigation of a Military Cemetery from the War of 1812. Edited by Susan Pfeiffer and Ronald F. Williamson. Toronto: Dundurn Press, 1991

Soldiers of 1814: American Enlisted Men's Memoirs of the Niagara Campaign. Edited by Donald E. Graves. Youngstown, NY, 1995

Spiers, Edward M. *The Army and Society, 1815–1914.* London: Longman, 1980

Spurr, J.W. "Sir James Lucas Yeo: A Hero on the Lakes." *Historic Kingston* 30 (Jan. 1982): 30–45

Stacey, C.P. "The Ships of the British Squadron on Lake Ontario, 1812–1814." *CHR* 34 (Dec. 1953): 311–23

– "Upper Canada at War, 1814: Captain Armstrong Reports." *OH* 48 (winter 1956): 37–42

Stagg, J.C.A. "Enlisted Men in the United States Army, 1812–1815: A Preliminary Survey." *William and Mary Quarterly*, 3rd ser., 43 (1986): 615–45

– *Mr. Madison's War: Politics, Diplomacy, and Warfare in the Early American Republic, 1783–1830.* Princeton, NJ: Princeton University Press, 1983

Stanley, G.F.G. *Canada's Soldiers, 1604–1954.* Toronto: Macmillan, 1954

– "The Significance of the Six Nations Participation in the War of 1812." *OH* 55 (Dec. 1963): 215–31

– *The War of 1812: Land Operations.* Canadian War Museum Historical Publication, no. 18. Ottawa: National Museums of Canada, 1983

Steppler, Glenn A. "A Duty Troublesome Beyond Measure: Logistical Considerations in the Canadian War of 1812." MA thesis, McGill University, 1974

Stickney, Kenneth. "Logistics and Communications in the 1814 Niagara Campaign." MA thesis, University of Toronto, 1976

Strachan, Hew. "The British Army 1815–1856: Recent Writing Reviewed." *JSAHR* 63 (1985): 68–79

– *European Armies and the Conduct of War.* London: Allen and Unwin, 1983

Stray, Albert. "Canadian Volunteers Burn Old Niagara." *Canadian Genealogist* 6 (Dec. 1984): 220–42

Sutherland, Maxwell. "The Civil Administration of Sir George Prevost 1811–1815: A Study in Conciliation." MA thesis, Queen's University, 1959

Symons, J. *The Battle of Queenston Heights; being a Narrative of the Opening of the War of 1812, with Notices of the Life of Major General Sir Isaac Brock, K.B., and Description of the Monument Erected to his Memory.* Toronto: Thompson and Co., 1859

Taking Command: The Art and Science of Military Leadership. Edited by Samuel H. Hays and William N. Thomas. Harrisburg, Pa: Stackpole Books, 1967

Thompson, David. *History of the Late War between Great Britain and the United States of America.* Niagara, UC: T. Sewell, 1832; reprint, S.R. Publishers, 1966

Thoumine, R.H. *Scientific Soldier: A Life of General Le Marchant, 1766–1812*, London: Oxford University Press, 1968

To Preserve and Defend: Essays on Kingston in the Nineteenth Century. Edited by G. Tulchinsky. Montreal and London: McGill-Queen's University Press, 1976

The Town of York, 1793–1815: A Collection of Documents of Early Toronto. Edited by Edith G. Firth. Ontario Series. Toronto: Champlain Society, 1962

Tuetey, Louis, *Les officiers sous l'ancien régime, nobles et soturiers.* Paris: Plon, 1908

Tupper, Ferdinand B., ed. *The Life and Correspondence of Major General Sir Isaac Brock, K.B.*, 2 nd ed. London, 1847

Turner, Wesley B. "The Career of Isaac Brock in Canada, 1802–1812." MA thesis, University of Toronto, 1961

– *The War of 1812: The War That Both Sides Won.* Illustrated Military History of Canada. Toronto: Dundurn Press, 1990

Upper Canada. The Journals of the Legislative Assembly of Upper Canada for the Years 1792 ... [to 1821]. *In* Archives of Ontario, *Report*, 6th, 8th-10th (Toronto: King's Printer, 1911–14). (Journals for 1809, 1813, and 1815 are missing)

– The Journals of the Legislative Council of Upper Canada for the Years 1792 ... [to] 1819. *In* Archives of Ontario, *Report*, 7th (Toronto: King's Printer, 1911)

Van Creveld, Martin. *Supplying War: Logistics from Wallenstein to Patton.* New York: Cambridge Press, 1977

Van Rensselaer, Solomon. *A Narrative of the Affair of Queenstown, in the War of 1812* ... New York: Leavitt, Lord, 1836

Viger, Jacques. "Diary of Captain Jacques Viger." *Waterdown Daily Times*, 4 June 1963.

Walden, K. "Isaac Brock, Man and Myth: A Study of the Militia Myth of the War of 1812 in Upper Canada, 1812–1912." MA thesis, Queen's University, 1971

Wallot, J.-P. "Une émeute à Lachine contre la 'conscription,'" *Revue d'histoire de l'Amérique française* 18 (1964): 112–37, 202–32

Walsh, Thomas. *Journal of the Late Campaign in Egypt, including Descriptions of that Country, and of Gibraltar, Minorca, Malta, Marmorice, and Macri; with an Appendix containing Official Papers and Documents.* London, 1803

War Along the Niagara: Essays on the War of 1812 and Its Legacy. Edited by R. Arthur Bowler. Youngstown, NY: Old Fort Niagara Association, 1991

War on the Great Lakes: Essays Commemorating the 175th Anniversary of the Battle of Lake Erie. Edited by W.J. Welsh and D.C. Skaggs. Kent, Ohio: Kent State University Press, 1991

Ward, S.G.P. "General Sir George Murray." *JSAHR* 58 (1980): 191–208

– *Wellington's Headquarters: A Study of the Administrative Problems in the Peninsula, 1809–1814.* London: Oxford University Press, 1957

Wavell, Archibald P., 1st Earl Wavell. *Generals and Generalship.* The Lees Knowles Lectures delivered at Trinity College, Cambridge, in 1939. Toronto, 1941

Way, R.L. "The Day of Chrysler's Farm." *Canadian Geographical Journal* 62 (June 1961): 184–217

Weekes, William M. "The War of 1812: Civil Authority and Martial Law in Upper Canada." *OH* 48 (1956): 147–61

Weigley, Russell. *History of the United States Army.* New York: Macmillan, 1967

Wellington at War, 1794–1815: A Selection of His Wartime Letters. Edited by Anthony Brett-James. London: Macmillan, 1961

Whitehorne, Joseph. *The Battle for Baltimore, 1814.* Baltimore: The Nautical & Aviation Publishing Co., 1997

– *While Washington Burned: The Battle for Fort Erie 1814.* Baltimore, Md: The Nautical & Aviation Publishing Co., 1992

Whitfield, Carol, *The Battle of Queenston Heights.* Canadian Historic Sites: Occasional Papers in Archaeology and History, no. 11. Ottawa, 1974

– *Tommy Atkins: The British Soldier in Canada, 1759–1870.* History & Archaeology, 56. Ottawa: National Historic Parks & Sites Branch, Parks Canada, 1981

Wilder, Patrick A. *The Battle of Sackett's Harbour, 1813.* Baltimore, Md: Nautical & Aviation Publishing Company of America, 1994

Williams, Edward G. "The Prevosts of the Royal Americans." *Western Pennsylvania History Magazine* 56 (1973): 1–38

Wilson, Robert T. *History of the British Expedition to Egypt; to Which is subjoined, a Sketch of the Present State of the Country and Its Means of Defence.* 2nd ed. London, 1803

Winder, William H. *Statement of Occurrences on the Niagara Frontier in 1812.* Washington: D. Green, 1829

Wishart, Bruce. "Sir James Yeo and the St. Lawrence: 'A Remarkable Fine Ship,' Sea-Dogs at War, 1812–1814." *Beaver* 72 (Feb./March, 1992): 12–22

Wohler, J. Patrick. *Charles de Salaberry: Soldier of the Empire, Defender of Quebec.* Toronto: Dundurn Press, 1984

Yaple, R.L. "The Auxiliaries: Foreign and Miscellaneous Regiments in the British Army, 1802–1817." *JSAHR* 50 (1972): 10–28

Index